Ch.... ...u Evolution

Wonder and Wisdom

Celia Deane-Drummond

SCM PRESS

© Celia Deane-Drummond 2009

Published in the UK in 2009 by SCM Press
Editorial office
13–17 Long Lane,
London, EC1A 9PN, UK

Published in the United States in 2009 by Fortress Press

SCM Press is an imprint of Hymns Ancient and Modern Ltd (a registered charity)
St Mary's Works, St Mary's Plain,
Norwich, NR3 3BH, UK
www.scm-canterburypress.co.uk

British Library Cataloguing in Publication data

A catalogue record for this book is available
from the British Library

978 0 334 04213 6

Typeset by PerfecType, Nashville, Tenn.

Christ and Evolution

To Arthur Peacocke

Contents

Acknowledgments

In 2007, I was awarded an Arts and Humanities Research Council (AHRC) grant to complete this book in the academic year 2007–2008. I am grateful to the University of Chester for being willing to accommodate an eight-month sabbatical leave in the period, without which this book could never have been finished. I am also grateful to St. Deiniol's Library for providing the tranquility and scholarly atmosphere that allowed me to focus my attention on my writing. I am also particularly grateful to Ben Quash, who graciously read and commented on four draft chapters of this book (chapters 1, 4, 6, and 7) that focused more specifically on the work of Hans Urs von Balthasar.

Some of this work has been tested in different forms at conference venues. Sections of chapter 2 were presented at the Lincoln Theological Institute research seminar at Manchester University in February 2008. I am grateful to Peter Scott for the invitation to take part in this seminar and for helpful feedback from those who took part. Parts of chapter 5 built on work that was started as integral to the J. K. Russell Fellowship, which I gratefully received following the invitation of Robert Russell in order to benefit from a conference focused on my ongoing research entitled "The Evolution of Sin and the Redemption of Nature" at the Center for Theology and the Natural Sciences in Berkeley, California, in March 2007. A modified version of the conference paper was also published in the February 2008 issue of *Theology and Science* 6 (no. 1), including responses from the conference, under the title "Shadow Sophia in Christological Perspective: The Evolution of Sin and the Redemption of Nature." I am particularly grateful to the respondents, Marc Bekoff, Robert Russell, James Haag, Nathan J. Hallanger, and William O'Neil, who all graciously gave of their time in helping me to sharpen up these ideas. I am also grateful to Chris Southgate and Denis Edwards, who generously allowed me to have access to their most recent articles before they were published. Robert Russell was also kind enough to offer comments on chapter 6.

I presented a modified version of chapter 8 entitled "Human Identity in Christological Perspective: Living as *Imago Christi*" for a European research network meeting, "Science and Religion Interaction in the 21st Century," focusing on the human person, which took place in Athens in September 2007. I am grateful to Professor Arygyris Nicolaides for the invitation to take part in this meeting, as well as for the feedback from other scholars working in this area. In May 2008, I also presented aspects of chapter 8 at a special lecture at the Teloglion Foundation of Art, Aristotle University of Thessaloniki, *entitled* "What Is the Future of the Human? A Theological Interrogation of the Posthuman Perspective." I am grateful to Professor Nicolaides for finding funds for this event from the British Council and the Institut Français, as well as the John Templeton Foundation. I am also grateful for the invitation from Eric Weislogel to give a lecture that drew on some material from chapter 8, entitled "What Is Human Wisdom? A Challenge to Transhuman Evolution," for the 2008 Metanexus Conference entitled "Subject, Self, and Soul," which took place at the Universidad Pontificia Comillas, Madrid, in July 2008. The feedback from the audiences on these occasions was valuable in shaping the final form of this book.

Finally, I need to thank my husband, Henry Curtis, and my daughters, Sara (seven) and Mair (two), who have had to tolerate the dedication needed to finish this book. This book has proved to be one of the most challenging ones I have ever attempted, and my hope is that the sacrifices that have proved necessary to bring this book to completion will bear fruit in many ways.

July 31, 2008, Memorial for Ignatius of Loyola

Preface

Publication of this book coincides with the 150th anniversary of the publication of Charles Darwin's *Origin of Species* and the 200th anniversary of the birth of Charles Darwin in 1809. The timing was fortuitous rather than deliberate on my part. Yet inasmuch as this book sets out to explore the implications of Darwinism and contemporary neo-Darwinian theories for Christology, it seems appropriate to honor Charles Darwin by giving him the first word in this book. Arthur Peacocke was correct to note that, historically, the conflict between Darwin's theory and Christian belief was not as stark as subsequent biologists and popular perception have supposed.[1] He suggests that T. H. Huxley's enmity toward Christianity was related to the desire to free professional biologists from any stranglehold of ecclesial control. Peacocke's reply, following Aubrey Moore, that Darwin is really a disguised friend is based on a profound belief that Darwin forces religious believers to think more carefully about the meaning of the incarnation and gives them a renewed sense of the sacramental presence of God understood as immanent in the world.[2]

Those reading the most recent vitriolic outpourings of Richard Dawkins, such as in his most recent book *The God Delusion*, might be forgiven

---

1. A. Peacocke, *The Palace of Glory: God's World and Science* (Adelaide: ATF, 2005), 59–60.

2. See other works by Peacocke that develop the idea of Darwin as disguised friend; for example, A. Peacocke, *Evolution: The Disguised Friend of Faith?* (Philadelphia: Templeton Foundation Press, 2004).

for wondering what kind of friend Darwin might be for religious faith, unless that friendship is seen in a paradoxical way of providing the opportunity to speak about what Christian belief in a Creator really entails.[3] This, of course, raises the issue of how far and to what extent Dawkins can speak either for Darwin or for Christian belief. Dawkins is particularly naïve in portraying Christian theism as founded on claims that lack a rational basis while denying the cultural ferment in which his own narrative is placed. While Christian commentators have more often than not pointed to considerable flaws in his understanding of theism, or even the cultural agenda behind his theories, they are less inclined to pay attention to the scientific or philosophical basis for his evolutionary arguments.

The premise of this book is that there is much more to be said about evolution and Christianity than simply taking the path of *either* friendship *or* hostility toward Darwin. Moreover, such debates regularly miss or push to the background proper consideration of that central tenet of Christian theology, namely, our understanding of the place and significance of Christ, or Christology. Perhaps in a paradoxical way, those who make it their profession to reflect on the significance of Christ in different cultures have also largely failed to give proper attention to the significance of either science in general or evolutionary ideas, in terms of both biological science and wider cultural meanings.[4]

F. LeRon Shults's book *Christology and Science* has appeared in print as this book goes to press, and inasmuch as it seeks to correct this anomaly, it is a welcome addition to the literature. I share many of Shults's premises inasmuch as he seeks to reform Christology in the light of current scientific research and argues for the importance of philosophical analysis in mediating between the two disciplines.[5] The particular philosophical traditions

---

3. This is not what Peacocke meant when he spoke of Darwin as a friend. See Richard Dawkins, *The God Delusion* (London: Bantam, 2006).

4. See, for example, Graham Ward's book on Christology and culture, where in spite of the considerable merits of this volume, engagement between Christology and scientific discourse is missing entirely, even though, arguably, the latter has served to shape Western culture ever since the Enlightenment. G. Ward, *Christ and Culture* (Oxford: Wiley/Blackwell, 2005).

5. Shults has critiqued in far more detail the philosophical basis for traditional Christology, as well as widening the scientific agenda to include cultural anthropology and physical cosmology. While evolution has sometimes been interpreted to include the latter, I prefer to focus here on biological evolution inasmuch as it raises its own questions and issues that would be lost in a broader perspective. F. LeRon Shults, *Christology and Science* (Aldershot: Ashgate, 2008).

that I call upon for this task are wonder and wisdom, though of course each term deliberately carries theological resonance—what Terence Deacon might term *symbolic meaning*.[6] I also, like Shults, argue against traditional views of Christology that focus simply on divine and human essence, or that link with literal views of Adam and Eve that are naïve hermeneutically and also incompatible with modern evolutionary biology. I, too, seek to widen the agenda for Christology so that it serves as more than just a focus on the incarnation narrowly conceived and includes reflection on the atonement and eschatology, as well as weaving in the doctrine of the Holy Spirit, so that Christology is interpreted in a Trinitarian way. Shults offers suggestive links between evolution and incarnation, cultural anthropology and atonement, and physical cosmology and eschatology. This typology is helpful in many respects. However, I believe that evolutionary biology has significance for themes beyond that of the incarnation—that is, it bears on a discussion of atonement and eschatology, as will be clear later in this preface and as developed in subsequent chapters, and I also give a much more prominent place to creation as such, rather than limiting discussion of evolution largely to reflection on the emergence of mind.[7] I also have taken rather more liberty to discuss controversy within scientific discourse, in that I believe it is helpful to recognize that we are not dealing with a single partner; rather, those engaged in dialogue are themselves riven in sharp debates with one another.[8]

I am, however, rather more critical than Shults of those theologians such as Pierre Teilhard de Chardin and Karl Rahner who have explored

---

6. T. Deacon, *The Symbolic Species: The Co-evolution of Language and the Brain* (New York: Norton, 1997).

7. I recognize that Shults's intention here was somewhat different, in that he seeks in his chapter on evolutionary biology to go behind what might be called the human nature of Christ, and how this might be understood in evolutionary terms. I also explore this issue in this book, and I share his preference for Wisdom Christology, though I push this to greater limits inasmuch as it opens up to include creation themes rather more explicitly.

8. While in some respects I warm to Shults's idea that we should view the dialogue between Christology and science as that between two lovers, recognizing and respecting difference, this analogy becomes a little strained once we realize the considerable diversity on both sides even within one subject domain. For this reason, I prefer to see the meeting of the ways as a mutual seeking after wonder and wisdom in both, as a *shared task* that unites and respects difference, seeking to influence instead of bringing union, rather than promoting any special preference for the other, that is, a special preference of science for Christology and vice versa. See Shults, *Christology and Science*, 3.

the relationship between evolutionary biology and Christology. Teilhard de Chardin's writings were more detailed compared with Rahner, but his almost excessive Christomonism and marriage to a particular version of evolutionary biology arguably showed that it was entirely possible to link both concepts, but in a way that many later writers have strongly criticized, even those who are otherwise warm to his overall project.

Inasmuch as Teilhard's understanding of evolution is outdated in many respects, this book begins with a brief introductory overview of evolutionary ideas and concepts, focusing particularly on those areas that will be significant in shaping the engagement with Christology that is to follow. This is not intended to indicate that the science has a privileged position in the discourse, but rather, it is important background for understanding the more constructive theological task that I attempt in subsequent chapters. It is therefore deliberately named an *introduction*, rather than a specific chapter. I have not dwelled on the historical details of Darwin's theory or its historical reception. Others are far better qualified to comment on this aspect.[9] I have tried to highlight where contemporary evolutionary theorists part company with Darwin's basic principles and the extent to which his core ideas remain intact, even through considerable revision. While Gould's macroevolutionary account of punctuated equilibrium remains controversial, it demonstrates the ferment that still surrounds evolutionary theory. I also suggest that it hints at an approach to evolution in the form of drama.[10]

The first chapter charts the different routes that theologians have taken in mapping the relationship between Christology and evolution. While, as I mentioned, this has not been given sufficient attention among contemporary theologians; Karl Rahner in his vast corpus of writing devoted only a single essay to this topic, and Jürgen Moltmann has touched on this issue to the extent that it is worthy of analysis. Both authors part company with Pierre Teilhard de Chardin, though both are influenced by his approach. I will argue in this chapter that while Teilhard was correct to put evolution on the theological agenda, his approach is ultimately indebted to a cosmic

---

9. See, for example, Ronald Numbers and John Stenhouse, eds., *Disseminating Darwinism: The Role of Place, Race, Religion and Gender* (Cambridge: Cambridge University Press, 1999). This essay collection focuses on the reception of Darwinism in the English-speaking world in the late nineteenth and early twentieth centuries.

10. Evelyn Hutchinson, *The Ecological Theatre and the Evolutionary Play* (New Haven: Yale University Press, 1965).

creation story that serves to generate an epic narrative approach to history. Instead, I will argue that an alternative way of relating Christology to evolution is one that takes its cues from theodrama as the primary source of inspiration. The rest of the book unfolds what this theodrama might entail.

The second chapter provides more reasons why it is important to be somewhat wary of narrative approaches to evolution and Christology by paying attention to the flowering of a particular approach to evolution in evolutionary psychology. This development, spawned from social Darwinism and sociobiology, is gaining momentum in both biological and popular circles. However, it is certainly not uncontested, and I pick up the criticisms that have been laid at the door of evolutionary psychology from a number of different perspectives, including biology, anthropology, and philosophy. In engaging more explicitly from a theological viewpoint, I argue that evolutionary psychology seeks to fill the gap that is left in the absence of Christology; it is an idolatry taking the shape of an *anti-Christology* inasmuch as it shows up the need for an adequate soteriology and eschatology.

The third chapter turns to the drama of the incarnation itself. Rather than remove the paradox implied by belief in the incarnation by accommodating such belief to what might be believable from a scientific perspective alone, I argue for the retention of the idea of radical difference between God and creation such that God assuming humanity is no longer viewed as a loss of omnipotence, since the basis of consideration is no longer comparable with anthropocentric notions of power. This allows for a kenotic Christology that is less about God giving up attributes than about God offering Godself in loving relationship by being fully present in the human Jesus. In speaking of the drama of the incarnation, there is no longer the tension created by classical notions of two natures of Christ, for the unity of divine and human comes through divine action expressed in the human life of Jesus. I also draw particularly on the work of the Orthodox theologian Sergii Bulgakov to argue for using Wisdom (Sophia) as a basis for reflection on the incarnation, since Wisdom allows for identity with and distinction from the rest of the created order.

The fourth chapter pays greater attention to the work of Hans Urs von Balthasar, who arguably has forged a case for the importance of theodrama in contemporary Roman Catholic scholarship. However, this particular chapter deals less with this aspect and more with his companion volume in the trilogy, *The Glory of the Lord.*[11] This is a deliberate step inasmuch as, like Balthasar, I believe that proper consideration of what might loosely be described as a theology of nature is appropriate as long as it is suitably qualified by proper attention to revealed theology. This chapter is not, as in traditional natural theology, about God and nature as much as it is about *Christ* and nature, and how such a discourse can serve to unravel what classical concepts such as cosmic Christology or Christ as Pantocrator might mean in an evolutionary world. In particular, I will suggest that the depth of the incarnation as inclusive of all creation is expressed through consideration of Christ as the form of beauty, alongside consideration of the classic transcendentals of truth, goodness, and beauty that Balthasar seeks to recover in a contemporary context. In addition, his use of what might be termed the *double analogy of being* preserves an adequate distinction between God and creation while showing forth the intimacy of God with creation as expressed in christological terms. Such intimacy is expressed in the love of God shown forth even in what might be termed the beauty of the ugliness of the cross and Christ's descent into hell.

The figuring of Christ as the beauty of the ugliness of the cross and sinking into hell raises the issue of atonement and its meaning not just for humanity, but for wider creation as such. As a window on the life of the earliest hominids, and also as a means for reflecting more intently on the significance of Christ's reconciling work for creation at large, I engage in chapter 5 explicitly with the work of animal behaviorists, including the primatologist Frans de Waal and the ethologist Marc Bekoff. I argue that such work is significant inasmuch as it forces us at least to reconsider the possibility that nonhuman animals show a form of morality in their worlds and express what might be termed latent vices and virtues. This opens up the question as to how Christ's death as atonement might be best understood. It also opens up wider issues about the place of Christ's death in theodicy as such, especially that informed by evolutionary suffering. I propose the use of shadow sophia (wisdom) as a symbolic way of representing the tapestry of evil in its different and varied contexts. Such an approach, by being grounded in the concrete death of Christ, tries to avoid purely theoretical philosophical reflection that makes little or no connection with theology or history.

---

11. The trilogy consists of the multivolume works *The Glory of the Lord* (Edinburgh: T&T Clark; San Francisco: Ignatius, 1982–1991), *Theo-Drama* (San Francisco: Ignatius, 1988–1998), and *Theo-Logic* (San Francisco: Ignatius, 2000–2005).

The resurrection of Christ from the dead and its meaning have attracted some attention from those engaged in the science and religion discourse. The sixth chapter deals explicitly with the evolutionary significance of Christ's resurrection and how it might be understood in an evolutionary world, where natural death is both the end of an existing life and a condition without which nothing could live. I argue for the inclusion of evolved beings in the theodrama, rather than their relegation to the position of the "stage." I also argue that such accounts need to be grounded in the biblical narrative, inasmuch as Jesus' encounter with Mary Magdalene in John's Gospel reflects John's portrait of Christ as Jesus-Sophia. This leads to a consideration of the role of women in the narratives of the resurrection, and inasmuch as the significance of women has been written out of the account, it mirrors an exclusion of natural imagery as well.

The seventh chapter returns to the theme of wonder, which formed the basis of reflection in chapter 4, in order to develop an eschatology that is grounded in the experience of the human community but looks wider to consider the natural world as such. This discussion includes proper attention to the role of the Holy Spirit, such that Christian hope with its distinct expectation of the future is oriented towards expectation of participation in the life of the Trinity. Such future hope is in stark contrast with the secularized eschatology of evolutionary psychology. While drawing on the work of Hans Urs von Balthasar, I am sharply critical of his stereotypical portrayal of women. Yet his attention to cosmic aspects of the significance of Christ, which has not always been appreciated by commentators, can serve as a basis for reflecting on the nature of future hope for other creatures in the community of creation.

The final chapter explores more fully the extension of evolutionary psychology in transhumanism, and the implications that this has for human identity. I argue that human identity needs to be grounded in adequate reflection on Christ as one who humbled himself, taking on the form of a servant, as a way of expressing the meaning of both the human and the divine. Inasmuch as transhumanism shows up a lack of appreciation of the natural origins of humanity by projecting a perfection that seems to loose its ties with creaturely reality, it amounts to a form of secular gnostic speculation. It is therefore an *anti-human* stance, one that sits in opposition to the kind of humanity that Christ expressed and is available for human communities through the Holy Spirit. The contingency that is an important factor in evolutionary theory—however much this might be qualified by notions of a directional signal of one sort or another—shows up the fallacy of this kind of approach, for it is a vain attempt to remove what is not possible to remove, namely, contingency. Other contingent forms that are more political in orientation surface, showing up the narrowness of the basis for arguments toward transhuman perfections. Hence, while aspects of the posthuman discourse may rattle the boundaries that have been constructed between human and nonhuman, including the artificial, the way this had been read off in evolutionary terms in transhuman discussion amounts to an undoing of the human, a loss of human identity. It shows up once more the urgency of the task of relating evolution and other aspects of theology.

I have argued in this book for the use of theodrama as an exercise in constructive theology and a means of relating Christology to evolution. I have been constantly troubled by the difficulty of doing justice to both areas of discussion. This book is more an exercise in the development of a Christology that takes due account of evolutionary theory without succumbing to an identification with or alienation from it. It therefore does not take the same sort of shape as what has been traditionally termed "science and religion" dialogue, if this is taken to mean scientific theories as they relate to religious belief as such, perhaps refining or even discarding elements of the latter belief. Instead, I offer the reader a way of thinking creatively and critically about Christ and evolution without pretending one discourse can be fused with the other; there remains an appropriate distance between them inasmuch as both have their own proper areas of discourse that do not always connect with the other. Failure to recognize this comes through in synthetic theological theories or in secularized attempts to meet religious needs. I also believe that theologians need to go further than debating the clash between evolution and creationism as alternatives, focusing just on the first chapters of Genesis, even if this is relevant as a clearing ground for further discussion. I am also acutely conscious of the difficulty of this task, and it soon became apparent as to *why* there is a lacuna in this area of study; the challenge is enormous. Inasmuch as this book is an attempt to offer a word into this lacuna, it is a first step. It is, if you will, an attempt to offer an account of Christian wisdom in this difficult and contested field, though I have also named wonder as another focal point in order to do justice to elements that might otherwise get forgotten.

My earlier book *Creation through Wisdom* attempted to develop a theology of creation as a reply to more truncated accounts that simply fitted theology into scientific reasoning.[12] In developing that account, I also opened up areas for ethical reflection, but it did not move so much from ethics to theology as the other way around. I only touched on Christology in the context of a wisdom theology of creation, and could not deal with its ramifications in any detail, nor did I specifically engage in evolutionary theory. I did, however, by writing in a way that would open up an engagement with practical, ethical questions, seek to ground my theological discussion. The present book is more narrowly focused on Christology but, at the same time, moves beyond this to consideration of issues in a theology of nature, anthropology, and eschatology inasmuch as they intersect with Christology. Like my earlier monograph, this book raises implications that are ethical without specifically developing ethical discourse. In common with David Ford, I believe that Christian wisdom at its best takes proper account of scripture, as well as being self-consciously interdisciplinary in orientation.[13] Inasmuch as this book is about seeking, it expresses wisdom in its most primary biblical sense of the cry of Wisdom.

It should also be noted that I have not dealt with other religious perspectives inasmuch as these might serve to challenge the particular approach to theology taken here. I hope that those who expected to find such discussion will bear with the limitations of space that such a work entails. Moreover, unlike some, I am not persuaded that in order to engage in dialogue with those of other religious traditions, a lowest common denominator approach is the most fruitful. One has the impression that the failure to deal adequately with Christology in science and religion discourse reflects a certain nervousness by some theologians as to whether such a topic would be too offensive to those outside the Christian tradition.[14] Yet I would be equally surprised if a Buddhist tailored his or her account of theology in order to conform to my perspective; rather, true dialogue need not eschew an open, respectful discussion of differences where these arise.

---

12. C. Deane-Drummond, *Creation through Wisdom: Theology and the New Biology* (Edinburgh: T&T Clark, 2000).

13. While I have referred to particular scriptural texts in this book, I have not expanded on this theme in the same way as David Ford, who argues for a more self-conscious use of scripture. However, inasmuch as I am also attempting to gain access to knowledge through an open but critical engagement with others, I share in the spirit of his project. See D. Ford, *Christian Wisdom: Desiring God and Learning in Love* (Cambridge: Cambridge University Press, 2007).

14. This point has also been noted by Shults. Shults, *Christology and Science*, 2.

I am also acutely aware that I could have taken on this task in a different way. The spirit of what I am attempting here is perhaps best expressed by the metaphor that Arthur Peacocke used on occasion: naming creation as the work of God understood as a great composer or musician.[15] He also wrote specifically on the relationship between music and creation in his coauthored book, *The Music of Creation*.[16] I have chosen instead to use the language of *drama* in order to capture something of the way I envisage God at work in the world, partly because of the theological resources available through the work of Hans Urs von Balthasar, and also because drama lends itself to becoming profoundly historical and in this sense coheres with the historical movement of evolution. A casual glance through the book I have written here will show some areas of continuity, but also areas of considerable discontinuity with Arthur Peacocke's overall position. Yet in dedicating this book to his memory, I am acknowledging not just a sincere appreciation for his commitment and energy in this field, warmth as a human being, and transparent openness to discussion and alternative positions. I am also acknowledging the personal debt I owe him as a scholar, for it was hearing him speak at Durham University in the 1980s, while I was still a lecturer in the botany department, that first moved me to thinking seriously about this field. Inasmuch as I am offering this book as a way of continuing the conversation, my hope is that others, too, will find fragments that prove useful for their own reflection.

---

15. See, for example, Arthur Peacocke, "Biological Evolution: A Positive Theological Appraisal," in *Evolutionary and Molecular Biology: Scientific Perspectives on Divine Action*, ed. R. J. Russell, W. R. Stoeger, and F. Ayala, 357–76 (Vatican City: Vatican; Berkeley: CTNS, 1998).

16. Arthur Peacocke and Ann Pederson, *The Music of Creation* (Minneapolis: Fortress Press, 2005).

Introduction: The Challenge of Darwinian Evolution

While the year 2009 will stand out as a focus for celebrating 200 years since the birth of Charles Darwin and 150 years since the publication of his celebrated *Origin of Species*, evolution as a concept has been around for much longer than this and has, arguably, influenced classical as well as contemporary thought. The history of evolutionary ideas is not the focus of this chapter, even though this would be a worthwhile exercise in itself. Instead, I will offer here only a brief introduction to the significance of Darwin's ideas to contemporary evolutionary biology, along with key unresolved areas of debate. I will argue for the particular significance of ideas relating to the interplay of what might be termed the core principles of Darwin's notions of agency, efficacy, and scope and the revisions proposed by Stephen Jay Gould. I will comment particularly on Eldredge and Gould's theory of punctuated equilibrium at a macroevolutionary level, inasmuch as it shows up the inadequacy of more gradualist versions of Darwin's theory, and insofar as it points to a very loose analogy with more dramatic accounts of history that I will return to in chapter 1. I will outline here the context of a more general discussion of evolution and theology, inasmuch as the latter has dominated science and religion discourse. I will deal with the specific atheistic intent of some popular writers in ultra-Darwinism in chapter 2.

Darwinian Natural Selection Comes of Age

While Charles Darwin was exposed to the milieu in which naturalists, such as William Paley, sought to find evidence for the existence of God through their perception of the intricate design of the natural world, his research forced him to come to some very different conclusions about the meaning of the diversity he encountered.[1] His key idea was not so much evolution *as such* but evolution by natural selection. No one denied the observations of overproduction of offspring, variation, and heritability. Darwin's novelty was to explain *how* these observations could contribute to a theory of evolution by natural selection, where natural selection was the prime syllogistic inference. Moreover, the process of natural selection helped explain William Paley's difficulty of accounting for what seemed to be the design of organisms, including both their diversity and complexity. Biologist Francisco Ayala has gone as far as suggesting that the prime purpose of natural selection was not so much an evolutionary theory, but a theory about design.[2] Darwin also based his argument on what was familiar to the audience in terms of plant breeding, and then extended this to reflect on the natural world. The difference in the latter case is that natural selection is the process through which apparent design is achieved, a process that depends on natural variability and then preferential survival and reproduction of those individuals with characteristics best adapted to their environment. Darwin argued that complex organs and other characteristics emerged gradually, rather than suddenly or all at once. He admitted a strong sense of wonder in what he discovered and, in an oft-cited phrase, exclaimed:

> There is grandeur in this view of life, with its several powers, having been originally breathed into a few forms or into one; and that, while this planet has gone cycling on according to the fixed law of gravity, from so simple a beginning

---

1. For a discussion of the history of ideas leading up to Darwin's discoveries, see Keith Thomson, *Before Darwin: Reconciling God and Nature* (London: Yale University Press, 2005).

2. Francisco Ayala, *Darwin's Gift to Science and Religion* (Washington: Joseph Henry, 2007). While it is understandable that he wishes to retrieve this emphasis on design in the light of current debates, particularly in America, about intelligent design, I am less confident that design language as such is as useful as he suggests, in that it might imply that evolution is purposive, which clearly it is not.

endless forms most beautiful and most wonderful have been, and are being, evolved.[3]

It is also important to recognize that natural selection alone is not progressive; that is, it does not promote change directly *unless* the environment changes. In this, it was very different from the rival theory of Jean-Baptiste Chevalier de Lamarck (1744–1829), who believed in the direct inheritance of characteristics derived from particular uses during a lifetime. Lamarck's theory also included the concept of necessary developments from lower to higher forms by envisaging an innate metaphysical tendency in life to improve over time.[4] Darwin's theory, by contrast, did not rely on any metaphysical explanations; rather, he sought to ground evolutionary processes in a materialistic philosophy that did not require metaphysical concepts for its success. Ayala argues that the significance of Darwin's work was that it served to complete the Copernican revolution so that it became extended to the sphere of biology. Now material explanations were sufficient, and there was no need to use supernatural or metaphysical explanations in order to understand the natural living world.[5]

Stephen Jay Gould has helpfully summarized Darwin's central logic as consisting of three principles.[6] The first principle is that of *agency*. In this case, the apparent benevolence of the natural evolutionary process in terms of characteristics suited to the environment, or "design," flowed not from a deliberate external force, but as an indirect side effect of natural selection working to remove organisms that were less fit for the environment in which they were placed. The second key principle is that of *efficacy*, that is, the extent to which natural selection can be proved to be the main causal element in biological evolution. At the time when Darwin's *Origin* was first proposed, many biologists acknowledged the existence of natural selection but believed that its role was too weak to account for the sheer variety of

---

3. Charles Darwin, *On the Origin of Species*, facsimile of 1st ed., with intro. by Ernst Mayr (New York: Athenaeum, 1967), 489–90. For further discussion of wonder as the experience of scientists, see C. Deane-Drummond, *Wonder and Wisdom: Conversations in Science, Spirituality and Theology* (London: DLT, 2006).

4. His theory has some common ground with that of Henri Bergson (1859–1940), in *Creative Evolution* (1907), trans. Arthur Mitchell (London: Macmillan, 1912).

5. Ayala, *Darwin's Gift*, 42.

6. See his vast volume, S. J. Gould, *The Structure of Evolutionary Theory* (Cambridge, Mass.: Belknap/Harvard University Press, 2002), which discusses this topic (pp. 12–15) and others in considerable depth.

species. They proposed that some other positive force was likely to be operative, "pushing" an organism's development toward specific ends. Darwin, by contrast, argued that the very slow *negative*, or eliminative, process of natural selection was sufficient to create organisms that are fitted to the environment. The third principle is that of *scope*, that is, whether natural selection is sufficient to explain the full panoply of taxonomic diversity, even though, for example, transition between similar types—such as the transition from a wolf to a dog—might be explained in such a manner.

Alfred Wallace (1823–1913) also discovered natural selection independently from Darwin, but later than Darwin's original discovery, which had not yet been made public. There were, however, important differences between them, in that Wallace believed natural selection was *always* progressive, while Darwin believed such change was not inevitable, since some organisms remained unchanged for many millions of years, and some organisms that existed millions of years ago, such as the ancient Silurian animals, did not differ much from living species.[7] Another problematic area concerned mental evolution in humans and their moral and religious endowment. Darwin's *Descent of Man*, published in 1871, was rather less guarded than his earlier *Origin of Species*. Here he speculated about the origin of human religious sensibility in evolutionary terms. Wallace agreed with Darwin initially and suggested that natural selection acted on human intellectual and moral capabilities.[8] Five years later, he had changed his mind, and he proposed that natural selection operated initially, but once human mental capacities were sufficiently advanced, the human mind became the means through which humans adapted to changing environments to suit human needs. He also seemed to doubt that natural selection was responsible for the appearance of conscious life: "The moral and higher intellectual nature of man is as unique a phenomenon as was conscious life on its first appearance in the world, and the one is almost as difficult to conceive as originating in any law of evolution as the other."[9]

---

7. Ayala, *Darwin's Gift*, 45.

8. A. R. Wallace, "The Origin of Human Races and the Antiquity of Man Deduced from the Theory of Natural Selection," *Anthr. Rev.* 2 (1864): clviii–clxxxvii.

9. A. R. Wallace, review of *Principles of Geology*, by Charles Lyell (10th ed., 1867, 1868) and *Elements of Geology* by Charles Lyell (6th ed., 1865), *Quarterly Rev.* 126 (1869): 359–94, quoting p. 391. See also A. R. Wallace, "The Limits of Natural Selection as Applied to Man," in *Contributions to the Theory of Natural Selection*, 332–71 (London: Macmillan, 1870).

Wallace believed that characteristics that seemed to confer little or no survival value could not have come about through natural selection, including in his list characteristics such as a large brain and attendant capacities such as formation of ideal conceptions of space and time, artistic feelings of pleasure in form or color, and abstract reasoning such as mathematics. He believed that such characteristics could have had no use for human beings "in [their] early stages of barbarism." He concluded, instead, that "a superior intelligence has guided the development of man in a definite direction, and for a special purpose."[10] While Wallace was influenced by spiritualism in making the latter comment, it reflects the present tendency to view the choice between seeking either an explanation through natural selection or some other mystical explanation that is clearly not grounded in science.

Darwin's *Descent of Man* responded to Wallace on a number of fronts and argued for the presence of higher mental functions in animals, including tool use, a sense of beauty, language, and religion. He suggested that morality was important for the success of tribes. Following Darwin, the possibility of natural selection working at the level of the group was aired, but an alternative was also sought through the belief that humanity can take control of its own evolution by encouraging those with positive characteristics to breed.[11] Eugenics fell out of fashion subsequently, but by the 1960s, evolutionary ideas as a basis for explaining human behavior became fashionable once more.

In this context, it is worth noting how Herbert Spencer took up and used Darwin's ideas. He not only introduced slogans such as "survival of the fittest," but also speculated about the social and economic implications of Darwin's work. It is his views that later flourished as social Darwinism, and I will discuss its contemporary extension in evolutionary psychology in more detail in chapter 2. It is also important to note Charles Darwin's own reaction to this appropriation, claiming of Spencer that "his deductive manner of treating any subject is wholly opposed to my frame of mind."[12]

In the nineteenth century, the main areas of controversy concerned the three core principles of natural selection: agency, efficacy, and scope. It would be incorrect, therefore, to portray religious belief in opposition

---

10. Wallace, "Limits of Natural Selection," 359.

11. The development of eugenics is outside the scope of this introduction. I have discussed it in C. Deane-Drummond, *Genetics and Christian Ethics* (Cambridge: Cambridge University Press, 2006).

12. Cited in Ayala, *Darwin's Gift*, 46; original source not identified.

to Darwin's theory of evolution at this stage, for even within the scientific community, there was considerable debate and opposition to his ideas.

While Charles Darwin's theory of natural selection in the *Origin of Species* was based on careful observations, it was only much later, with the rediscovery in 1900 of Gregor Mendel's famous experiments on peas, that scientists began to work out the possible genetic mechanism for natural selection. The mutation of genes is the fundamental source of variety that confers advantage, which is then translated into longevity and higher reproductive success. Where mutations are disadvantageous, the opposite follows, and one can expect eventual elimination by natural selection. By the twentieth century, in what has been variously named the Modern Synthesis, Darwin's ideas came to be accepted. Yet in the latter half of the twentieth century, there was an important transition, which can be termed a hardening toward more absolute positions that drew on natural selection, and an exclusivist commitment to explaining even complex behavior in terms of adaptationist scenarios. This hardening is still in evidence in some quarters, as I will return to in chapter 2's more focused discussion of an offshoot of sociobiology known as evolutionary psychology.

In such a context, evolution by natural selection is thought to be dominant, with subsidiary processes that qualify its importance. At least four factors are known to limit adaptations:

1. *Gene flow.* This is the movement of organisms born in one place to another geographic region. In the new location, they may be maladapted to local conditions or may have characteristics that prove advantageous. If these populations are isolated, then either maladapted or advantageous alleles may persist, and responding to new environmental conditions normally takes time.

2. *Constraints.* The constraints on evolutionary change may be due to the particular history of the species, its development, physiology, physical constraints, or constraints of chemical processes. In developmental terms, for example, genetic imprinting means that in germ cells, some genes are "silenced," that is, fail to express. Parental imprints are erased later in development, so the imprinting becomes characteristic of the sex of the individual. Across different evolutionary pathways, there are common developmental control systems, so the formation of a body plan is remarkably similar between very divergent organisms, ranging from insects to mammalian species. The evolution of developmental systems presents puzzles for biologists that are still being unraveled, and it leads to

parallelisms, which are similar patterns of evolution across related species with shared developmental constraints.

3. *Genetic drift and founder effects.* Genetic drift describes changes in organisms or populations that are brought about by random changes in genetics that do not have any particular advantage or disadvantage in reproductive terms. Founder effects describe genetic bottlenecks, often following catastrophic events. After a mass extinction, for example, a species founder can achieve a higher status, as in the radiation of mammals after the extinction of dinosaurs at the end of the Mesozoic Era.

4. *Deviation from expected gene frequencies.* The normal segregation of 1:1 expectation following Mendelian genetic frequency is rarely found in very small populations, so that the distribution of alleles from parents is not predictable. A few individuals who form a new group may bring about another founder effect. These individuals may show a difference in gene frequency compared with that in the parent population.

The evolution of sex also presents a puzzle for biologists, for there is no general explanation as to why sex has evolved. It does allow more rapid evolution to take place, since it offers the possibility of a greater combination of different beneficial characteristics. Sex selection was one of Darwin's key ideas in how evolution took place, namely, through the development of particular characteristics that enhance mating success. While there is considerable evidence for sexual selection across a range of different species, relatively little is known about the genetic basis for most of the traits.[13] For organisms to qualify as a species, there must be separation at morphological, behavioral, and genetic levels. Organisms within a species share a common ancestor and may show diagnostic difference in particular characteristics or traits, or have particular phenotypic or genetic clusters. Species are also characteristically interbreeding where sex has evolved.

Another puzzle for the explanation of evolution through natural selection was one that Darwin considered, namely, why populations remained stable and did not increase as rapidly as one might expect in favorable conditions.[14] Darwin spoke vaguely of predation and disease or food shortages.

---

13. For a good general guide to the evolution of sex and sexual selection, see, for example, Stephen C. Stearns and Rolf F. Hoekstra, *Evolution: An Introduction* (Oxford: Oxford University Press, 2005), 177–263.

14. For a discussion, see Timothy Shanahan, *The Evolution of Darwinism: Selection, Adaptation and Progress in Evolutionary Biology* (Cambridge: Cambridge University Press, 2004), 38–53.

Some biologists, including David Lack, proposed that population density was kept in check by individual responses to particular prevailing conditions of food scarcity, predation, disease, and climate. Others, including Vero Copner Wynne-Edwards, proposed an active regulation of population density by natural selection working at the level of the group. He suggested that particular epideictic displays, such as flocking in birds or schooling in fish, were a way of monitoring the optimum group size. He was criticized heavily by John Maynard Smith, who insisted that group selection was unnecessary as an explanation; moreover, the individuals would lack the necessary cognitive skills to plan at group level in the way Wynne-Edwards suggested. Since then, through the work of David Sloan Wilson, there has been something of a revival of the possibility of group selection. Controversially, he argued that religion itself is a form of group adaptation, natural selection working at the level of the group/community.[15] Such discussions reflect debates over the level at which natural selection acts, be it the level of the gene, organism, group, species, and so on.

Finally, more popular conceptions that there remain "missing links" in the evolutionary record are largely illusory, at least as far as the gap between apes and humans is concerned. Ayala comments, "Not one, but hundreds of fossil remains belonging to hundreds of individual hominids have been discovered since Darwin's time and continue to be discovered at an accelerated rate."[16] The oldest fossil hominids are about 6 million to 7 million years old; known as *Australopithecus*, they have an upright stance, smaller cranial capacity, and a skull that shows some apelike and some human characteristics. *Paranthropus* and *Kenyanthropus* lived around the same time, but the former became extinct. *Homo* species appeared later, about 1.5 million to 2.0 million years ago in the case of *Homo habilis* and *Homo erectus*, the latter having a slightly larger brain. Several other species of hominids, living up to 500,000 years ago, have been identified. The transition to *Homo sapiens* is likely to have begun about 400,000 years ago, but *Homo erectus* remained until about 250,000 years ago in China, and maybe later in Java.[17] There are also other hominid species in the ancestral tree, known as co-lateral relatives, that are not direct ancestors but bear some of the same characteristics. Neanderthals were present in Europe more than

---

15. David Sloan Wilson, *Darwin's Cathedral: Evolution, Religion and the Nature of Society* (Chicago: University of Chicago Press, 2002).

16. Ayala, *Darwin's Gift*, 95.

17. Ibid., 97.

200,000 years ago. The consensus now seems to be that modern humans arose in Africa about 150,000 years ago[18] and then spread to other regions of the world, gradually outcompeting other hominid species, including Neanderthals. China, Europe, and America were colonized about 60,000, 35,000, and 15,000 years ago, respectively. While the details of evolutionary history of hominids and other species remain the subject of active research, it would be incorrect to surmise that there are large gaps or that the evolutionary origin of humans is in question.

Darwin has "come of age" inasmuch as most working biologists assume his theory is correct. There are drawbacks to this view of life, in that it can become dominant over other ways of thinking about the living world, such as natural kinds. Such natural kinds are not fixed by evolutionary descent but come from a perception of a universal characteristic that then has its particular instance in particular ways.[19] Refusal to allow any other interpretation other than that arising from evolutionary biology amounts to what Conor Cunningham has termed the "supernaturalistic fallacy," where religion or metaphysics is ruled out of court as nonexistent if it does not match up to scientific analysis.[20] The expression of this kind of attitude has its flowering, I suggest, in evolutionary psychology, though it is ironic, perhaps, that the latter has resisted the logical consequences of Darwinian contingency and reverted to a language of design and engineering in order to make its case. John Dupré is similarly critical of the rejection

---

18. Dating and DNA analysis of skeletons and modern human samples suggest a figure of 156,000 years ago. However, the small number of samples used means that the date may be inaccurate by tens of thousands of years. See ibid., 102 n. 3, 209.

19. John Dupré takes up a discussion of this issue in his *Humans and Other Animals* (Oxford: Clarendon, 2002), 3. Examples of natural kinds might be moths, lilies, hawks, and rabbits, none of which map onto the modern classification system according to evolutionary biology. He resists the elitist attitude of science that assumes that its classification system is the superior one.

20. For an entertaining and thoughtful essay, see Conor Cunningham, "Trying My Very Best to Believe Darwin, or The Supernaturalistic Fallacy: From Is to Nought," in *Belief and Metaphysics*, ed. Peter Candler and C. Cunningham, 100–141 (London: SCM, 2008). In a playful comparison with the naturalistic fallacy (is to ought), he argues here that if Darwinian scientists claim that something does not exist, then we are moving from is to nought. Such scientism clearly needs to be roundly rebuffed and is expressed in Francis Crick's astonishing hypothesis as applied to the mind, though I have some doubts if all working biologists, including those who hold to Darwinian theories as fruitful in biological terms, necessarily or inevitably think this way. This seems to be Cunningham's eventual conclusion as well, in that he agrees that ultra-Darwinians are not true to their originator, a point I will return to in chapter 1.

of transcendence by sociobiologists, who see it as "metaphysical mystery mongering." This is, he argues, because they "remain trapped in the reductionistic, deterministic metaphysics of Darwin's scientific predecessors."[21] Nonetheless, this is not the only way to envisage evolutionary change, and inasmuch as evolution can be understood as allowing for *emergence*, it offers an alternative way of approaching evolution that at least permits the existence of the transcendent, at least in philosophically consistent ways, as well as *convergence*, which also seems to allow for the transcendent, as discussed further below.[22]

Is Evolution a Narrative or Drama?

The account that Darwin gives of evolution by natural selection is one of slow and gradual increments, a meandering process whereby changes in environmental conditions for whatever reason permit the process of natural selection to accomplish a slow and gradual adaptation by individuals that are at a greater survival advantage and hence produce more offspring. This account finds its literary equivalent in narrative, though arguably even this categorization softens the more dramatic encounters tending to either violence or cooperation between individuals that are necessary for evolutionary change. Any dramatic elements are, of course, removed entirely if the narrative becomes reduced to the level of the gene, where genes are tracked in order to trace evolutionary change. Geneticists have also since found that even trying to use genes for tracking is extremely complex, in that the expression of genes may be sensitive to environmental conditions, not all genes are stable, some are linked to sexuality, others are suppressed through parental imprinting, and so on and so on.[23] The characteristics conferred by a particular genetic combination may also be put to other uses later on in evolutionary history, so that it would be incorrect to assume that particular characteristics simply emerge by new mutations when the need arises, for they may already be latent in the genome.

---

21. Dupré, *Humans and Other Animals*, 171.

22. See, in particular, Martinez J. Hewlett, "True to Life? Biological Models of Origin and Evolution," in *Evolution and Emergence*, ed. N. Murphy and W. R. Stoeger, 158–72 (Oxford: Oxford University Press, 2007).

23. A full discussion is not relevant to the central theme of this book, and I give a brief summary of contemporary genetic concepts in Deane-Drummond, *Genetics and Christian Ethics*.

It is also worth pointing out that the way Darwin envisaged evolution by natural selection is, in many cases, now being qualified by revisions to his theory. This discussion is significant, as it qualifies the discussion of those who have adopted more exclusivist interpretations of human behavior in terms of evolution by natural selection. This is one reason why Richard Dawkins's reduction of natural selection to the genetic level fails, for while it can provide a means of what might be termed "bookkeeping," as Gould points out, "replicators cannot specify the causality of selectionist processes, which must be based on the recognition and definition of interactors within environments."[24] His critique goes deeper still, in naming selection among cell lines as only of ancestral importance, for it is the organism that in effect suppresses selection at this level in the interests of its integrity, so that "failure of this suppression leads to the pyrrhic victory of cell lineages that we call cancer."[25] As noted earlier in this introduction, Darwin believed that the agency of natural selection operated at the level of organisms, though Gould also considers that in the longer version of his *Origin*, Darwin allowed for the possibility of selection at the species level. The question that needs to be addressed is not just the level at which selection works—be it gene, organism, species, deme, or clade—but also whether this is sufficient as a means of explaining transitions between species, or whether there is a requirement for what might be called auxiliary theories.

Hence, the *scale* at which measurements are made means that some changes take place not just at the level of the organism, but also at the level of the species. The latter is known as *macro*evolution and is measured over a long time scale of species extinction and generation of new species, or speciation. Stephen Gould describes how he was increasingly frustrated by the mantra of natural selection as the means for explaining *all* evolutionary change, so that where there were gaps in the paleontological record, the assumption was simply that this represented a gap in the data, rather than a genuine transition. To respond to this, he proposed, together with Niles Eldredge, the idea of punctuated equilibrium, where periods of relatively slow change were interspersed with periods of rapid change and speciation. He compares the theory of punctuated equilibrium in terms of the importance to his own research with the *Apologia Pro Vita Sua* of Cardinal Newman.[26] He is not, he claims, suggesting by this theory a radical

---

24. Gould, *Structure of Evolutionary Theory*, 72.
25. Ibid., 73–74.
26. Ibid., 37.

departure from Darwin's core theory of natural selection, but rather what he terms key revisions, such that the core principles remain intact.[27] He also prefers to speak of Darwin's theory as a *framework* rather than as a *foundation*, reflecting a more open-ended approach to alternatives compared with more absolutist stances. He wavers, however, in how far he sees this central idea of punctuated equilibrium as being a challenge to natural selection, for

> substantial changes, introduced during the last half of the 20th century, have built a structure so expanded beyond the original Darwinian core, and so enlarged by new principles of macroevolutionary explanation, that the full exposition, while remaining within the domain of Darwinian logic, must be construed as basically different from the canonical theory of natural selection, rather than simply extended.[28]

Yet we can ask ourselves how his theory can remain within the logic of Darwinian evolution by natural selection even as he proposes such a radical difference in macroevolution. It is therefore necessary to explore more fully what he means by punctuated equilibrium in order to assess both its novelty and consistency within a Darwinian framework.

Gould's macroevolutionary theory of punctuated equilibrium works only at the level of *species* rather than at the microevolutionary level within species, which can, according to Gould, still be subject to the usual explanatory basis of natural selection. Microevolution, in contrast, reflects heritable changes in genes, organisms, or populations; these changes are either adaptive or neutral, and they result from natural selection or other processes such as genetic drift. Where changes in traits are reflected in reproductive success, *adaptive* evolution occurs. Where such changes are not reflected in reproductive success, *neutral* evolution occurs. In the latter

---

27. Gould describes his own particular odyssey in terms of seeking a reformulation of a basic Darwinian core in Hegelian terms, such that it combines both aspects of Darwin's theory and challenges to his theory, so that he intends his own contribution to be a new and richer synthesis. The question that concerns us here is not so much the history of science as such, interesting though this might be, but the kind of analogies that might be suggested by auxiliary theories such as punctuated evolution. In addition, the ferment that continues in contemporary evolutionary biology shows the implicit danger of tying talk about God too closely to specific strands in evolutionary science. See ibid., 23.

28. Ibid., 3.

case, as long as those organisms or populations are not at a disadvantage, then some accumulative changes will take place. Macroevolution threatens the absolutism in Darwinism, rather than Darwin's theory at what might be called the root level. Darwin's own explanation of the apparent stasis of species and their abrupt replacement with other species was simply a sign of lack of evidence. Yet the lack of any obvious evolutionary change is such that biostratigraphers record the overlapping appearance of given fossils in order to indicate the date of rocks.[29] Species that have unusually short duration but wide geographic spread can act as marker or "index" fossils. Gould argues that paleontological literature "abounds in testimony for predominant stasis," and more often than not, such stasis is viewed as an embarrassment, as it could not fit easily within a standard Darwinian explanation. Accordingly, the majority of microbial species appear and disappear in the fossil record without antecedents or precedents.[30] Much the same applies to more complex forms, such as Australian Carboniferous brachiopods, including the later Mesozoic brachiopods and also Paleozoic invertebrates such as trilobites, or Late Cenozoic fossil beetles.[31] Of course, Darwin was aware to some extent of the sudden transitions, but assumed a gradualism and smoothness in natural selection over time, believing that the slowness is such that it is undetectable in geological formation over several million years, and that any examples are a result of imperfections in the fossil record.

Yet if the record is imperfect, how does this explain a *lack* of apparent change, that is, the stasis that is recorded? In the grip of a strong Darwinian paradigm, Gould laments that most paleontologists saw this stasis as a signal of failure to detect evolution, and so did not publish their results. The relatively rare cases of apparent gradualism, such as the increased coiling of the *Gryphaea* in Lower Jurassic rocks in England, became cases used in textbooks, but Gould proposes that these cases also proved false upon reexamination.[32] Gould believes that the tendency toward what he has termed publication bias—that is, a positive discrimination in favor of what are deemed positive results, in this case, that for gradualism—has seriously distorted the kind of data available for publication. Significantly,

---

29. Ibid., 751.

30. Ibid., 753.

31. Gould cites Derek Ager as a world leader in Mesozoic brachiopods who, after a lifetime effort, found few, if any, evolving lineages. Ibid., 753–54.

32. This research informed Trueman's claim for gradualism. See ibid., 762.

he suggests, "Apparent silence—the overt nothing that actually records the strongest something—can embody the deepest and most vital meaning of all."[33]

Punctuated equilibrium operates at the level of geological time, and a more general punctuated style of change is also characteristic of mass extinctions triggered by, for example, bolide impacts. The geological immensity of time scales involved is hard to grasp, and it means, for example, somewhat graphically that "the entire history of human civilisation stands to the duration of primate phylogeny as an eyeblink to a human lifetime."[34] According to this hypothesis, little or no change would be expected during the lifetime of a given species, though *species* is more often than not defined in anatomical terms in the fossil record. The range of fluctuations that one might expect in this record would correspond approximately to that variation found in contemporary populations within species or a close relative. The punctuation phase is that assessed according to the limits of geological time, or a bedding plane, normally taking several thousand years in most cases, and only very rarely years or seasons. Given that the average species lifetime is about four million years, its appearance is very rapid and therefore can be given the analogy of "birth." A comparison with species that seem to show gradual change shows that about nine out of ten species of Ordovician trilobites arise by punctuation. Other experimental data come from study of African rift valley lakes, where high sedimentation rates permit tracking of the punctuation process from a given ancestor.

Since 1972, when Eldredge and Gould published their first article on punctuated equilibrium, evidence, according to Gould, has gradually accumulated that species seem to emerge by splitting off from an ancestral line, rather than by gradual change.[35] Gould proposes, "A new species must pass through a short period of ambiguity during its initial differentiation from an ancestral population, but, in the proper scaling of macroevolutionary time, this period passes so quickly (almost always in the unsolvable geological moment of a single bedding plane) that operational definability

---

33. In this, he shows a much greater sensitivity to cultural influences on scientific practice compared with those scholars who are, arguably, hardened toward an exclusivist approach to Darwinian theory, even while making a claim for detached objectivity. He also compares this silence to historical instances of significant silence, including that of Jesus before Pilate. See ibid., 765.

34. Ibid., 766.

35. Gould gives numerous references for this; see ibid., 824–74.

encounters no threat."[36] While branching has been recognized for some time, the weight it was given in evolutionary terms was to generate diversity, rather than as an *agency* that is subject to selection. The alternative theory was that change happened during the lifetime of a species, that is, in the *anagenetic* mode, rather than at speciation as such.

Punctuated equilibrium is primarily about the *time scale* of particular events, rather than a novel theory of change, for it conceives that speciation happens relatively quickly followed by stasis, rather than the usual account of anagenesis followed by allopatric geographical separation. Although Gould complains bitterly about how his theory has been misunderstood, it is clear that his claim that "selection" during punctuated equilibrium operates at the species level is perhaps somewhat misleading, if this implies that two species somehow "compete" with each other such that one produces the most "offspring" in the manner normally understood as integral to Darwinian natural selection. He is at pains to point out that evolutionary patterns are not simply extrapolated from what happens at the individual level of genes, cells, organisms, or local populations. At the same time, macroevolution is supported by this theory; that is, the transition to a new species is significant in evolutionary terms. Instead, what would be more accurate to state is that rapid genetic change in a given species is *coincident* with speciation, so that what had been thought to be a gradual anagenic process over the lifetime of a species is now compressed into geologically very short time scales.

Punctuated equilibrium certainly does not give any support whatsoever for creationism, and the fact that some creationists have inappropriately used this theory to support their ideas shows not only their ignorance, but also, perhaps, why some evolutionary biologists are wary of giving it their support.[37] Francisco Ayala is particularly vitriolic in his attack, and he believes that any direct evidence for macroevolution is not yet forthcoming, and that so-called macroevolution between species could still be explained according to classical neo-Darwinian principles without alteration.[38] Punctuated equilibrium also fits in with an allopatric theory

---

36. Ibid., 776–77.

37. I mean by this not that evolutionary biologists are ignorant of the science, but the view that any theory that might even illegitimately support such a position should be treated with caution.

38. See, for example, Francisco J. Ayala, "Punctuated Equilibrium and Species Selection," in *Back to Darwin: A Richer Account of Evolution*, ed. John B. Cobb, 185–92 (Grand Rapids: Eerdmans, 2008). Ayala gives the example, also used by Gould, of an

of speciation, whereby the separation of a new "daughter" species from the "parental" species occurs by geographical or other forms of isolation. The key here is that the process of speciation itself needs to be thought of as rapid.[39]

Yet Gould takes his theory further than this "weak" version of punctuated evolution that I have been suggesting, in proposing that species can be thought of as equivalent to "individuals" when they arise through allopatry and rapid change, are stable over long periods, and are then followed by extinction. He names two versions of macroevolution. The first, weaker theory holds that the differential success of species, while "individual" in descriptive terms, still ultimately depends on conventional Darwinian theories about organisms struggling in a given population. The second, stronger version holds that fitness is defined by the interaction of species with their environments, that is, at a much larger scale than microevolution. Gould's strong theory has come under criticism from other evolutionary

---

optimal fish species that has specialized and is successful in Darwinian terms, living side by side with a more genetically variable species that, when the time is right, finds that the ability of some of its members to survive the drying-out process proves advantageous, so what was a minor species survives in evolutionary terms as a new lineage. Ayala's retort is that such a minor species could equally have adapted to drying out, and this then accounts for its survival, rather than its genetic variability as such. However, it seems to me that the change in environmental conditions that triggered the relative survival advantage of another species is less likely to be explained by early specialization in the way that Ayala suggests, as in this case, the minor species would have evolved in the first instance in such a way that it was grossly unsuited to its environment. In other words, I support Gould's idea that it is necessary to conceive of evolvability of species as being of significance. Those species that are the most able to cope with environmental change will survive, and this leads to one species replacing the other in a pattern that suggests rapid change followed by stasis. The characteristics that make for evolvability are also likely to include a genetic component, but that does not mean it is incorrect to look at patterns of species replacement over the long term as a way of articulating evolutionary change. In other words, punctuated equilibrium could be seen not so much as introducing new fundamental mechanisms, but as a descriptive account of patterns of species replacement. Far more adventurous is the idea that there are factors working at this higher macro level that are unknown at the level of the individual organisms. Gould believes that this is the case and that, as for other mechanisms operating beyond the species level, definitive proof is almost impossible to obtain. Yet it seems to me that the emergence of complexity is such that this should not be ruled out and most likely needs to be included.

39. Thoeretically, punctuated equilibrium could also cohere with sympatric speciation, but Eldredge and Gould choose the more conventional model of allopatry deliberately.

biologists who refute some of his evidence. His reply against those who hold to anagenic theories is the persistence of ancestral lines, which one would not expect if transformation took place within a species in its entirety. Yet as I have shown here, it seems entirely reasonable to recognize a "weak" version of punctuated evolution without going so far as to give a species a particular identity such that it is, in ways not fully understood, in competition with other species. Claims for the latter need not discount the possibility of punctuation per se, though I remain agnostic about the extent to which there is clear scientific evidence for the stronger version of this theory, which Gould clearly prefers.

The proposal that evolution also acts at the level of the species, including catastrophic mass extinctions, has important consequences in other respects, for it seems to open up different processes that allow for the possibility of directional change. Gould puts the matter succinctly thus:

> I try to resolve the paradox of the first tier (the empirical failure of Darwin's logically airtight argument for a vector of progress) by arguing that punctuated equilibrium at the second tier or phyletic trends, and mass extinction at the third tier of faunal overturn, impose enough of their own, distinct and different, patterning to forestall the domination or pure imprint of extrapolated micro-evolutionary results upon the general pageant of life's history.[40]

Of course, as I previously mentioned, not all biologists accept his view that Darwinian theory acting at the microevolutionary level is insufficient to explain what might be termed the broad directionality in evolution toward increasing complexity. In this, Gould seems to be allowing for the emergence of some kind of restraint in the evolutionary process at large. This challenges the second principle of Darwin's theory, namely, that of complete efficacy, since it seems to allow for evolution by processes other than natural selection acting at the level of the organism. Gould believes that while some lineages show an increase in complexity, others do not, though it would be incorrect to suppose that he rejects any directional sense toward complexity.[41]

---

40. Gould, *Structure of Evolutionary Thought*, 50.

41. Niels Gregersen characterizes Gould as a skeptic toward the idea of complexity in evolution. It seems to me that Gould is correct to challenge any universal appeal to complexity, and inasmuch as he still allows for some direction to evolution, as noted here and through ideas such as constraint, the contrast between his position and that of

Gould begins his discussion of constraint by resisting first that it is in opposition to Darwin's theory, and second that it needs to be considered in positive terms, taking as its root a classic meaning rather than simply a negative concept.[42] These ideas have a historical basis in that, in Darwin's time, competing theories claimed that positive forces over and beyond natural selection were required in order to effect change. Yet following the success of Darwin's theory, most biologists have resisted the idea of constraint understood in anything other than limits to the power of natural selection under certain circumstances. One such simple example that is still Darwinian is that of trade-offs between two positive characteristics in evolutionary terms, or biomechanical limits. Other so-called genetic or developmental constraints reflect the level of variability present as raw material for natural selection. Gould believes that internal constraints exist both as a consequence of physical principles and as a result of particular histories that lead to what he terms "inhomogeneous filling of morphospace as flow down ancient channels of deep homology"; that is, more is going on here than simple adaptation to current ecological landscapes.[43] The observation of common patterns of morphology led D'Arcy Thomson to argue that physical laws act rather like Aristotelian final causes, with natural selection acting as the means to reach such a pattern, that is, efficient cause.[44] Gould admits that there are some instances where this may apply, but it is certainly not sufficient as an explanation.[45]

Historical constraints do not challenge the central tenets of Darwinian theory inasmuch as such constraints are viewed as direct adaptations in the ancestral taxon. But Gould argues that it is *after* their initial appearance that a more positive meaning may appear, expressed as easier access to adaptive solutions, or negative constraint expressed through limitation

---

others such as Francisco Ayala is rather less stark. Niels Gregersen, "The Complexification of Nature: Supplementing the Neo-Darwinian Paradigm?" *Theology and Science* 4, no. 1 (2006): 5–31.

42. Gould, *Structure of Evolutionary Thought*, 1026. He draws on the biblical book of Job here for this classical meaning, more as a source of literature than as anything more profound.

43. Ibid., 49.

44. Ibid., 1207.

45. He names instances where structural constraint may apply as including the origin of life itself and its early history up to the generation of the prokaryotic cell, the formation of broad and recurrent patterns that are not phylogenetically constrained, and the right-skewed distribution of life's complexity.

of potential.[46] Yet in general, Gould believes that microevolution according to Darwinian natural selection acts in a way that effectively locks organisms into transient specialist modes and thereby reduces the capacity to evolve later when conditions change. This reduces prospects for long-term success. Occasionally there is general improvement, such as biomechanical improvement that is flexible enough for further usefulness. At the genetic level, certain genes for development, such as the Hox genes in bilateral phyla, provide flexible developmental rules that are then shared by all complex animal phyla but expressed in very different ways, so that the ancestral agnathan gill arch becomes the functioning malleus of the mammalian middle ear.[47] Yet Gould believes that this still represents constraint to the extent that some skeletal element of form and position is needed. He also argues strongly against any notion that such relatively limited flexibility is sufficient to explain the macroevolutionary success of species; hence selection works at this level and not just at the microevolutionary level.

The immediate question that comes to mind is whether the interactions that take place at the species level, assuming they exist, can meaningfully be termed as operating according to natural selection, given that this is defined in terms of individual organisms' fitness for survival in order to reproduce. In other words, while we might go with Gould far enough in supposing that some sort of interactions do perhaps genuinely take place at levels beyond that of the individual organisms, to name species "individuals" in the way he contends seems rather more tenuous. The ability of species to use features evolved for one function in order to adapt to another is what he terms exaptation, the features themselves being spandrels.[48]

A further area of considerable debate is that of convergence, the phenomenon attested to on numerous occasions that organisms show certain parallels of form and function when faced with equivalent environments, but have different evolutionary histories. The difference between parallelism and convergence becomes clearer in light of the central distinction between homology and homoplasty: homologous structures are similar because of a common ancestor, while homoplastic structures are similar by independent evolution. In parallelism, we find that internal constraint provides the formal influence, whereas in convergence, the operation of

---

46. Gould, *Structure of Evolutionary Thought*, 1173.

47. Ibid., 1273.

48. I will return to a fuller discussion of the significance of this in relation to evolutionary psychology in chapter 2.

natural selection is on two different substrates such that the resulting similarity could not come from internal factors. Sometimes parallelism is used to describe the gray area between homology and homoplasty, such that there is still a common underlying generator of structures, even if the structures themselves are arrived at by independent selection. Gould believes that many examples of what look like convergence actually share homologous genes and developmental pathways. Such homology is then explained more accurately by parallelism, especially in studies of the evolutionary genetics of development (termed *evo-devo*). In this, "internal constraints of homologous genes and developmental pathways have kept fruitful channels of change open and parallel, even in the most disparate and most genealogically distant bilaterian phyla."[49] An alternative theory of convergence proposed by Simon Conway Morris is that many observed cases of convergence are not primarily disguised parallelism, but rather, in encountering similar problems, natural selection works in order to generate the same solutions to these problems.[50] This theory does not so much overturn Gould's alternative proposal but suggests it is insufficient as an explanation. A question for debate is the extent to which each operates in the course of evolutionary history.

Conway Morris's case rests on numerous examples of convergence, though it can be interpreted as supporting Darwinian evolution inasmuch as natural selection works to effect the same results. Conway Morris is also convinced that evolution is far less random than Stephen Gould claimed when he proposed that if life's tape were to be rerun again, then the chances of humans appearing would be extremely remote.[51] Conway Morris claims in the first place that the notion of exaptation—that is, that some gene sites are more prone to change than others—implies less randomness in mutations than commonly assumed.[52] In the second place, Conway Morris

49. Gould, *Structure of Evolutionary Thought*, 1069.

50. Simon Conway Morris, *Life's Solution* (Cambridge: Cambridge University Press, 2003).

51. See Simon Conway Morris, "Evolution and Convergence," in *The Deep Structure of Biology: Is Convergence Sufficiently Ubiquitous to Give a Directional Signal?* ed. Simon Conway Morris, 46–67 (West Conshohocken: Templeton Foundation Press, 2008). Although Gould's sense of the randomness of evolution pervades his overall picture of evolutionary history, it is also significant, perhaps, that his understanding of constraint and punctuated evolution as following a pattern is suggestive of a theory that is more than simply an endorsement of randomness as an overarching idea.

52. Other aspects of evolutionary processes are far from "random," such as historical

suggests that the mass extinctions that occurred in end Cretaceous and end Permian might not have been strictly *necessary* in order to allow mammals and other humans to evolve. He engages in a thought experiment such that if, for example, no bolide struck but the climatic changes still took place, then in the glacial period that would have ensued, mammals would have migrated to warmer regions, but this could still be out of the range of the great reptiles confined to tropical zones. Moreover, if evolution were just allowed to run its course again, he believes that something like intelligent humans would eventually emerge.

Convergence also seems to operate at different scales, that is, from the molecular scale through to particular social characteristics. Two examples suffice here. The first is the translucent crystalline protein of the eye. The bivalve mollusk uses a crystalline derived from aldehyde dehydrogenase, while vertebrates use one related to heat shock proteins. In these cases, the proteins show convergent function but no sequence similarity, but the promoter sequence does show convergence. Lizards and birds also show mammal-like properties in different ways—in the former through, for example, viviparity and similarities in the placenta, the latter in warm-bloodedness, parental care, vocalization, and so on, even though the brain structure is itself very different. Conway Morris speculates that the existence of convergent evolution is not simply a directional signal—that is, in a loose way, Darwinian evolution acting like a compass that points in a particular direction—but also that there may be deeper realities in the world that are universal, a metaphysics. He eschews, then, what he sees as the corrupting and corrosive force of a rejection of all metaphysics in science and the humanities, the adoption of suspicion toward any universalism in biology, and postmodern relativism as the only framework of meaning in the humanities.

The stress on randomness as the underlying process of evolution in Gould is clearly in stark contrast to the possibility of a universal order toward which evolution searches like a wavering needle on a compass. Nonetheless, the difference between Gould and Conway Morris is perhaps not quite as sharp as some commentators have suggested.[53] Gould

---

constraints according to evolutionary history that Gould also acknowledges, though for him, the ancestral divergence and subsequent development would have been subject to random environmental factors.

53. While I appreciate Gregersen's generally astute analysis, I part company with his characterization of Conway Morris as adopting a "law like" biochemistry, in contrast to

does allow for constraint, in both a physical and a historical sense, and he also seems to see an overall directional pattern in macroevolution. This qualifies his comments on the randomness and contingency of microevolution. The difference between Gould and Conway Morris seems to relate to Gould's total rejection of any universal pattern as ensuing from phenomena of convergence, and his insistence that historical constraints arise in the ancestral phyla in a contingent manner, rather than as a "solution" to a given problem. Both Conway Morris and Gould claim to be firmly rooted in Darwinian theory while seeking to revise aspects of that theory in the light of their observations; ironically, perhaps, both have worked extensively on the Burgess Shale. But where Gould finds in the theory of punctuated equilibrium a more satisfying biological explanation of the mismatch between observation and theory, Conway Morris is drawn to consider the possibility of other, yet unidentified metaphysical laws, while at the same time eschewing vitalism or intelligent design. Natural law theory perhaps comes closest to the instinct of universal order hinted at by Conway Morris.[54] Although, strictly speaking, natural law in the classic sense does not specify fixity in the way sometimes supposed, it does not necessarily capture sufficiently the dynamic movement of evolutionary processes, such as that found particularly in Gould's punctuated equilibrium theory.

I will suggest in the following chapter that a theodramatic approach is the most convincing way of relating evolution with Christology. Such an approach both allows for the directionality that Conway Morris has indicated is characteristic of evolution as a whole, and permits the flexibility that is necessary in order to capture the sense of contingency that is characteristic of evolution and of history in general. Jeffrey Schloss is an evolutionary biologist who concedes that evolutionary history is like a

---

Gould's macroevolution of species, though I agree that both are seeking to revise neo-Darwinian ideas. Gregersen, "Complexification of Nature," 15. Conway Morris seems to be using biochemistry to illustrate constraints at the molecular level prior to dealing with other levels, but Gould does not deny that such constraints exist, and Conway Morris seems to view a more pervasive sense of convergence at different levels, including the social level, that is more than simply one governed by physical/chemical laws.

54. I have argued that natural law provides an analogy for Conway Morris's position, while not claiming that this is sufficient as a way of treating the relationship between evolution and theology. See C. Deane-Drummond, "Plumbing the Depths: A Recovery of Natural Law and Natural Wisdom in the Context of Debates about Evolutionary Purpose," in Conway Morris, *Deep Structure of Biology*, 195–217.

drama, with a cast involving living organisms as actors, where the environmental "stage" is itself changed over time.[55] Viewing evolutionary history as drama is also able to accommodate the idea of punctuated evolution, which speaks of more dramatic changes, at least in geological time, rather more readily than a simple narrative structure, which tends to view the backdrop as a more fixed "stage." Typical neo-Darwinian views stress the improvisation of the script of the play, while others see more directionality. Gould seems to concede *some* directionality operating at the macroevolutionary level, but he also acknowledges constraint in a positive way that is not always sufficiently recognized. Conway Morris, in contrast, seems to give more priority to constraint, over and above Gould, who views any processes of constraint arising somewhat fortuitously. The point is that both evolutionary models fit well with the metaphor of evolutionary change as *drama*; in Conway Morris's case, the script seems to be written, at least in general terms, in advance, while in Gould's case, the playwright improvises at every turn. The most radical interpretation of punctuated equilibrium as that which expresses species selection also can be accommodated, but it is not strictly necessary in order to recount evolutionary history in dramatic terms.

Regardless of the perspective, the slip toward retelling such a drama as a metanarrative is strong.[56] I share Niels Gregersen's proposal that we need to adopt what he terms a "patchwork view of scientific explanations"; that is, to resist attempts to come up with a single theory that does not do justice to the perplexing complexities of evolutionary history.[57] However, his characterization of Gould as encapsulating simply a Lady Luck hypothesis that is hostile to religion, in contrast to Conway Morris's potential for theism, is in many respects tempting but rather too simplistic.[58] Instead, as I will be arguing in this book as a whole, there is a need to treat universal ideals in biology with considerable caution, and Gould's approach, taken as a whole, can still be consistent with theological reflection—that is, it is not *inherently* atheistic. Ian Barbour argues the case for process theology as a mediating category between Gould's emphasis on

<hr />

55. Jeffrey P. Schloss, "Divine Providence and the Question of Evolutionary Directionality," in Cobb, *Back to Darwin*, 330–50.

56. While I am appreciative of Jeffrey Schloss's use of drama to recount evolutionary history, he fails to appreciate sufficiently the difference between viewing evolutionary history as drama and viewing it as narrative, a point that I will return to in chapter 1.

57. Gregersen, "Complexification of Nature," 5–31.

58. Ibid., 16.

randomness and Conway Morris's position on contingency.[59] I suggest that process theology may be able to perform such a function, though not all its protagonists have kept such a balance, as discussed in the section on religious quandaries over evolution below in this introduction, and it also seems to fail to give an adequate account of Christology. In leaning toward a narrative approach, process thought sets up similar problems of universality criticized in classical accounts, even if it draws back from classic notions of eschatology in a way that has more in common with Darwinian evolution. In particular, the adaptationist metanarrative that is particularly pervasive in evolutionary psychology has, if anything, adopted an inappropriate metaphysic and a hidden secularized eschatology in that it has led to an account of evolutionary biology in the social sphere that loses touch with the openness to evolutionary alternatives that forms the core of Darwin's principles. I will discuss this issue in more detail in chapter 2. This does not mean, however, that metaphysics is ruled out of court entirely, as long as it is suitably qualified. But before attempting this more constructive task, we need to situate such discussion by a brief reference to the broader setting of the debates between evolution and religious belief.

Religious Quandaries over Evolution

Rather than survey the full spread of religious debates about evolution, I intend to touch on more recent scholarship inasmuch as it sets the scene for the more focused discussion of Christology in the chapter that follows. Most of the debates have focused on how far evolutionary theory is compatible with theological concepts of God as Creator, divine providence over creation, and theological anthropology, whereby humanity is perceived as being in a special sense the image of the Creator. Darwin's theory seemed to remove all need for a Creator God, diminish any sense of divine providence in the wake of evolutionary ills and suffering, and qualify the importance of humans by situating human life as a brief episode in a long and complex evolutionary history.

There are various reactions to this dilemma. One approach is to deny the relevance of evolutionary biology to theology, so that while biology

---

59. Ian G. Barbour, "Evolution and Process Thought," *Theology and Science* 3, no. 2 (2005): 161–78.

talks about evolutionary mechanism, theology talks about the meaning of life and the relationship between God and human history.

A second is to react against evolution as if it is an enemy to religious thought, and attack by attempting to substitute an alternative so-called scientific explanation, where the early books of Genesis, for example, are interpreted in particular ways for scientific purposes. This trend, known as creationism, is particularly rife in America. Its popularity may relate to literalistic interpretations of scripture, though—ironically, perhaps—the so-called insights from this interpretation go far beyond what can be read from the biblical text itself.[60] In such a context, it is hardly surprising that counterreactions, such as those from Richard Dawkins, sound more convincing to the public mind, though his perception of God rests on a very simplistic theological interpretation.

Related to this discussion is what has been coined the "intelligent design" movement, whereby an explanation for complexity is sought through an intelligence that is believed to direct evolution in particular ways, such that a complex assemblage of organs such as the eye is possible. As indicated earlier, Darwin has already provided evidence that such intelligence is not required in order to explain complexity, and in this sense, most scientists remain unconvinced, so that where material explanations are not forthcoming, they are likely to be found in due course. Of course, any evidence that such *intelligence* is materially based in the manner that William Dembski suggests is almost impossible, and such theories, while sounding scientific, follow in the tradition of Lamarck inasmuch as they seem to presuppose metaphysics. It is one reason, perhaps, why intelligent design has come under such heavy fire from many quarters, though it is still a topic of active discussion in the United States, as its campaigners have presented it as an alternative to evolution in schools. William Dembski is perhaps its most sophisticated protagonist, though he has come under heavy criticism from the philosopher Michael Ruse.[61]

A third approach is to engage with those in the second camp (creationism and counterreactions) and show up their deficiencies, either by attacking authors such as Dawkins for their naïve approach to theology, or by attacking creationism or intelligent design for its naïve approach to

---

60. A full discussion of creationism and replies by theologians is outside the scope of this introduction.

61. For discussion, see Robert B. Stewart, *Intelligent Design: William A. Dembski and Michael Ruse in Dialogue* (Minneapolis: Fortress Press, 2007).

science. Alister McGrath has written extensively on Dawkins and his various illusions.[62]

A fourth approach is a more active attempt at resolution of the difficulties by portraying God as in some sense the author of evolution. Although this is sometimes called theistic evolution, it is more accurately a theology of evolution, in that the former joins a particular metaphysics with evolution.[63] The shape that this discussion takes will almost always put most emphasis on the immanence of God in creation; that is, God need not be thought of as remote from biologically based evolutionary processes just because the latter provide all that seems to be required to explain the evolution of humans and other species. Although this discussion has its precedents in Henry Drummond's *Ascent of Man* written in 1894, authors come from different theological backgrounds, but all resist the notion that God somehow intervenes in evolutionary history.[64] Of course, this resistance to interventionist notions of God is much wider than biological evolution, and it reflects a desire to portray the interaction between God and nature as in alignment with known laws of physics, chemistry, and biology, rather than working against these laws through what has traditionally been termed miraculous interventions in nature.[65] Of course, this begs the question of what the interaction of God with the natural world might mean, and Robert Russell offers the possibility of the influence of God at the quantum level, affecting the mutations that take place by influencing the probability of their occurrence.[66] This mediates between more conservative

---

62. A. McGrath, *Dawkins' God* (Oxford: Blackwell, 2005); and Alister E. McGrath and Joanna Collicutt McGrath, *The Dawkins Delusion: Atheist Fundamentalism and the Denial of the Divine* (Downers Grove: InterVarsity, 2007), provide good summaries of arguments against Dawkins.

63. This is discussed in Antje Jackelen, "A Critical View of 'Theistic Evolution,'" *Theology and Science* 5, no. 2 (2007): 151–65. See also Martinez Hewlett and Ted Peters, "Why Darwin's Theory of Evolution Deserves Theological Support," *Theology and Science* 4, no. 2 (2006): 171–82.

64. Henry Drummond, *The Lowell Lectures on the Ascent of Man* (London: Hodder & Stoughton, 1984).

65. A series of five volumes titled Scientific Perspectives on Divine Action compiled by the Center for Theology and the Natural Sciences and the Vatican Observatory is particularly helpful in this regard. See especially Robert John Russell, William Stoeger, and Francisco Ayala, eds., *Evolution and Molecular Biology: Scientific Perspectives on Divine Action* 3 (Vatican City: Vatican Observatory; Berkeley: CTNS, 1998). See also Ted Peters and Nathan Hallanger, eds., *God's Action in Nature's World: Essays in Honour of Robert John Russell* (Basingstoke: Ashgate, 2006).

66. R. J. Russell, "Special Providence and Genetic Mutation: A New Defence of

views of God acting directly in history and their liberal alternatives, while avoiding the idea of God breaking natural laws. However, as someone trained in biological science, I find the possibility that God might influence mutation in a particular direction for usefulness perhaps many thousands of years hence somewhat strange. The evolutionary record shows not only the development of adaptations later on in the history of that species, where earlier mutations are now put to good use, but also their conservation in development, so that the same genes are now used in the same way for different species. It would seem to anticipate, if it is to work, that God knows the whole history of the intervening period, which goes against how I would interpret the action of God in creation and history. Moreover, if God is somehow influencing the probabilities of mutation at a quantum level, such mutations are no longer random in the true sense and would seem to go against natural selection of randomly distributed variants. If randomness remains, then the actual influence at this level is obscure.

The alternative around this quandary is to envisage a "top-down" approach, where evolutionary emergence of complexity is viewed as somehow being influenced by the next level. The highest level is envisaged as God, impinging on less complex levels. Theological discussion around emergence has proved to be particularly intense.[67] Arthur Peacocke was one of the pioneers of this particular view of God's action with the world, and his influence continues to be felt in present discussion.[68] This work is still somewhat philosophically based inasmuch as while there is clear evidence for the emergence of complexity, scientific proof of "top-down" causation is harder to demonstrate.[69] Arthur Peacocke adheres to a "naturalistic" understanding of the relationship between God and the world, in that it takes as its cue the emergence of different levels or layers of complexity as

---

Theistic Evolution," in Russell, Stoeger, and Ayala, *Evolution and Molecular Biology*, 191–223.

67. See, for example, Nancey Murphy and William Stoeger, eds., *Evolution and Emergence: Systems, Organisms and Persons* (Oxford: Oxford University Press, 2007). This book deals with emergent phenomena in general, not just evolutionary emergence.

68. See, for example, A. Peacocke, *All That Is: A Naturalistic Faith for the Twenty-first Century*, ed. Philip Clayton (Minneapolis: Fortress Press, 2007).

69. See, for example, discussions in Murphy and Stoeger, *Evolution and Emergence*, especially Alwyn Scott, "Non-linear Science and the Cognitive Hierarchy," 173–97. Scott considers varieties of downward causation from strong to weak varieties, and prefers the more moderate variety that has some analogy with more moderate versions of emergence.

organisms evolve to higher and higher levels of consciousness. The interaction of God with the world would then be analogous to the way evolution as a whole has shown the capacity for increased complexity and "top-down" causation. Christopher Knight argues that such a position still implies a form of "intervention"—though this word is too strong, and "influence" might be a better term here. However, it is not an influence that breaks known or existing laws, so it is easier in many ways to accept in parallel with contemporary scientific views of evolution.[70] The difficulty with this view as stated is that if the influence is there but has no impact other than affirming what happens in evolutionary processes anyway, then one wonders what the purpose of that influence might be. Also, if this is the primary way God interacts with the world, then the character of God becomes read off from the evolved world of nature as a whole: God's action is mirrored through a particular understanding of the world as emergent. Yet what gives us such confidence that our interpretation of the world as evolved reflects adequately the *primary* character of who God is in the manner suggested? Such a view implies a form of natural revelation that takes precedence over special revelation.[71] Indeed, Peacocke's account of Christology seems to be softened in order to fit Christ into this picture, so that Christ emerges as one example of God incarnate in the world as a whole, where "incarnate" seems to mean a general impact of God on the workings of the world.

An alternative to bottom-up or top-down approaches is to return to more classical notions of God and envisage God working simply through evolution as a secondary cause, much in the manner of Thomistic discussion.[72] There is much to commend this route, in that it allows for distinctions to be drawn between God and creation while recognizing their interaction. The difficulty with this view is whether the creation of laws, including natural selection, sufficiently represents God as engaged in the creative process. It would be all too easy to view God as somehow leaving the world to its own devices after creating secondary causes.

Process theologians seek to find God in the evolving processes of the natural world as such, at least in God's contingent nature. John Haught's

---

70. Christopher Knight, *The God of Nature: Incarnation and Contemporary Science* (Minneapolis: Fortress Press, 2007).

71. I will argue in chapter 4 that Hans Urs von Balthasar's use of analogy of being offers one way through this difficulty.

72. This seems to be the view of Denis Edwards, as expressed in his *God and Evolution: A Trinitarian Theology* (New York: Paulist Press, 1999).

God after Darwin summarizes his theology of evolution, drawing heavily on the process thought of A. N. Whitehead.[73] Haught reacts against any classical notion of natural theology that more often than not viewed the deity as in some sense both benign and bringing order.[74] Instead, correctly in my view, he argues that an understanding of the way evolution and theology interact needs to take into account the contingency and turmoil of life processes. He proposes to solve this problem by speaking of divine creativity in terms of the vulnerability of God, and speaking of nature as promise, rather than design or order. In other words, he resists the language of design inasmuch as it promises more than it can keep with respect to the way Darwin, at least, embraced the contingency of evolution by natural selection. Moreover, he is palpable in his resistance to the intelligent design camp, for he argues more strongly still that it is a mistake to find in design a mirror of the way God works, for as such, this detaches God from the novelty found in creation, its source of creativity and ultimately life itself. He also considers the evolutionary account of Darwin to be a gift inasmuch as it promises to point humanity to a much larger narrative, beginning with the earliest history of the cosmos, so that life and its processes are integrated into this larger epic of evolution.[75] Although very occasionally he uses the language of drama, it is embedded in an overall thesis that both biblical narrative and nature are stories to be read together, and what he terms "biblical wisdom" is trust in an incomprehensible Mystery that grounds the universe, self-abandoning and vulnerable love that gives itself away to the universe, and an invitation by this Mystery to future fulfillment in a way that is surprising and unpredictable.[76] This is very different from the way the Bible interprets wisdom as such, and seems to take its form from process thought, alongside concern for a suffering God.[77]

73. John Haught, *God after Darwin: A Theology of Evolution*, 2nd ed. (Boulder: Westview, 2007). See also J. Haught, *Deeper than Darwin* (Cambridge: Westview, 2004).

74. Haught, *God after Darwin*, ix–x.

75. Ibid., 2. Haught is certainly not the only author who has viewed cosmological history and connected it to the history of life in this way. Other authors include, for example, Brian Swimme and Thomas Berry. See, for example, Brian Swimme and Thomas Berry, *The Universe Story* (San Francisco: HarperCollins, 1992). The cosmic creation story has also become popular among ecotheologians. I offer a review of the latter in C. Deane-Drummond, *Ecotheology* (London: DLT, 2008).

76. Haught, *Deeper Than Darwin*, 65.

77. I have discussed biblical wisdom in the context of science and religion discourse in C. Deane-Drummond, *Creation through Wisdom* (Edinburgh: T&T Clark, 2000).

Of course, this evolutionary epic itself shows some measure of an ordered progression that Haught wants to endorse, particularly through his notion of aesthetic principles that he finds emerging in evolution. Yet for him, the randomness of the process remains inasmuch as it shows God not as a coercive divine power, but as one who is widely experimental, expressing infinite love through its persuasion, rather than coercion.[78] For him, the emergence of intense beauty, along with suffering and tragedy, is taken eternally into "God's own feeling of the world," such that all evolutionary events "abide permanently within the everlasting empathy of God."[79] Yet I would contend that Haught's theology of evolution is much more influenced by cosmological ideas and the philosophy of A. N. Whitehead, which suggest a strong directionality to evolution, than by Darwin's position. This contrasts strongly with Darwin's theory, where evolution wandered on its way in a kind of "random walk." Haught argues that Darwinian evolution inevitably presupposes cosmic change,[80] and while this is true after a fashion, the time scale in which evolutionary changes have taken place is dwarfed by cosmic considerations, and evolutionary biology is subject to local variations on a scale that is very different from the cosmic scale that Haught underwrites. The language of "depth" that he uses implies that evolutionary biology on its own misses something by not connecting to the cosmic "story," but it seems to me that this jars with what biologists seek to discover in their own terms and "flattens out" the complexity and intricate diversity of evolution discussed in this introduction by considering it in terms of a strongly directional cosmic purpose. The most that we might say of biological evolution is that it is under some sort of constraint to evolve in a certain way.[81] Haught instead, following Freeman Dyson and Whitehead, envisages a positive movement along an axis according to an aesthetic principle.[82] For him, the point of the universe is to express this beauty, viewed as ever intensifying in the experience of God.

---

78. Haught, *God after Darwin*, 45.

79. Ibid., 47.

80. Haught, *Deeper than Darwin*, 60.

81. Conway Morris, *Life's Solution;* and Conway Morris, *The Deep Structure of Biology.*

82. Haught, *God after Darwin*, 137.

PART 1
THE DRAMA OF INCARNATION

1

Christology and Evolution as Theodrama

Pierre Teilhard de Chardin, Karl Rahner, and Jürgen Moltmann have all contributed to the narrower concern of relating Christ to evolution. However, for reasons that will be clear in this chapter, I will not be drawing primarily on these sources for this book. Instead, I will argue for a different way of appropriating evolutionary ideas into a theological discourse using *theodrama*, rather than *narrative*, as a framework for discussion. Such theodrama, drawing particularly on Hans Urs von Balthasar, allows for theological aesthetics/wonder as both the first word before the performance and the last word in terms of its goal. Wonder as a mediating category in consideration of christological and evolutionary ideas is not all that needs to be said, however. Wisdom as one of the earliest Christologies has the advantage of coming close to the historical Jesus as teacher and sage. Yet for the purposes of this chapter, I will argue that Wisdom also needs to be thought of in terms of kenotic Christology as a way of highlighting the theodramatic quality of the relationship between God and the cosmos. In the light of this discussion, theodrama in a metaphorical way serves to highlight those aspects of evolution that are perhaps pushed to one side by other readings that seek to generate grand narratives.

1.1 Christology and Evolution

Classical debates on the person and nature of Christ struggled to articulate the meaning of the human and divine nature of Christ while keeping within the Chalcedonian framework of who Christ is, namely, one person and two natures. It was possible to lean in the more Alexandrian direction, where the emphasis was on the importance of the divinity of Christ and the Word made flesh, or in the Antiochene direction, where more emphasis was placed on the humanity of Christ and the human soul taken up by the Word from the moment of incarnation. If the first view tended to squeeze out the possibility of a human soul, the second ended up with two persons in Christ, the divine indwelling the human. Historically, the story was likely to have been rather more complicated than this account implies, with authors such as Cyril of Alexandria adopting some ideas on Christ's rational soul that seem closer to the Antiochene tradition.[1] The point here is that such a framework then leads to further discussion about how one might consider the human nature that is assumed by Christ—is it an abstract universal, or does it only make sense in the particular?—along with related discussion about anhypostasia and enhypostasia, with the former putting more emphasis on the possibility of a human nature existing as an abstract universal human nature, and the latter emphasizing the particular human nature as pertains in Christ's person.[2] Other ways through the problem of relating the divine and human natures in Christ posit that the two are related through mutual indwelling, that is, perichoresis, so that each indwells the other in a manner analogous to the relationships of the Trinity.[3] All these discussions are closed insofar as they represent internal theological debates about what might be logically possible, given certain premises. They seem to bear little or no relationship to evolutionary biology except inasmuch as the concept of two natures becomes incredible or difficult to understand.

It is hardly surprising that those who are engaged in the dialogue between evolution and theology are more attracted to liberal accounts of Christology, where Christ is portrayed as a man unique only inasmuch as he is uniquely obedient and open to God. Arthur Peacocke, for example, suggests that in his oneness to God, Jesus is an archetype, a chief exemplar

---

1. For discussion, see Oliver Crisp, *Divinity and Humanity* (Cambridge: Cambridge University Press, 2007), 38–40.

2. An *anhypostatos physis* is a human nature that exists independently from an individual or person. In this scenario, Christ's personhood requires the assumption of human nature by the Word. From the moment of incarnation, there is *enhypostatos*, that is, human nature in a particular person. In some discussions, the human nature of Christ is seen as being taken up into the Word. See, in particular, ibid., 72–89.

3. Crisp also devotes a whole chapter to considering this issue. Ibid., 2–33.

of what it is for a human to be united in self-offering to God.[4] In Jesus, we find God's character as Love displayed, and this in its turn is expressed in the life, death, and resurrection of Jesus, where resurrection is interpreted in terms of what happens in the minds of the disciples. Drawing heavily on the theology of Geoffrey Lampe, Peacocke views Jesus as the evolutionary point where perfect humanity appears for the first time, but it is perfection in relationship. Jesus, here, is portrayed as one whose deity *emerges* as a result of carrying out the divine will, and is seen as in direct parallel to the normal workings of emergent reality in other spheres. Jesus becomes "the manifestation of what, or rather of the One who, is already in the world though not recognised or known."[5] Jesus' humanity evolved into a form of "transcendence" and then is recognized by others as having divine cogency. Although Peacocke maintains, therefore, a "top-down" approach to the interaction of God and the world, analogous to evolutionary emergence of "higher" levels of interaction, his Christology is "bottom-up," inasmuch as Jesus seems to *become* a fully God-informed subject, rather than being endowed with divine subjectivity from the beginning. Of course, this is the only option he really has, for it would be hard to imagine, in a general sense, how Christ might acquire divine characteristics through general top-down providential activity.

Ian Barbour is similarly exercised against traditional notions of two natures, so that "what was unique about Christ, in other words, was his relationship to God, not his metaphysical 'substance'"; even though he had "two wills," he was also able to exercise human "freedom and personal responsibility."[6] Also, similarly drawing on Lampe, he suggests that Jesus is best understood through a Spirit Christology, where Christ emerges as the archetype and pattern of union between God as Spirit and the spirit of humanity, and moves toward the final goal of creation, where humanity will be formed in the likeness of Christ, the model "Adam." Christ represents, therefore, a new "stage" in evolution and a new stage in God's activity. But

---

4. A. Peacocke, *Creation and the World of Science* (Oxford: Clarendon, 1979), 248.

5. A. Peacocke, *All That Is: A Naturalistic Faith for the Twenty-first Century*, ed. Philip Clayton (Minneapolis: Fortress Press, 2007), 37. Of course, the idea that Christ might become known as divine through his obedience and openness to God reflects a liberal tradition that goes as far back as Albert Ritschl. The point is that the evolutionary story of emergence is made paradigmatic, and the work of God, including the description of the meaning of theological terms such as grace, as well as an understanding of Christology, then becomes compatible with this, rather than the other way around.

6. Ian Barbour, *Religion in an Age of Science* (London: SCM, 1990), 210.

on what basis is humanity going to be conformed to the likeness of Christ if Christ has simply emerged through evolution? On this basis, redemption seems to be reduced to what happens to creation, expressed entirely in evolutionary terms. The newness of Christ is related to, first, his personal relationship with God, second, his ideas, and third, the response by the community around him. But is this sufficient? Would I really be inclined to worship Jesus as Lord, in the manner given in John's Gospel, if this is *all* that can be said about Christ?

Using process thought, Barbour also suggests that the difference between humanity and animals is similar to the difference between humanity and Christ, in that it is a difference of degree rather than an absolute difference, so in this way, "Christ is the distinctive, but not exclusive revelation of the power of God."[7] Inasmuch as he follows process writers in claiming that Christ's free decision and faithful response are needed, this fits in with an affirmation of his full humanity. I would agree with Barbour that the difference as far as Christ's humanity is concerned is one of degree, so that while Christ is perfect in his relationship to God, his humanity is fully grounded in evolutionary biology as far as his human personality is concerned; he suffers and grieves and is tempted like all of us. What is much weaker is a sense of Christ as divine gift, in spite of the language of process authors such as Cobb or Griffin, where Christ becomes God's "supreme act," yet such an act seems integral to evolutionary processes. Christ's uniqueness is reduced to "the content of God's aims for him and in his actualisation of those aims."[8] Hence, the classic notion of Christ as God incarnate has virtually disappeared.

The influence of Jesuit priest and paleontologist Pierre Teilhard de Chardin is palpable in such accounts. He was, without doubt, one of the pioneers of relating theology to evolution, and Christ to evolution in particular. Yet his vision was informed by a particular metaphysical way of perceiving the world that owed its origin less to Darwin's theory of evolution by natural selection than to Spencer's notion of progressive evolution, mentioned in the introduction. In this, Teilhard's writing suffers considerable drawbacks, for it imposes a cosmological unidirectional metaphysical theory on the nonlinear processes of Darwinian evolution. Yet for Teilhard, bringing evolution into line with Christology was a task that impinged on Christology as such. Hence, he believed that it was necessary to shed the

---

7. Ibid., 213.
8. Ibid., 235.

traditional account of Adam and Eve, with its preoccupation with original sin, and the "shadow of the cross," and to concentrate instead on viewing Christ in evolutionary terms.[9] Once we shift to an evolutionary worldview, evil becomes a "natural feature," so that evil comes about inevitably as a secondary effect.[10] Teilhard's experience in the trenches no doubt brought him face-to-face with a raw sense of evil and suffering, but he believed that theology needed to view it as a "necessary appearance in the course of the unification of the multiple," by which he seems to mean the emergence of complexity. Instead, evil is a "shadow, which God inevitably produces simply by the fact that he decides on creation."[11] In this, Teilhard anticipated much of the discussion on natural evil in contemporary thought. The cross in this way becomes not just expiation for moral sin, but the structural overcoming of the resistance to unification, that is, a "resistance to the rise of spirit inherent in matter."[12]

Of course, such a view depends on the accuracy of his evolutionary ideas that there is an inherent push toward unification, a view that arguably stems more from ideals of progress than from Darwinian theory as such. It is also in the light of this vision of progress that he situates the significance of Christ, for he proposes that such a center is necessary if the cosmos is to progress, and in this way, Christ is recognized as the crossroads where "everything can be seen, can be felt, can be controlled, can be vitalised, can be in touch with everything else. Is not that an admirable place in which to position (or rather recognize) Christ?"[13] He also argues that Christ needs to be seen as the progression toward which evolution has been working since the beginning, in the development of consciousness and hominization, and that evolution of humanity is continuing, such that it awaits a new future, but that future is anticipated in Christ. In this way, he presses for a reinterpretation of redemption so that it becomes equated with the consummation of evolution, where Christ is at the head as king, revitalizing the world.[14] In this way, he speaks of the blood of Christ as one

---

9. Pierre Teilhard de Chardin, "Christology and Evolution," in *Christianity and Evolution* trans. R. Hague, 81–82 (London: Collins, 1971).

10. This way of dealing with evil through an evolutionary, redemptive account is one that I will return to in later chapters.

11. Teilhard, "Christology and Evolution," 84.

12. Ibid., 85.

13. Ibid., 87.

14. Pierre Teilhard de Chardin, "Christ the Evolver, or a Logical Development of the Idea of Redemption," in *Christianity and Evolution*, 138–50, esp. 144–45.

that "circulates and vitalises, even more than it is shed. The Lamb of God bearing, together with the sins of the world, the burdens of its progress."[15] It would be incorrect to suggest that he removes all references to expiation for sin; rather, he believed that the first word has to be about creation and the ascent of creation and, as a consequence of this, fighting against evil, as well that moral evil found in humans. In other words, he interprets the incarnation of God in Christ primarily in evolutionary terms, and the cross of Christ primarily on a cosmic stage first, rather than speaking of it in terms of human misdemeanors.

It would, however, be incorrect to suggest that Christ is simply explained by evolution. Rather, Christ is also in some way emancipated from time and space, so that "in one of its aspects, different from that in which we are witnessing its formation, it has always been emerging above a world from which, seen from another angle, it is, at the same time, in the process of emergence."[16] He also envisages the future as impinging on the present, so that "this is what renders the movement not only irreversible, but irresistible."[17] Before humankind emerges, such attraction is "received blindly"; afterward, it is partially conscious in reflective freedom, leading eventually to religious belief.[18] Teilhard's God, understood as a "prime psychic mover" who works from the lowest levels of creation to humanization, anticipates process thought.

Teilhard also had a high view of the potential of science to contribute to the transformation of the future that he saw in Christ as Omega. For him, human progress and the kingdom of God offered two streams working in synergy in such a way that they "fertilise each other, and so, by synthesis, make Christianity break through into a new sphere." His vision of the future was undeniably optimistic, as he believed a form of "Super-humanity, Super-Christ, and Super-charity" would coalesce.[19] The first is

---

15. Ibid., 146.

16. Pierre Teilhard de Chardin, *Let Me Explain*, trans. R. Hague et al. (London: Collins, 1966), 84.

17. Ibid., 85.

18. Ibid., 86. It is worth noting that while the evolutionary emergence of religion is an area of more recent debate, Teilhard believed that the psychic elements in evolutionary processes were connected to divine action that beckoned from the future, expressed eventually as Omega.

19. Pierre Teilhard de Chardin, "Super-Humanity, Super-Christ and Super-Charity: Some New Dimensions of the Future," in *Science and Christ*, trans. R. Hague (London: Collins, 1965), 151–73.

a "higher biological state that mankind seems destined to attain," and this state is likely to be collective, rather than an individual characteristic such as an increase in brain size.[20] The state of Super-humanity coincides with "Super-Christ," and Super-charity seems to be related to a universalization of love that includes "devotion to an evolutive and universal Christ."[21]

Of course, many of his later interpreters have stripped away Teilhard's Christomonism inasmuch as it seems to detract from a more earthen view of Christ that we find in process thought, while keeping his vision of progress intact, though now muted in more modest ways. Teilhard believed that the Latin tradition of Christology was too legalistic; instead, he pressed for a more organic notion of Christ's significance, the universal Christ. Yet inasmuch as Teilhard recognized the significance of Christ in his divine nature as well as his human nature, he needs to be commended. For him, Christ is coextensive with both the peaks of spirit and the depths of matter; his is a cosmic Christology that follows the writing of Paul's letter to the Colossians, as well as the tradition of the Eastern Church, along the lines of, for example, Maximus the Confessor. In all, he sought to synthesize theology and evolution, such that we make our way to heaven "through earth," so that the choice of serving two masters is no longer present.[22] Although he drew back from any claim that science on its own could discover Christ, he believed that Christ fulfilled the yearning of science and the expectation of the natural world.[23] Given his own background as scientist and priest, it is easy to envisage how he could come to such a conclusion.

---

20. Ibid., 157–58. He envisages this as a multitude of "thinking elements," and while this may echo something of the power envisaged in the Internet, the analogy is only loose inasmuch as the Internet is not a collective consciousness in the way he imagined. Further, he argued for a "single heart" for collective humanity (160), a goal that is far more remote now in terms of the rise in individualism and social lack of cohesion, at least in the Western world.

21. Ibid., 169.

22. Teilhard, "Christology and Evolution," 93.

23. Pierre Teilhard de Chardin, "Science and Christ, or Analysis and Synthesis: Remarks on the Way in Which the Scientific Study of Matter Can and Must Help to Lead Us Up to the Divine Centre," in *Science and Christ*, 34–36. He also claims that biology can, when taken to the limit, enable us to emerge into the transcendent, a position developed with rather more theological rigor in the work of Karl Rahner. See Pierre Teilhard de Chardin, "Can Biology, Taken to Its Extreme Limit, Enable Us to Emerge into the Transcendent?" in *Science and Christ*, 212–13.

The question marks about Teilhard's approach relate to six issues: (1) his understanding of evolution as progressive, which seems to rest on metaphysical theory and cosmology rather than the evolutionary biology of Charles Darwin; (2) his outdated evolutionary theory and its anthropocentrism inasmuch as his interpretation of its direction toward the human is not strictly accurate, even if the present landscape of the world shows *Homo sapiens* to be the most dominant species; (3) his tight association of evolution and Christology, such that Christ becomes embedded in the process as such, thus endorsing that process, rather than being freely given by God to creation; (4) his Christomonism, where Christ becomes remote from any understanding of the historical Jesus; (5) his neutralization of evil through his treatment of it as a necessary part of the process; and (6) his somewhat naive and optimistic view of human progress and science in particular, whereby all its endeavors could necessarily be synthesized with the goals of the kingdom of God.[24]

Karl Rahner has taken up some threads from Teilhard de Chardin and used them creatively to develop his own understanding of the relationship between Christology and evolution.[25] While Teilhard wrote as a mystic, priest, and scientist, Rahner's work is academically rigorous, particularly in its attention to philosophy and systematic theology. Ironically, perhaps, he makes little attempt to go into the details of evolutionary theory and processes that Teilhard held so dear, even if Teilhard's views are in many respects superseded in current theory. Rahner engaged with the principles that he saw behind evolutionary thought in his essay "Christology within an Evolutionary View of the World."[26] His stated aim there was not to prove that the incarnation of Christ was simply *compatible* with evolution, or that the incarnation could be *deduced* from evolution, but rather to show that there was "an intrinsic affinity and the possibility of a reciprocal correlation between the two, without

---

24. His views are perhaps more in line with those of physicists and cosmologists, who speak of the anthropic principle, though in reality this means the principle of life. In addition, he remains a prophetic visionary inasmuch as he seemed to anticipate the World Wide Web through his understanding of a further evolutionary stage of human consciousness and communication. Such global cultural shifts can hardly be identified with the coming kingdom of God in the way that he anticipated.

25. His views are also interwoven with his understanding of anthropology, which I will return to in chapter 8.

26. K. Rahner, "Christianity within an Evolutionary View of the World," in *Foundations of Christian Faith*, trans. William V. Dych (London: Darton, Longman & Todd, 1978), 78–203.

making the Christian doctrine of incarnation a necessary and intrinsic element within the contemporary view of the world."[27]

He recognized how difficult the task would be, in that "all the problems of reconciling Christian teaching and its interpretation of existence with the life style and mentality and experience of today's world are rolled up into one and concentrated in our topic."[28] He believed that many people feel estranged from metaphysical statements proclaimed by the church, so in this sense, he rejects use of mythology or language that is remote from ordinary experience. On the one hand, he wants to avoid dualistic ways of thinking that make nature into an adversary of humans, while on the other hand, he wants to affirm the redeeming work of Christ as rooted in nature and society, so that Christ as savior is "a part of the cosmos, a moment within its history, and indeed at its climax."[29] He suggests that those theories that connect Christ simply with Spirit (inasmuch as he draws close to the spirit of the world) and then bring about its salvation are still ultimately gnostic in character, for such theories ignore the fact that Christ becomes *flesh* and matter. For him, the Logos bears matter in just the same way as the soul bears matter in the human person, and this matter is integral to the history of the cosmos.[30] In particular, this means that the action of God in creation is of a piece with the action of God in incarnation; both are "two movements and two phases of the one process of God's self-giving and self-expression, although it is an intrinsically differentiated process."[31] In this way, God *might* have created the world without the incarnation, "for although every such essential transcendence of self is the goal of the movement, it is always related to the lower stage as grace, as the unexpected and unnecessary."[32]

---

27. Ibid., 179.

28. Ibid.

29. Ibid., 195.

30. Ibid., 196. Rahner was not engaged in more recent debates about whether it is possible to speak of the soul at all in the light of current knowledge about human consciousness. See, for example, M. Jeeves, ed., *From Cells to Souls and Beyond: Changing Portraits of Human Nature* (Grand Rapids: Eerdmans, 2004); W. Brown, N. Murphy, and H. N. Malony, eds., *Whatever Happened to the Soul? Scientific and Theological Portraits of Human Nature* (Minneapolis: Fortress Press, 1998); and Mark Graves, *Mind, Brain and the Elusive Soul: Human Systems of Cognitive Science and Religion* (Aldershot: Ashgate, 2008). However, it seems that his understanding of soul was not dualistic in that he envisaged the soul as embedded in matter rather than separated from it.

31. Rahner, "Christianity within an Evolutionary View," 197.

32. Ibid.

The true humanity of Christ is reflected in his finiteness, participation in the history of the cosmos in "the dimension of spirit and of freedom," as well as in the history that leads ultimately to death. However, Christ is *also* God's self-communication, which "attains an irrevocable and irreversible character."[33] It is this that implies a hypostatic union between God and humanity, so that from God's side, there is absolute self-communication, while from the world's side, there is self-transcendence. Rahner then asks if Christ's incarnation represents a higher level of self-transcendence of the world or the way in which divinization of a creature needs to take place if such self-transcendence is to take place at all. He opts for the latter, so that the incarnation is a singular moment in the universal bestowal of grace. Here he slips into more traditional theological language, so that in the self-communication of God in incarnation, a human reality is assumed. Yet he also suggests that the reality of Jesus is such that God's offer is accepted; in other words, there seems to be freedom on the part of Jesus to reject the offer. For Rahner, the "unsurpassable and definitive offer and acceptance" must mean that "it is not only established by God, but it is God himself."[34] He also speaks of the incarnation as occurring just once and the human reality of Jesus being "graced in an absolute way," so that Jesus' "human reality belongs absolutely to God," which is, for him, the hypostatic union.

Rahner's Christology is ingenious in that it allows us to envisage a fully human Christ, who by receiving God's offer of absolute self-communication becomes one with God, and this is the meaning of the incarnation. In many ways, this is a highly successful resolution of the difficult problem of how to connect Christ with evolutionary ideas in such a way that no violence is done either to theology or to evolution. The elaborate theories of Teilhard are not present here, but Christ still represents a key moment in the evolutionary process and the history of the cosmos. There are, however, some difficulties with his interpretation. One difficulty relates to Rahner's notion of divine offer as connected to the experience of grace in the life of Jesus, so that Jesus seems to *become* divine, so that "this union is distinguished from our grace not by what has been offered in it, which in both instances, including that of Jesus, is grace. It is distinguished rather by the fact that Jesus is the offer for us, and we ourselves are not once again the offer, but the recipients of God's offer to us."[35] If this is the case,

---

33. Ibid.
34. Ibid., 202.
35. Ibid.

then why could not such an absolute offer of divine self-communication and reception happen again? While he claims graphically, "I can accept the words of the Johannine prologue with a faith so steadfast that I am ready to die for it," he also believes that a "Christology of ascent" is the most convincing, even within a framework of diversity of views. And while in his earlier essay, he resists taking his cue from Teilhard, he also suggests, "It would do no harm for a present day Christology to take up the ideas of Teilhard de Chardin, and to elaborate them with more precision and clarity, even though in his work it is not very easy to find an intelligible and orthodox connection between Jesus of Nazareth and the Omega Point of world evolution."[36]

In what sense might Christ be the *redeemer* of the world, except inasmuch as he was necessarily the first to receive fully that grace and so is able to offer himself to others? In other contexts, Rahner speaks of Christ as the "ultimate Word of God's forgiveness and promise of himself to us," but this is still anthropocentric in its scope.[37] Is Christ *only* connected with creation inasmuch as he shares in its evolutionary, material history? While he hesitates to claim that Jesus represents a "moral unity" with the Father, the language of an "irrevocable kind of union between this human reality and God" seems artificial in this context, especially as this seems to be connected more with the mission of Jesus and his self-identity, so that the one who proclaims is united to his proclamation. He also speaks of Christ's death as manifesting alienation from God rather than expressing some external imposed penalty. Yet he recognizes the need for Christology to show that Christ's death does not make Christ acosmic but serves to usher in a new relationship with the world, freed from limitations of a history confined to a single point in space and time characteristic of his earthly existence.[38] How this might relate to his evolutionary vision of an ascending Christology remains unresolved, though he hints that he recognizes the difficulty of connecting God's ek-sistence[39] in the world with the humanity of Jesus.

---

36. Karl Rahner, *Theological Investigations*, vol. 21, *Science and Christian Faith*, trans. Hugh Riley (London: Darton, Longman & Todd, 1988), 227.

37. Ibid., 215.

38. Karl Rahner, "Current Problems in Christology," in *Theological Investigations*, vol. 1, *God, Christ, Mary and Grace*, trans. Cornelius Ernst, 149–200 (London: Darton, Longman & Todd, 1961), 195.

39. Ibid., 195–96.

Jürgen Moltmann develops his own position on the specific relationship between Christology and evolution in dialogue with Teilhard de Chardin and Karl Rahner. In earlier work, he has outlined a theology of evolution inasmuch as he takes care to distinguish the initial act of creation in the beginning, *creatio originalis*, from the overall continuous creation in evolution. The latter is a "making," more properly called *creatio continua*, an activity of God in history.[40] He also believes that *creatio nova*, the new creative act of God, is "initially only perceived in human history," but there are parallels in the history of nature. In speaking of evolution of the cosmos, he aligns the creative work of the Spirit with the evolutionary processes of the world, so that "the evolutions and catastrophes of the universe are also the movements and experiences of the Spirit of creation."[41] In other places, he expresses a similar idea: "The whole cosmos must be described as corresponding to God. . . . Because it is effected through God the Spirit, and exists in God the Spirit, it also moves and evolves in the energies and powers of the divine Spirit."[42] Here he holds back from a full-blown pantheism by retaining a Trinitarian understanding of God the creator, so that the Spirit in creation is the Spirit of God. Self-organization and self-transcendence of life are particular manifestations of the Spirit, including the evolutionary movement toward greater complexity. More explicitly, he states here that the movement of creation and evolution should not be considered as in opposition to each other, so that "we have to see the concept of evolution as the basic concept of the self-movement of the divine Spirit of creation."[43]

There is, however, a fundamental difficulty here in that the evolution of life per se is not spiritual in the way he suggests; at least, the only residues of such a view are found in the work of nineteenth-century writers Wallace and Lamarck, whose metaphysical approaches have long since been abandoned by scientists. It is also clear that tying in the work of the Spirit in an *explicit* way with evolutionary theory presents similar theological problems that he finds implicit in the work of Teilhard de Chardin. The

---

40. J. Moltmann, *God in Creation*, trans. M. Kohl (London: SCM, 1985), 208–9.

41. Ibid., 16. He also distinguishes creation, understood as the miracle of existence, from evolution, which he views as a form of "making," and offers another way in which they do not clash, since they "belong on different levels" (196). However, he is also prepared to speak of evolution as continuous creation, creation that is not yet finished, as opposed to the initial creation of all that is in the beginning.

42. Ibid., 212.

43. Ibid., 19.

first problem he identifies in the latter's work relates to his particular way of interpreting redemption in evolutionary terms. And while to claim, as Moltmann suggests, that "Teilhard transferred salvation history as it was understood by Christian faith to the history of life and the cosmos" ignores the fact that Teilhard was also careful to add atonement of human sin to his more cosmic speculations, it is fair to suggest that this more traditional treatment in Teilhard seems to be something of an afterthought; it is the second word rather than the first.[44] The second problem that he identifies, and one that he does not sufficiently address in his own speculations about the work of the Spirit in evolution, relates to the Christification of the whole cosmos, expressed in the sacramental and Eucharistic presence of Christ in all matter:

> [Teilhard] has overlooked the ambiguity of evolution itself, and therefore to have paid no attention to evolution's victims. Evolution always means selection. Many living things are sacrificed in order that the "fittest"—which means the most effective and the most adaptable—may survive.[45]

Complex life systems emerge, but at heavy expense: "Milliards of living things fall by the wayside and disappear into evolution's rubbish bin."[46] Of course, Teilhard did consider suffering and evil in the process of evolution, but he considered it to be a price worth paying and that Christ took on the pain of evolution as it emerged in ever more complex forms of unification. His real mistake was to assume that such suffering was somehow acceptable because it seemed to be necessary for the continuing evolution of life, so that all of life was in some sense "cruciform."

This is also particularly evident in another of Moltmann's criticisms of Teilhard, namely, his somewhat disturbing endorsement of human butchery, including the dropping of the atomic bomb at Hiroshima, as an example of the possibility of human evolutionary change.[47] Yet perhaps this is also a good example of the kind of attitude that has now become so prevalent in social Darwinism and evolutionary psychology; while Teilhard is clearly wrong, his views were prophetic inasmuch as he anticipated a

---

44. J. Moltmann, *The Way of Jesus Christ*, trans. M. Kohl (London: SCM, 1990), 292.

45. Ibid., 294.

46. Ibid.

47. Ibid., 295.

stream of thought that emerges from extrapolation of Darwinian ideas into the human and social realm. Such a view would have horrified Darwin, as I indicated earlier. Moreover, Teilhard's cosmic evolutionary vision seems to be drawn more from cosmology than from evolutionary biology and neo-Darwinian theory as such, and like Moltmann, he failed to consider adequately the tensions between them. For Moltmann, Teilhard's Christ is simply a cruel "*Christus selector*, a historical world judge without compassion for the weak, and a breeder of life uninterested in the victims."[48]

In the light of these reflections, Moltmann returns to his notion of the way the Spirit works in evolution, and he attempts to salvage his earlier idea of the identity of evolution and pneumatology, but now is careful to emphasize that the way in which the Spirit works is through the development of richer and more complex forms of life, so that it is in this sense that "the creative energy of the ground of the whole cosmos can be theologically perceived."[49] Yet the other side of this history is the history of the victims, and Christ has to be perceived "as a victim among evolution's other victims. . . . There is no conceivable human evolution in the near or remote future which could give any meaning to the mass deaths of the fallen and the murdered in the two world wars of this century."[50] In this way, Christ becomes not only the redeemer of humanity, but evolution's redeemer as well.

Yet there is a problem here that Moltmann has not fully taken into account. In the first place, the creative ground of evolution depends on the random process of natural selection in order to emerge, so tying the work of the Spirit to that creativity while ignoring its basis, or seeking to solve the problems with this basis through identification of Christ with the victims of evolution, seems somewhat artificial. He also, like Teilhard, does not distinguish adequately between evolutionary processes in the natural world and those taking place in human societies; in reality, the interconnection between cultural and natural tendencies is much more complex, so the two processes cannot be lumped together in an amorphous way, as if they were the same, even though evolution is the language used to describe both. Nevertheless, it is clear that Moltmann is more resistant to the anthropocentrism that still prevails somewhat in Teilhard's thought, for he argues that the human being is not the meaning and purpose of evolution, but

---

48. Ibid., 296.
49. Ibid.
50. Ibid.

rather all creation finds its purpose in God, in the anticipated Sabbath.[51] Third, if Christ is viewed *simply* as a victim of evolution, alongside other victims, what is the basis of hope for the redemption of evolution that is desired? He has in effect entangled both his pneumatology and Christology in the evolutionary process, and while this is considerably more sophisticated than Teilhard de Chardin's approach, it suffers from a similar drawback as process thought in associating God with creation in such a way that distinctions begin to fade from view. In effect, while he has tried to distance himself from cruder versions of what he terms theologies of evolution and process—placing *creatio continua* in the space between *creatio originalis* as one that preserves and *creatio nova* as one that prepares for its perfection—in the end, it is the eschatological dimension that seems to win out.[52]

Unlike process theologians, Moltmann intends to retain a sense of distinction by holding on to more classic notions of *creatio ex nihilo* (creation out of nothing), complemented by the rather more radical Jewish notion of *tzimtzum*, or inner withdrawal in God, interpreted as a kenotic understanding of the relationship between God and the world. It is in this sense that he can speak of the self-humiliation of God becoming expressed in creation and incarnation.[53] Nonetheless, such views sit somewhat uneasily with his much stronger sense of the identification of God with evolution in the way just presented here. This is also exemplified inasmuch as he is prepared to speak of God as suffering with evolution, so that

> it is not through supernatural interventions that God guides creation to its goal, and drives forward evolution; it is through his passion, and the opening of possibilities out of his suffering. Seen in terms of world history, the transforming power of suffering is the basis for the liberating and consummating acts of God.[54]

Moltmann shares a common presupposition with many others that God works in the world by not intervening with natural laws. However, his understanding of the positive value of the suffering of God in driving forward evolution seems inconsistent with his later idea of the suffering of

---

51. Moltmann, *God in Creation*, 197.

52. Ibid., 209–10.

53. For discussion of his views on *creatio ex nihilo*, see *God in Creation*, 86–93. On *tzimtzum*, see J. Moltmann, *The Trinity and the Kingdom of God* (London: SCM, 1981), 108–11.

54. Moltmann, *God in Creation*, 211.

God being confined to the passive suffering of Christ in sharing with the victims of evolution.

Moltmann finds in Rahner's schema of self-transcendence a lack of attention to redemption similar to what he detected in Teilhard.[55] He objects to what he sees as the "smooth" passing from the history of nature to human history, including a seeming endorsement of the technological civilization of contemporary times. He rejects the anthropocentrism that seems implicit in Rahner's account, with the possibility that nature may become just "material" for human usefulness. Of course, Rahner does not have to be read in this way, and theologians such as Denis Edwards find in Rahner's work inspiration for reflection on contemporary ecological problems and issues.[56] Nonetheless, it is easy to see why Moltmann finds aspects of Rahner's thought disturbing, in that he seems to accept evolution as a given and to have a much weaker sense of the importance of Christ's redeeming role in evolution, as already noted. Here Moltmann has a strong sense of redemption coming from ahead, but one that permeates the whole of the evolutionary process. In this way, the *Christus Redemptor* is the Christ in his coming.[57] This eschatological tone to Christology and its cosmic scope are original and in many respects are a considerable improvement over either Teilhard's or Rahner's more truncated vision. Yet has he gone too far in this respect? In his enthusiasm for the new creation, the possibility of the redemption of all of evolutionary history seems somewhat far-fetched, even as seen with the eye of faith. Is it necessary, therefore—or even helpful, for that matter—to envisage such a grand restoration?

1.2 Theodrama and Evolution

The final section of this chapter lays out the theoretical basis for interweaving Christology and evolution in a way that provides an alternative to the positions just discussed. Moltmann criticizes Rahner for accepting evolution as simply a given that cannot be challenged, but then goes on to criticize various theological interpretations of evolution, rather than challenging its theoretical basis. Like many other authors in this field, he is also more inclined to discuss the process of cosmological evolution rather than

---

55. Moltmann, *Way of Jesus Christ*, 299.
56. See, for example, D. Edwards, *Ecology at the Heart of Faith: The Change of Heart That Leads to a New Way of Living on Earth* (Maryknoll: Orbis, 2006).
57. Moltmann, *Way of Jesus Christ*, 303.

biological evolution. This leads to his interweaving of evolution and theology through historical narrative, viewing the history of nature as a story to be told in a way that is comparable to the human story. This comparison is similar to Haught's position, discussed earlier, and is also presupposed in both Teilhard and Rahner, even though their theologies take very different forms. In one sense, I agree heartily with the idea that the natural world can be interpreted as sharing historical features that run to some extent in tandem, or even in continuity, with human history. But what if a theology of history becomes much more vivid and true to itself as theology through a *different* reading of history, one that draws specifically on drama rather than a narrative account of God's ways with the world, which has characterized all the accounts of evolution named earlier in this chapter?

The first, most basic question to be addressed is whether theology is compatible with history. Given the influence of scientific understanding on modern historical scholarship, this is also indirectly a question about the compatibility of theology and science. Yet the history is the same; what is different is that theologians will read it in a different way, so that, as Ben Quash suggests, people are prepared

> to see the dense, historical world as having an origin and an end in the creative purposing of God, a God who can relate personally to his creatures. People are ready to acknowledge the idea that there can be revelation: a prevenient ground for our knowledge and perception that is not the product of our knowledge and perception, which is neither accidental nor impersonal but which freely, and even lovingly, communicates itself.[58]

Such a reading gives history an eschatological key, and theodramatics is a way of thinking about eschatology and history together in their relationship with each other.[59] Drama is about human actions and particular events in particular contexts, and theodrama is that which is connected to God's purpose. A theodramatic approach will always be in one sense eschatological in orientation. Attention to drama draws out the specific significance of human agency, the particular context, and also the wider plot or time dimension. Consideration will therefore include that of the *subjects*

---

58. Ben Quash, *Theology and the Drama of History* (Cambridge: Cambridge University Press, 2005), 2.

59. Quash, *Theology*, 2–3. The basic interpretation of theodrama as applied to human history that I am using here follows Quash's very helpful summary.

themselves; the acting area in which they perform, or the *stage*; and the movement of the play, or *action*. Another key issue that arises here is that of freedom and what this means in the Christian life. If God is perceived as one who possesses divine freedom, this means that any narration of history cannot be simply an inevitable chain of events while preserving the sense of the importance and validity of individual freedom. In this, theodrama resists making either subjects, through family genealogies, or structures, through a systematization in mechanistic or organic models, the most important keys to the interpretation of history.

But what if we allow theodrama to include not just human history, but evolutionary history as well? Such an expansion has the advantage of viewing other evolved creatures as more than simply the stage on which human action and freedom are worked out. Of course, the degree of awareness of divine action will be different according to different levels of consciousness and capacity for decision, but if creatures are placed in kinship with humanity, the evolution of life becomes an integral aspect of the drama between God and God's creatures. Moreover, in the light of such a dramatic reading, an overly systematized account of evolutionary process begins to look far too thin.

Ben Quash suggests that a nondramatic reading in human history leads to "synchronic" principles that amount to a form of betrayal, for they "fail to give due attention to particulars, to the individuals, the exceptions to rules, the resistances to explanation and the densities of meaning that ask for recognition in a good description of historical reality."[60] Yet such synchronic readings of *evolutionary* history are rife; examples include the Christomonism of Teilhard, the aesthetic principle of process thought, even the organic model of Gaia, or even more general ideas, such as the "balance" of nature.

The difficulty, of course, when it comes to the millions of years of evolutionary history, is that human imagination finds it hard to appreciate the dynamics of the particular in any given "scene" of the drama. Also, given that evolution takes place over a long period of time, the "play," if it is to do justice to the individual characters concerned, will find itself dealing with long epochs of history when such characters have come and gone in different scenes presented. In other words, the characters that may be picked out for discussion are selective and illustrative inasmuch as they represent just

---

60. Ibid.

one small fraction of the overall evolutionary process. Sometimes it may prove preferable, therefore, to use a close examination of those creatures that we know, in order to provide an analogy of what earlier creatures may have been like. A good example of this is the study of primates in order to give clues as to the life of early hominids.[61] Yet such study also helps open up the realization of human ignorance about the drama itself, by focusing on the punctuated phases of evolution where improbable events came together in a way that means only one lineage survived and not others. Such events, which effectively wiped out myriads of species, many of which may not even yet be identified by present research, means that the tragic nature of the evolutionary drama comes into view. A theodramatic approach takes proper account of the tragic, one that is vivid in terms of the evolutionary history of the earth, but now brings this into juxtaposition with an understanding of how God works in the tragic in human history. It therefore will resist any generalization of evil or attempt to wash over the contingency of events.

To highlight the advantages of a theodramatic approach, it is also worth considering the tendency for narrative accounts to become *epic*. Evolutionary history, with its tremendously long time scale, is almost always sucked into such an interpretation. While in some sense, narrative accounts are inevitable in order to get an insight into the overall evolutionary process at large, the manner in which these slip surreptitiously into epics needs to be treated with considerable caution. In other words, I do not believe that we can avoid at least some narrative description, but such description needs to be self-aware inasmuch as it recognizes the tendency for it to be taken over by the genre of the epic.

What do we mean by epic? While an interpretation of this would be worthy of a more complete study, for present purposes, it is sufficient to highlight those characteristics of epic that are considered problematic in the light of the development of theodrama.[62] In the second of his trilogy, *Theo-Drama*, Balthasar considers whether there is some standpoint from which we can merely be observers of a sequence of events, including the events of Christ's death and resurrection. In such a view, he suggests, we "smooth out the folds and say that Jesus' suffering is past history; we can only speak of

---

61. There are, of course, disadvantages in such an approach, especially as much of the cultural history of early humans is dependent on speculation.

62. Quash takes the view that Balthasar is influenced by Hegel's distinctions among epic, lyric, and dramatic. See Quash, *Theology*, 40–41.

his continued suffering in an indirect sense, in so far as those who believe in him are referred to, metaphorically, as his members."[63] However, Christian spirituality is more often than not expressed in terms of particular experiences of the individual—what Balthasar terms the "lyric" mode, where all thoughts of universal significance found in epic thought fall from view.

The councils of the church may frame their theological deliberations with prayer, but this does not deal with the problem that they are delivered in an epic mode. Even a theology that focuses on scripture can lead in the same direction, that is, if it sees itself as an objective (epic-narrative) account that has taken place and is now done. Reactions against such "arrogance" in theopraxy are, Balthasar believes, simply a one-sided reaction.[64] Instead, the theodramatic considers the ongoing *action* of God in history, as witnessed particularly in the lives of the apostles and in the early church.

Lurking behind Balthasar's attraction to theodrama, the spirituality of Ignatius of Loyola comes into view.[65] While this spirituality served to shape the dynamics of the human-divine encounter, Ignatius' sacramental view of the world allowed for a positive attitude toward all of creation, God's presence being found in all things. It is no surprise, therefore, that Balthasar also perceived this dramatic account of God's action as extending back not just to the creation of Adam and Eve, but also to the creation of the world and forward to the future revelation of what is to come, expressed through apocalyptic literature. He suggests:

> It so overarches everything, from beginning to end, that there is no standpoint from which we could observe and portray events as if we were uninvolved narrators of an epic. By wanting to find such an external standpoint, allegedly because it will enable us to evaluate the events objectively (*sine ira et studio*), we put ourselves outside the drama, which has already drawn all truth and all objectivity into itself. In this play, all the spectators must eventually become fellow actors, whether they wish to or not.[66]

---

63. Hans Urs von Balthasar, *Theo-Drama*, vol. 2, *Dramatis Personae: Man in God*, trans. Graham Harrison (San Francisco: Ignatius Press, 1990), 54 (hereafter cited as *TD* 2).

64. Ibid., 57.

65. Ben Quash is not alone in believing that Ignatius exerted a genuinely shaping influence on Balthasar, including his fascination with drama. See Ben Quash, "Ignatian Dramatics: First Glance at the Spirituality of Hans Urs von Balthasar," *The Way* 38, no. 4 (1998): 77–86.

66. Balthasar, *TD* 2, 58.

Balthasar argued that an epic recounting of the dramatic world events had in the background a sense of opposites balancing out and can be thought of as nirvana, kismet, nothingness, or evolution. Hence, evolutionary ideas help feed into a mind-set where those listening adopt "a kind of calm, yielding resignation, a lofty benevolence: this is how things are, have always been and always will be."[67] Somewhat surprising is his view that the epic attitude of resignation is somehow incorporated into the drama of Christian life, though, for him, it is always transformed into "readiness to step into whatever role in the play God has in mind."[68] Balthasar seems, therefore, to interpret epic along Hegelian lines, where there is an element of necessity at the heart of events.[69] At its worst, epic becomes the "genre of false objectification" and "reifies what is given to it to know. It substitutes monological narration for dialogue, without supposing that this is a loss for truth. And it tends towards determinism."[70] The idea of evolution as incorporating some sort of *necessity* is a typical reading of evolutionary history in some quarters as well. As will become clear in the chapter that follows, the reading of the evolutionary history in epic terms becomes particularly acute in evolutionary psychology. It, too, suffers from the genre of false objectification, and inasmuch as it makes claim to offer its listeners a way of dealing with the meaning of human existence, it attempts to perform a religious function.

1.3 Evolution and the Kenotic Christ

Interpreting the action of God in the human and evolutionary history and in the history of Jesus Christ in dramatic terms lends itself to the development of a kenotic Christology. Such a Christology has the advantage of affirming the full humanity of Christ while, at the same time, affirming his divinity. It therefore does not lead to the kind of quandaries associated

---

67. Ibid., 59.

68. Ibid. He has in mind here the difference between Ignatian *indifferencia* (indifference) and Greek *apatheia* (passionlessness). It is of note that Quash interprets the Ignatian concept of indifference as a demonstration of an epic lack of human freedom (see Quash, *Theology*, 77), though in the context just cited, Balthasar seems to imply a clear distinction from *apatheia* and a transformation that includes the possibility of refusal.

69. See Quash for an excellent discussion of the influence of Hegel on Balthasar. Quash, *Theology*, 42.

70. Ibid.

with two-natures theories that bedeviled the classic discussion, as noted in Barbour's analysis. There are different ways of representing what kenosis might mean, though at the outset I position myself in favor of those who argue for kenosis as a self-emptying of God in Christ, rather than a "giving up" of divine powers in the manner of some early Anglican kenotic theories.[71] Moreover, I also am more inclined to resist any notion of kenosis as requiring *tzimtzum*, or a form of inner withdrawal or spatial self-limitation in God, as followed by Jürgen Moltmann, mentioned above in section 1.1.

Both Balthasar and Sergii Bulgakov develop kenotic Christology, and the latter uses Wisdom language that I find particularly helpful inasmuch as it allows an explicit connection with the doctrine of creation. The question that arises here, however, is how far might one be justified in making such a claim, given the experience of the early Christian church and its own very gradual development of Christology, such that it took some time for Jesus to be perceived in divine terms? I suggest that the language of wisdom is helpful here, for not only does it illustrate the way Jesus eventually came to be thought of as Wisdom incarnate, but it also shows how the language of wisdom *connects* Jesus with his history on earth and, in this sense, resists the kind of speculation that finds expression in Teilhard de Chardin, where Christ becomes detached from history in an epic seemingly remote from his ordinary human experience. At the same time, this account of the development of Wisdom Christology should not remain *confined* to the earliest interpretations of Christ's significance, in a way that might tend toward the

---

71. For a discussion of these theories, see, for example, Thomas R. Thompson, "Nineteenth-Century Kenotic Christology: The Waxing, Waning and Weighing of a Quest for a Coherent Orthodoxy," in *Exploring Kenotic Christology: The Self-Emptying of God*, ed. C. S. Evans, 74–111 (Oxford: Oxford University Press, 2006). The kind of kenotic Christology popular among Anglican clerics, which presumed a real self-emptying of divine attributes and powers, is far from the thought of Balthasar or Bulgakov in their development of kenotic Christology. Stephen Davis takes the view that the kenosis should be distinguished from the incarnation, limiting the period of kenosis to that of Jesus' lifetime, while the incarnation is not so limited. S. Davies, "Is Kenosis Orthodox?" in Evans, *Exploring Kenotic Christology*, 114. Bulgakov also seems to follow the route of a more limited kenosis, but it only disappears with the coming of Pentecost, and the Spirit, too, shares in kenotic characteristics. I will discuss this in more detail in chapter 6. Balthasar, in contrast, associates kenosis with the self-emptying of Christ on the cross and his descent into hell. Edward Oakes offers a helpful discussion of the kenotic character of Balthasar's Christology. E. Oakes, "He Descended into Hell: The Depths of God's Self-Emptying Love on Holy Saturday in the Thought of Hans Urs von Balthasar," in Evans, *Exploring Kenotic Christology*, 218–45.

view that Christ's divinity somehow evolved in the minds of believers of the early church. Instead, it serves merely as the *context* in which Jesus can be viewed in the drama of divine action and response, though expressed through the language of wisdom.

One of the oldest sayings of Jesus found in Q is "Sophia is justified by her children" (Luke 7:35). Elisabeth Schüssler Fiorenza suggests that this has its setting in the inclusive table community of Jesus with sinners, tax collectors, and prostitutes.[72] Schüssler Fiorenza believes that Jesus was identified with the wisdom prophets, who were persecuted and killed (compare Luke 11:49). Luke 13:34, which speaks of the lament over Jerusalem where the prophets are killed and stoned, echoes the same tradition, though it is important to point out that this lament is directed against the governing authorities, rather than specifically against Israel or Judaism as such. The well-known invitation of Jesus that begins, "Come to me, all who labor and are heavy laden" (Matt. 11:28 RSV), is also an invitation of Sophia.

This passage is one of a number of sayings that form a sayings tradition that is subject to considerable debate among biblical scholars as to its reconstruction and social-historical contextualization.[73] The first stage, which depicts Jesus as a sage in the Cynic tradition, is superseded by a stage that envisages conflict between Sophia and Israel. John the Baptist and Jesus follow in the tradition of Sophia sages, but at the same time, there is a sense of discontinuity, for in Luke 11:31, Jesus is perceived as greater than the wisdom teacher Solomon. Schüssler Fiorenza—correctly, in my view—urges against an interpretation that jumps too quickly to seeing the distance between Jesus and the prophetic ministry of others who were messengers of Sophia. At the same time, Schüssler Fiorenza is wary of the shift in Matt. 11:25-27 that identifies Jesus as the Son of the Father who mediates revelation in an exclusive way:[74]

"I thank you, Father, Lord of heaven and earth, because you have hidden these things from the wise and the intelligent and have revealed them to infants; yes, Father, for such was your gracious will. All things have been handed over to me

---

72. Elisabeth Schüssler Fiorenza, *Jesus: Miriam's Child, Sophia's Prophet* (London: SCM, 1995), 140.

73. See, for example, William R. Farmer, *The Gospel of Jesus: The Pastoral Relevance of the Synoptic Problem* (Louisville: Westminster John Knox, 1994).

74. Schüssler Fiorenza, *Jesus*, 143–44.

by my Father; and no one knows the Father except the Son and anyone to whom the Son chooses to reveal him." (Matt 11:25-27)

Aspects of this passage relate to Jewish Wisdom traditions that speak of Wisdom as receiving everything from God; she is the one who knows and is known by God. Another theological tradition is also likely to be at work here, namely, the Logos tradition of Philo, which understands the Logos to be the firstborn son of Wisdom and also of God.[75] Schüssler Fiorenza concludes, "The Q people (men?) who articulated this saying replaced the inclusive sophialogy of the earliest Jesus traditions with an exclusive understanding of revelation."[76] Yet is it necessary to interpret the Father-Son relationship in the exclusivist sense that Schüssler Fiorenza assumes to have been the case? It could equally be asserted that the intimacy of a father-son relationship is now, through Sophia, opened up to all, the "any-one" of Matt. 11:27. Schüssler Fiorenza seems to admit as much by speaking of numerous early Christian sapiential abba/father sayings that could have been open to men or women. Nonetheless, eventually the tradition of speaking of Jesus in sophianic terms was squeezed out and replaced with a Logos Christology.

What Schüssler Fiorenza seems to be resisting is the translation of the human history of Christ into an epic narrative, represented by Logos Christology, one that she also believes is particularly androcentric inasmuch as the Logos represents the masculine. Her critique will certainly need to be borne in mind in engaging with authors such as Hans Urs von Balthasar and Sergii Bulgakov, both of whom associate the Logos with a male principle and the Holy Spirit with a female principle. A focus on the dramatic account of God's action in Christ resists equating Jesus simply with the prophetic stream in the manner of Schüssler Fiorenza, while at the same time giving full credence to what might loosely be described as his human nature and human history. The difficulty with Schüssler Fiorenza's account is that confining the wisdom of Jesus to that of sage and prophet means that the full significance and impact of Christ are muted; the drama is no longer present except in a mirror held up with that drama encountered in human history. In other words, the distinctive action of God in Christ fades from view. Such distinctions between God and creation, yet

---

75. John S. Kloppenborg, "Wisdom Christology in Q," *LTP* 34 (1978): 129–47.
76. Schüssler Fiorenza, *Jesus*, 144.

resolved paradoxically in the kenotic Christ, need not be interpreted in the patriarchal manner that she assumes to be the case.

Yet I will also argue that the dramatic encounter of Christ with the world is best situated in the context of an understanding of the theological meaning of beauty in the world, that is, an encounter with natural wonder. It is, in other words, a reminder once again that the first scene in any theo-dramatic account has to be one that begins by being grounded in the natural world as such, rather than either human beings or even the presence of the Christ child. While Balthasar has suffered rather more criticism for his *Glory of the Lord* compared with his *Theo-Drama*, for the present purposes at least, the *Glory* can be interpreted as the first act in the drama of human history. It is, as it were, the initial contemplative stance at the start of the performance that then allows a full appreciation of the dramatic account as it unfolds. In using the language of the "stage" for creation in *Theo-Drama*, Balthasar fails to follow through the potential fruitfulness of his contemplative theology and thereby encourages a detachment from the story of creation by his subsequent interpreters.

Finally, a kenotic Christology necessarily includes not only an account of who Christ is, but also a pneumatology, so that Christology is interpreted in the light of the Trinity. While some scholars have used Trinitarian language in order to represent the way God acts in human and evolutionary history, I have used this language sparingly inasmuch as I am intending to develop more specific reference to the figure of Christ and his significance.[77] Moreover, without due care, the language of the Trinity can easily take on an epic style, such that it becomes a mythology that reinterprets all human and natural interrelationships, including their histories redescribed in evolutionary terms. I am less convinced now than I was earlier that seeking to find Trinitarian images in the world is all that helpful, any more than finding nature as cruciform is helpful. However, as will become clear later in this book, I am also aware that a discussion of Christology without proper attention to the work of the Holy Spirit in particular is a mistake. Just as the final goal of theodrama is both anticipation and an appreciation of practical expression in ethics, this is also how I have sought to present the challenge of relating Christology and evolution: namely, it is a challenge that insists on retaining hope for the future but also probes our own identity as evolved human persons living in an evolved world.

---

77. For a Trinitarian approach to creation, see, for example, Moltmann, *God in Creation*, 94–97; *The Trinity and the Kingdom*, 105–13.

1.4 Conclusions

The conclusions of this chapter are necessarily tentative, in that it represents more a proposal of how Christology and evolution might be considered together in a way that does not do violence to either subject. The first question already addressed in the introduction was the context of the literature in science and religion, inasmuch as the shape of discussion has more often than not taken the form of how to relate God to evolution, where Christ appears in continuum with that evolutionary account. While such a diminished portrait of Christ's significance is not unusual, certainly in the liberal tradition, it fails to do justice to the profound Christian belief that Christ is not only human but also God incarnate. At the same time, theologians who have considered the relationship between Christ and culture have, in general, largely failed to take into account the significance of what might be termed the evolutionary way of looking at the world, which is so much a part of contemporary Western thought. There are some exceptions to this, discussed in the present chapter, in that evolutionary ideas have been taken up in the thought of Pierre Teilhard de Chardin, Karl Rahner, and Jürgen Moltmann.

The pioneering work of Teilhard needs to be acknowledged inasmuch as he recognized the insufficiency of a purely scientific way of thinking about the natural world. His attempt at resolution through a tight synthesis between evolution and Christology, and indeed, salvation history at large, fails in a number of respects, not least insofar as it entraps God in a particular epic wrought from human scientific discourse. Rahner's account is considerably more sophisticated, though he too assumes evolution as a given and seeks to present Christology in such a way that Jesus' divinity emerges through self-transcendence of grace in a manner identical to that found in other human beings. The only difference seems to be that, in Christ, divine grace is fully received and accepted, and this acceptance of divine offer is what makes Christ divine. Moltmann finds difficulty with both Rahner's and Teilhard's accounts in that they seem to endorse evolution and remove it from the redemptive acts of Christ in history. However, by aligning Christ with the victims of evolution, and the Spirit specifically with the overflowing of novelty and complexity in evolution, Moltmann is, in effect, still entangling God in evolutionary history in a manner that is problematic as far as its free creativity and redemption are concerned. Thinkers influenced by process thought, such as John Haught, fare little better inasmuch as Haught views the evolutionary process in the light of an aesthetic principle, so that in spite of the language of the identity of God with suffering, the promise of creation is connected with the aesthetic emergence of beauty, seemingly dependent on that suffering and represented by the figure of Christ.

In offering such criticisms, I am aware of the real and pressing difficulty in the task of relating Christology and evolution without subsuming one under the other or distorting one in favor of the other. As an alternative that attempts to avoid some of the limitations of the preceding views, I seek to develop a view of evolutionary history that considers it in the light of theodrama, rather than as epic narrative in the manner indicated in the accounts just described. Of course, some narrative elements are inevitable, but such elements need to be viewed in a theodramatic way, rather than sublimated into an epic description of events.

The author who has most influenced me in this respect is Hans Urs von Balthasar. He seems to have thought of evolution as purely an epic account that was impossible to retrieve in theodramatic terms. Certainly, as the next chapter will show, the tendency toward epic description of evolutionary theories is rife. However, this does not mean that *all* evolutionary accounts are therefore redundant. In fact, using Balthasar's theological aesthetics, I will suggest in chapter 3 that his work lends itself to thinking about the natural world in a positive way, but thinking about the natural world is still qualified by reference to the Christ event. Such an event needs to be situated in a theodrama if it is to avoid becoming epic in its proportions, a danger inherent in all natural theology. Much of the discussion of the remainder of this book seeks to do just that, namely, work out what it means for evolution and Christology to be an integral part of the theodrama, where wisdom and wonder become means of linking the action of the Director, those on the stage, and the experience of the audience. The Christology that I prefer in this context is a kenotic Christology rather than one that simply emerges from evolutionary history, from below, even if it takes into account the specific history of Jesus in reflecting on him in terms of wisdom. Moreover, nonhuman creatures are not simply the "stage" for human activity but become included in the drama as such.

2

Christology Secularized: A Theological Engagement with Evolutionary Psychology

This chapter investigates in more detail the specific claims of evolutionary psychology, which sets out to express human cognition, moral behavior, and religious practice in evolutionary terms. I will demonstrate in this chapter that the claims of evolutionary psychology and related theories of mimetics championed by Richard Dawkins are seriously questioned from the perspective of many other evolutionary biologists, social anthropologists, and philosophers. In other words, evolutionary psychology may use Darwinian rhetoric, but in many respects, it fails in Darwinian terms. I share many of these concerns, and I will offer, in addition, a philosophical and theological critique that considers this trend from a theological perspective as a form of idolatry that offers a specific account of humanity in biologized essentialist terms, a secularized theory of atonement, and a secularized eschatology.[1] Moreover, it proves ultimately irresponsible in its attempts to project human guilt onto our far-flung ancestors and in its naturalistic endorsement of immoral behaviors. It opens up, in other words, the need for a Christology that deals, arguably, with the religious issues raised by the claims of evolutionary psychology and the atheism that is implicit in much of its writings. While not wanting to deny that Christ, as every other human being, shares in the evolutionary history of the world in a general sense, and humanity in a particular sense, this chapter will set the scene for the more detailed engagement with Christology that will be developed in subsequent chapters.

---

1. I will come back to the eschatological aspects of evolutionary psychology as projected in transhumansim in chapter 8.

2.1 Introduction

The birth of sociobiology, which uses evolutionary ideas as applied to human behavior, has gripped the public imagination mostly through the writings of key authors such as E. O. Wilson's *Sociobiology and the New Synthesis* (1975) and Richard Dawkins's *The Selfish Gene* (1976).[2] One of the difficulties that both authors addressed was how to explain altruism in evolutionary terms, specifically assuming the centrality of natural selection. Bill Hamilton proposed the concept of kin selection, so that behaviors that seem to be disadvantageous to an individual will be of benefit to the kin.[3] One would expect, according to this scenario, a greater degree of commitment to costly behavior, the closer the relative. Of course, this does not apply to nonrelatives, so R. L. Triver's concept of reciprocal altruism attempts to fill this gap, where deeds are done on the basis that in due course some other benefit will be returned.[4] Even more sophisticated mathematical analyses use game theory and tit-for-tat explanations as a theoretical basis for given behaviors.[5]

---

2. E. O. Wilson, *Sociobiology: The New Synthesis* (Cambridge, Mass.: Belknap/Harvard University Press, 2000), first published in 1975; Richard Dawkins, *The Selfish Gene* (Oxford: Oxford University Press, 1989), first published in 1976. See also E. O. Wilson, *Consilience* (London: Abacus, 1998). These books were, of course, an improvement on the loosely assembled ideas of earlier books such as Desmond Morris's *Naked Ape* (1967), whose description of innate behavior stemming from early primate existence seemed to justify existing social inequalities, or Konrad Lorenz's book *On Aggression* (1963), which implied war is inevitable in humans and is an expression of human instincts.

3. Bill Hamilton is arguably the one who put kin selection on a mathematical basis. He argued that altruistic behavior toward kin is related to the closeness of kin to the individual concerned in terms of the relative survival of copies of genes in each case, so that the relationship between parent and offspring is 50 percent, while that of nephews or half siblings or grandchildren is 25 percent. This would be played out in practice such that the benefit to an offspring would be twice that of the loss sacrificed on its part by the parent. See W. Hamilton, "The Genetical Evolution of Social Behaviour," in *Narrow Roads of Gene Land: The Collected Papers of W. D. Hamilton*, vol. 1, *Evolution of Social Behaviour* (Basingstoke: Macmillan, 1996), 31–45.

4. R. L. Trivers, "The Evolution of Reciprocal Altruism," in *Natural Selection and Social Theory: Selected Papers of Robert Trivers*, 18–55 (Oxford: Oxford University Press, 2002).

5. See, for example, Martin Novak, *Evolutionary Dynamics: Exploring the Equations of Life* (Cambridge, Mass.: Belknap/Harvard University Press, 2006). I am referring here to the specific extension of this theory to sociobiology and its relatives.

Yet there are important differences between Wilson and Dawkins. While the former argued that genes strictly control cultural tendencies, that is, hold "culture on a leash," Dawkins adopted a dual inheritance model in which cultural ideas are passed between individuals by memes, and biological, genetic traits are inherited through genes. Both models are, nonetheless, in parallel in the sense that both are envisaged to operate through analogous selection mechanisms. Since the 1970s, sociobiology has mushroomed into different schools of thought: human behavioral ecology, evolutionary psychology, and gene-culture evolution. I will devote most space to a critique of evolutionary psychology, as this branch of sociobiology is arguably the one that is enjoying a flourishing that seems to have penetrated even further into academic discourse than the original sociobiological theories.[6]

To put the task of evolutionary psychology in its sociobiological context, it is worth briefly mentioning human behavioral ecology. The main focus of this work is the environment in which people live and the ways ecological and social factors affect human behavior and produce cultural differences within and between populations.[7] Much of the research focused initially on the foraging behavior of small communities remote from Western societies. The assumption made is that most aspects of human behavior depend on social and ecological resource limitations, and the strategy that leads to most benefits and least costs will be the one favored by natural selection. In a given community, a higher social status is correlated with higher lifetime reproductive success. Evolutionary psychologists criticize this approach by arguing that it is not clear where in the mind such behaviors originate. Yet the observation of behavior in human behavioral ecology can be recorded and measured as adaptive, and in this sense partly reflects the behaviorist approach, which has since largely gone out of fashion.[8]

---

6. The number of textbooks devoted to evolutionary psychology provides evidence enough of the growing significance of this field among biologists. See, for example, Lance Workman and Will Reader, *Evolutionary Psychology: An Introduction* (Cambridge: Cambridge University Press, 2004); D. M. Buss, *Evolutionary Psychology: The New Science of the Mind*, 2nd ed. (London: Allyn & Bacon, 2004); and Louise Barrett, Robin Dunbar, and John Lycett, *Human Evolutionary Psychology* (Basingstoke: Palgrave Macmillan, 2002). Historical issues are also discussed in Henry Plotkin, *Evolutionary Thought in Psychology: A Brief History* (Oxford: Blackwell, 2004).

7. For a useful summary, see Kevin N. Laland and Gillian R. Brown, *Evolutionary Perspectives on Human Behaviour* (Oxford: Oxford University Press, 2002), 109–52.

8. Space does not permit discussion of this school of thought.

Evolutionary psychologists also resist the idea that natural selection can act at the level of behavior, but they argue that it is operative at the level of psychological mechanisms. Others will dispute this and suggest that natural selection can act on all aspects of the phenotype, from physiological and psychological through to behavioral characteristics.

2.2 Facets of Evolutionary Psychology

Evolutionary psychology proposes several key ideas. First is that, under-lying human behavior, there are evolved psychological mechanisms that have functioned as adaptations and therefore have been favored by natural selection. Second, most, if not all, of these adaptations took place in the environment of evolutionary adaptedness (EEA), purported to be in the Pleistocene Era some 1.7 million to 10,000 years ago. During this period, specific mental organs or modules evolved in particular areas of the brain or domains as an evolved response to ancestral problems. Leda Cosmides and John Tooby were two of the foremost writers in this vein, writing in the late 1980s; but other key authors, including Harvard professor Steven Pinker, have since joined them.[9]

For authors such as David Buss, the mind has hundreds of specific evolved psychological characteristics that are assumed to be stable and universal characteristics of human nature.[10] Such characteristics include facial expressions; spoken language with phonemes, morphemes, and syn-tax; status roles and division of labor; and incest avoidance regulations. There are, according to this view, distinct mental domains for language, mate choice, sexual behavior, parenting, friendship, resource accrual, dis-ease avoidance, predator avoidance, and social exchange, to name just a few.[11] Buss summarizes this by reference to what he calls the four Rs:

9. Leda Cosmides and J. Tooby, "Cognitive Adaptations for Social Change," in The Adapted Mind: Evolutionary Psychology and the Generation of Culture, ed. Jerome K. Barkow, Leda Cosmides, and J. Tooby, 163–228 (Oxford: Oxford University Press, 1992); S. Pinker, How the Mind Works (London: Penguin, 1997); and L. Cosmides and J. Tooby, "From Evolution to Behaviour: Evolutionary Psychology and the Missing Link," in The Latest on the Best: Essays on Evolution and Optimality, ed. J. Dupré (Cambridge, Mass.: MIT Press, 1987). More popular accounts are given in Robert Wright, The Moral Animal: Evolutionary Psychology and Everyday Life (London: Little, Brown, 1994).

10. Buss, Evolutionary Psychology.

11. Laland and Brown, Evolutionary Perspectives, 162.

(1) pursuit of resources; (2) reproduction; (3) relatedness, meaning here inclusive fitness;[12] and (4) reciprocity (in social groups).

Evolutionary psychologists debate among themselves as to (a) what particular problems might pertain in Pleistocene conditions and (b) which computational theory to use for given behaviors. Cross-cultural studies have reported that mate choice by women is influenced by financial prospects, while mate choice by men is influenced by physical attractiveness, but both sexes found mutual attraction, dependable character, emotional stability, and pleasing disposition were the most important. Evolutionary psychology predicts that children reared by people other than biological parents will be more often at risk, that human societies will show more lethal violence among men, and that males will be more inclined than women to take risks.

Of special interest is the extension of evolutionary psychology to religious belief. Pascal Boyer is an influential writer in this vein, and his *Religion Explained* charts out an evolutionary account of religious belief and practices.[13] While Boyer writes more as a social scientist than an evolutionary psychologist in the strict sense, his approach draws on this theory inasmuch as he speaks of mental systems and their adaptive functioning in a manner that presupposes it is basically correct.[14] Boyer considers the standard secular accounts of why religion exists, such as it provides explanations of puzzling events or experiences, or provides comfort in the face of mortality, or provides social order, or is a cognitive illusion.[15] All of these, he suggests, fail to address the issue of why religion is there at all. He suggests, rather, that there is not so much a "religious" domain in the mind as there are religious ideas *distributed* among different mental systems, such that they impinge on thoughts, emotions, and particular behaviors, more often than not in a way familiar to one's social milieu.

---

12. See introduction for explanation of terminology.

13. Pascal Boyer, *Religion Explained: The Human Instincts That Fashion Gods, Spirits and Ancestors* (London: Heinemann, 2001).

14. Boyer refers to evolutionary psychology as a "tool-kit," while suggesting that evolutionary psychology, in the strict sense of tracing back particular traits to our earliest ancestors, is "still very much in its infancy." Boyer, *Religion Explained*, 135. He is also enthusiastic about Steven Pinker, Robert Wright, and Matt Ridley in his annotated list of further reading, 382.

15. Boyer, *Religion Explained*, 6–7.

Scott Atran writes in a similar vein in his *In Gods We Trust*.[16] Like Boyer, Atran sees religion as coming from "the ordinary workings of the human mind as it deals with emotionally compelling problems of human existence."[17] Also like Boyer, he believes that standard explanations of religious belief fail to explain why supernatural-agent concepts are culturally universal, how it is possible to validate belief in supernatural agents that seem illogical, and how people can be prevented from detecting from moral order. He also makes the case for a "naturalistic" approach to anthropology. He argues that evolution sets the framework for religion and culture but does not determine its development in an absolute sense.

Atran believes that Boyer represents those who concentrate on cognitive theories of religion and counterfactual beliefs. This focuses on the way the mind works in particular ways in processes of cultural transmission. Atran suggests that this ignores motivation. A second group, which includes authors such as Sober and Wilson, focuses on religious belief in terms of individual or group costs and benefits, paying relatively little attention to cognitive architecture. A third group studies religious belief by focusing on experiential theories and states of altered consciousness, so that neurophysiological responses are tracked during mystical and other states. Finally, a fourth group is concerned with psychosocial dynamics of liturgy and ritual. None, Atran argues, adequately answers the question as to *why* religious belief in the supernatural is able to underpin moral order in a way that no secular ideology is able to do for very long.

Yet his explanation for the existence of supernatural agency seems far from satisfactory. For him, supernatural agencies are "in part, by-products of a naturally selected cognitive system for detecting agents—such as predators, protectors and prey—and for dealing rapidly and economically with stimulus situations involving people and animals."[18] He also suggests that core beliefs of religions seem to be favored by memory in a way that favors their cultural survival. Like Boyer, he rejects the idea of specialist brain activity for routine religious experience. He also rejects Dawkins's idea of memes as applied to religious belief and is more inclined to evolutionary

16. S. Atran, *In Gods We Trust: The Evolutionary Landscape of Religion* (Oxford: Oxford University Press, 2002).
17. Ibid., viii.
18. Ibid., 15.

psychology.[19] However, he rejects the idea that religious traditions have a systematic relationship to genetic fitness, preferring instead that an original obsolete function is now used for another, now religious function; in other words, it is an exaptation. Yet he also holds that humans will converge toward certain forms of cultural life, including religious life, which is set to some extent by the ancestral evolutionary landscape. Such constraints include "emotional feelings and displays, on modularised conceptual and mnemonic processing, and on social commitments and attentiveness to information about co-operators, protectors, predators and prey."[20] Supernatural agents arise culturally from a general biologically evolved "agent detection" module(s). However, Atran also relies on a cultural interpretation of this process—that is, people will act together in order to manipulate the agent detection module in historically contingent ways. He suggests that a few counterintuitive beliefs (such as belief in a supernatural agent), if combined with intuitive beliefs, are more easily recalled over time. Although claiming at the outset that religious belief has no survival advantage, he concludes that self-sacrifice stabilizes moral order in a given group, giving people faith in one another's good will.

Steven Mithen has contributed to this discussion from an archaeological perspective.[21] Assuming the archaeological record is complete, current research suggests that religious belief is pervasive as far back as Neolithic human societies. Like Atran, Mithen asks why religion is so pervasive in all human societies, even in prehistory. He offers his readers a stark contrast: either there has been an intervention by a supernatural agent, or there has been some reason why religious belief has evolved, as it had survival value.[22] Of course, theologians will cringe at this simplistic understanding of

19. Ibid., 265. He is using evolutionary psychology in a narrow sense as that which is distinctive from mimetics and other co-evolutionary theories, as discussed above.

20. Ibid., 266.

21. See S. Mithen, *Prehistory of the Mind: A Search for the Origins of Art, Science and Religion* (London: Thames & Hudson, 1996); S. J. Mithen, "The Supernatural Beings of Pre-history and the External Storage of Religious Ideas," in *Cognition and Material Culture: The Archaeology of Symbolic Storage*, ed. C. Renfrew and C. Scarre, 99–107 (Cambridge: McDonald Institute of Archaeological Research, 1998); S. J. Mithen, "Paleoanthropological Perspectives on the Theory of the Mind," in *Understanding Other Minds*, ed. S. Baron-Cohen, H. Tager-Flusberg, and D. J. Cohen, 97–106 (Oxford: Oxford University Press, 2000); and S. J. Mithen, *The Singing Neanderthals: The Origin of Music, Language, Mind and Body* (London: Weidenfeld & Nicolson, 2005).

22. This is most explicit in S. Mithen, "The Prehistory of the Religious Mind," in

God as a supernatural agent, intervening in the world, but the extent to which this was actually the belief of these earliest *Homo* species is impossible to discern with any accuracy. What is of particular interest here is that Neanderthals were not, apparently, religious in any formal sense, although Mithen argues that they did have musical sensibility, it seems, communicating with one another through singing.[23]

The particular focus for the present discussion is Mithen's adoption of evolutionary psychology as the rational basis for the evolution of religious belief in early humans. He encounters considerable difficulty in using the cognitive Swiss army knife model of Leda and Cosmides, in that the flexibility of responses in prehistory is not what one would expect if mental behavior were fixed in given modules in the way that strict evolutionary psychology suggests. However, rather than go down the route of total cognitive fluidity, he understands the mind as existing much as a cathedral, with passages between the different mental modules, allowing communication between them.

Of course, for a theologian, the analogy with a cathedral is instantly appealing, and certainly the idea allows for a narrative to be told about how early and late humans differed in their abilities to think in complex ways, seemingly accounting for some empirical observations about the differences in cultural behavior, including, perhaps, religious behavior. In particular, Mithen argues that the mental domains associated with, for example, social activity are separated from those associated with tool use and beliefs about the natural world in primates and Neanderthals, but in modern humans, we find considerable cognitive fluidity between the different cognitive domains. The species *Homo sapiens* evolved about 200,000 years ago, but it was only with the evidence for partial burials that were very different from those of Neanderthals, discovered at Mount Carmel between 100,000 and 80,000 years ago, that we find some concrete evidence of religious activity. Yet Mithen concludes that ideas about supernatural beings were later than this, likely around 35,000 years ago with the first representational art of the Upper Paleolithic in Europe. He believes that the kind of religious sensibility that evolved was that associated with imagistic religious belief, rather than doctrinal modes of religiosity.[24]

Theology, Evolution and the Mind, ed. N. Spurway (Cambridge: Scholars Press, 2009). See also my response in this volume.
23. See Mithen, *Singing Neanderthals*.
24. Here he follows Harvey Whitehouse. See H. Whitehouse, *Modes of Religiosity: A Cognitive Theory of Religious Transmission* (Walnut Creek, Calif.: Altamira, 2004).

The question that concerns us here is whether it is really necessary or indeed helpful to use evolutionary psychology to try to explain
religious belief. Indeed, the cognitive fluidity necessarily associated with
the emergence of the possibility of religion implies a much more general evolutionary process of the brain, which led to a very generalized
cognitive fluidity, rather than one dependent on prior modular units or
domains. There are unanswered questions here as well, such as why religious belief in the supernatural appeared when it did, when the supposedly more fluid cognitive architecture had already been in place for some
time. There is no need to introduce a "God concept" here in order to fill
in the gaps; rather, the evolution of the mind in such a way that religious
belief becomes possible is something one would have anticipated if God
intended to communicate with particular agents. In other words, while
I am not persuaded that evolutionary psychology "explains" religion, I
am more certain that the basic *capacity* for religious belief, and complex
thought more generally, is grounded in an evolutionary account of brain
development.[25] But this does not answer properly the question as to *why*
religion evolved, or its cause; it merely states that it is *possible* for more
advanced forms of religion to evolve in *Homo* species rather than in, for
example, other hominids.

---

25. An ambitious large-scale multimillion-pound multidisciplinary project initiated
in September 2007, boldly entitled "Explaining Religion," is currently under way, coordinated by Professor Harvey Whitehouse from the Institute of Cognitive and Evolutionary Anthropology at Oxford University. This project networks academics from nine
different European partners and draws on evolutionary psychology, as well as other disciplines. Its intention is to integrate the world's leading centers for psychological, biological, anthropological, and historical research on religion. It will attempt to map the
extent to which belief in God might improve reproductive success or lead to other social
benefits, such as enhancement in reputation. Other research relates to the neurobiology
of the brain. See http://www.icea.ox.ac.uk/research/cam/projects/explaining_religion/,
accessed April 2, 2008. The European commission, which has sponsored this research,
suggests that this work will also be used to "model future evolution," presuming, of
course, that evolutionary science has succeeded in explaining both religious belief and
diversity. See http://www.icea.ox.ac.uk/research/cam/projects/explaining_religion/
exrel.pdf, accessed April 2, 2008. Of course, how far and to what extent different partners will come to a consensus on this remains to be seen; ethnologists have traditionally
been opposed to much of evolutionary psychology, as Harvey Whitehouse is only too
well aware. See H. Whitehouse, ed., *The Debated Mind: Evolutionary Psychology versus
Ethnography* (Oxford: Berg, 2001). Also of relevance is H. Whitehouse and James Laid-
law, *Religion, Anthropology and Cognitive Science* (Durham: Carolina Academic Press,
2008).

2.3 Is Jesus an Evolutionary Psychologist?

The claim that evolutionary psychology merits attention inasmuch as it opens up the possibility of religious belief has been taken further in the work of theologian Patricia Williams, who claims not just that Jesus is shaped by evolutionary psychology in terms of his basic capacity for religious belief, but that his *inner identity* takes the form of an evolutionary psychologist. Those who take up evolutionary psychology are, by implication, imitating Christ! She argues her case by using what she believes is a scholarly reconstruction of the Jesus figure as found in the Gospel accounts.

The first element she names is the use of resources, and she finds evidence in the Gospel records for Jesus' concern with such matters. Yet it seems to me that such concern does not so much nail Jesus as an evolutionary psychologist as it recognizes that he is aware, like everyone else, of the need to take into account the commonsense natural limits of resources as well as to raise social questions about human greed. The portrait of Jesus as one who recognizes and responds to male dominance need not come from his recognition of evolutionary instincts in the manner suggested by Williams. Indeed, her uncritical reading of evolutionary psychology leads to an equally uncritical appropriation as applied to the Gospel record. While she correctly interprets Jesus as one who not only defended women but also challenged the lustful approaches to women that characterized that society, this hardly "fits" evolutionary psychology as much as it challenges this way of behavior toward women. It is also unclear why Jesus would challenge the supposed evolutionary psychology that dominates the society; in this sense, it would make him an evolutionary freak.[26] In every instance, Jesus seems to defy the biological ties that make up human relatedness and society. Williams states that this means he was a good evolutionary psychologist; he knew that what comes "naturally" is not necessarily a good thing. But this would hardly make him a "good" evolutionary psychologist; rather, it would mean that he is trying to overcome tendencies purported to affect behavior as studied in evolutionary psychology.

Even more surprising, perhaps, is Williams's claim that Jesus rejected reciprocity and justice in favor of love and generosity. It seems to me that

---

26. Gerd Theissen takes up the idea that Jesus can be thought of as an evolutionary mutation. In his reading of the Bible, Jesus' attitude of solidarity is diametrically opposed to natural selection. See G. Theissen, *Biblical Faith: An Evolutionary Approach* (London: SCM, 1984). I engage with Theissen's work in more detail in chapter 8.

Jesus *was* concerned about injustices in society, and that his call was to look beyond the demands of justice and the law, rather than to dispense with them altogether. More to the point in this context, such examples again show up Jesus not so much as an exemplar for evolutionary psychology, but rather as one who went back to the creation mandate prior to the legis- lation of the Torah; that is, he understood God and all creatures as in loving relationship with each other, according to the tradition of the goodness of God's creation. In other words, his motivation was based on a critical and radical reading of his Jewish tradition, rather than dispensing with that tradition and replacing it with something else. Naming Jesus as somehow indebted to insights from evolutionary psychology, even though, of course, he would not know the formal science, misses the point.

Williams also seems to assume that atonement theory is necessar- ily about the infliction of God's punishment on Jesus, demonstrating the unjust killing of an innocent man. Such portrayals are not the only way of considering the meaning of the atonement.[27] Moreover, while socio- biologists claim that "selfish" genes do not necessarily equate with selfish behavior, the metaphor all too often wears thin, exposing an underlying belief that self-interest is what dominates human behavior and actions.[28]

---

27. See chapter 5.

28. Lisa Goddard has taken this further in her careful and rigorous analysis of the selfishness paradigm throughout sociobiological works. See Lisa Goddard, "An Inter- rogation of the Selfishness Paradigm in Sociobiology Including Its Explanations of Altruism and a Response to Its Interpretation of New Testament Love" (Ph.D. diss., University of Liverpool, 2008). Goddard also distinguishes self-love and egoism, and challenges Williams's equation of reciprocal kin relationships with sin, in contrast with the position of Stephen Pope, who relates sociobiological views on altruism with theo- ries about natural law. See S. Pope, *The Evolution of Altruism and the Ordering of Love* (Washington, D.C.: Georgetown University Press, 1994). His most recent work is S. Pope, *Human Evolution and Christian Ethics* (Cambridge: Cambridge University Press, 2008). While Goddard does not deal specifically with evolutionary psychology in her thesis, it is of note that both Williams and Pope seem largely to accept evolutionary psychology as providing a valid interpretation of human behavior. The difference relates to their interpretation of Christian witness. For Pope, Christian altruism is largely an extension of that which motivates natural human nature, while for Williams, Christ's teaching is a radical rebuttal of that tendency. Williams, of course, faces the difficulty of how the cultural teaching of Jesus is compatible with evolutionary psychology; one would have expected it to disappear according to its own paradigm. Pope faces the charge of the relative difference Christ makes to human acting and behaving, in line with the evolutionary Christologies already discussed in the previous chapter. Both authors, by largely accepting evolutionary psychology, have failed to probe deeper into possible alternative ways of relating Christology and evolutionary theory. I have reviewed Pope's

Not only is this message a simplistic account of human behavior; it also is diametrically opposed to Christ's teaching on radical altruism.

It also seems to me that Williams is misappropriating a particular version of evolutionary psychology for her own particular ends, namely, to find a way of creating a seamless account of science and biblical faith. Human behavioral ecology has reminded us of the context of the wider ecology of the land and resources in descriptions of human behavior. It is *this* branch of evolutionary discourse that is possibly worth taking into account in the context of consideration of the historical Jesus, even though we might be cautious of its attraction to evolutionary explanations of particular behaviors. In other words, like evolutionary psychology, it goes much too far in making correlations between land resources and human action. However, it is a reminder of the need to be sensitive to the possible impact of wider ecological conditions prevailing in different regions of Galilee.

Bearing in mind the limitation of inappropriate correlations, it is possible to suggest that the influence of the ecological, cultural, and political diversity of Israel at the time of Jesus' historical ministry is worth considering in attempts to retrace the historic Jesus, without taking up the mantle of evolutionary psychology.[29] For example, his earliest ministry in the desert with his cousin John contrasts with his later ministry in the ecologically much richer region of Galilee. A farm excavated near Nazareth from the Roman period shows a relatively comfortable lifestyle, so that Jesus' claim for simplicity and itinerant lifestyle imply that he challenged prevailing values of the culture that sought family stability and relative comfort. Jewish peasant interests were squeezed where land was granted to returning army veterans, but Jesus describes such people as experiencing a blessing, not a curse. Sean Freyne speculates that in the valley by the Lake of Galilee, dominated by a flourishing and relatively wealthy fishing industry, Jesus' itinerant message may have been more readily received, compared with that of the settled farmers of Nazareth, who were tied more closely to the land and threatened with possible eviction. Jesus is portrayed as one who was both an innovator and also deeply appreciative of ancient Jewish accounts of the natural world and its processes belonging to Yahweh.

Human Genetics elsewhere; see C. Deane-Drummond, review of *Human Evolution and Christian Ethics*, by S. J. Pope, *Theology* (2009), in press.

29. Sean Freyne has discussed this aspect in his book *Jesus: A Jewish Galilean; A New Reading of the Jesus Story* (London: Continuum International, 2004), 27–57.

It is more likely, then, that the earliest followers of Jesus perceived him as a sage, one who imitated to some extent the literary pattern of other sages in the trial, death, and vindication of the wise one.[30] According to this interpretation, the Suffering Servant motif in Isaiah and *maskilim* (wise teachers) of Daniel would have inspired Jesus as background figures and analogues in his own public ministry. There are some shared values with that of wisdom in openness to outsiders, critique of wealth, and rejection of triumphal attitudes toward God's alignment with Israel's cause. There was a link between the Jewish heritage and early Christian reception of Jesus' ideas, though it would be incorrect to portray the earliest Christian community as simply about belief. Rather, "living a life as Jesus had lived became an essential component of the early Christian kerygma, orthopraxis, or proper behaviour, became as important as, indeed, was an expression of orthodoxy or right belief."[31] If evolutionary psychology has reminded us of the importance of linking belief and practice, theology has tended to separate the two and view one (belief) as a prerequisite of the other (practice).

2.4 Critical Perspectives on Evolutionary Psychology

Although authors such as Boyer and Atran have not taken up all aspects of evolutionary psychology in their interpretation of moral order and religious belief, and Patricia Williams offers a strange amalgam of affirming evolutionary psychology even while naming the teaching of Jesus as challenging its overall direction in human behavior, I suggest that it is important for theologians to consider many deep problems in this way of thinking, not least because it claims to provide a way of thinking meaningfully about all aspects of human experience and behavior. As I have indicated, it is also important that theologians do not simply identify with evolutionary psychology, as if failing to do so will somehow betray an evolutionary understanding of biological life or be Luddite in its approach to new scientific developments. I will claim here that it is possible to affirm biological/Darwinian evolution without necessarily subscribing to the claims of evolutionary psychology.

As pointed out in the introduction, Darwinian evolution by natural selection is barely a sufficient explanation, due to the complexities of other

---

30. Common patterns include Dan. 3, 6; Wis. 2–5; 2 Macc. 7; and Gen. 37–39. See Freyne, *Jesus*, 168.

31. Ibid., 173.

parallel processes. However, in a minimal sense, it is possible to argue for the overall validity of Darwinian evolution without either extending it so that it becomes a paradigm for human cultural diversity or, as I will suggest later in this chapter, distorting it so that it becomes more closely associated with Spencerian ideals of progress. Although evolutionary psychology does not claim any belief in any supernatural being, its dominance in some quarters, at least in the Western world, suggests a particular deep commitment that has religious overtones. It follows, in other words, in that stream of thought of social Darwinism that seems to give moral purpose to evolution itself and suggests why some commentators have gone so far as to call these interpretations of evolution the "God-Surrogate."[32]

Yet there are other particular reasons why evolutionary psychology proves problematic.

Evolutionary Biology

Not all biologists agree with the way evolutionary psychology interprets human cognition as functional, evolved mental units or modules. Geneticist Steven Rose, for example, goes so far as to suggest that evolutionary psychology is largely erroneous in its account of evolution, development, and neural function.[33] He also traces evolutionary psychology to those strands of biological determinism that pervaded twentieth-century genetics. These strands included, first, the idea that socially relevant differences between individuals and groups, such as sexual orientation or intelligence, could be accounted for by genetics, and second, the concept that there are universals in human nature, such as male aggression or female coyness. While recognizing that evolutionary psychologists are not strict genetic determinists, they try to use a particular version of Darwin's theory in order to account for observations, for it is used to interpret forms of social organization as adaptations parsed by natural selection, even if not always tied in with particular genes for particular behaviors.[34]

---

32. E. Gellner, *Plough, Sword and Book: The Structure of Human History* (London: Collins/Harvill, 1988), 144.

33. Steven Rose, "Escaping Evolutionary Psychology," in *Alas Poor Darwin: Arguments against Evolutionary Psychology*, ed. H. Rose and S. Rose, 247–65 (London: Jonathan Cape, 2000). See also J. Panksepp and J. B. Panksepp, "The Seven Sins of Evolutionary Psychology," *Evolution and Cognition* 6 (2000): 108–31.

34. Rose uses the word *nativism* to describe the way evolutionary psychologists talk about the architecture of the mind. This implies a connection to eugenics that many

Overall, Rose strongly criticizes the way evolutionary psychologists claim a genetic basis for behavior, what he terms "pseudo-genes," with a putative basis in genetic fitness, without any empirical support for such claims. A consistent failure in evolutionary psychology is, then, to mistake enablement for causation. In other words, the brain *enables* certain behaviors, but it does not *cause* them. A good example would be the preference for green, cited by evolutionary psychologists as that which has arisen in EEA and been named as a universal preference across different peoples from very different cultures. Rose somewhat scathingly comments that such research is more often than not drawn from research on undergraduate students, whose preference for green most likely reflects a mythic desire to escape from life's problems. Of course, a reply to this charge would be that more research could be done on people of other cultures. However, even this would not prove, first, that such preference arose when it is claimed to have done, and second, that there is a basis for such preference in particular behavioral modules favored by natural selection and often assumed to have a particular genetic basis.

A frequent claim of evolutionary psychology is to speak in terms of genes for particular behaviors. As well as the problems just suggested, this view of the relationship between genetics and behavior gives a false impression, for naked replicators are simply abstractions; they require cells, enzymes, and a metabolic web to work, so that the relationship between genotype and phenotype is nonlinear.[35] Living systems are not "sandwiched between the demands of their genes and the challenges of their environments"; rather, they are far more complex and subtle than this implies.[36] Instead, organisms actively construct the environments around them, constantly transforming these environments in active ways. In other words, there is a balance between specificity and plasticity, so

---

evolutionary psychologists would strongly resist, though the manner in which it is portrayed in more popular writings does, in my view, lend itself to such criticism.

35. The point being argued here is that while there are known genes that, when faulty, will lead to particular diseases, including mental disease, there is rarely, if ever, a one-to-one correspondence between genetics and particular behaviors. Genetics involves a complex process of editing and regulation. Often one gene is responsible for many different products, as is certainly the case considering the relatively low number of genes found in human species and their commonality with other related species, such as primates. The differences in this case reflect differences in regulation of expression of these genes.

36. Rose, "Escaping Evolutionary Psychology," 256.

that just as there are developmental changes in the connections between eye and brain after an infant is born (which designates specificity), so the wiring of the visual cortex and what is perceived also are shaped by early experiences (that is, plasticity). Rose sums up his criticism neatly in the following sentence:

> A living organism is an active player in its own destiny, not a lumbering robot responding to genetic imperatives whilst passively waiting to discover whether it has passed what Darwin described as the continuous scrutiny of natural selection.[37]

Moreover, genes work together in order for an organism to survive, so even where there is a genetic basis for particular traits, packages of genes are selected, not single genes in the manner implied by evolutionary psychology. Furthermore, as discussed in the introduction, natural selection is not the only mode of evolutionary change that exists; there are other mechanisms, including genetic drift, founder effects, and so on, which evolutionary psychology ignores. Finally, Rose criticizes the focus on cognitive information processing among evolutionary psychologists and their lack of attention to emotion, as well as envisaging a brain "designed" according to an architectural blueprint. This, he suggests, gives a false impression that the brain is inflexible, which is the opposite of how the brain needs to be conceived. He also points to empirical studies that have shown changes in so-called universals such as women preferring men with wealth or men being violent. Rose asks, somewhat scathingly, has there been a sudden change in mutation rates, or have the people decided to rebel against their selfish replicators? A more likely explanation is, he suggests, one that stresses the fluidity and plasticity of the brain, rather than its adherence to preset preferences set up in the Pleistocene Era.

Does the split between genetics and mimetics offered by Richard Dawkins and others provide any resolution? In this case, it is clear that Dawkins's position suffers from many of the same weaknesses in biological terms as standard accounts of evolutionary psychology. Often mimetics is included in textbooks on evolutionary psychology, and it is largely a matter of definition as to how broadly it is defined.[38] In the first place, genes are portrayed as the sole units on which natural selection acts, which itself is

---

37. Ibid., 257.
38. See, for example, Workman and Reader, *Evolutionary Psychology*, 350–57.

misleading, for natural selection acts at higher levels than this view implies. Of course, the most controversial position is that natural selection acts at the level of the group. Dawkins supposes that because there is a genetic component to a given complex function, then natural selection is responsible, and he does not adequately consider other evolutionary mechanisms.

Dawkins also presents natural selection as a process that has a particular direction. In practice, however, natural selection is not active as such; rather, it is a passive outcome of those interactions where the particular phenotypes that are most suited to the environment survive. It is therefore both illegitimate and misleading in evolutionary terms to give quantitative coefficients to genes as a reflection of their supposed genetic "power" to influence the result of selection.[39] Much the same could be said of the way evolutionary psychology attempts to mathematically quantify its results by correlations that are ultimately based on theoretical speculations rather than in empirical evidence of a particular genetic basis for behavior. Dawkins's own reference to the phenotype should not detract from the overall thrust of his writing, which is seeking to promote one thing: "Everything of functional importance and complexity is an adaptation fashioned by natural selection working for the good of selfish replicators. The caveats, the qualifications, the 'ifs' and 'buts' are not part of the grand illusion."[40]

The regulation of gene expression by shared modules has highlighted the complexity of gene function, along with transpositions between genes or regulatory units that show sources of genetic variation that are non-Mendelian. *Molecular drive* is the name given to describe the potential of new genetic variants to spread through sexual populations. This differs from Darwinian-Mendelian evolution, where mutations are portrayed as one-off occurrences waiting for the sieving effect of natural selection. Dawkins's view that complex functions are "improbable perfections" arising through natural selection of adaptations is also false on a number of counts, not least because the genetic components behind complex functions are likely to be already in use across other cellular processes; that is, they are adopted for subsequent use. Moreover, to speak of probabilities is an error, as there is only one tree of life, so probabilities cannot be assigned to singular events. When genomic turnover leads to the appearance of two very similar genes or developmental processes, the organism is buffered

---

39. This point has been made well by Gabriel Dover, "Anti-Dawkins," in Rose and Rose, *Alas Poor Darwin*, 53.

40. Ibid., 55–56.

against potential mutations. In such conditions, some previously inaccessible component of the environment may be adopted, leading to an alternative means of arriving at novel biological function.

Overall, there is a much looser relationship between organisms and environment than previously thought:

> The inherent flux and redundancy of the genetic material, coupled with the widespread sharing of molecular constructs that underpin diverse biological functions, ensures that there is a much looser relationship between organisms and environment than was supposed when there was only natural selection as the motor of evolutionary change.[41]

Human Prehistory

Evolutionary psychologists commonly rely on certain assumptions about the era of evolutionary adaptedness. While this makes fascinating reading, it is all speculation. It is hardly surprising that this has come under attack from different sources, most noticeably from evolutionary biologists such as Stephen Jay Gould, who has described the practice as "Just So Stories."[42] By this, he means that more or less any attribute can be read back into the EEA as an adaptation to a particular set of conditions that was presumed to prevail at the time, namely, an African savannah. However, it is clear that the prevailing conditions where humans lived were far more varied than evolutionary psychologists assume to be the case—including deserts, rivers, oceans, forests, and arctic tundra. The kind of cooperative, coordinated, and socially organized and linguistically guided hunting and gathering that prevails in modern hunter-gatherer societies, and is assumed to be a model of early human society, may not apply.[43] Also, many of the so-called adaptations are also characteristic of other primate species, so it is incorrect to assume that they first appeared in the EEA.

Gould believes that much greater stress needs to be put on cultural learning and that this form of learning is not passed down in a Darwinian manner. If we follow the mimetic alternative of Dawkins, then this is incorrect as well, since cultural habits are passed on in a Lamarckian

---

41. Ibid., 64.

42. Stephen Jay Gould, "More Things in Heaven and Earth," in Rose and Rose, *Alas Poor Darwin*, 85–105.

43. Laland and Brown, *Evolutionary Perspectives*, 177–84.

fashion; that is, children acquire those changes introduced by their parents. He also suggests that most if not all universal behaviors are *spandrels,* that is, nonadaptive by-products of an evolutionary process that are then adopted for other uses. It is therefore incorrect to suggest that such secondary uses *explain* the spandrel, for spandrels fall outside the sphere of ultra-Darwinian approaches to evolution. Hence, while Gould seems to concede that there may be a genetic element to some behaviors, he suggests that they cannot be explained in terms of particular adaptations for given conditions in the ancestral period in the manner suggested by evolutionary psychology.

Social Anthropology

As one might expect, many social anthropologists are extremely wary of the way evolutionary psychology portrays human cultures. Tim Ingold is among the critics who reject the idea that culture is somehow added to a biological matrix.[44] Of course, this assumes that there are cultural variables distinct from biological tendencies, and within evolutionary psychology, we find some variation from those who are drawn to a separation of the two in mimetics and those who try to keep culture firmly based in biological predispositions. Ingold suggests that culture is a measure of differences between peoples in their relationships to each other and the environment, rather than something added to organisms. He cites the way we walk as an example of how mistaken it is to speak of this in cultural or biological terms; rather, it is a developmental achievement of the whole organism in its environment. He prefers, therefore, models of evolution that give a higher place to relational aspects, echoing more controversial ideas of authors such as Brian Goodwin.[45] Whether or not we choose to adopt such an evolutionary theory, the point seems plain enough, namely, that far more consideration needs to be given to the context of individuals in their relationships with others, rather than considering behavior as isolated examples of particular selection patterns.

Susan McKinnon, writing from a feminist perspective, is even more strident in her criticism of evolutionary psychology, describing the science as "complete fiction" that is "created by the false assumption that their own

---

44. T. Ingold, "Evolving Skills," in Rose and Rose, *Alas Poor Darwin,* 225–44.

45. See, for example, Brian Goodwin, *How the Leopard Changed Its Spots: The Evolution of Complexity* (London: Phoenix, 2001).

cultural values are both natural in origin and universal in nature."[46] In other words, she believes that evolutionary psychology conducts itself in a way that is shaped by particular social and cultural biases that effectively marginalize other cultural values and "[suppress] a wide range of past, present and future human potentialities." These are sharp charges indeed, and her arguments are worth exploring in some detail. Her main argument is with those versions of evolutionary psychology that view cultural processes in terms of inherited psychological mechanisms that are themselves reduced to genetic traits. The way the mind works is in dispute in the first instance; for McKinnon and many other social anthropologists as well as biologists, the brain is flexible in its ability to respond to given events, rather than subject to predisposed innate tendencies.[47] There are, however, other models of cognition that do not presuppose some sort of preloaded software in the mind.[48]

McKinnon also believes that the theory of mind and culture proposed by evolutionary psychologists cannot account for the evolutionary origin and history of the mind and its function, as well as the contemporary diversity and variation of human social function. We have dealt with the former critique from the perspective of evolutionary function and history. She is particularly critical of assumptions about gender and genetics that underlie the theories of universal psychological mechanisms. She believes that much of the writing of evolutionary psychology adopts a rhetoric that reflects particular cultural ideas that are then embedded in deep genetic and evolutionary history, as a means of privileging such ideas and giving them a prescriptive moral force.[49] I doubt very much if evolutionary

---

46. Susan McKinnon, *Neo-liberal Genetics: The Myths and Tales of Evolutionary Psychology* (Chicago: Prickly Paradigm, 2005), 4.

47. Similar objections have been aired by others; see, for example, Barbara Herrnstein Smith, "Sewing Up the Mind: The Claims of Evolutionary Psychology," in Rose and Rose, *Alas Poor Darwin*, 129–43.

48. See, for example, Esther Thelen and Linda B. Smith, *A Dynamic Systems Approach to the Development of Cognition and Action* (Cambridge, Mass.: MIT Press, 1994). See also Kathleen R. Gibson, "Epigenesis, Brain Plasticity, and Behavioural Versatility: Alternatives to Standard Evolutionary Psychology Models," in *Complexities: Beyond Nature and Nurture*, ed. Susan McKinnon and Sydel Silverman, 23–42 (Chicago: Chicago University Press, 2005). A related issue is the development of human cognition. It is clear that much brain development takes place after birth and that its complexity is constructed rather than predetermined. See Annette K. Smith, "Why Babies' Brains Are Not Swiss Army Knives," in Rose and Rose, *Alas Poor Darwin*, 144–56.

49. McKinnon, *Neo-liberal Genetics*, 12.

psychologists are aware of such an influence on their writing; they certainly seek to dismiss all criticism from such quarters in a somewhat sneering fashion, claiming that only those on the far left and other radicals object to their ideas. The lack of openness to the possibility that there might be particular cultural biases entering their scientific research is unfortunate, though their approach can be criticized on their own terms, that is, on scientific grounds, as I have already suggested.

What is clear is that the so-called universal patterns of sexual and gender relations claimed to exist by evolutionary psychologists fail to record the fact that these purported universals are also most dominant in these scientists' own culture and society. Evolutionary psychology has also reversed the premises of natural selection as lacking purpose, by speaking in terms of "design" at regular intervals. Moreover, while anthropologists view human beings as having an active capacity for intelligent intervention in the world, evolutionary psychologists reduce this function to a passive reception of biological tendencies evolved in prehistory. The language used to describe natural selection is one of "policy maker," "engineer," with particular "goals."[50] While there are disclaimers about genes having agency, the language used implies that genes do have such agency. In this scenario, selfish genes are covered up by self-deceiving cultures. It is the genes, apparently, that seem to portray the self-interest characteristic of neoliberal culture, where public good is replaced by individual responsibility. Culture is added on where there is supposed deviation from the norm anticipated by genetic universals.[51]

McKinnon argues, instead, that kinship relationships do not support the idea that human social relationships follow some sort of genetic codification. Many societies and cultures follow unilineal descent, that is, descent traced through the male or female line. In this scenario, by the third generation, only a quarter of the original genetic kin are present, and by the fifth generation, one-sixteenth, while relatives in other lineages, such as the children of sisters, have a higher coefficient of one-quarter. Overall, some genetic kin end up in other lineages, while some strangers end up in one's own lineage. This contravenes the logic of genetic self-maximization and kin selection, which presumes resources will be spent on genetically close

---

50. Ibid., 16.
51. Ibid., 42–44.

relatives rather than distant kin or strangers.[52] In some societies, the residential group, rather than genetic ties, decides who is kin or nonkin. On the Tanimbar Islands, children are allocated to houses based on a system of exchanges that accompany marriage. In other cultures, such as the Langkawi, kinship is related to feeding, so that when food is shared, it is envisaged as being transferred to one's blood. In these scenarios, kinship is more about doing than biological origin. In Western societies, the biological is privileged over the behavioral as a basis for kinship. In this way, McKinnon argues,

> what evolutionary psychologists have done is to reduce a symbolic, culturally mediated system to what they deem to be a natural, culturally unmediated one. Yet the diversity of cultural understandings of kinship and the range of kinship formations cannot be accounted for as a natural system operating by means of a fixed genetic calculus.[53]

Overall, McKinnon suggests that evolutionary psychology is compelling to Euro-American minds, as it reflects those beliefs that are embedded in its culture, including, for example, innateness of gender difference, sexual double standards, naturalness of neoliberal values of self-interest, competition, rational choice, survival of the fittest, evolutionary origins of man as hunter, and life's complexity having a single key. While some of this critique is overdrawn in places, I suggest that the underlying cultural presuppositions that are reflected in the way evolutionary psychology functions deserve far more attention by those claiming to support its premises. It is well known that Darwin, Wallace, and others introduced their own prejudices considering other human cultures by speaking of "savages" and other "primitive peoples." Their interpretation of human culture thus was inevitably biased toward their cultural values. Much the same could be said of evolutionary psychology.

Philosophy

The philosophical engagement with evolutionary psychology in part depends on which branch of evolutionary psychology is under discussion. Mary Midgley has been vocal in her attack on sociobiology, ever since

---

52. Ibid., 51–53.
53. Ibid., 56.

E. O. Wilson first colonized the field. Dawkins's development of sociobiology in the form of meme theory has also come under her scrutiny.[54] While biologists such as S. J. Gould want to attack meme theory on the basis that it is inappropriate to use natural selection to describe all evolutionary change, Midgley believes that extending biological science into cultural analysis is inappropriate. She believes that the Cartesian split between fact and values cannot be solved simply by one-half (science) "swallowing up" the other, but by avoiding making that split in the first place. She suggests that the questions that are asked in social dilemmas are a very different kind from those needed for chemistry or biology, so that extending memes to cultural analysis is mistaken, as it assumes there is a close connection between the two spheres. She rejects, then, what she detects as a "Darwinian universal" that pervades meme talk, including authors such as Daniel Dennett, who describes Darwin's theory as a "universal acid" eating through traditional concepts. For her, such a position is "reductionism incarnate."[55] Rather, attempts to frame such concepts in a universal way are actually quite traditional and resemble the metaphysical structures of Herbert Spencer that Darwin himself rejected. Darwin also allowed for other means of modification, not just natural selection in the manner projected in evolutionary psychology. If we seldom pass on a meme unaltered, how far can it possibly resemble genetics? She suggests that, in describing humans as "meme machines," we are taken into the philosophical world of fatalism.

John Dupré adds to the criticism of evolutionary psychology by suggesting that evolutionary psychology more often than not seems to advocate a form of essentialism that is a radical departure from an appropriately empiricist approach to science, as evidenced in the stereotypical view of sex and gender.[56] He joins the criticism of mental modules inasmuch as they rest on flimsy a priori evidence, so much so that he claims ironically that "we should treat this school of genetic determinism with all the respect that thinking people have come to accord its predecessors."[57] He does not, however, reject the possibility of task-specific modules outright; in other words, he believes we are not in a position to decide either way. He is even

---

54. For a summary of her position in this respect, see Mary Midgley "Why Memes?" in Rose and Rose, *Alas Poor Darwin*, 67–84. For a biographical support for her views on Darwin, see, for example, Nora Barlow, ed., *Autobiography of Charles Darwin, 1809–1882* (New York: Harcourt Brace, 1958), 109.

55. Midgley, "Why Memes?" 82.

56. John Dupré, *Humans and Other Animals* (Oxford: Clarendon, 2002), 9–10.

57. Ibid., 211.

more skeptical of the atavistic character attributed to them, and inasmuch as they are genetically based, they would lack the flexibility to respond to changing environments. On this point, he seems to be supported by more recent research on brain function, which suggests that the importance of genetics relates more to general properties and anatomy, such as the location of the retinal nerve and vision processing, whereas other neurological functions depend on the neurons that were active or available when the environmental change or learning took place.[58]

Mark Graves gives a concrete example that spells this out clearly:

> The area of the brain responsible for generating speech is physically adjacent to the region responsible for hand movement, not the language area responsible for understanding speech. At the psychological level, mental functions can be characterised as systems, but those systems map in complex, flexible, "plastic" ways to the systems of the biological and physical level, not the direct one-to-one mappings proposed by evolutionary psychologists and others.[59]

While I would agree with Dupré that information—including, for example, cellular, physiological, and cultural information—is never simply moving one way from genes to environment, to assume that there is an *equal and reciprocal* flow of information from environment to gene takes this rather too far,[60] as we end up with a Lamarckian basis for inheritance. He is also not alone in considering the cooperative elements in evolutionary change; there is no reason to read into evolutionary theory competitive individualism in the manner suggested by some ultra-Darwinists.[61]

Peter Munz has joined in this discussion by proposing due consideration of the assumption of evolutionary psychology that a general-purpose mind could not have evolved, as it does not seem to be obviously adaptive.[62] Munz believes that evolutionary psychology is an example of positivism by seeking to explain our ability to acquire knowledge as a direct result of Darwinian natural selection.[63] In traditional positivism, observations

---

58. Mark Graves, *Mind, Brain and the Elusive Soul: Human Systems of Cognitive Science and Religion* (Aldershot: Ashgate, 2008), 160.

59. Ibid.

60. Dupré, *Humans and Other Animals*, 210.

61. I will return to the cooperative elements in evolution in chapter 5, where I pick up a discussion of the cooperative life of nonhuman animals.

62. This point is made in, for example, Pinker, *How the Mind Works*, 525.

63. Peter Munz, *Beyond Wittgenstein's Poker: New Light on Popper and Wittgenstein*

"installed correct knowledge of one's environment in the human mind."[64] In the Darwinian version, adopted by evolutionary psychology, natural selection performs the same task, except now knowledge about the environment is "installed" in the genes. Both positivisms ignore the possibility of genuine knowledge coming from freely invented hypotheses that are falsifiable. According to this positivistic formulation, knowledge is acquired without, it appears, competition between different ways of picking up the same information. After watching and learning, the recognition is genetically installed. This adapted mind is very different from Popper's concept of mind; Popper believed that the mind is "not only neither programmed nor adapted, but also, and above all, a mind whose most characteristic feature is to make mistakes."[65] Such mistakes may be proposing more than the available information warrants or misreading the available information by proposing ideas that contradict what is the case. Popper also relies on Darwin, but in a very different way, to stress that proposals emerge in the brain without relying on what has gone before, and this then preceded selection on the basis of particular proposals being eliminated.

Munz also suggests that a coordinating function of a modular mind sometimes proposed by evolutionary psychologists is also very different from what is being proposed here, namely, a flexible mind that is capable of an imagination that can go beyond given information. Munz argues that once a large brain evolved, it became possible to develop what he terms three-dimensional language, that is, language not just about events and objects, but about events and objects that have not happened or are not yet there.[66] He also argues that biologists who claim that a brain is an adaptation

---

(Basingstoke: Ashgate, 2004), 138. He also argues that evolutionary psychology commits the same error as Wittgenstein's *Tractatus*, that only sentences that refer to facts are meaningful. Wittgenstein later rejected this and argued that meaning is not dependent on our ability to establish a particular reference. See ibid., 168–69.

64. Ibid., 149.

65. Ibid., 139.

66. Ibid., 144. He proposes that the large brain was initially a liability rather than a response to the exigencies of social life, the size of social groups, or the ability to symbolize. Such authors include, for example, Nicholas Humphrey, Robin Dunbar, and Terence Deacon. Of particular note is N. K. Humphrey, "The Social Function of Intellect," in *Growing Pains in Ethology*, ed. P. P. G. Bateson and R. A. Hinde (Cambridge: Cambridge University Press, 1976); R. Bryne and A. Whiten, eds., *Machiavellian Intelligence: Social Expertise and the Evolution of Intellect in Monkeys, Apes and Humans* (Oxford: Clarendon, 1988); R. I. M. Dunbar, "Determinates in Group Size in Primates: A General Model," in *Evolution of Social Behaviour Patterns in Primates and Man*, ed. W.

through natural selection make a similar point to Leibnizian doctrine that there must be a God who made the best possible world, or to theologians who claim that all is for the best, as God designed the world. Instead, he argues that the increase in brain size was an accident that survived because humans were able to invent three-dimensional language that proved useful. The emergence of three-dimensional language took place, he argues, in societies that developed particular cultures. With a three-dimensional language, "it became possible to assemble the separate cerebral reactions to colour, movement, location, duration and so on into a coherent representation of something which the brain in itself has not taken in as such." This "evolution of a general-purpose mind capable of forming hypotheses about events which have not been experienced and of making predictions"[67] is, it seems to me, more plausible than the speculation of evolutionary psychology that assumes every mental process has been parsed individually by natural selection. The evolution of three-dimensional language was only possible because of cultural development. In biological terms, this coheres with Gould's notion of exaptation, previously discussed.

Munz also addresses the issue of why the revival of positivism in the form of evolutionary psychology has taken hold in the way it has in so many different quarters. He suggests that there are two reasons for this. In the first place, it seems common sense to suggest that we learn by allowing ourselves to be instructed. In the second place, he suggests that the guise of Darwinism is crucial. It is ironic, because the first condition—namely, that we learn by instruction—is anti-Darwinian, in that Darwin spoke of selection rather than instruction as a means of acquiring knowledge.

2.5 Evolutionary Psychology: A Theological Critique

While Munz's critical analysis of the success of evolutionary psychology goes some way toward explaining its popularity, I suggest that there is another reason why it has taken grip, and that is that the theory itself has religious overtones. In the first place, it addresses questions of meaning,

G. Runciman, John Maynard Smith, and R. J. M. Dunbar (Oxford: Oxford University Press, 1996), 50; T. Deacon, *The Symbolic Species* (London: Allen Lane/Penguin, 1997). Munz's suggestion seems to me to be as plausible as these alternatives. For further discussion, see C. Deane-Drummond, "Shadow Sophia in Christological Perspective: A Reply to Responses," *Theology and Science* 6, no. 1 (2008): 61–71.

67. Munz, *Beyond Wittgenstein's Poker*, 146.

proffering itself as a "theory of everything," including our intellectual, social, and religious behaviors. It, in common with its earlier formulations as sociobiology, seeks to explain love, jealousy, infidelity, rape, status seeking, violence, gender differences, and good and evil. Such language becomes more explicit in terms of its religious metaphors by seeking to explain the world in terms of cosmic principles as well as ultimate purpose and design.[68] Evolutionary psychology takes advantage of the way the gene itself has become a cultural icon that has taken on spiritual significance, so that it becomes the means through which human life, history, and fate are explained and understood.[69]

This has profound implications, for once we see behavior as simply driven by biological predispositions, then any sense of blame, guilt, or responsibility becomes groundless and intellectually suspect. However, if we follow Munz in his argument that evolutionary psychology is a revival of positivism based on a mistaken idea of the way the mind works, then the practical implications of this mistaken view are profound. For there can be no escape from human responsibility in the manner suggested by evolutionary psychology. This is perhaps yet another reason for its popularity in Western cultures, for it provides a convenient secular account of soteriology; our guilt is purged through reference to our long-distant ancestors. No human action can be tied in with free choice of human beings; rather, it is built into our mental functioning in the earliest period of human evolutionary history. While an explication of obesity based on supposed ancestral preferences for sugar and fat may seem to be relatively harmless, much the same approach could be used to explain other instances of greed, overconsumption, and even violence that have traditionally come under religious and moral scrutiny. It is hardly surprising that feminists such as Susan McKinnon raise such strong objections to the mantra of evolutionary psychology as just discussed, for while some versions will view culture as an "add-on" through meme theory, others purport to reduce virtually all human behaviors to genetic predispositions.

Inasmuch as evolutionary psychology seems to reinforce the stereotypes of sexual difference and essentialist roles of men and women, a theological

---

68. Dorothy Nelkin discusses these aspects in "Less Selfish Than Sacred? Genes and the Religious Impulse in Evolutionary Psychology," in Rose and Rose, *Alas Poor Darwin*, 14–25.

69. See Dorothy Nelkin and M. Susan Lindee, *The DNA Mystique: The Gene as Cultural Icon* (New York: Freeman, 1995).

response will join in the chorus of critics from social anthropology. A doctrine of creation and an affirmation of all creation through a doctrine of incarnation seek to protect the diversity in human life, rather than reduce it to essential roles or biologically predisposed tendencies. While theology can equally suffer from the same tendencies toward essentialist thought, especially where human freedom is inappropriately suppressed in the name of the greater freedom of God, such as that of predestination, any endorsement of fatalistic tendencies needs to be strongly resisted. Such tendencies, both in theology and in science, lead to a failure to take responsibility and, in some cases, might even endorse violence. Dawkins is therefore mistaken to find in religion the exclusive basis for violent behavior.[70] Instead, those forms of "nativism" that dogged nineteenth-century genetics and now find a new form in evolutionary psychology epitomize the tendency toward univocal explanations of human behavior.

Evolutionary psychology has also sought to give an explanation for the emergence of morality and religion as a way of binding that morality and ultimately evacuating it of any significance. While there is certainly something to be said for finding moral sense in some nonhuman animals, and even the development of what might be termed "vices" and "virtues," there is a difference between this and projecting an evolutionary explanation into all forms of moral reasoning in human societies.[71] Richard Joyce shows the philosophical end point of adopting the view of an adapted mind: "What if it reveals that the very terms under which he is conducting his deliberation owe their characteristics not to *truth*, but to social conditions on the savannah 1,000,000 years ago?"[72] His answer to his own question is straightforward, namely, that we can no longer have confidence in our moral judgments. Hence, not only is our guilt projected onto our ancestors in the way I have suggested, but the very basis for making claims for truth are no longer reasonable and are subject to skepticism. Joyce presents his case as one who is agnostic, rather than atheistic or theistic, so in other words he believes that we do not know that judgments are false, yet we cannot have confidence in their validity. The moral outcome thus seems to be one of profound doubt; we do not know how to behave anymore or

---

70. He repeats such a charge in several places, including, for example, R. Dawkins, *The God Delusion* (London: Bantam, 2006), esp. 281–308.

71. I will come back to the specific significance of ethological research to the way theories of atonement might be developed in chapter 5.

72. R. Joyce, *The Evolution of Morality* (Cambridge, Mass.: MIT Press, 2006), 222.

in what ways to behave. Such a position would be expected to lead to profound apathy in moral conduct and, ultimately, to a loss of hope. Hence, while evolutionary psychology on one level seems to deal with guilt and moral conduct, such as sexual behavior and relationships, on another level, it leaves the individual powerless to make moral judgments.

While there are other ways of accounting for religious experience in naturalistic terms, as discussed in Atran's account, the evolutionary basis for the appearance of religion is most relevant. Anthropologists who are influenced by evolutionary psychology will claim that their proposals do not suggest anything about the falsity or otherwise of particular religious beliefs. Rather, their intention is to seek to interpret religious behavior in evolutionary terms. In a very general sense, it is clear that religion has "evolved" in human communities in the sense that there was little evidence for particular religious practices in the very earliest human communities. However, to tie this in with natural selection and genetics seems to me to be mistaken. Scott Atran tries to offer something of a mediating position by suggesting that what has been selected is not religious belief itself, but some other characteristic that is then exapted for religious purposes, as discussed earlier. Either way, he assumes that the evolutionary psychology model of how the mind works is broadly correct.

More often than not, evolutionary psychology and its close relative, mimetics, are linked with a much more aggressive atheism that seeks to undermine the basis of all religious beliefs. Richard Dawkins's book *The God Delusion* and the numerous responses to this book illustrate the extent to which this form of evolutionary theory seems to find a home within an atheistic worldview.[73] Tina Beattie, in particular, places Dawkins along with other more aggressive evolutionary biologists in the camp of the new atheists, arguing that the prejudices against religion expressed by Dawkins and other popular philosophers in this vein hark back to prejudices against cultures that are different, which were also latent in Charles Darwin's attitude toward other races and cultures.[74] I agree with this analysis inasmuch as Dawkins shows himself up as one who expresses almost complete

---

73. Dawkins, *God Delusion*. Of course, the responses to this book have largely concentrated on his atheism, rather than rejection of belief in Christ as such. For a satire, see J. Cornwall, *Darwin's Angel: An Angelic Riposte to "The God Delusion"* (London: Profile, 2007). Cornwall remains unconvinced that religious belief simply "emerged" though evolutionary selection pressures.

74. Tina Beattie, *The New Atheists* (London: Darton, Longman & Todd, 2007), 43–45.

ignorance of theology. The atheism expressed here is the mirror image of the outmoded theism that is claimed to be a threat. Inasmuch as it attempts to take hold and captivate the religious imagination, it represents a form of idolatry, but one that is as unsophisticated as the simplistic theism it seeks to replace. However, Beattie's relatively broad approach does not consider adequately the particular manifestation of evolutionary science that Dawkins's position represents and the challenges that can be posed to this position even within this discourse. Hence, she rather too readily, in my view, correlates the Victorian prejudicial attitudes of Darwin against other cultures and Dawkins's own hostility toward religion.

Of course, Darwin's own position against other races is reprehensible, but in spite of this prejudice, some important insights about the common evolutionary history of humanity with other species emerged. He is also not openly hostile toward those who are different. While prejudice and an inflated sense of superiority toward those who are deemed ignorant may be a common factor, I very much doubt if Dawkins's atheistic agenda has the same roots, since Dawkins is not sufficiently Darwinian in the way he approaches evolutionary theory, and takes his cue more from the progressive thought of Herbert Spencer, discussed in the introduction. In other words, it is the distortion of Darwinian thought, combined with all-too-human prejudice stemming no doubt from early childhood experiences, that seems to inform Dawkins's attitude toward religious belief. The underlying philosophical reasons why Dawkins and other ultra-Darwinists are hostile to religion are less likely to stem from their specific affinity with Darwin and more likely to be related to affinity with pre-Darwinian materialist philosophies that have been around for centuries.[75] Such a philosophy confronts in a stark way the belief that supernatural agency is all-important, even in evolutionary terms. Beattie is therefore closer to the mark when she suggests that the hostility expressed by Dawkins and others toward religious believers needs to take into account the bitter struggle between creationists and evolutionary science.[76]

---

75. For more detailed analysis, see Conor Cunningham, "Trying My Very Best to Believe Darwin, or The Supernaturalistic Fallacy: From Is to Nought," in *Belief and Metaphysics*, ed. C. Cunningham and Peter Candler, 100–141 (London: SCM, 2008).

76. Beattie, *New Atheists*, 35. Of course, while creationism is predominantly American in its influence, Dawkins would be aware of the possibilities that this attitude will spread to other nationalities. The fact that it has become an issue in schools in the United Kingdom in the past ten years or so gives some support to his anxiety in this respect.

It is also important to distinguish between the way Darwin's ideas have been misappropriated for social ends and the wider significance of evolutionary biology. Beattie claims that Darwin's theory ultimately "has always been used to serve the interests of a ruling male elite [rather] than to challenge social, racial and sexual hierarchies."[77] I am less convinced that such general conclusions can be reached without much more detailed historical analysis of Darwin's influence, which is of a par with Copernicus in challenging preconceived hierarchies of the human in a global context. Indeed, misuse of a particular theory hardly warrants its dismissal; just as Dawkins incorrectly attacks theism on the basis of a naive understanding of some interpretations of theology, so the misappropriation of Darwin in social Darwinism should not provide a reason for theologians to eschew either Darwinism's usefulness or its appropriateness as a matter of serious engagement. I remain therefore unconvinced of Beattie's seeming equation of Charles Darwin with social Darwinism for reasons discussed in the introduction.[78]

On one level, of course, evolutionary explanations of religious behavior need not be threatening for religious believers, for they simply account for that behavior in naturalistic terms, rather than claiming that it is impossible or a fiction. Religion becomes a natural outcome of the way humans have evolved through natural selection. It is one reason, perhaps, why Justin Barrett remains unabashed in his claim to be a religious believer. His book, *Why Would Anyone Believe in God?* illustrates clearly both his engagement with evolutionary psychology and his belief in God.[79] He is entirely correct to suggest that whether God does or does not exist cannot be proved by science,[80] so that the claim that Christ is human and divine, for example, cannot be disproved by scientific analysis—or evolutionary psychology, for that matter. I also agree that there is nothing problematic, per se, in the claim that the human capacity to believe in God comes naturally to human minds. The content of different religious beliefs is, of course, far more sophisticated than this, so evolutionary psychology at best can only ever lay claim to so-called universal aspects of religion, if such aspects genuinely exist, which I doubt. I also agree with Barrett

---

77. Ibid., 25.

78. Ibid., 26.

79. Justin L. Barrett, *Why Would Anyone Believe in God?* (Lanham/Plymouth: Altamira, 2004).

80. Ibid., 123.

that the child is just as likely to know something of God as is the "adult" who has mystical experiences.[81] The difficulty comes in Barrett's purported explanations of how that religious mind is perceived to work and the way that evolutionary psychology tries to capture the whole essence of that experience. Religious belief is far more than simply "natural," though it can include the "natural," and as I have already argued, it may not be "natural" in the way supposed by evolutionary psychology, as the mind is far more flexible than it implies.

In other words, while it is entirely *possible* to affirm both religious belief and evolutionary psychology, the latter, by seeking to explain religion purely in naturalistic terms, according to the "design of our minds,"[82] seems to remove the drama that is the basis for Christian living. God seems to be a God who is the outcome of our projected needs and evolutionary history, rather than representing an encounter with the divine in a way that transforms and changes human beings—a "new creation," in Pauline language. In this view, Jesus Christ, who thought of himself as divine, must, according to evolutionary psychology, be suffering a grand delusion, for how can he possibly find in himself an "agency detection" system that is also necessarily outside himself? Belief in God is something we can possibly conceive of as compatible with evolutionary psychology, but what about belief in the human man Jesus, whose followers claim shares in the divine nature? Has agency detection been transferred to human and divine somehow simultaneously, due to the dissatisfaction with purely transcendent reflective theories, inasmuch as they seem to jar with human experience or with nonreflective belief in the way Barrett outlines?[83] It is here, in Christology, that the sticking point with evolutionary psychology seems to be finally reached, for it could not come to terms with a human being who is also divine without seriously jarring with its own representation of how religious beliefs are formulated.

There is, of course, nothing particularly problematic about saying that belief in God is natural, in that our natural cerebral endowment lends itself to religious thoughts and beliefs. What is more controversial is

---

81. His rejection of mystical experience (ibid., 123) as a basis for true religion is, however, somewhat odd, given the pervasive accounts of mysticism in different religious traditions. It most likely demonstrates his own particular prejudice from his religious background.

82. Barrett, *Why Would Anyone Believe?* 124. This perception of a mind as "designed" shows his indebtedness to evolutionary psychology.

83. For his discussion, see ibid., 1–19.

that it is possible to be fully committed to both an evolutionary psychology stance toward such beliefs and belief in God. While such a stance is unusual among evolutionary psychologists and anthropologists influenced by evolutionary psychology, the claim that it is still possible to be religious and fully committed to evolutionary psychology needs to be met with a certain amount of caution. If evolutionary psychology is to sit comfortably alongside religious belief, either the religious beliefs themselves would need drastic modification, or the explanatory power of evolutionary psychology would need to be held in abeyance from its more sweeping generalizations about the nature and origins of religious belief. Hence, while a radically transformed and humbled evolutionary psychology might be possible, I have seen no evidence of this variant as yet in the literature I have encountered.

In the first place, the strongest forms of evolutionary psychology might seem to endorse all forms of religious belief and practice as "natural," while the diversity of such beliefs and their cultural expressions can hardly be fitted into the kind of schemes envisaged. Underlying such suppositions is a naturalistic fallacy that relates goodness to what is the case. Universal similarities, where they exist, are just as easily explained through general theories of the mind that selected the one that was most convincing, rather than some predisposition to forms of thinking based on earlier prereligious tendencies for "agent detection" in animals. It seems doubtful that any such detection systems for "cheats," "agents," or other specific capacities really exist as naturally selected modular capacities of brain function. The only capacities that we might reasonably anticipate to be evolved capacities are the general capacities for emotion, such as fear, anger, and so on, that Darwin also recognized were not unique to human species.[84] Evolutionary psychologists have more often than not ignored a discussion of the origin of emotions by concentrating on the evolution of cognition. Yet religious experience taps into all aspects of human functioning, not just the cognitive functions. It is one reason why, in the chapters that follow, I not only stress the importance of considering Christology as a dramatic encounter with the divine, but also bring in affective aspects of how to think about who Christ is through imagination, drawing on the notion of wonder as well as wisdom.

---

84. See chapter 5.

2.6 Conclusions

In this chapter, I have sought to engage with that strand in evolutionary theory known as evolutionary psychology. I considered this theory in most detail because it is, arguably, taking over the cultural landscape in certain quarters and claiming an authority based on evolutionary biology and Darwinism in particular. I have suggested that those theologians who have treated evolution as a friend rather than a foe to religious belief need to be rather more aware of the dangers of the particular form of naturalism that evolutionary psychology represents before they claim to adhere to a naturalistic faith that seems to endorse evolutionary theology without constraint. While it is possible, of course, to claim that evolutionary biology is just one level of explanation and theology is another, such a division of cultures is naive inasmuch as it fails to recognize the profoundly religious needs that are met by grand theories such as evolutionary psychology or even its close cousin, the meme theory of Richard Dawkins. Moreover, much of its discourse tends to reinforce particular attitudes toward behavior that are decidedly un-Christian and even immoral by many standards of ethics.

Of course, there are varieties of evolutionary psychology, and some may be more innocuous than others, but its most pervasive advocates also, I suggest, have a particular ideological agenda that needs to be challenged. In particular, the positivism that lurks behind the overall project of evolutionary psychology squeezes out the possibility of other forms of valid knowledge in a way that is stifling for theology rather than liberating for it. This is not to suggest that Darwinism per se is problematic. On the contrary, a Popperian version of Darwinism can show that it is possible to take up other strands of Darwin's thought and arrive at a more flexible interpretation of how the mind works in creating and inventing new ideas and discarding ones that are unsuccessful. We can also go so far as to suggest that a "three-dimensional" language was in all likelihood a crucial prerequisite for the emergence of religious concepts and beliefs. We might question, however, how far even this logic might apply to theology, for even those ideas that are least successful at the time may find further relevance much later in another historical context in a way that does not apply to science. In this sense, all nascent ideas remain like potential exaptations, waiting to be taken up in a subsequent era, if a loose analogy with biology is permitted.

From the discussion so far, even taking a thin slice of discourse about understanding Christ as prophet of wisdom, it is clear that such ideas cannot be viewed as the direct result of natural selection somehow geneti-cally programmed as instructions, but as ideas that were thrashed out in experience in the early history of the first Christian communities. Further-more, I suggest that some of these ideas, such as envisaging Jesus as prophet of Sophia, are useful in filling out the human portrait of Jesus. If evolu-tionary biology in general has warned against too rigid an interpretation of Christ's human and divine nature, where nature bespoke something unchangeable, then the wisdom tradition at least helps to connect who Christ is in his humanity not just with the historical tradition of prophecy, but also with the evolved world as such.

But then we are left with the question of how a perception of Christ in human terms could change so that Christ is also thought of as divine. Can considering Christ as divine Wisdom incarnate help us solve this puzzle? Moreover, how might it be possible to avoid simply pitching Christology as a grand narrative in competition with other narratives, such as that found in evolutionary psychology? It is to these considerations that we turn in the chapter that follows.

3

Christ as Divine: Incarnate Wisdom

In what way might it make sense to describe Christ as divine in theological terms, and how might Christ's human nature and divine nature be related, given current understanding of humanity in evolutionary terms? In other words, while, as I noted in the previous chapter, many of the claims of evolutionary psychology overreach supposed evolutionary paradigms into the realm of culture and religious belief, is there a way of expressing belief in the divinity of Christ that also allows for an understanding of human nature as radically embedded in evolutionary history? I will draw on the work of Kathryn Tanner to point to a kenotic Christology that is less about God "giving up" particular attributes or divine and human essences and more about a theodrama expressed in a radical, deep incarnation of God assuming human and thereby creaturely being in Christ. I will then ask how the earliest Christian community came to think of Christ as divine and having a cosmic role, according to recent biblical scholarship, with particular reference to the motif of Wisdom. The classic Orthodox tradition used the concept of Logos and *logoi* as a way of relating Christ's divinity to creation. I will explore Sergii Bulgakov's use of divine Sophia and creaturely sophia alongside his use of the Logos tradition and his role for Mary in the incarnation. I will argue that a critical appropriation of his theology needs to include taking rather more account of contemporary natural science as well as aspects of feminist scholarship.

3.1 What Does Christ's Divinity Mean?

Just as an understanding of Christ's humanity reflects presuppositions about what humanity might be in theological terms, so an understanding of his divinity reflects prior conceptions about what it is to be divine. Kathryn Tanner is a theologian who has recognized this in a particularly sharp way and argues convincingly, in my view, that two prior considerations are necessary. In the first place, an understanding of the radical transcendence of God means that God is wholly other than creation, and in the second place, there is a noncompetitive relationship between creatures and their Creator.[1] Given this position, the theoretical question that this seems to raise for theology is, How can God become incarnate without losing something of the divine "nature"? Theologians responding to this pressure have proposed (1) particular forms of kenotic Christology understood as God giving up some of God's properties in order to become a creature; or (2) a historicization, understanding God as somehow becoming Godself through being bound up in human history.[2] But as indicated in chapter 1, it seems to me that this does not necessarily mean that the idea of kenosis is now obsolete; rather, it depends on how it is interpreted. Another tendency, which Tanner does not really address but which follows a pattern similar to the ones she criticizes, is what might be termed (3) the ecologization of God, where God becomes Godself through being bound up not just in human history, but in the evolutionary and ecological dynamics of planet Earth.[3] The latter ecologization of God is of particular relevance in considering the particular significance of the incarnation, for if God is already identified as God in the processes of evolution and ecology, there seems to be nothing new represented in the incarnation as such.

It is important to note that all three tendencies are connected with a resistance to the idea of the divine understood in the classic way of God as

---

1. K. Tanner, *Jesus, Humanity and the Trinity: A Brief Systematic Theology* (Edinburgh: T&T Clark, 2001), 2.

2. Tanner names in the former category early Anglican kenotic theories, and in the latter those theories of the social, politicized Trinity, as that found in the work of authors such as Jürgen Moltmann. See Tanner, *Jesus, Humanity and the Trinity*, 10.

3. Such a trend can be found in the work of authors such as Anne Primavesi, who views Godself as being intimately connected with the earth, and resists all traditional notions of transcendence on the basis that they are dualistic. Moreover, she ties the workings of God into a particular way of viewing the earth as a system, as that found in Lovelock's hypothesis. See, for example, Anne Primavesi, *Gaia as God's Gift* (London: Routledge, 2003).

transcendent other than creatures, a resistance that translates in christological terms to a fear of docetism or in much feminist theology to a fear of patriarchy. But the impact of all these views is that the soteriology is altered; for example, it raises the question of how a God who is so united in ontological terms with human history and evolution can act in a salvific way. The solution, Tanner suggests, is instead to insist on the prior *radical difference* between God and creatures, so that God is not opposed to the characteristics of human beings but is far beyond any such contrasts. In this way, Tanner believes that "only what is not a kind—and therefore not bound by the usual differences between natures—can bring together in the most intimate unity divinity and humanity."[4]

Rather than imagining God as possessing some abstract omnipotence, in the manner that would be in opposition to the limited power of humans, this view understands God as assuming human weakness, so that the hypostasis of the Word is not restricted by its substance nature in such a way that it *cannot* take on a created nature. In other words, the difference between God and creatures is such that "the divine substance is not defined, as finite substances are, by a nature exclusive of others."[5] Moreover, this *difference* should not be taken to imply *distance*: "What makes God different from creatures is also what enables God to be with what God is not, rather than shut up in self-enclosed isolation."[6] Hence, it would be wrong to see God's transcendence as somehow "outside" or "above" the world, as if God could never relate to that world, or to view incarnation as a loss of transcendence.

While Tanner refrains from using the term, it seems to me that this radical identification with humanity in Christ, so that Christ is fully human, assuming weakness without loss of transcendence, is also at heart a *kenotic Christology*. Indeed, the language of kenosis is helpful, as it is a reminder that this act of God in incarnation is about a generous self-giving, a self-giving that is expressed in a drama of love that is also receptive to the other's giving in a way that is rather less obvious in Tanner's account. In Tanner, the incarnation comes over more as being about the prior naked power of God to be so absolutely different from creatures that any human response seems obliterated in the giftedness, even if that power allows God to assume frail human nature.

---

4. Tanner, *Jesus, Humanity and the Trinity*, 11.
5. Ibid., 12.
6. Ibid., 14.

In much the same way, Tanner proposes that it makes little sense to dissect the characteristics of Jesus and ask where his divinity begins and humanity ends, for the two are not in competition with each other, as they are not comparable. Instead, she suggests that Jesus' divinity and humanity are on different planes or levels of reality, so that one is the source of the other. Just as Jesus is the human life lived on a horizontal plane, so the Word assumes this whole human phase of life on a vertical plane, without viewing one as somehow replacing the other. Jesus is the *deified* human or, more accurately, *becomes* deified, in the sense that the human is assumed by God, but since the divine and human characterize the whole of Jesus' human life, the divinity of Christ is veiled or "invisible," just as God's action in the creation of the world is invisible and, as it were, is acting behind the scenes. In this sense, she suggests that trying to see ways in which the character of Jesus points to an isolated divine nature would be incorrect, for this would jeopardize his human nature. The unity of *subject* in the divinity and humanity of Jesus distinguishes his life from that of a graced human being.

This remains a very traditional view inasmuch as she still speaks of "substances" in human and divine nature and their resolution in personal terms, in a way that is highly problematic in an evolutionary context. It is therefore far more fruitful to push toward an understanding of Christ as one who expresses his divinity through his activity as a human being, a view that is also buried in Tanner's account. It is here that Hans Urs von Balthasar's portrait of Christ coheres with that of Tanner, but he succeeds where she fails in shifting the agenda from ontological to obediential terms; hence we arrive at "a union of divine and human activity in Christ."[7] In this way, the Word on the human plane suffers and acts, but the Word does not suffer and do those acts in precisely the same way as a human being would, for this would "bring divinity down to a human level"; instead, the Word as subject means that what Jesus does is attributed to the Word.[8] I would also want to take this further, inasmuch as any rhetoric about a human and divine nature as such makes less sense in an evolutionary world, even if Tanner's notion of "different planes of reality" softens any classical thought of fixity of nature.[9]

---

7. See Mark McIntosh, *Christology from Within: Spirituality and the Incarnation in Hans Urs von Balthasar* (Notre Dame: University of Notre Dame Press, 1996), 5.

8. Tanner, *Jesus, Humanity and the Trinity*, 26.

9. Le Ron Shults has helpfully summarized the difficulties with envisaging classical

There are also difficulties with her position more generally, inasmuch as her stress on the absoluteness of God's transcendence is logical in terms of maintaining the classical distance between God and creation but veers toward an epic narrative that is detached from everyday experience and lacks consciousness of the situated nature of all theologizing, which is brought out so well in the theologians, such as Moltmann, whom she heavily criticizes.[10] Instead, taking up the theme of Jesus as acting subject, which Tanner also suggests, means that Jesus' divinity and humanity are perhaps best shown forth through theodrama, expressed in a concrete, particular way in his life and ministry on earth.[11]

Tanner also argues that the deification of the humanity of Christ does not happen all at once; rather, this takes place gradually through the course of his human life and death. It is a historical process, because humanity is historical. This means that the Word assumes a humanity that is imperfect

---

christological essences for human or divine nature and the classic debates surrounding Chalcedon (451 C.E.) that point toward Antiochean or Alexandrian alternatives and their limit boundaries. L. Shults, *Christology and Science* (Aldershot: Ashgate, 2008), 24–31.

10. Balthasar accuses Moltmann of succumbing to an epic narrative shaped by Hegelian dialectic in his social doctrine of the Trinity. See Hans Urs von Balthasar, *Theo-Drama* 2, trans. Graham Harrison (San Francisco: Ignatius, 1994), 321–22 (hereafter cited as *TD* 2); and Hans Urs von Balthasar, *Theo-Drama* 5, trans. Graham Harrison (San Francisco: Ignatius, 1998), 227–29 (hereafter cited as *TD* 5). Inasmuch as Moltmann's theology relies on speculation that equates God's identity with the creation, cross, and resurrection—in other words, the economic Trinity *is* the immanent Trinity, and "God is entangled in the process and becomes a tragic, mythological God" (*TD* 2, 322)—there is some merit in this criticism. However, it seems to me that Balthasar goes rather too far in his attack, in that Moltmann's emphasis on the risen Christ in other works shows that the story of God does not simply end in tragedy, but Moltmann always wants the resurrection to inform his account of the cross and vice versa. In addition, the stringent criticism of Moltmann could also in some respects be applied to his own thought, in that there are also epic strands in his own thinking, as discussed elsewhere in this book. The relevant issue in this context is that social doctrines of the Trinity do not necessarily escape from the problems associated with epic thinking, which are in some respects rather more likely to be associated with Christologies from above.

11. Tanner refrains from using the term *theodrama*, but some aspects of her thought point in this direction, and for reasons already discussed in chapter 1, I find this the most convincing approach as a way of linking divine and human action. It is a pity that this aspect is not given a higher place in her thinking, since she tends to slip into narrative language that betrays epic tendencies. In addition, Tanner, following Barth, still seems to view creation as the ground of God's action with humans, so that once humanity appears, creation is largely forgotten, while I am arguing for a much more significant role for creation as such.

but is gradually transformed over the course of his life. In this way, incarnation is, as it were, *spread out* over the course of Jesus' life, history, and death, rather than identified with one moment, namely, conception or birth, even though it is accurate to suggest that it begins at conception and birth. Moreover, she argues that the co-inherence of divinity and humanity in the assumption of humanity by the Son is similar to the kind of co-inherence enjoyed in Trinitarian relationships and better imitates the incarnation than does God pervading the created world in a more general sense. In this way, the incarnation *deepens* the way God contains and pervades creation, without jeopardizing the inequality between God and creation. This shows some parallels with Balthasar's attraction to a Trinitarian basis for Christology; for him, it is the filial response to the Father that unites both the human activity of the Son and the divine Son in Trinitarian relationships.[12]

3.2 Wisdom Incarnate in Biblical Scholarship?

Tanner's analysis works well as a clear systematic theological treatment of the incarnation and draws heavily on the work of patristic scholars, as well as modern theologians, such as Karl Barth and Karl Rahner. It is far less successful when it comes to integrating the work of biblical scholars who have sought to tease out the very different Christologies that emerge in the context of the New Testament. The purpose of this section is to highlight those facets of the biblical debate that might be significant for a more systematic treatment of Christ understood in kenotic terms as the drama of incarnate Wisdom. In other words, might there be a way of thinking about Christ as Wisdom incarnate that, while taking account of the important logical conundrums of systematic thought, also takes some account of the lived drama and history of interpretation in the earliest Christian communities?

Jack Suggs was one of the first scholars to present the idea through redaction criticism that the understanding of Jesus in Matt. 11:25-30 was not simply Jesus understood as Wisdom's last envoy, as Rudolf Bultmann had proposed, but was more than this—namely, Wisdom incarnate.[13]

---

12. Hans Urs von Balthasar, *Explorations in Theology*, vol. 1, *The Word Made Flesh* (San Francisco: Ignatius, 1989), 170–71.

13. W. Jack Suggs, *Wisdom, Christology and Law in Matthew's Gospel* (Cambridge, Mass.: Harvard University Press, 1970). Felix Christ, who claimed to have found the

Suggs also noted the identification of Jesus with the Torah. Suggs has since found himself under criticism from other biblical scholars.[14] Fred Burnett, for example, looked carefully at the later passages in Matt. 23 that in the first place identified Jesus as Wisdom of God (Matt. 23:34-36) but then followed this immediately by proclamation of judgment (23:37-39). The discourse on the second coming in Matt. 24:3 follows immediately, so that Son of Man Christology and Wisdom Christology coalesce.[15]

Burnett, Suggs, and others have been criticized either for failing to take into account the strong Son of God Christology in Matthew or for claiming in an unjustified way the universality of identification of Jesus with Wisdom in Matthew. An alternative interpretation is that Jesus is identified with Wisdom in Matthew precisely in order to weaken the more gnostic influences in the Wisdom myth, rather than to specifically exalt Wisdom.[16] A further alternative is that the replacement of Jesus in those passages that refer to Wisdom in Matt. 23:34-36 is there to reinforce the view that Jesus, like Wisdom, is acting under the authority of God.[17] This ties in with the main thrust of the series of controversies in Matt. 21 onward, which are set up in such a way so as to challenge Jesus' authority. The earlier passages in Matt. 11:25-30 that seem to identify Wisdom with Jesus—for Matthew places on the lips of Jesus a saying appropriate to Wisdom—are set in the context of Israel's repudiation of Jesus' ministry. In such a context, it made more sense to emphasize the theme of Jesus as Son of God, one who has been designated by God as agent of revelation. Hence, the appropriation of Wisdom motifs in Matthew does not necessarily mean that Jesus is

---

idea of Wisdom incarnate in Luke, Q, and earlier traditions, also supported this idea. See Felix Christ, *Jesus Sophia Die Sophie Christologie bieden Synoptikern*, ATANT, Bd. 57 (Zurich: Zwingli, 1970). Christ was later criticized for his failure to distinguish adequately among Wisdom speculation in Matthew, Luke, and Q.

14. There are some notable exceptions. For example, Celia Deutsch draws on his work in C. Deutsch, "Hidden Wisdom and the Easy Yoke: Wisdom, Torah and Discipleship in Matthew 11.25-30," *JSOT*, suppl. ser., no. 18 (1987).

15. Fred W. Barnett, *The Testament of Jesus-Sophia: A Redaction Critical Study of the Eschatological Discourse in Matthew* (Washington, D.C.: University Press of America, 1981).

16. For a sharp review, see Marshall Johnson, "Reflections on Wisdom's Approach to Matthew's Christology," *CBQ* 49 (1987): 57–71.

17. This position is developed in a doctoral thesis by Frances Taylor Gench later published as F. Gench, *Wisdom in the Christology of Matthew* (Lanham, Md.: University Press of America, 1987).

identified with Sophia, but rather seems to be there to reinforce the Son of God Christology as one who mediates God's revelation.[18]

Of course, such an interpretation of Jesus as Son of God parts company with Elisabeth Schüssler Fiorenza, who, as we saw in chapter 1, intends to pick up what she sees as a forgotten strand in Matthew's thought—namely, Jesus as Wisdom's envoy.[19] Schüssler Fiorenza's Christology of Wisdom therefore puts virtually exclusive emphasis on Jesus' humanity and views the connection between Jesus and revelation in God as expressive of an oppressive dualism. It seems to me that such Son of God Christologies are not oppressive in the way she imagines, for they only become so if, as follows from Tanner's discussion, the difference between God and humanity is wrongly equated with distance, and dualism is used an occasion for oppression.

Yet in order to tease out more fully the significance of Wisdom for Christology, it is necessary to consider both the breadth of possible meanings for Wisdom in pre-Christian Judaism and the ways that Wisdom has been used in other New Testament texts. In other words, disputes about the extent to which Matthew might have appropriated a Wisdom Christology do not rule out of court the possibility that a conception of Jesus as Wisdom incarnate surfaced elsewhere. The variety of New Testament Christologies needs to be respected. Furthermore, the variety of meanings for Wisdom in the pre-Christian Jewish literature also opens the possibility of a variety of meanings for Wisdom incarnate. James Dunn, who has done much to investigate this issue on a broad scale, outlines four possible pre-Christian understandings of Wisdom: as divine being, as hypostasis, as personification of divine attribute, and as personification of the cosmic order.[20] His conclusions are modest, namely, that in Jewish literature, there is no clear evidence that Wisdom has gone beyond that of personification of divine attribute. Wisdom may use the language of Stoic reason, but in a way that resists any equation of wisdom with pantheistic ultimate reason, for the Wisdom of God is the one who creates the world (Wis. 7:15). Dunn believes that there are two broad alternatives: either Wisdom is a being subordinate to Yahweh, or Wisdom language is used in a picturesque way to describe the way that Yahweh creates, namely, in wisdom. He also

---

18. Ibid., 207.

19 Elisabeth Schüssler Fiorenza, *Jesus: Miriam's Child, Sophia's Prophet* (London: SCM, 1995), 140.

20. James Dunn, *Christology in the Making*, 2nd ed. (London: SCM, 1989), 168.

believes that it is very unlikely that Wisdom was viewed as a divine being independent of Yahweh.[21]

How might the Gospel of John's far more explicit alignment of Wisdom and the Logos be understood? The understanding of Wisdom as in some sense preexistent provides John with the language through which to articulate his notion of the Logos. Martin Scott has suggested, "She existed in the heavens before the world was formed, and shares responsibility for the orderly nature of creation. This is precisely the role given by the opening words of John's Prologue to the Logos."[22] There are other parallels in John as well, such as the descent-ascent trajectory found in Hebrew texts such as Prov. 8, Sir. 24, and *1 En.* 42.[23] Additional similarities include the sending of both Wisdom and Jesus as a gift of God, in both cases so that humanity might find communion with God.[24] While there are scant references to a relationship of love between God and Wisdom, Wis. 8:3-4 suggests this in a way that pushes beyond an understanding of Hebrew wisdom as merely a personification of a divine attribute.[25] Furthermore, Scott believes that the feminine aspect of Sophia needs to be emphasized, so that "Sophia is effectively God in feminine form, equivalent to the more common Jewish expression of God in masculine form, Yahweh."[26] There are also other striking parallels between Wisdom and Jesus in, for example, passages that extol Jesus as the bread of life in John 6:27, echoed in Prov. 9:1-26. Other images of Jesus in John, such as the vine and water, also have echoes in Wisdom literature, where Wisdom is described as a river (Sir. 24:30-34) and a vine (Sir. 24:17). John's extensive appropriation of Wisdom reflects the universal appeal of wisdom for John's audience, which included a mixture of Greeks and Jews.

---

21. Ibid., 170–76. For my own brief discussion of the place of wisdom in the Hebrew Bible, see C. Deane-Drummond, *Creation through Wisdom* (Edinburgh: T&T Clark, 2000), 19–22.

22. M. Scott, *Sophia and the Johannine Jesus* (Sheffield: JSOT/Academic Press, 1992), 96.

23. Stephen Barton, "Gospel Wisdom," in *Where Shall Wisdom Be Found?*, ed. S. Barton, 104–10 (Edinburgh: T&T Clark, 1999).

24. M. E. Willett, *Wisdom Christology in the Fourth Gospel* (San Francisco: Mellen Research University Press, 1995), 60–62.

25. Ibid., 79.

26. Scott, *Sophia and the Johannine Jesus*, 77. I do not think it is necessary to envisage a separate ontology for God in feminine form; rather, I believe that God moves in a category beyond gender; hence both kinds of language are needed in order to describe more fully who God is.

The most striking difference between John's portrayal of Wisdom and that of Jewish literature is the idea of Christ's death as *also* exhibiting divine Wisdom. While Wisdom literature readily taught that human beings can learn from suffering, the identification of suffering and death with wisdom and glory takes us deeper into the idea of Jesus as preexistent Wisdom that not even death could extinguish. M. E. Willett remarks, "The Gospel transforms the cross from humiliation (as in the synoptics, Acts and Paul) to glorification. . . . The cross is glory because it is pre-existent Word who is on the cross."[27]

Yet it would be incorrect to suppose that the preexistence of Wisdom/ Word is the only means through which John elevates the cross; rather, the light of the resurrection seems to shine back on the crucifixion, showing it in a new, glorious light. The final vindication of Christ through the resurrection echoes the theme of kingship found in the Wisdom literature, and this motif may have been influential in this context.[28] The wisdom traditions seem to allow John to weave traditions of creation, incarnation, and salvation history into a single canvas. Hence, while his Christology is clearly a Logos Christology, it is simultaneously a Wisdom Christology in a manner that is more obviously the case than in the account of Matthew, whose appropriation of Wisdom remains somewhat ambiguous, as previously discussed. It may be the case that the varied traditions of Wisdom lent themselves to different interpretations by the Gospel writers, so that while, for John, understanding Wisdom in the strong preexistent sense served his purposes well, for Matthew, writing from another context, Wisdom served to reinforce the authority of Jesus as sent by God, rather than serving in an explicit way to describe the identity of Jesus.

The hymn to Wisdom in the first chapter of the letter to the Colossians is, arguably, one of the strongest examples of the close links drawn between Christ and Wisdom and their interweaving in the work of creation.[29] The context of this hymn is one in which the author addresses a situation where the person of Jesus was depreciated and his ordinary humanness stressed to such an extent that his divinity was obscured. In addition, the opponents addressed in this letter sought to separate the cosmic from the

---

27. Willett, *Wisdom Christology*, 52.

28. Ibid., 121–22.

29. See Michael Trainor, "Celebrating Diversity: The Hymn to Christ in a Letter from Ancient Colossae (Col 1:15-20)," in *Biodiversity and Ecology as Interdisciplinary Challenge*, ed. D. Edwards and M. Worthing, 65–71 (Adelaide: ATF, 2004).

anthropological world in a form of world-denying asceticism. Paul[30] countered this view by celebrating the extent and scope of Christ's significance in cosmic terms. The first part of this hymn expresses a cosmic Christology as that which encompasses the whole creation; Jesus Christ is the one through whom and for whom the whole creation was made. The second half of the hymn points to cosmic redemption; all things will be reconciled in Christ.

Jesus as the "icon" of God (Col. 1:15), normally translated "image" of God, does not mean image in the physical sense, but rather the preincarnate Christ or Christ in his glory, having the connotation of *manifestation* of God.[31] In this reading, it is more likely to be drawn from wisdom traditions, such as Wis. 7:26, which speaks of wisdom as the image of God's goodness, rather than Gen. 1:28, which speaks of humanity as the image of God. The "first-born" (1:15) could mean the priority in time or rank, though most commentators prefer the latter, since temporal priority is hardly what the author is trying to emphasize here. In preexistent form, the image could hardly reveal God in the way suggested. The creation of all things "through" him (1:16) has the sense of Christ as a mediating agent, while in other contexts, the term is often used to express Christ as mediator between humanity and God.

Of course, some interpreters have given this passage a thoroughgoing anthropocentric reading, so G. B. Caird writes that the framing of the hymn in redemptive categories is crucial, "since man was destined by God to be Lord of the universe, this is the secret also of the whole creation,"[32] and "only in union with the 'proper man' could the universe be brought to its proper coherence."[33] James Dunn also seems more inclined to weaken the cosmic scope of this passage, for he claims that it is the continuity of the activity of Yahweh that is celebrated, so that the movement is from creation to Christ, rather than the other way around.[34] Yet this interpretation

---

30. Scholars divide on whether this letter was written by Paul or an author with Pauline sympathies after Paul's death, but the authorship is not pertinent to this discussion.

31. Homer Kent, Curtis Vaughan, and Arthur Rupprecht, *The Expositor's Bible Commentary with the New International Version, Colossians* (Grand Rapids: Zondervan, 1996), 89.

32. G. B. Caird, *Paul's Letters from Prison* (Oxford: Oxford University Press, 1984), 175.

33. Ibid., 178.

34. Dunn, *Christology in the Making*, 190. He also resists any notion of Christ's preexistence here, though while this is probably true for the interpretation of "firstborn" in verse 15, it seems less likely when applied to the idea of "icon" or "manifestation."

assumes that redemption is necessarily confined to humans, restricting the meaning of "all things" to those principalities and powers that are of importance in the cohesion of the human world, and thus Christ's scope is limited in this respect. Given the challenge that this writer is addressing— namely, a reduction in Christ's authority—it seems far more likely to be broader in scope and to include creation as such. Other biblical scholars have been quite prepared to concede that "all things" does refer to all creatures; indeed, such an idea was already in the prophetic literature such as Isaiah and Jeremiah.[35]

What are the origins of this magnificent hymn? Many scholars have adhered to the theory that the first stanza (1:15-17) is an ancient hymn to Wisdom / divine Word that was adapted by the author to celebrate the status of Christ. An alternative ingenious theory is that Paul adapted to Christian use a rabbinic midrash on Gen. 1:1, "in the beginning (*be-reshith*) God created," and Prov. 8:22, "the LORD begat me as the beginning (*reshith*) of his way."[36] The three meanings of *be-* are in, by, and for; and the three meanings of *reshith* are beginning, sum total, and firstfruits. From this followed that God created the world in, by, and for wisdom, and wisdom was the firstborn of all creation, its sum total, head, and source. The equation of wisdom and Torah in the Jewish tradition meant that Paul could also claim this applies to Christ, as fulfillment of the Torah, as he seems to have done in other passages, such as 1 Cor. 10:1-4 and Eph. 4:7-11.

The second stanza then moves to a focus on the human community; Christ is named as the one who is capable of reconciliation in both the cosmic community and the human community, with authority over all imaginable powers.[37] The universe, according to the hymn, is revelatory of the presence of Jesus, and as God's icon, the universe is also revelatory of the presence of God. Some commentators have suggested that the "fullness" dwelling in 19a refers to the fullness of God. Yet an equally plausible interpretation is that this refers to the creation, so that Jesus is the fullest expression of creation as well as being an icon of God. Trainor suggests, "What creation is about is revealed in him, in his relationship to God. In

---

35. Markus Barth and Helmut Blanke, *Colossians: A New Translation with Introduction and Commentary*, trans. Ashid B. Beck, Anchor Bible Series (New York: Doubleday, 1994), 246.

36 Translation taken from G. B. Caird, *Paul's Letters from Prison* (Oxford: Oxford University, 1984), 175–76.

37. Trainor, "Celebrating Diversity," 68–69.

Jesus the cosmos is taken to a new height; it is sanctified and revelatory of God's own being."[38]

Such a view is to interpret the text so that we can view the world as the writer did in a way that still has fresh relevance for contemporary theological reflection on the evolutionary history of the planet, as well as contemporary debates on ecology. In this sense, it does not matter if the biblical writer had no knowledge of contemporary science; rather, when we come to the text with certain questions, fresh insights bear fruit. Along with John's Gospel, the epistle to the Colossians enables wisdom to be used in such a way that we can view the incarnation of Christ as *deep incarnation*, linking Christ not just with humanity, but with the whole of the cosmos, including and especially the evolutionary world of created beings.[39]

3.3 Worshipful Perception: Seeing Christ as Divine

Of course, we are left with the question that has haunted biblical scholars: How could Jesus have ever come to be thought of as God? This question is significant, as it provides an important bridge into more contemporary appropriations of biblical texts in modern systematic theology.[40] While a detailed discussion of this topic is outside the scope of this book, the particular area of relevance here is the possible role, if any, of viewing Christ through the motif of Wisdom in facilitating the development of devotion to Jesus in the tradition.

Philippians 2:6-11, like the hymn in Colossians, is one of a family of hymns that expresses the faith of the earliest Christian community about

---

38. Ibid., 70.

39. Niels Gregersen has also used *deep incarnation* to describe the evolutionary significance of the cross as "bearing the costs of the hardships of natural selection," so that God assumes not just a human nature, but a human-animal body and a scorned social being, and with it, therefore, the "whole macrocosm of evolutionary history." N. Gregersen, "The Cross of Christ in an Evolutionary World," *Di* 40, no. 3 (2001):193. He also argues strongly that the focus on the cross in Luther is against a legalistic theology, rather than antinatural as such. He asks, significantly, whether we can combine high Christology with deep incarnation. Building on Martin Luther, Gregerson is similarly drawn to extending the soteriological significance of Christ, which I will return to again in chapter 5..

40. Larry Hurtado has explored this issue in some detail. See, for example, L. Hurtado, *How on Earth Did Jesus Become a God? Historical Questions about Earliest Devotion to Jesus* (Grand Rapids: Eerdmans, 2005). This fascinating book explores early devotion to Jesus in its historical Jewish context, as well as its social and political significance.

the significance of Jesus.[41] Larry Hurtado believes that the lofty claims in this passage seem to be assumed by Paul and imply that, even before this letter was written, the high status of Jesus was assured.[42] He resists the idea that Philippians simply adapts a pervasive Wisdom myth, but rather, the charismatic interpretation of Isa. 45:18-25 forms the background to this passage in the light of an existing belief that God has exalted Jesus to heaven and designated him Lord over creation.[43] Philippians 2:6 speaks of Jesus' self-humbling and taking on the role of a servant in the context of one whose being is "in the form of God." The two options most discussed in biblical scholarship are either that the form of God means, simply, the image of God and reflects a Christology drawing on the account of Adam in Genesis, or that the form of God is a referent to preexistence.[44] The latter would support the view that these verses express an incipient faith in the incarnation understood in the traditional sense of God assuming human flesh. In this respect, I am rather more convinced by the second interpretation, as the evidence for the first seems rather weak; using the expression "the form of God" as a means to link Jesus with Adam seems to be without any analogy anywhere else.[45] The letter to the Philippians, written some twenty to thirty years before the Gospel of John, indicates that the idea of Christ as divine was around very early on indeed, and if Paul presumed, as he seemed to do by the use of existing hymnology, that Christ's preexistence could be taken for granted, then this would make such beliefs earlier still. Hurtado also admits that while Wisdom and Word were often exalted in Second Temple Jewish circles, these figures were not treated as objects of devotion in the manner that was applied to Jesus, so that this treatment was without any prior analogy. He also suggests, "Devotion to Jesus cannot adequately be seen as simply the consequence of attributing to him a special place in relation to God in creation, governance and redemption of the world."[46] In other words, worship of Jesus seemed to precede theological

---

41. I will return to a more detailed discussion of the significance of this text in chapter 8.

42. Hurtado, *How on Earth*, 87.

43. Ibid., 91–93. I will be returning to a fuller discussion of the significance of this passage for relating Christ to anthropology in the final chapter.

44. While I will return to these options in a later chapter, all that is important to note here is that the first option tends to stress the humanity of Jesus, and the second option his divinity.

45. For a useful analysis of this debate, see Hurtado, *How on Earth*, 99.

46. Ibid., 23–25.

formulations about his significance and emerged more like a "volcanic eruption" than a slow development in response to specific beliefs about him. Worship of Jesus thus took the pattern of drama rather than slow, evolutionary development.

Hurtado believes that too much attention in biblical scholarship to particular christological beliefs has obscured the devotion to Jesus in which such beliefs began to flourish. These specific practices included (1) hymns about Jesus sung in Christian worship; (2) prayer to God through Jesus and in his name, as well as direct invocations to Jesus; (3) use of the name of Jesus in Christian rites, such as baptism, exorcism, and healing; (4) Christian meals where Christ is named as Lord of the gathered community; (5) confession of Jesus in the context of worship; and (6) Christian prophecy understood as (a) oracles of Jesus and (b) the Holy Spirit of prophecy understood as expressing the Spirit of Jesus.[47] Hurtado views the emergence of devotion to Jesus in Second Temple Jewish tradition as having its roots in powerful religious experiences that have some analogies with similar phenomena found in new religious movements more generally. He resists the idea that new ideas were somehow "imported" from other traditions; rather, they form a major reconfiguration within a particular religious tradition. Nonetheless, he draws an analogy with biological mutations in naming religious development that took place, in a somewhat unfortunate way, in my view. For while this analogy may suggest continuity, a *genetic* analogy implies a blueprint model that he is trying to resist, and the use of genetic language for religious change has unfortunate connotations in view of trends in evolutionary psychology discussed in the previous chapter.[48] Instead, the emergence of a new tradition takes place in the *context* of worship and religious experience, which has, it seems to me, far more similarities with the now somewhat discredited Lamarckian interpretation of acquired characteristics, rather than neo-Darwinian forms of inheritance.[49] In addition, the belief in one God most characteristic of Judaism

---

47. Ibid., 27–30.

48. Ibid., 29. Of course, it seems unlikely that he is following or identifying with sociobiology, but this relatively casual use of mutation language reflects a lack of awareness of the investment in genetic analogies made by sociobiological theorists.

49. The complexity of inheritance is such that some scientists are arguing for what might arguably called modified versions of Lamarckian inheritance in certain specific cases, especially transposons and other mobile genetic elements, which seem to be remarkably sensitive to environmental influences and, when applied to the germ cells at least, would be likely to influence patterns of inheritance away from that expected

remained intact, so that "he was given devotion that expressed the distinctively Christian recognition that Jesus was God's unique emissary, in whom the glory of the one God was singularly reflected" and to whom God "the Father" now demanded full reverence "as to a god."[50]

In such a context, does this mean that considerations of the Wisdom motif in early Judaism are now redundant for Christology? I suggest that the answer is that the elevation of Jesus needs to be viewed in the context in which Wisdom came to be interpreted by the earliest Christian community. Hence, Dunn is correct in resisting Schweizer's claim that Wisdom formed the basis for a bridge between Christ as exalted and Christ as preexistent, but that is because Christ was *already* presumed as preexistent. His conclusion that Wisdom in Jewish literature is best interpreted as a personification of a divine attribute, rather than as divine being or hypostasis, reinforces the point that Hurtado makes—namely, that (1) worship of Jesus is a significant innovation compared with treatment of other comparable figures in the Hebrew literature, and (2) belief in the one God takes precedence.

James Dunn prefers a Wisdom Christology that stops short of any notion of Jesus as divine, for his notion of Wisdom is suitably modest.[51] For example, he suggests that the Wisdom imagery helped to link Jesus with God, in that through the language of Wisdom, Jesus is one who portrays what God is like and serves as a revelation of God as both creator and redeemer.[52] This could be thought of as an initial formulation of the doctrine of the incarnation, understood as God's love experienced in the fullest sense in Jesus. Dunn consequently views the concept of Jesus as preexistent

---

according to neo-Darwinian evolutionary models. In addition, cultural traits, if thought of in mimetic terms, are not so much "mutations" as "acquired characteristics." See the previous chapter for further discussion of the evolution of religion in sociobiology and anthropology.

50. Hurtado, *How on Earth*, 30.

51. See also his more recent study, James D. G. Dunn, *Jesus Remembered* (Grand Rapids: Eerdmans, 2003).

52. Dunn, *Christology in the Making*, 261–63. Dunn is correct to insist that any notion of a "myth" of God incarnate as having been somehow taken from pagan myths about other gods was false, as it would presuppose a notion of wisdom as somehow independent of Yahweh, rather than a vehicle through which to express divine immanence. Hence, while he plays down the strong sense of Christ as divine in the early Christian community, he parts company from the liberal school that treats notions of incarnation as an early Christian myth in parallel with other gnostic religious speculations of the time.

and divine as a much later development than Hurtado presumes, emerging only in the later decades of the first century.[53] Dunn therefore suggests that the only explicit statements of faith in the incarnation are in the relatively late Logos Christology of John, which, as we have seen, also shows parallels with Wisdom literature. Moreover, he traces the dissimilarity to the Wisdom tradition by suggesting that John was drawing on a tradition characteristic of Philo in presenting Logos as preexistent without infringing his monotheism.[54]

However, there is an alternative Wisdom Christology that follows more naturally from Hurtado's analysis. If Jesus was given devotion and subsequently titles appropriate to God, then Jesus' attributes were ones that *also* would be shared by God, namely, divine Wisdom. In this way, Wisdom as a background motif in John and Colossians, for example, was used to stress the continuity with the Jewish tradition but in ways that served to elevate his divine status and authority and unity with the one God as much as to express divine immanence, that is, the way God is actively involved with the world without compromising transcendence.[55] Yet the elevation of the divinity of Christ did not result in a sense of remoteness from humanity; rather, the novel transition in John 1:14, which Dunn notes carefully, is the transition from impersonal personification, as found in the figures of the Wisdom tradition, to *actual person.*

3.4 Wisdom from Above: Wisdom in the Christology of Sergii Bulgakov

Of course, the identification of the Logos with Wisdom in the Gospel of John can have the unfortunate effect of (a) replacing a Wisdom Christology with an exclusive Logos Christology in such a way that Wisdom Christology is simply replaced by the notion of the Logos, and (b) presuming that Wisdom is not also present elsewhere, that is, seeing it as exclusive to

---

53. James D. G. Dunn, "The Making of Christology: Evolution or Unfolding?" in *Jesus of Nazareth: Lord and Christ; Essays on the Historical Jesus and New Testament Christology*, ed. Joel B. Green and Max Turner, 437–52 (Grand Rapids: Eerdmans; Carlisle: Paternoster, 1994). I find Hurtado's account of much earlier devotion to Jesus more convincing.

54. Dunn, *Christology in the Making*, 241.

55. Dunn prefers the idea of personification of *function* rather than *attribute* in order to emphasize the association of wisdom with divine immanence rather than transcendence. See ibid., 176.

Christ, rather than present also in the Holy Spirit or God the Father. The notion of Logos/*logoi* in the Orthodox tradition has proved very appealing for many theologians concerned with trying to find a language that connects the action of God with God's creation. Feminist writers, such as Elisabeth Johnson, have argued against such trends by suggesting that replacing a female term, Sophia, with a male term, Logos, only reinforces the patriarchal presentation of Christian faith.[56] We have already noted Schüssler Fiorenza's critical stance toward any language of Sonship, viewing the Gospel of John not so much as a pinnacle of creative theological reflection as a marginalization of the traditions of Wisdom displayed in other Gospel accounts, such as Matthew.[57] However, I suggest that ditching the tradition of John in favor of the weaker accounts of Wisdom in Matthew actually lowers the significance of both Jesus and associated Wisdom. Instead, a reappropriation of the language of the Logos/Wisdom can, I suggest, serve to *elevate* Wisdom to her rightful place, namely, as incorporated into an understanding of who God is, rather than either a separate, lesser, divine being or identified with creaturely existence as such.

Sergii Bulgakov, perhaps more than any other theologian in the twentieth century, attempted to do just this; that is, he elevated the notion of Wisdom into a full-blown sophiology. His discussion of Christology enlarges a core conception in his theology, namely that of Christ as Divine-humanity. Yet his discussion of the Word is also colored by his stress on Christ through the imagery of the Lamb.[58] As with other contemporary writers, he views the imperative of the incarnation as coming primarily from God's love for the creation, rather than simply in response to human sinfulness. In his cogent commentary on Sergii Bulgakov, Aidan Nichols aptly remarks:

> The initiatives of the Holy Trinity are never just responses to dilemmas people set for God. What he prefers to say is that from everlasting God knew how one of the possibilities built into the creation was the possibility of the world segregating itself from him. And this he did know, and the manner in which

---

56. Elisabeth Johnson, *She Who Is* (New York: Crossroad, 1994), 152.

57. Schüssler Fiorenza, *Jesus: Miriam's Child, Sophia's Prophet*, 153.

58. Sergii Bulgakov's arguably most significant works comprised his trilogy, *On Divine Humanity*, first published in 1933, 1936, and 1945. These include *The Lamb of God*, trans. B. Jakim (Grand Rapids: Eerdmans, 2008) (hereafter cited as *LG*); *The Comforter*, trans. B. Jakim (Grand Rapids: Eerdmans, 2004) (hereafter cited as *TC*); and *The Bride of the Lamb*, trans. B. Jakim (Grand Rapids: Eerdmans, 2002) (hereafter cited as *BL*).

he determined the incarnation should take place shows as much. In concrete terms the incarnation was carried out precisely as an act of redemption. From all eternity the divine Son was marked out by the Father as an immolated Lamb of God, the Lamb who would be sent to be sacrificed.[59]

The Son is therefore sent into the world through the activity of the Father; it is, in Balthasar's language, an aspect of theodrama.

Yet the significance of the incarnation is not limited to eventual soteriology. The incarnation required the active cooperation of Mary, as one who was able to conceive "not by her human powers but because the Holy Spirit reposes in Her and upon Her. . . . Hypostatic incarnation, which is perfectly appropriate for the Second hypostasis as hypostatic sonhood, is inappropriate for the Third hypostasis . . . the Son of God is kenotic hypostasis, the eternal Lamb."[60] Further, Mary was worthy of becoming the recipient of the Holy Spirit by her spiritual openness and what Bulgakov terms her sophianic maturity.[61] It is the *receptivity* of Mary through the work of the Spirit that enables the incarnation to take place, and it is this aspect that has, arguably, been forgotten by many writers in the Protestant tradition. This aspect is ignored completely by Kathryn Tanner, for example, who, in many other respects, draws heavily from the patristic tradition. While I would want to resist the idea that receptivity is necessarily exclusive to femaleness as such, in that it implies a certain stereotypical view of women about which feminists have some cause for complaint, this does not mean thereby that receptivity as such is now redundant or should not be included in the overall theodrama. The act of the incarnation is not so much God acting through an exclusive power over the other, but God in love eliciting human cooperation. For Bulgakov, in Mary, original sin "lost its power" by receiving the Word.[62]

---

59. Aidan Nichols, *Wisdom from Above: A Primer in the Theology of Father Sergei Bulgakov* (London: Gracewing, 2005), 80.

60. Bulgakov, *LG*, 177.

61. Ibid., 199–201.

62. Bulgakov argues in relation to original sin that it was necessary to "weaken this sin to the point of rendering it inactive" in order for Mary to be worthy to receive the grace of God in the incarnation. He also states that a "hereditary holiness" accumulated in the centuries leading up to this event, so that she was "full of grace" even prior to the incarnation. Ibid., 178. He also claims, "Hereditary sin, the envelopment of spirit by flesh, is transmitted through fleshly begetting, which corresponds to man's sinful state." Ibid., 181. His association of sex and original sin, while common in the tradition, seems unnecessary and, in my view, more readily admits to the charge of unwarranted

In answer to the question of how the hypostasis of the Word can take on human nature, Bulgakov, like Tanner, resists the temptation to refer to God's omnipotence, but his solution is rather different. Instead of stressing the absolute and radical difference between God and creation in order to argue for the possibility of incarnation in a different realm, Bulgakov elevates the humanity of God as found in Jesus Christ *back* into the realm of the Godhead. He argues, in the first place, that the hypostasis of the Logos has also become the proper hypostasis of his human nature. But then he is left with the question as to *why* the human hypostasis remains human and is not simply the hypostasis of the Logos. To get around this difficulty, he proposes that the Logos is in a primordial sense human. In this way, "insofar as it hypostatizes the human nature the hypostasis of the Logos is, in a special sense, a human hypostasis too, that it is proper not only to God but also to Man, that is, the God man."[63] In this way, "to be a human hypostasis, the hypostasis of the Logos must be human or, more precisely, co-human," so that the hypostatization "corresponds to a primordial interrelation."[64] This allows, in other words, humanity to *receive* a hypostasis that is divine while still remaining a human being.

Bulgakov uses the Platonic categories of proto-image and image in order to preserve the distinction between God and humanity, while at the same time, this serves to elevate the human hypostatic spirit so that this "fundamentally distinguishes him from the animal world," inasmuch as its origin is "uncreated" and "divine," from "God's breath."[65] Yet the connection between humanity in God and that in human beings as such is also expressed sophianically, so that "Sophia is also the heavenly humanity as the proto-image of the creaturely humanity; insomuch as she is eternally hypostatized in the Logos, she is His pre-eternal Divine-Humanity."[66] The vocation of the human being is (1) to be bearers of the Wisdom of God through natural grace and (2) to become divinized and so enter the condition of Divine-humanity, or theanthropy.

For Bulgakov, the Logos enters the world through self-humiliation, kenotically entering the world.[67] There are similarities between the

---

patriarchy compared with other purported tendencies, such as the use of Logos language, though we will come back to discussion of the latter.

63. Ibid., 186.
64. Ibid.
65. Ibid.
66. Ibid., 187.
67. It is important to point out that kenosis for Bulgakov does not imply in any

incarnation and the creation of the world in that both are acts of condescension, but the difference is related to the thesis that while the world face of the Logos is imprinted in the world in a general sense, it is only in the incarnation as such that the Logos becomes "in-humanized."[68] Further, "in the creation of the world, the world remains outside of God, solely as the *object* of his salvific action, whereas, in the Incarnation, God receives creaturely becoming into his own life and thus becomes the *Subject* of this becoming, while preserving the eternal fullness of His proper natural-sophianic essence."[69] Precisely how the eternal God can become united to temporal becoming remains mysterious. Yet inasmuch as Mary's human nature enjoys the "highest degree of sophianity possible," she shares in the incarnation, so Bulgakov argues that the proper image of the incarnation is not simply a solitary Christ, but mother and child. He also resists an abstract view of the assumption of human nature by Christ; for him, the "assumption of the integral humanity signifies not the abstract assimilation of certain human properties, corporeal and psychic, but the concrete assumption of me, you, them."[70] It seems to me that this aspect is just as important as his attempt to deepen the sense in which humanity interpenetrates the divine; in this case, the divine is fully integrated into *all* of humanity in the concrete, so that he can say, "The Lord took His humanity not from impersonal nature but from each of us personally. He thus became one with His humanity, introducing it into His own hypostatic being. And only on this basis can it be said: 'Christ lives in me.'"[71]

For Nichols, the most distinctive aspect of his Christology is its stress of Christ as theanthropic-Divine-humanity. In the incarnation, the Word surrenders the joy flowing from the love of the hypostatic God for divinity in exchange for the suffering of the world.[72] The Son, in making this consent (see Phil. 1), allows his divine life as the Word to belong to the hypostasis of the Father. The manifestation of the Son now becomes expressed through a human hypostasis, expressing a miracle of divine love. In a rather complicated maneuver, Bulgakov suggests that the Son in an objective sense

---

sense that God "gives up" some divine attributes. Rather, what changes is the condition in which the Word lives out the divine nature.

68. Bulgakov, *LG*, 193.

69. Ibid., 197.

70. Bulgakov, *BL*, 109.

71. Ibid.

72. This is a novel interpretation of Heb. 12 as "instead of" rather than "because of." See Nichols, *Wisdom from Above*, 101.

remains the Second Person of the Trinity, but in a subjective sense views himself as being wholly invested with the Father.[73] The Logos recognizes himself through the lens of his humanity. Like Tanner, Bulgakov views the humanity of Jesus as not simply passive in relation to his divinity; rather, his humanity inclined ever more fully to its own transformation and could only receive the plenitude of divine glory after the resurrection.[74] Similarly, Bulgakov argues that Jesus' divine nature was not removed from suffering, but neither did it suffer in the same manner as humanity; instead, it co-suffered in a spiritual sense, including drawing in the two other persons of the Trinity, the Holy Spirit and the Father. Yet this was not a "compulsory" or "necessary" suffering, as it flowed from a primary relation of sacrificial love.[75]

Bulgakov's Christology, as outlined so far, both coheres with Chalcedon and has novel elements. While his affirmation of Christology understood in terms of two natures requires modification in the light of earlier dis-cussion of evolutionary science, the notion of "fixity" in the manner that the classical tradition affirmed is certainly not uppermost in his thinking. Bulgakov seems to allow, for example, for the idea of possibility in God, but not at the expense of an Orthodox insistence on the unchangeable nature of God. In this sense, he, like Balthasar, manages to avoid more theoretical classical positions that simply honor the divine omnipotence, while resist-ing the idea that in the incarnation, nothing of significance happens as far as God is concerned. For example, he views Christ's humanity as reaching back into the Godhead itself in a way that is reminiscent of more contem-porary speculation, though more often than not, this is viewed as a post-resurrection encounter, rather than through the Logos having a preexistent tendency toward humanity in the manner Bulgakov implies. Nichols's comment that Bulgakov's understanding of the kenotic Christ has "little (if not quite nothing) to do with the Antiochene Christology"[76] needs, therefore, a qualification in this respect, for even if he resists the direction that such Christology implies, namely, an elevation of Christ's humanity to

---

73. Bulgakov, *LG*, 263. Hence "From the moment it awakened in Him, Jesus's per-sonal I could only be, and was, the direct divine consciousness." In other words, kenosis is excluded from this aspect of Jesus' human life. This personal I is defined by his con-sciousness of being begotten by the Father. Ibid., 264.

74. I will return to a discussion of the significance of wisdom for the resurrection in chapter 6.

75. Bulgakov, *LG*, 259–60.

76 Nichols, *Wisdom from Above*, 97.

the divine, this does not preclude an important stress on the humanity of Christ as that which then impinges on Trinitarian relationships.

Other commentators have also noted that Bulgakov "seeks to carve out a greater role for man in the preparation of our salvation and in the transfiguration of creation than previously allowed by official Orthodox doctrine."[77] The idea of humanity is therefore crucial to his scheme, but in the context of evolutionary biology, how far does he give sufficient weight to the creation of beings *other* than humans? Is the anthropocentrism read out of his Christology that then reaches into the Godhead unhelpful in the context of an evolutionary understanding of human becoming?

To address this question, we must address the central place of his sophiology, or his understanding of Wisdom. I will argue that the importance of Sophia in Bulgakov goes somewhat further than simply informing the "ground" for the possibility of the incarnation, as Aidan Nichols suggests, since Sophia is identified not just with the active process involved in creative activity as such, but *also* with the goal of the process in the community of persons united sophianically with Divine-humanity.[78] His view on Sophia is also vital inasmuch as it helps to connect what would otherwise be a strong anthropocentric orientation to one that includes the wider creation. In other words, viewing Sophia as simply the ground for the possibility of the incarnation reinforces the bias toward a more exclusive notion of divinization of the human in *Theanthropos* that fails to reflect the deep sophianicity that Bulgakov believed was characteristic of the created order as such.

Bulgakov's theology of creation envisages creaturely sophia expressing both the Logos and the Holy Spirit, but the hypostatic nature of both is disguised, as it were, through the hypostasis of the Father.[79] Bulgakov suggests

---

77. B. Jakim, translator's introduction, in Bulgakov, *BL*, xii.

78. For Nichols's interpretation of the role of wisdom in the incarnation, see *Wisdom from Above*, 99. "Created wisdom, and its special relation with uncreated, is a ground of possibility for the encounter between God and man in the Incarnation. It helps to explain how the Incarnation could take place. But it is not that encounter— that unique union, itself." While it is certainly true that in his *Lamb of God*, Bulgakov devotes considerable attention to the personal aspects of what it meant for Christ to be theanthropic, it seems to me that the sophianic context in which he develops this understanding in subsequent works announces not just the ground, but also the direction and significance of the incarnation. Boris Jakim seems to agree with this interpretation, as he also gives a stronger role for Sophiology. See Jakim, translator's introduction, in Bulgakov, *BL*, xii.

79. Bulgakov, *TC*, 195. For further discussion, see C. Deane-Drummond, *Ecotheology* (London: DLT, 2008), 64.

that the Father is the creative origin of the world, but the Second and Third Persons of the Trinity participate in creation through Sophia, since all three persons share Sophia. Sophia is associated both with the spoken words of the Word in creation and with the action of the Spirit, transfiguring creation toward life, beauty, and glory.[80] Significantly, perhaps, he also posits the action of the Spirit as being in some sense prior to that of the Word, so that proto-matter emerges from the action of the Spirit and becomes "the maternal womb in which the forms of this world are conceived."[81] Yet he draws back from considering that the Holy Spirit itself is acting here at the dawn of creation, as he wants to retain the idea that the Father alone acts hypostatically in relation to creation. Rather, the Spirit is not so much the hypostatic revelation of the Holy Spirit, but the spirit of God, the action of the Third Person as revealed *through* Sophia. The Son and the Spirit have their hypostases disguised, as it were, by acting through Sophia in the creation of the world. In this, Bulgakov can claim, "Three hypostatic flames are lit in a row, one behind the other and therefore they are seen as a single flame; and this single flame is the I of the Father."[82] Both the hypostasis of the Son and that of the Spirit consent to this action, but they are concealed by the hypostasis of the Father.

Furthermore, Bulgakov views the incarnation as extending beyond just the significance of Christ's history on earth, for "the Incarnation, in which all human beings are co-resurrected in glory together with Christ, makes this sophianic proto-image of every human being transparent and clear."[83] In this way, at the resurrection, divine Sophia will be made manifest in creaturely sophia. Hence, Christ understood as human and divine is expressed not just through the language of the Logos, as noted in his work *The Lamb of God*, but also through the language of Sophia.

However, he does not just woodenly identify Logos with Sophia, a view that he consistently criticizes in the work of Origen.[84] Rather, he insists that divine Sophia needs to be distinguished from creaturely sophia, and that the Logos, who is hypostatic and the Second Person of the Trinity, is distinguished from divine Sophia, who expresses the nonhypostatic divinity in God and is the self-revelation of the entire Trinity. For him, the "place

---

80. See, for example, Bulgakov, *TC*, 191–92.
81. Ibid., 194.
82. Ibid., 195.
83. Bulgakov, *BL*, 451.
84. Bulgakov, *TC*, ch. 1; Bulgakov, *BL*, 15.

of the Divine Person in the creaturely Sophia is allotted to man," which gives humanity a highly elevated place, for the creaturely world expresses a "cosmo-anthropic world."[85] Creaturely sophia is "only a hypostatizedness," rather than a hypostasis. Thus, although technically guarding against any thought of universal personhood in creation, this aspect of his thinking is thoroughly anthropocentric, in common with much of the patristic tradition. However, it is not necessary to take up this aspect of his theology, which in an evolutionary context remains unconvincing.

Rather oddly, perhaps, Bulgakov proposes that the specific image of God in man is not sophianic, but is somehow added to sophianicity as its subject by the divine Personality. While this is not in any sense in opposition to divine or creaturely wisdom, his view of divine image bearing as an unfathomable gift of God serves to emphasize the difference between humanity and other creatures, with God acting creatively in humans in order not just to repeat his nature, as in creaturely sophia, but to express God's hypostatic image, allowing for a personal relationship, "co-I's."

Even more speculative and less convincing is his idea that the Logos is multiplied in male hypostases, while the Holy Spirit is multiplied in female hypostases.[86] The association of the Logos with masculinity and the Holy Spirit with femininity is stereotypical and unhelpful in many respects.[87]

Such a rendition of Sophia also allows Bulgakov to propose divine ideas of the world in Trinitarian form, rather than simply restricted to the Logos. This permits him to view the significance of Christ's incarnation as *cosmic*, extending beyond the human community but in a way that is not simply confined to the work of the Second Person of the Trinity. In this way, he claims, "through the union in Christ of the divine and human natures, the Divine and creaturely Sophia, redemption is also the sophianization and glorification of creation."[88]

To perceive more clearly the role of Sophia in his Christology, it is also worth noting his own summary as expressed in his later book, *Sophia: The Wisdom of God*, published a few years after *The Lamb of God*.[89] Here he spells out more clearly that the basis for the union of two natures in Christ

---

85. Bulgakov, *BL*, 85.

86. Ibid., 87, 91.

87. I will come back to a fuller critique of the stereotypical nature of Bulgakov's theology in this respect subsequently.

88. Bulgakov, *BL*, 451.

89. Sergii Bulgakov, *Sophia: The Wisdom of God*, trans. Patrick Thompson, O. Fielding Clarke, and Xenia Braikevite (Hudson: Lindisfarne, 1993).

is sophianic, so "the real basis of the union of the two natures in Christ seems to lie in their mutual relationship as two variant forms of divine and created Wisdom."[90] Hence, the metaphysical absurdity—and, arguably, its incompatibility with contemporary evolutionary views that the two-natures doctrine supposes—is relieved through sophiology. Moreover, it helps to explain the manner of the incarnation in kenotic terms, not in the sense of ceasing to be God, but "in the Incarnation the Word divests himself of this glory, and confines the life which is his in divine Wisdom within the measure of the created wisdom in the process of coming to be. *He remains in the nature of God, but devoid of his glory.*"[91] In addition, the union of divine and created Wisdom in the person of the Word forms the basis for the reconciliation of the world to God, as expressed liturgically in the Eucharist.[92] More graphically, he suggests that the link between divine and creaturely Wisdom in the person of Christ points to the link between heaven and earth and the anticipation of the penetration of the world by divine Wisdom. It is, therefore, entirely appropriate to view Bulgakov's understanding of Christology as Wisdom Christology as well as Logos Christology, and it should not be thought of as simply a static Christology, but one that expresses the dynamic movement between God and creatures as such, and their ultimate goal. In this sense, it is possible to characterize Bulgakov as a theologian whose use of Sophia is still deeply sensitive to the drama of salvation history, even if he did not explicitly work out his theology in the language of theodrama in the manner characteristic of Balthasar. Moreover, the unity of creaturely sophia and divine Sophia in the person of Christ reflects both the precondition and goal not just for humanity, but for the whole cosmos, so that the cosmos—not just humanity in isolation—is caught up in the drama of incarnation and redemption.

3.5 Mary as God-Bearer in Sophianic and Evolutionary Perspective

Although Bulgakov remains committed to the boundaries set by the Chalcedonian definition of Christ, the development of his Christology through the twin notions of Divine-humanity and Sophia is significant inasmuch as it can be brought to bear on contemporary discussion of evolution. While

90. Ibid., 88.
91. Ibid., 90.
92. Ibid., 95–96.

the evolutionary story of humanity stresses increase in complexity, the biblical account refers to an original perfected state. Bulgakov believes that the clash between these accounts can have a destructive impact on the spiritual life. Like many contemporary writers, he views the biblical account as having different degrees of historical accuracy; the earliest chapters of Genesis are, he suggests, symbolic in form as "an echo or anamnesis of prehistoric or metahistoric events," rather than simply "empty legend."[93] Hence, while on the one hand he resists excluding the *possibility* of a more perfect human existence, as he believes that assuming that this is not the case is unwarranted scientific positivism, on the other he views the creation of the world as an expression of creaturely sophia, groping in a nonhypostatic manner through evolutionary processes. He believes that creaturely sophia understood as a "world soul" working through an evolutionary process is blind and instinctive, since it lacks the personal character that he believes is possible only with the appearance of humanity.

Of course, scientists would shudder at any serious consideration of a "world soul" somehow animating evolutionary processes, and in many respects, I find this language unhelpful, as it implies a form of vitalism that is in direct contradiction with evolution rather than compatible with it. Also, although he rejects the idea that evolutionary progress continues through prehistory to present civilization, his view of the human person as superior and the crown of creation is still very traditional and anthropocentric. He is also traditional in his treatment of the differences between the sexes, and his suggestion that women receive their personal "I" from the Spirit and men their personal "I" from the Logos, through association rather than in a direct sense, does not seem plausible, as it confines the feminine to the Spirit in a way that is both very traditional and unhelpful.[94]

The place of Mary in his Christology is, I suggest, fruitful for further discussion in evolutionary as well as ecological terms, for it points in a rather more concrete way to the possibility of divinization of the human.[95] It provides, I suggest, a counterweight to the top-down, somewhat theoretical

---

93. Bulgakov, *BL*, 170.

94. For discussion of this aspect, see S. Coakley, "Femininity and the Holy Spirit," in *Mirror to the Church: Reflections on Sexism*, ed. M. Furlong, 130–32 (London: SPCK, 1988).

95. I have discussed his understanding of Mary and its ecological significance in C. Deane-Drummond, "Sophia, Mary and the Eternal Feminine in Pierre Teilhard de Chardin and Sergei Bulgakov," in *Teilhard de Chardin on People and Planet*, ed. C. Deane-Drummond, 209–25 (London: Equinox, 2006).

approaches to the incarnation that tend to dominate in classical accounts and in Bulgakov's own *Lamb of God*. Moreover, Mary is one who shares fully in the creaturely sophia of all human beings; she exemplifies, as it were, what it is possible for human beings to become through redemption in Christ. Bulgakov viewed her as "a second Eve," who gives Christ his human flesh. More important, perhaps, he views Mary as one who can demonstrate what the Holy Spirit is like, even though the Third Person is not *personally* incarnate in the same way as the Logos is incarnate in Christ. Mary is so interpenetrated by the Spirit that she becomes completely deified. Hence, she "is not the personal incarnation of the Holy Spirit but becomes his personal, living receptacle, an absolutely Spirit-bearing creature, a Spirit-bearing human being."[96] In this, she enables the divinization of the human race, and thence to the created world as such,

> the Mother of God, since she gave her son the humanness of the second Adam, is also the mother of the race of human beings, of universal humanity, the spiritual centre of the whole creation, the heart of the world. In her creation is utterly and completely divinised, conceives, bears and fosters God.[97]

Mary is the "feminine counterpart" to the humanity of Christ. Hence, Christ cannot be separated from his mother, for to do so "is in effect an attempted violation of the mystery of the Incarnation, in its innermost shrine."[98] Bulgakov roundly rejects any suggestion that Mary is divine Wisdom by insisting that divine Wisdom is in her only insofar as she allows the Holy Spirit to descend on her; she is its consecrated temple. Only in this sense that she is God-bearer can she be thought of as divine. Rather, Bulgakov emphasizes that the Virgin is venerated as *created wisdom*:

> She is created Wisdom, for she is creation glorified. In her is realised the purpose of creation, the complete penetration of the creature by Wisdom, the full accord of the created type with its prototype, its entire accomplishment. In

---

96. Sergii Bulgakov, extract from "The Burning Bush: An Essay in the Dogmatic Interpretation of Some Features in the Orthodox Veneration of the Mother of God" (1927), entitled "The Burning Bush," in *A Bulgakov Anthology*, ed. James Pain and Nicolas Zernov, trans. Natalie Duddington and James Pain (Philadelphia: Westminster; London: SPCK, 1976), 92.

97. Bulgakov, *Sophia*, 119–20.

98. Ibid., 123.

her creation is completely irradiated by its prototype. In her God is already all in all.[99]

Yet Mary seems to acquire this title of created wisdom by virtue of the fact that she is mother to Christ, that Christ's humanity came to him from his mother. As Christ represents both divine Sophia and creaturely sophia, so "it is in this sense, as sharing the human nature of the God-human, that his holy Mother is the created Sophia."[100] Mary is divinized, clothed with divine Wisdom, yet the ultimate expression of creaturely wisdom, uniting her not just to humanity, but to the whole cosmos. Bulgakov names Mary as expressive of perfected creaturely sophia, with the Holy Spirit infusing her personality so that it becomes "dissolved" in the Spirit.

For Bulgakov, the Spirit works with creaturely sophia at the beginning of creation before the first "Let there be" of God's creative act. She is like the first mother who brings forth life to all that exists in the created, evolved world. The bringing forth of life in creation becomes a Trinitarian act, not just "Mother" in place of "Father," but a movement of Trinitarian love through Sophia. Bulgakov's reflection on the role of Mary in the incarnation and of her significance is a reminder that the incarnation cannot be thought of apart from the work of the Spirit and apart from the willingness of humanity to receive God in the manner that Mary exemplifies.

There are, of course, some difficulties with his account. In the first place, his views of women are somewhat stereotypical, and his association of femininity exclusively with the Holy Spirit, rather than with other persons of the Trinity, has some unfortunate consequences. Not least is his frankly odd discussion of personhood as that coming from different persons of the Trinity to men and women. He does not, however, incorrectly assume identity between God and humanity, apart from that found in God-humanity in Christ, but rather expresses the idea of alignment. His association of Christ as Logos with male persons also has undesirable consequences, though he is careful to point out that the humanity of Christ is inclusive of both genders, rather than exclusive.[101] Association of

---

99. Ibid., 126.

100. Ibid., 127.

101. Bulgakov, *LG*, 140. Here he claims, "In man, a clear distinction is established between male and female, expressed in the fact that the female was made out of one of the male's ribs (not directly out of the dust of the earth) and, in general, in the fact that the male plays the dominant role, since he bears the image of the demiurgic hypostasis, the Logos. Male and female, differing as two distinct images of man, bear, in their

Christology with imperialist, even patriarchal models of the human household has been the subject of intense feminist criticism.[102] His account is also speculative, metaphysical, and, arguably, lacking in contact with the very earthly presence of Christ in his lived humanity, apart from reflection on the passion narrative. His portrait of Mary in particular is also similarly portrayed in idealistic language, apparently detached from the simple history in which she, as a young teenager, discovered that she was with child and unmarried. Yet it is worth considering how just as God is present in human weakness in the form of Christ, so also perfected humanity as represented in Mary is not to be shorn from her humble origins. While in Bulgakov the balance is tipped rather too far toward idealization of Mary, it is perhaps preferable to the opposite tendency of allowing consideration of her significance to fall from view entirely. Indeed, Mary, as fully human and yet divinized, shows what creaturely sophia can become in relationship with divine humanity in Christ.

It is therefore not surprising that feminists who have taken up the notion of Jesus-Sophia have often preferred to cast him in terms that stress the association of Sophia with his public ministry as prophet of Sophia, rather than propose more speculative accounts that link Sophia with the Logos.[103] Elisabeth Johnson gets around the difficulty of the limited scope of such analysis by expanding the extent of Christ's significance through a more cosmic interpretation of the work of the Spirit in Christ after the resurrection, so that Christ becomes a "pneumatological reality, a creation of the Spirit."[104] Yet Johnson also allows for more traditional categories to describe Jesus, arguing—correctly, in my view—that the incarnate Jesus

---

unity, the fullness of humanity and, in this humanity, the fullness of the image of God: they bear the imprint of the dyad of the Son and Holy Spirit, who reveal the Father. In their ability to reproduce, they contain the image of multi-unity that is inscribed in the human race as a whole." His association of the male with the Logos and the female with the Holy Spirit reinforces the dominance of the former, though, compared with Balthasar, for example, he gives a higher place to the Holy Spirit in his overall theology, as well as refraining from the more elaborated discussion of the significance of sexuality and woman as the "answer" to the man that appears in Balthasar. I will come back to a discussion of the latter in chapter 7. For my critical discussion of the association of the Holy Spirit with femaleness, see Deane-Drummond, *Creation through Wisdom*, 132–35.

102. Johnson, *She Who Is*, 151–54.

103. Such a preference is found in Elisabeth Schüssler Fiorenza (see chapter 1), and also in Johnson, *She Who Is*, 156–61.

104. Johnson, *She Who Is*, 162.

thought of in sophianic language can speak of the "graciousness of God imaged as female."[105] Moreover, the doctrine of incarnation is a reminder of the importance of "bodiliness" to God.[106] While I am less resistant to the use of the language of the Logos than Johnson is, I suggest that the Logos needs to be interpreted in a sophianic way in the manner of John's Gospel. Furthermore, as discussed earlier, Sophia, if confined to the Logos, loses its potency.

One of the strengths of Bulgakov's account is not just his Trinitarian approach to Sophia, but also the way he links his speculative thought with specific practices and liturgy of the church. This trend connects his thought with the more recent emphases in biblical scholarship on the importance of devotion to Jesus in the earliest Christian communities. Bulgakov offers a Christology that is traditional yet, by incorporating sophianic themes, opens up the possibility for inclusive interpretations of Christ's significance.

3.6 Conclusions

In any retrieval of the classical concept of Christ's divinity, the question that comes to the surface is how Jesus can be thought of both as a human being and as divine at the same time. In particular, in what way might this make sense, given the evolutionary history of the earth, and humanity as included in that history? An alternative to evolutionary Christology is one that still respects the radical nature of the incarnation in the classic sense of God assuming human nature, but then what might this nature mean in an evolutionary world? Certainly the assumption of human nature implies, according to the evolutionary story, the assumption of living creaturely being in the sense of a shared history of becoming. Yet any division between human and divine nature in Christ seems forced.

Kathryn Tanner's resolution is to stress the utter difference between God and creation, such that any thought of omnipotence as being somehow related to finite power is ruled out of court. Instead, the utter difference between God and creation means that it is no longer possible to reject the idea that God can assume human nature, for it is not so much God giving up certain qualities or becoming entangled in the world as God taking on a weak, finite state in a deliberate way in order to identify fully with

---

105. Ibid., 165.
106. Ibid., 168.

the creation God has made. Leaving aside the question of the nature of this making for a moment, she also suggests that Christ is both human in his horizontal plane and divine on the plane of the Logos, and that Christ becomes divine in his human nature, even though he is always at the same time divine person in the Logos. This Logos Christology has the advantage of clarity, but the nature of the interaction between God and the world seems more like an epic account than a drama of salvation, motivated by the love of God for the world.

Does a Wisdom Christology fare any better in this respect? Certainly a Wisdom Christology has the advantage of holding together very different biblical traditions, some of which highlight the very human story of Jesus in comparison with the prophets of wisdom, as in Matthew, while others point to a closer identification between Wisdom and the divine, as in the Logos Christology of John. Feminist scholars such as Schüssler Fiorenza are drawn more to the traditions where Jesus is presented as a sage, but her argument against any appropriation of Son of God Christologies seems unconvincing and dependent on her own particular feminist agenda that rejects elements of the tradition by associating it with patriarchal social structures. Bulgakov was certainly guilty in the sense that he failed to take into account misogynist aspects of the tradition, but this does not mean that concepts such as the transcendence of God should be ruled out of court in the name of antidualist purity. Rather, the distinctions that he draws between God and creation, and their link through creaturely sophia, take a new dimension in Christ, who is not just God-humanity, but also the integration of divine Sophia and creaturely sophia that anticipates the sophianization of the cosmos. In Mary we find a deeper affirmation of the possibilities latent in creaturely sophia, both in Mary's receptivity to the divine Word and in her divinization, so in this sense, she becomes an icon of hope for the realm of nature as inclusive of humanity, rather than the other way around.

Bulgakov's sophianic interpretation of creation therefore lends itself to a wider appreciation of the value of creation in the drama of salvation. While he does not use the language of theodrama, the links he makes between creation, incarnation, salvation, and redemption present a portrait of God as divine Wisdom, active in the world through creaturely sophia. His Trinitarian understanding of Sophia also resists the kind of Christomonism that is characteristic of authors such as Teilhard de Chardin. Moreover, the expression of Jesus as Sophia can be anticipated in the history of the church inasmuch as the way Christ came to be thought of as divine emerged in the context of a worshipping community. Sophia connects with this liturgy and allows the expression of Jesus as divine to take shape.

This is not so much an evolution of religious belief arising out of the need to believe in a supernatural figure, as discussed in the evolutionary psychology of religion, since belief in God was already present, and there was considerable resistance to the idea of a human being sharing in the divinity. Rather, it arose out of particular experiences and encounters with Christ in the lives of the early apostles and the early witnessing community of faith. But given this faith, are there appropriate ways of reflecting on the relationship between the natural world and God as revealed in Christ other than through the language of Sophia outlined in this chapter? Indeed, does the very language of the drama of the action of Sophia in the world imply a deeper wonder that is available to be seen by all, not just those who are committed to religious belief? Is there, in other words, any place for what has been traditionally called natural theology? And how might this fit in with the overall thesis of this book, that an evolutionary world is best understood in relation to Christology through an inclusion of the natural world in the theodrama, rather than an exclusive reference to humanity alone, as has been the habit of much theological reflection? It is to these topics that we turn in the next chapter.

4

Deep Incarnation: Christ, the Form of Beauty

Even a cursory consideration of the evolved world in all its tremendous diversity and complexity gives heightened awareness of what might be termed natural wonders and, in their wake, the human experience of wonder. Although evolutionary scientists, as scientists, rest their case on careful observation and experiment, the excitement that follows in the wake of discovery of new connections between species in the paleontological record, more often than not, is simultaneous with the experience of wonder and may even form an ingredient in the overall motivation for further research. But how might this be related to Christian theology and, in particular, to an understanding of Christ as deeply inculcated in the natural order? I will give particular consideration here to the work of Hans Urs von Balthasar, whose consideration of beauty in relation to that in Christ provides a means for working through the dynamics of this relationship.

Wonder is an even broader term than *beauty* and could be said to be prior to its recognition.[1] Yet wonder accompanies both secular beauty and theological glory, and is at the background in the recognition of the transcendentals of being, beauty, goodness, and truth, which Balthasar weaves into his discussion. In the present context, wonder *in the mode of beauty* is

---

1. John's Gospel in particular portrays wonder or awe as accompanying belief or unbelief, but the sense in which I am using the term here is that of wonder as the preliminary to deeper philosophical inquiry. Both beauty and wonder in the theological sense point to Glory, but because beauty has a rather more specific philosophical and theological pedigree, I am drawing on beauty in this context, even though wonder, like beauty, could also be said to share in the analogy of faith.

of most concern. My contention in this chapter is that Balthasar's discussion of the analogy of being, alongside his consideration of the experience of Christ on Holy Saturday, opening out to affirmation of the Eastern tradition of cosmic Christology, can be appropriated to the specific discussion of the relationship between Christ and nature, and thence to Christ and nature understood in evolutionary terms. It is, in other words, impossible to address the more specific question of how Christ relates to evolved natural being unless we have first addressed the more general question of how Christ relates to nature as such.

Balthasar's strong use of metaphysics is distasteful for some, in that it flies in the face of the postmodern deconstruction of thought. However, inasmuch as postmodernity focuses entirely on context, it remains "curiously discarnate."[2] Balthasar's theology seeks to go beyond the modern and postmodern counterreaction by returning to the classic tradition but in a way that takes account of the cultural shifts since the Enlightenment.

4.1 Natural Beauty and the Analogy of Being

Is there any sense in which the intimation of beauty (or wonder) in the natural world, which is common across different religious traditions or even those claiming not to be in such a tradition, points to a sense of the divine? Consideration of this question takes us into the realm of natural theology. Unfortunately, insofar as this has been taken up in the science and religion dialogue, where there is more often than not an assumption that natural theology is sufficient, counterreactions in the form of exclusive claims for the superiority of revealed theology lead to an ever-widening chasm between theological triumphalism and secularized alternatives more dependent on science. Balthasar walks on a knife edge between these alternatives by proposing that the order of creation is predisposed to receive what was to follow in the form of divine revelation of the Word. This comes through most clearly in the following statement:

> Man's spiritual speech presupposes the speech of nature, and the speech of revelation presupposes for its part the speech of God's creation, in fact, this analogy of being, and in consequence, a natural knowledge of God, or expressed in

---

2. Rowan Williams, "Afterword: Making Differences," in *Balthasar at the End of Modernity*, ed. L. Gardener, D. Moss, B. Quash, and G. Ward (Edinburgh: T&T Clark, 1999) 174, see 173–79.

religious terms a natural, concrete sense of the creature for the being from which it proceeds, a *cognitio per contactum* (Thomas) which persists through each individual essence and the whole historical cause of peoples and cultures.[3]

He also suggests that there is particular significance in the evolutionary emergence of speech in animals and infants, but the human experience of free speech then becomes appropriated so that God speaks. In this way, "it is precisely this experience, in which human freedom, rising superior to nature, attains speech, that God appropriates in order to show man that he is his Lord and that he acts in perfect freedom."[4] While Balthasar shows his anthropocentric bent in proposing that humanity is the "summit of the whole material creation and its mouthpiece towards God," it is important that he also recognized the interconnectedness of the natural order and acknowledged that human life is *grounded* in the natural world in such a way that "it is only in our technological age that the confidential relationship between man and nature that bore him has in great part been shattered."[5]

Balthasar's great trilogy of multivolume works, *The Glory of the Lord*, *Theo-Drama*, and *Theo-Logic*, shows an indebtedness to Western metaphysics in the volumes' respective emphases on beauty, goodness, and truth, though they are written in such a way as to draw out the interconnected nature of all three qualities. Beauty, for Balthasar, is not so much the subject's judgment of taste, but a response to the form of reality perceived, holding to Aristotelian realism that supposes form radiates being.[6] In theo-

---

3. Hans Urs von Balthasar, *Explorations in Theology*, vol. 1, *The Word Made Flesh*, trans. A. V. Littledale and A. Dru (San Francisco: Ignatius, 1989), 84 (hereafter cited as *WF*).

4. Ibid., 85. I will come back to a discussion of how far and to what extent freedom can be afforded to nonhumans and the implication this has for theories of redemption. At the same time, it is clear that the level and complexity of both speech and freedom afforded to the human race exceed what is found in other species. The important point to note here is that the speech of God was possible at that moment in evolutionary history when human speech was sophisticated enough to understand the speech of God, which Balthasar understands as revelation by intervention in human history. While the language of intervention is eschewed by many of those in the science and religion dialogue, Balthasar would no doubt justify his use of such language through his resistance to the trappings of modernity.

5. Ibid., 82.

6. Hans Urs von Balthasar, *The Glory of the Lord: A Theological Aesthetics*, vol. 1, *Seeing the Form*, trans. E. Leivá-Merikakis (Edinburgh: T&T Clark; San Francisco: Ignatius, 1882), 19–20 (hereafter cited as *GL* 1).

logical terms, beauty finds its expression as glory. The link with theology is grounded in a Johannine interpretation of the doctrine of creation and the incarnation, so that the Word breaks the divine silence, speaking first in creation of the cosmos and then in the incarnation.[7] The layout of his trilogy shows the common ground between God and the created world that is the basis of all analogous relationships. Scholars of Balthasar have paid rather less attention to his specific treatment of the natural, created order than to other aspects of his theology.[8]

His analogy of being expands on the thought forms of Aquinas, yet what amounts to a parallelism of sign and signified leads to a dualism that Balthasar believes can be abolished by introducing categories of the beautiful.[9] In this way, "the light does not fall on this form from above and from outside, rather, it breaks forth from the form's interior."[10] Just as Ignatian spirituality is in the background of Balthasar's conception of the dramatic, so too it forms an undercurrent in his understanding of analogy as being more than speech about God, in that it points to participation of the creature with God in such a way that leads to increasing awe.[11] In other words, it is not simply a pointing to a form beyond itself, but "form is the apparition of this mystery, and reveals it while, naturally, at the same time, protecting

---

7. Ibid., 28.

8. It is fair to suggest that Balthasar did not focus on this himself, but as this chapter will point out, the discussion of this area in his work lends itself to further development and comment. For a helpful overview of his work as a whole, see Ben Quash, "Hans Urs von Balthasar," in *The Modern Theologians*, ed. D. Ford and R. Muers, 106–23 (Oxford: Blackwell, 2006); and E. T. Oakes and D. Moss, eds., *The Cambridge Companion to Hans Urs von Balthasar* (Cambridge: Cambridge University Press, 2004).

9. He also draws on Aquinas's account of the beautiful, which includes the ideas of clarity; proportion, or what is needed for a particular end; and integrity or completion, the realization of perfection. Aquinas identified these marks of the beautiful with the Second Person of the Trinity. Thomas Aquinas, *Summa Theologiae*, vol. 2, *Existence and Nature of God*, trans. Timothy McDermott (London: Blackfriars, 1963), 1a Qu. 5.4; Thomas Aquinas, *Summa Theologiae*, vol. 19, *The Emotions*, trans. Eric D'Arcy (London: Blackfriars, 1967), 1a2ae Qu. 27.1; Thomas Aquinas, *Summa Theologiae*, vol. 46, *Action and Contemplation*, trans. Jordan Aumann (London: Blackfriars, 1966), 2a2ae Qu. 180.2; and Thomas Aquinas, *Summa Theologiae*, vol. 7, *Father, Son and Holy Spirit*, trans. T. C. O'Brien (London: Blackfriars, 1976), 1a Qu. 39.8.

10. Balthasar, *GL* 1, 151.

11. The influence of Erich Przywara also is significant in this respect. See Ben Quash, *Theology and the Drama of History* (Cambridge: Cambridge University Press, 2005), 171–74.

and veiling it."[12] Such categories of form apply both to artistic expression and to beauty as found in the natural world, so that form is found within it rather than simply behind it. Yet it is clear that Balthasar claimed not only to value the beauty in the natural world, but also to find in it a "life principle":

> Artistic beauty here provides only a one-sided analogy, in so far as God is certainly free to create and remains free while creating and after having created. But the analogy from natural beauty is needed to complete the picture, because in this case the necessary, internal and living relationship between expressive form and the self-expressing life-principle is the presupposition for the understanding of natural beauty.[13]

In other words, within the world, there is something invisible that is shaping that world and giving rise to natural beauty. He goes on to suggest that the form of beauty shows itself through the development of life:

> In a flower, a certain interior reality opens its eye and reveals something beyond and more profound than a form which delights us by its proportion and colour. In the rhythm of the form of plants, from seed to full growth, from bud to fruit—there is manifested an essence, and to reduce this essence to mere utilitarian principles would be blasphemous. And in the totality of things, as they ascend and maintain their equilibrium, there is revealed a mystery of Being which it would be even more blasphemous and blind to interpret by reducing it to a neutral "existence."[14]

This suggestion is somewhat astonishing in many ways, for Balthasar seems to be suggesting, like the Romantics, that understanding what nature is really like means acknowledging a natural mysticism that demands laying aside an orientation of objectivity toward the natural world. He recognizes the debt to this tradition by his statement, "As especially the Romantics and the German Idealists deeply know, we are all initiated into these mysteries because we ourselves are spirit in nature, and because all the expressive laws of the macrocosm are at work in ourselves."[15] Yet he parts company

---

12. Balthasar, *GL* 1, 151.
13. Ibid., 444.
14. Ibid.
15. Ibid.

with the Idealist tradition in having due humility about what the human spirit can perceive, so that "the spirit with all its clarity of vision is not initiated into all the depths of the womb like night of the world soul and of the *natura naturans*."[16]

He suggests, further, that the mystery of Being is revealed in the totality of things, so that the forms of nature are really understood only when the spirit is ready to "give up its own light" and "trust itself to the loving intimations" that are found only when the intellect "renounces its argumentativeness."[17] He also detects in the natural world a deeper law at work in the "game of life," which is expressed in humanity but not equivalent to humanity, so that he will be "acting best of all when he allows this great law to operate unobstructed through him." Such a law is both the "law of nature" and a "law of reality, of the Being of the world as such, which reveals itself in everything ordered by the law of nature all the more enigmatically because of the fundamental puzzle about why it exists at all."[18] Of course, evolutionary biologists are rather more reluctant to speak of "laws of nature," if understood in a fixed ontological sense. However, the ordering that arises through what might be called "restrained contingency" in the evolution of convergent forms does show a certain resonance with the tradition of natural law.[19] In a later volume of *The Glory of the Lord*, he comments on this puzzle again, arguing, incorrectly, that this is not a question posed by science and, correctly, that such an awareness leads to the experience of wonder.[20]

---

16. Ibid. It is not clear from this quotation whether he acknowledges the possibility of a world soul, for it is equally likely that he is simply borrowing this language from the idealists he criticizes.

17. Ibid.

18. Ibid., 445. Such passages show indebtedness to the tradition of natural law, even though he fills this out in metaphysical terms, and it is always qualified by the strand in his thinking that stresses the radical difference between God and creation.

19. See C. Deane-Drummond, "Plumbing the Depths: A Recovery of Natural Law and Natural Wisdom in the Context of Debates about Evolutionary Purpose," *Zygon* 42, no. 4 (2007): 981–98.

20. Balthasar suggests that the metaphysical question as to why there is anything at all "is not posed seriously by any science." He believes that wonder at the fact that there is something rather than nothing can be reduced to wonder at the ordering of Being in response to the beauty of the cosmos. Hans Urs von Balthasar, *The Glory of the Lord*, vol. 5, *The Realm of Metaphysics in the Modern Age*, trans. by O. Davies, A. Louth, B. McNeil, J. Saward, and R. Williams, ed. Brian McNeil and J. Riches (Edinburgh: T&T Clark; San Francisco: Ignatius Press, 1991), 613–14. Yet the puzzle of existence as such is dealt with by the field of cosmology. I discuss wonder in this sense in C. Deane-Drummond,

The question that needs to be asked is whether he has adequately considered the reality of the natural world that he eloquently describes through his contemplation of a flower, an image that he uses on a number of occasions. He would certainly resist any suggestion that the way science treats the natural world is sufficient, but he has largely ignored biological science in his appraisal of natural beauty and its relationship with other forms of artistic beauty. His discussion of a "life principle" verges on forms of vitalism that are inimical to biological and evolutionary science in a way that is quite frankly unnecessary as a challenge. Yet it seems to me that he is correct to argue that, in a certain sense, for us to appreciate the depth of the natural world, we need to be prepared to admit to a poetic form of knowledge and insight, one that enlarges the scope of appreciation of natural wonder and natural beauty. He is correct, in other words, to resist the idea that a "shallow functionalism" is sufficient. Yet while he seems to want to prevent theology from existing "in its abstraction" by refusing isolation from "the exact sciences," it is doubtful whether he has taken the time to consider precisely what the exact sciences might have to contribute to the discussion.[21] If he had taken rather more trouble to appreciate the ambiguity of natural beauty as it appears through an acknowledgment, even in a limited sense, of evolutionary biology, then it might have offered him a further way through to link this insight with that of revealed theology, for it is not just the form of Christ that shatters any secular image of beauty in the world; rather, the shattering of secular images of beauty also comes from within the world of nature as such.

However, lest we think that he might be promoting a form of pantheism, he quickly qualifies this statement by suggesting that any positive cataphatic theology is accompanied by thoroughly comprehensive negative apophatic theology, so that "natural religion abides by the cipher-code of the world's Being." He concludes, significantly, "We will never be able to determine exactly the extent to which this splendour, given with creation itself, coincides objectively with what Christian theology calls 'supernatural revelation,' which, at least for Adam, was not yet a specifically distinct revelation given in the form of words."[22]

Wonder and Wisdom: Conversations in Science, Spirituality and Theology (London: DLT, 2006), 19–37.

21. Balthasar, *GL* 1, 447.

22. Ibid., 449.

In other words, the natural inspiration coming from the world is "the locus and vessel of God's inspiration by grace."[23] Balthasar argues that it was only because of sin that the Word became an external word, which in the Old Testament is expressed as law and prophecy, and in the New Testament as the incarnate and ecclesial Word. He associates such expression of God in the world with the biblical tradition of wisdom; for him, the natural theology of the Bible is the Wisdom literature, where there is a double movement of the revelatory character of the created world and also its vanity.[24] At the same time, the wisdom at work in the cosmos is more than simply the wise ordering of the created world, a position that Balthasar believes is deistic. "Rather, it is the presence of the creating and graciously providential God in all worldly form."[25] This sense of a God continuously and actively engaged in all natural forms is consistent with an evolutionary account of the history of the cosmos and human history.

It is here, however, that another ingredient enters Balthasar's theology, namely, his insistence that the revelation as that found in Christ surpasses anything that might be found in the created world. The similarity should not, in other words, fail to do justice to the dissimilarity, so that

> just as the divine Persons do not confront one another as autonomous beings but, in God's one concrete nature, forever one divine Being, so too, in Christ, the covenant between God and creatures as a covenant of free partners is forever surpassed and indissolubly established, in anticipation, upon the hypostatic union.[26]

Balthasar, in making such a claim, is aware of two opposite tendencies: "despair of the dignity of existence" and failure to "keep the transcendental beauty of revelation from slipping back into equality with an inner worldly natural beauty."[27] Yet just as we might think that Balthasar is moving from worldly beauty to transcendental beauty, even if recognizing their difference, he turns any such metaphor on its head by posing these questions:

---

23. Ibid., 452.
24. Ibid., 448.
25. Ibid., 454.
26. Ibid., 480.
27. Ibid., 25, 41.

Is it really only a matter of metaphor when theology contemplates and describes as *ars divina* the divine *oikonomia* that begins with the creation, unfolds throughout the salvation history of the Old and New Covenants, and is consummated in the Resurrection? . . . Or should we not rather consider this "art" of God to be precisely the transcendental archetype of all worldly and human beauty?[28]

In other words, do we move from consideration of the natural order to what might be termed special revelation of God through Christ or vice versa? The influence of Karl Barth in the second movement is well known, with his firm *Nein* to all natural theology. Yet Balthasar refuses to shed so readily that Roman Catholic tradition and Ignatian spirituality that is grounded on an analogy of being.

Noel O'Donoghue finds Balthasar's seeming rejection of the concept of "pure nature," with no clear concept of natural law and natural ethics, "disastrous," for he contends that "it blocked off any real dialogue between the Christian and his millions of non-Christian fellows," and any relationship between the natural and the Christian self.[29] Yet I remain less convinced that Balthasar is as hostile to this tradition as O'Donoghue suggests. Balthasar's resistance to speaking about the natural world in purely utilitarian ways, alongside his acknowledgment of a sacramental approach to nature, which he gleans from Ignatian spirituality, would also resonate with many religious traditions other than Christianity. Balthasar does speak clearly of the need for natural philosophy in his book on the theology of Karl Barth.[30] However, O'Donoghue notes that in *The Glory of the Lord*, "there is a deep ambiguity here which is only tolerable because of the triumph of the *Herrlichkeit* as a work of orchestral imagination."[31] Yet is it fair to speak in the way that O'Donoghue does of the "theological arrogance of Karl Barth," which he detects has crept into the work of Balthasar? Certainly, while a contemporary reader can detect notes of triumphalism in Barth's work,

---

28. Ibid., 69–70.

29. Noel O'Donoghue, "Appendix: Do We Get beyond Plato? A Critical Appreciation of the Theological Aesthetics," in *The Beauty of Christ: An Introduction to the Theology of Hans Urs von Balthasar*, ed. B. McGregor and T. Norris, 253–66 (Edinburgh: T&T Clark, 1994), 258 n. 2.

30. Hans Urs von Balthasar, *The Theology of Karl Barth* (New York: Holt, Rinehart & Winston, 1971), 297 (hereafter cited as *TKB*).

31. O'Donoghue, "Do We Get beyond Plato?" 258 n. 2.

even his consideration of natural law was rather more sophisticated than many readers have supposed.[32]

Moreover, Balthasar is influenced by Ignatius of Loyola in mediating between Barth and other forms of natural theology, developing a focus on the dramatic without losing touch with a strongly grounded spirituality, which eventually found its fruits in his subsequent volumes of *Theo-Drama*. As I have argued in chapter 1, a rather greater analogy can be found between theological accounts that stress *drama* and evolutionary change, compared with *narrative*, than we might have anticipated.[33] A contemporary evolutionary account of the emergence of species is, in many respects, not so much a smooth evolutionary narrative as one that gives expression to surprising twists and turns of events, so that, in Stephen Gould's phraseology, evolution is "punctuated" with periods of rapid evolution interspersed by periods of relative inactivity.[34] Balthasar doggedly hangs on to his affirmation of the need for analogy in spite of the recognition of difference between what is possible in the human and divine spheres. In this way, he states clearly, "it is only when there is an analogy (be it only distant) between the human sense of the divine and divine revelation that the height, the difference and the distance of that which the revelation discloses may be measured in God's grace."[35] Indeed, he claims that we have failed to perceive adequately both the profound truth *between* the world and God, and the holiness of God, such that the breaking of God's law is "far more deadly than one can see from the standpoint of the world alone."[36] It is this that makes him qualify insights from political or aesthetic views, so that "the *charis* of God is far richer in grace, far more free, bestows a far greater transfiguration than any political aesthetic world of images made by men could ever have supposed."[37]

---

32. See N. Biggar and R. Black, eds., *The Revival of Natural Law: Philosophical, Theological and Ethical Responses to the Finnes-Grisez School* (Aldershot: Ashgate, 2002).

33. Narrative theology has become increasing popular, and inasmuch as it puts emphasis on *story*, it can be connected with the *evolutionary story*. This follows in the tradition of Teilhard de Chardin, as discussed in chapter 1.

34. For further discussion of this issue, see the introduction.

35. Hans Urs von Balthasar, *The Glory of the Lord: A Theological Aesthetics*, vol. 4, *In the Realm of Metaphysics in Antiquity*, trans. B. McNeil, A. Louth, J. Saward, R. Williams, and O. Davies (Edinburgh: T&T Clark; San Francisco: Ignatius, 1989), 14 (hereafter cited as *GL* 4).

36. Ibid., 23.

37. Ibid., 24.

4.2 Christ, the Form of Beauty

Balthasar is correct to suggest that we should not pass over the creaturely phase too readily before coming to consideration of God as revealed, and such revelation of the mystery of Being invites and prepares the human spirit to move away from preoccupation with itself.[38] The incarnation of the Word combines, in a paradoxical way, "the most extreme manifestness within the deepest concealment."[39] The manifestness is evident because God comes as a human being, the concealment because of the radical particularity of this event, so that "the translation of God's absolutely unique, absolute and infinite Being into the ever more dissimilar, almost arbitrary and hopelessly relativised reality of one individual man in the crowd from the outset appears to be an undertaking condemned to failure."[40]

It is also important to note that revelation in Christ does not come simply alongside creation, as if in competition with it, but rather appears *within* it, showing Christ's uniqueness through his ordinariness. The human nature of Christ is not "oppressed and violated" by divine absolute being. Balthasar wants to avoid the tendency that he detects in German idealism on the one hand, where creation is identical to revelation and a manifestation of the divine Being, a mere "stage in the utterance of creation itself," and the counterreaction through a dualism that separates the revelation of the Word of God in Christ from the natural revelation of creation.[41] He also resists a third possibility, that is, starting from principles drawn from revelation in creation and viewing the Word as the "crown and summit" of that revelation. Instead, the transcendence of Christ's Word has "something setting it wholly apart," so a simple reliance on interpretation of Christ's activities in psychological and philological terms misses the "feeling for form," which includes an aesthetic sense.[42] Rather, the human and the divine in Christ are united such that there is nothing human that is not the utterance and expression of the divine and nothing divine that is not revealed and communicated to us in human terms. Such a combination applies to the public acts of Jesus historically as well as to his inner life of obedience. Balthasar is keen to insist that the inner life of Jesus is shared with the rest of humanity, and "it is precisely this inner aspect that is most

---

38. Ibid., 450.
39. Balthasar, *GL* 1, 451.
40. Ibid.
41. Balthasar, *WF*, 47.
42. Ibid., 52–55.

essential, definitive in the whole economy of the redemption. For it is not true that the acts and states of the Redeemer . . . are only partially human acts."[43] In this way, he can speak of the acts of Christ as acts of his human nature, while also saying his humanity is a "function of his divine Person and so a fit instrument for all those acts which are required for the redemption of mankind."[44]

In Balthasar's view, Christ is the form of beauty that overturns prior conceptions of beauty by showing forth the inadequacy of the finite order[45] but at the same time shows forth their fulfillment. Given Balthasar's attraction to kenotic Christology,[46] where Christ is understood as one whose love leads to an emptying of himself, it is in the Paschal mystery that we find the fullest expression of the beauty of Christ. The beauty of Christ "includes the hard law of the necessity of suffering even to the point of Cross and Hell as the centre of God's free salvific will."[47] In the background is the "ultimate intention of God," yet such suffering is a "free necessity," and "no logic can be more necessary than the absolute Logos, since every logic has its origin in him. Therefore God's self-revelation, precisely at the point where it goes to the Cross and Hell, must knock down before it all innerworldly concepts of the beautiful, and then, by transcending them in a sovereign manner, give them norm and fulfilment."[48] Such recognition of the form of Christ assumes an understanding of that form as the God-man, which in its turn presupposes an act of faith in his divinity.[49] Aidan Nichols expresses this strand in Balthasar when he suggests, "If the God of Glory wished to show his beauty to the world in his incarnate image he must at once take up forms within the world and shatter them so as to express the Glory beyond beauty."[50] Yet, as the quotation from Balthasar indicates, the worldly pieces are not simply left in tatters, but rather Christ is also shown to be their norm and fulfillment.

---

43. Ibid., 57.

44. Ibid., 58.

45. Balthasar, *GL* 1, 34.

46. Ibid., 28.

47. Hans Urs von Balthasar, *The Glory of the Lord: A Theological Aesthetics*, vol. 7, *Theology: The New Covenant*, trans. McNeil (Edinburgh: T&T Clark; San Francisco: Ignatius, 1989), 316 (hereafter cited as *GL* 7).

48. Ibid., 316.

49. Balthasar, *GL* 1, 153.

50. Aidan Nichols, *The Word Has Been Abroad: A Guide through Balthasar's Aesthetics* (Edinburgh: T&T Clark, 1998), xix.

At first sight, we might ask how this could be the case, for it seems obvious that the beauty of the cross is no ordinary beauty but rather an expression of profound ugliness, so that all worldly aesthetics are shaken at their foundations.[51] Balthasar holds to the patristic idea of the Logos actively at work in the world, but at the same time, he holds that the secular word expressed in culture, art, philosophy, pedagogy, and technology "can yet be a response to God's call."[52] At this point, Balthasar's use of analogy proves even more important in interpreting these seemingly contradictory claims.[53] He holds that the analogy of being is consummated in the analogy of faith, so that when philosophy posits Absolute Being in relation to contingent finite being, this bears an analogous relation to theology positing the Absolute Being offering grace to sinful creatures. Given that theology proposes an Absolute God who reveals, the relationship with Being in philosophy is analogous rather than identical. Given that theology also knows that the finite being is the subject who is offered revelation, then contingent being in philosophy is only analogous to finite being in theology.[54] Stephen Fields proposes, "This double level of dissimilarity so attenuates any similarity between God and the world that at once it affirms the radical contingency of the finite order while it establishes a basis for a novel revelation that can challenge the hegemony of intramundane aesthetics."[55]

Following Denys, Balthasar holds that the self-communication of God that grounds the finite order is a self-manifestation of the reality of God's being. Yet behind God's being is a perfection of the Godhead that is even more universal, namely, goodness, beauty, and eros. The analogy between the world and God relates to God's being rather than to God's beauty. Hence, Absolute Beauty is revealed in the cross, while Absolute Being is the ground of intramundane beauty.[56] Balthasar appeals to Denys in linking God's beauty with God's passionate love, the revealed love of a Person.

---

51. Balthasar, *GL* 1, 35.

52. Balthasar, *WF*, 23.

53. For discussion of this point, see Stephen Fields, "The Beauty of the Ugly: Balthasar, the Crucifixion, Analogy and God," International Journal of Systematic Theology 9, no. 2 (2007): 172–83.

54. Balthasar, *TKB*, 217.

55. Fields, "Beauty of the Ugly," 178.

56. Fields notes that being and beauty as constituting a dissimilarity within similarity within the infinite Godhead is philosophically tenable, but an act of faith is required in order to see that divine beauty, the crucified Christ, and intramundane aesthetics are similar. Ibid., 180.

As Fields comments, "Shining forth in the scandal of the cross, this love, grasped in faith, transforms an image assessed as ugly by intramundane norms into an icon of beauty."[57] The ultimate norm of beauty is not so much in "harmony and form of being," but in recognition of a God whose passionate love is revealed in the crucified Christ, the form of beauty.

The fact that Balthasar did not hold to any sharp divide between worldly beauty and that of the cross is evident in his speaking of the analogous experience between the contemplation of a flower and perceiving and "receiving" of "a certain depth of life," on the one hand, and grasping and accepting Jesus' form as the "appearance of a divine depth transcending all worldly nature" on the other.[58] This perception requires the grace of God to be at work, by "participation in this same depth that makes him proportionate to the wholly new dimension of a form phenomenon which comprises within itself both God and the world."[59]

Is a description of Christ as the form of beauty too abstract to be helpful as a way of interpreting Christ's passion? Noel O'Donoghue has found fault with Balthasar's apparent lack of engagement with traditional philosophy, alongside a theological arrogance and failure to attend to the "seeing of the feminine eye" and "the feminine heart."[60] Gerard O'Hanlon takes issue with his lack of attention to the historical Jesus, and to concrete issues more generally, along with a neutral attitude toward patriarchy.[61] Certainly, for all his descriptions of the importance of reflecting on the suffering Christ, and his call for an honest facing of the reality of evil and suffering,[62] there are almost no concrete descriptions of actual occasions of suffering and evil. Others, too, have criticized his lack of critical attention to traditions of contemporary biblical scholarship, as well as his somewhat free, almost idiosyncratic approach to assembling mystical, systematic, and biblical material. His defiance of pressures to specialize, so rife in contemporary theology as elsewhere, reflects his own desire to resist those trends in modernity and contemporary science, which he believes undermine the

---

57. Ibid., 180.

58. Balthasar, *GL* 1, 153–54.

59. Balthasar, *GL* 1, 154.

60. O'Donoghue, "Do We Get beyond Plato?" 258, 262.

61. Gerard O'Hanlon, "Theological Dramatics," in McGregor and Norris, *Beauty of Christ*, 108–12.

62. Hans Urs von Balthasar, *The Glory of the Lord: A Theological Aesthetics*, vol. 6, *Theology: The Old Covenant*, trans. B. McNeil and E. Leivá-Merikakis (Edinburgh: T&T Clark; San Francisco: Ignatius, 1991), 170, 407 (hereafter cited as *GL* 6).

true beauty of theology.[63] Moreover, while some have found his attention to natural revelation problematic, others believe that his rejection of aesthetic theology is misplaced, and that rather more attention needs to be given to proper appreciation of the arts.[64]

Balthasar was also prepared to consider the aesthetics as evidenced in the sciences through his discussion of Pascal. He comments on the "religious sense of structure" that Pascal displays, which acts as a bridge between an ascetic Augustinianism and the exact sciences.[65] He views in Pascal that awareness of the mystery of the suffering love of Christ, along-side his mathematical skill: the dread in the face of the cosmos that Pascal finds in unbelievers has a parallel, according to Balthasar, with the "evo-lutionary materialist, for whom the form of the universe has emerged from formless matter."[66] However, as a mathematician, Pascal lacked the sensitivity to living systems that is evident in biologists, for his own dread was the radical discontinuity that he sensed between the human spirit and all orders of lower nature. His solution was to see a vertical relation in the lower orders that can be discerned only from above. Indeed, Balthasar approves of Pascal's *fides naturalis* (faith in nature) on the basis of a genius being able to discern relationships, though he qualifies this by suggesting it is "completely on the margin."[67]

Balthasar's interpretation of Christ as the form of beauty can be extended to include appreciation of not just creaturely suffering more generally, but also our standards of aesthetics as applied to the nonhu-man world. One of the reasons that Balthasar did not spell out specific instances of suffering in the historical sense may be that he wanted his readers to appropriate his thinking for themselves in their specific contexts. In the light of evolutionary biology, it is possible to name and describe many thousands of species that are now extinct, which evolved more often than not in the crucible of suffering, and many of which are not beau-tiful according to what may be judged as worldly aesthetic standards. In

63. For comment on this aspect, see Richard Viladesau, *Theological Aesthetics: God in Imagination, Beauty and Art* (Oxford: Oxford University Press, 1999), 11–12.

64. Ibid., 23.

65. Hans Urs von Balthasar, *The Glory of the Lord: A Theological Aesthetics*, vol. 3, *Studies in Theological Styles: Lay Styles*, trans. A. Louth, J. Saward, M. Simon, and R. Williams (Edinburgh: T&T Clark; San Francisco: Ignatius, 1986), 172 (hereafter cited as *GL* 3).

66. Ibid., 198.

67. Ibid., 200–201.

addition, many thousands are not described, as they have not yet been named or researched. Christ the form of beauty challenges humanity to appreciate not just those forms of creation that seem most appealing to us, but also those creatures that seem to us in aesthetic terms to be repellent or even repugnant. Understanding that form of beauty in analogous terms also preserves the distinction between creation and Creator in such a way that Christ can show solidarity with the suffering in the natural world, without becoming identified with it.[68] Balthasar wants to affirm, against Nietzsche, that beauty, truth, and goodness do exist in the created world, but at the same time, he offers a theological response to that suffering through his meditation on the mystery of the incarnation as expressed in the beauty of the cross. Balthasar sees the world in all its tragic dimensions, and it is only an extension of his position to view this tragedy as rippling out into the fabric of creation as such, in much the same way that the Logos of Christ is also echoed in the cosmos as a whole. As Francesca Murphy points out, the beauty of Christ is not simply that of a luminous icon, but represents the beauty of an action, an expression of the "dramatic movement within the Trinity to us."[69]

4.3 The Depth of Incarnation: Christ in Hell

It is also necessary, however, to consider Balthasar's understanding of Christ as the form of beauty not just internally, but also in relation to his understanding of the drama of Christ's coming, where we find retold both God's acts in human history and Christ's human response.[70] This drama reaches its climax in his account of Christ on Holy Saturday. Balthasar's discussion of Holy Saturday draws heavily on his contact with Adrienne von Speyr. David Brown believes that Balthasar is making the claim that the systematic work of theology can only be the task of the mystic.[71] I am less convinced that Balthasar is even conceiving of his work as systematic theology in the standard sense; rather, what he claims—and this claim is

---

68. I will take up a critical discussion of the natural world as "cruciform" in the following chapter.

69. F. Murphy, *Christ: The Form of Beauty* (Edinburgh: T&T Clark, 1995), 146.

70. Balthasar points this out throughout his trilogy, but also explicitly in Hans Urs von Balthasar, "In Retrospect," in *The Analogy of Beauty: The Theology of Hans Urs von Balthasar*, ed. John Riches (Edinburgh: T&T Clark, 1986), 217.

71. David Brown, *Continental Philosophy and Modern Theology* (Oxford: Blackwell, 1987), 21–22.

coherent, in my view—is that theology should not be divorced from religious experience, and that accounts of such experiences are a valid source for theological reflection, even if they, too, need to be tested out.[72] Few commentators doubt the influence that von Speyr had on his theology, as he acknowledges himself, or the novelty in his thinking that stems from such appropriation.[73] The question that is of most concern in this context is the impact this has on his understanding of the incarnation, and how this may or may not connect with his understanding of how Christ and nature—and thus how Christ and evolutionary forms—might be related to one another.

A religious experience of Holy Saturday as recounted by Adrienne von Speyr came after a mystical sharing in the Passion of Christ during Holy Week, Good Friday, and Holy Saturday, repeated year by year. In the days of Holy Week, she experienced not just fear, but also a sense of shame, outrage, humiliation, godforsakenness, and physical pain, knowing her separation from the Lamb of God through her sin, but also her close proximity to him. It was, according to Balthasar, "what I consider to be the greatest theological gift she received from God and left to the Church."[74] The experience of Christ in hell, as recounted by these mystical experiences, was an experience of hell as filled with all that is irreconcilable with God, with the world's godlessness, sin, where even Christ's action becomes passive so that it is "truly the obedience of a corpse."[75] This is one reason why, in his *Mysterium Paschale*,[76] he speaks of Holy Saturday as a "going to the dead" rather than a "descent into Hell," as the latter would imply an active descent on the part of Christ and a mythological view of heaven, earth, and hell in a three-layered universe that he seeks to reject. Hell seems to be sin somehow "separated" from humanity, with Christ walking through it in such a way that there is no trace, as there is no time or direction, and "traversing its formlessness, he experiences the second chaos."[77] Here we find no spiritual

---

72. Balthasar's determined effort to get Adrienne von Speyr recognized by the Roman Catholic Church may also have been connected to his own desire for official validation of this aspect of his theological corpus.

73. See Quash, "Hans Urs von Balthasar."

74. Hans Urs von Balthasar, *First Glance at Adrienne von Speyr*, trans. A. Lawry and S. Englund (San Francisco: Ignatius, 1968), 64 (hereafter cited as *FG*).

75. Ibid., 66.

76. Hans Urs von Balthasar, *Mysterium Paschale*, trans. Aidan Nichols (Edinburgh: T&T Clark, 1990), p. 148.

77. Ibid.

light of the Father, but "in sheer obedience," Christ still seeks the Father where he cannot be found.

This emphasis on obedience, to which we will return in later chapters, shows up in a naked way Balthasar's attraction to the Ignatian notion of indifference, but such indifference is, normally speaking, not so much just "letting things happen" as it is a positive choice to surrender. For Balthasar, Ignatius is significant in that indifference understood as abandonment (*apatheia*) is not so much the end as the beginning of an active pursuit of God's will.[78] In Balthasar's account of hell, however, we find no activity in the mode of obedience, but merely passive acceptance. But hell remains "a final mystery of the Father as the Creator," and in this sense, Balthasar believes that this is a sharing of the Son "experientially" in what was "reserved" for the Father. He is therefore insistent that hell is "in its final possibility, a trinitarian event. On Good Friday the Father hands the 'key' to it over to the Son."[79] For Balthasar, von Speyr's account of hell is "more horrible" than that of the medieval theologians, as it is the knowledge of losing God forever, "engulfed in the chaotic mire of the anti-divine." All human communication is lost; all faith, hope, and love are gone; and thought just becomes a "prattle of lifeless logic." Certainly, the account that Adrienne von Speyr gives to Balthasar of other visions, without having read the biblical account, so closely resembles the book of Revelation as to be uncanny.

---

78. In *The Glory of the Lord*, he compares Ignatius with the Rhineland mystics, where abandonment meant detachment from all created things for the sake of immediate union with God. For Balthasar, the human being and will were still active and present. Hans Urs von Balthasar, *The Glory of the Lord*, vol. 5, *In the Realm of Metaphysics in the Modern Age*, trans. O. Davies, A. Louth, B. McNeil, J. Saward, and R. Williams (Edinburgh: T&T Clark, 1991), 102–5 (hereafter cited as *GL* 5). Earlier in the same volume, he describes *apatheia* as a feminine capacity (80), as a "passive" readiness to accept every positive impression made by God (78), though his own position is one that more often than not stresses both receptivity and activity. Mark McIntosh also coheres with this, inasmuch as he claims that Ignatian indifference never means a human being ceases to be a "spontaneous and free human subject," also citing *GL* 5, 106. Mark McIntosh, *Christology from Within: Spirituality and the Incarnation in Hans Urs von Balthasar* (Notre Dame: University of Notre Dame Press, 1996), 66. McIntosh suggests that for Balthasar, obedience is always a "response of love" and "includes a divine gift of interior freedom and energy." Ibid., 76. Hence, it seems to me that Quash goes rather too far in claiming that indifference lacks daring and makes for the "freezing of subjects." Quash, *Theology*, 134. It is in his description of hell, however, that Balthasar brings to the surface the passive nature of Christ's being and willing, so much so that the possibility of an active willing on his part seems to have disappeared.

79. Balthasar, *FG*, 66.

It may be that these visions convinced him that her mysticism was genuine, though his suggestion that acting in obedience to the church "must have all the reality and relentlessness of the Cross itself, both in the authority which commands and in the faithful who obey"[80] sounds like an uncritical, somewhat suffocating acceptance of a manipulative church authority.

Balthasar's own account of Holy Saturday draws heavily on that of Adrienne van Speyr in his insistence that Christ is in solidarity with the dead in all their passivity, a view that parts company with more traditional accounts, which treat the activity of Christ as if he were living rather than dead. He also believes that the traditional accounts rely too much on mythology, a mythology that envisages some sort of struggle between divinity that descends and the underworld.[81] The most we might concede in New Testament accounts of Christ's proclamation in the world of the dead is a making known of a victory already won, rather than a victory obtained by the descent to hell.[82] His understanding of preaching to the dead seems for him to symbolize the fact that the Righteous One died for the unrighteous and those without hope. He also believes that the New Testament account stresses that Jesus is not simply abandoned in Hades, but the accounts of the resurrection show the whence, the return from the dead. In this way he claims that the "accent is placed on the whence—the phrase *ek nekron* occurs some fifty times in the New Testament—a whence which implies a point of departure, namely, being with the dead."[83] Matthew's interpretation of Jesus' death as a sign of Jonah is, Balthasar claims, further support for the idea that Jesus was genuinely with the dead between Good Friday and Easter Sunday.[84] In sum, the "body simply *must* be put

---

80. Ibid., 70. His own rigidity here may possibly be a reaction against the painful experience he bore when leaving the Jesuits. Ignatius had strong words to say about the importance of ecclesial obedience, but the way he lived out that obedience was tempered by an acknowledgment that his adherence to the papal authority was such that it always had to keep an eye on the primary goal to bring glory to God. In his actual dealings with papal authority, Ignatius often forced them to change their minds, showing himself a master of ecclesial diplomacy and political maneuvering. See Ignatius, "The Final Word on Obedience," in *Saint Ignatius of Loyola: Personal Writings*, ed. Joseph A. Munitiz and Philip Endean (London: Penguin Classics, 1995), 251–65; and Harvey D. Egan, *Ignatius Loyola the Mystic* (Wilmington: Michael Glazier, 1987), 171–77.

81. Hans Urs von Balthasar, *Mysterium Pascale*, trans. Aidan Nichols (Edinburgh: T&T Clark, 1993), 151 (hereafter cited as *MP*).

82. Relevant passages are, for example, 1 Peter 3:19 and 1 Peter 4:6.

83. Balthasar, *MP*, 153.

84. Ibid., 153, 156.

into the earth."[85] Following Thomas, the experience of his soul while the body was in the earth was that of Hades, a sharing in the penalty given to the soul, a place where those who lived before Christ also descended *ad infernum* (from the dead).[86] Aquinas views the soul and body as adapted to each other. While Balthasar seems prepared to speak of the soul in distinction from the body, in language that is traditional from a Roman Catholic perspective, his envisagement of Hades as outside time, and presumably space, means that the travail of the soul can be thought of in existential terms while the body is in the ground. An evolutionary account of the human person that would eschew any clearly separated soul, or any activity of the brain at all after death, would therefore be compatible with this view only if the person concerned was near death rather than completely dead. This is not what Balthasar intends. Discussion of Christ being with the dead on Holy Saturday therefore presupposes faith and is intended for consideration by Christian believers, without creating further difficulties by imagining a mythical underworld. It is intended to extend the compassion of Christ to those who have died, so that even the experience of being dead is not outside his experience.

Balthasar uses the language of a "second death" to describe the passive experience of Christ in hell, where he confronts the naked reality of sin, now loosed from its attachment to any human being.[87] Hell is distinct from Hades, as while the latter draws on the Old Testament concept of Sheol, the former is an outcome of Christ's death and amounts to a "second death" in confrontation with sin "contemplated in its bear reality as such (for sin is a reality!)."[88] This construal of sin in detachment from human beings or any creaturely beings seems rather odd, but at the same time, the complete loss of any sense that there might be "principalities and powers" of evil at work in the world should not be too readily dismissed. He also holds to the view that such a separation of sin is a consequence of the suffering on the cross, and the liberation of humanity from sin does not, it seems, destroy that sin, but instead generates a kind of "second chaos," so viewing that separated sin can also be claimed as a triumph, for it no longer has its hold on human lives.

---

85. Ibid., 160.
86. Ibid., 164.
87. Ibid., 172–73.
88. Ibid., 173.

Indeed, Balthasar believes that hell as such is depopulated, as otherwise it would be defeat; moreover, hell does not exist prior to Christ, as in effect, Christ has created hell, rather than Hades, by his sacrificial work on the cross. But if hell is depopulated in the way Balthasar suggests, then Christ is experiencing something that no dead person after him will experience, so in what sense can that mean he shows *solidarity* with the dead? Such solidarity seems to reside with being dead, being passive, and his solidarity is with those in Hades, a condition where humanity is cut off from God, rather than in hell, where naked sin dwells in the absolute. Christ's entry into hell is a result of the work of the Trinity through an active decision by the Father to create free human beings and to send the Son as human into hell as an expression of that freedom.[89] However, hell is not outside the bounds of possibility for human occupation, and Balthasar stops short of following to its limit the universalistic thrust of his argument but claims, at the same time, that the offer of salvation given in this life will also be available to those who have died, before and after Christ.

Another aspect of Holy Saturday is often missed by commentators, and that is the image of hell as in effect the "undoing of creation."[90] Hell is not so much the neutral void of nonbeing, as in the beginning of creation, but a second chaos, so that, as John Saward observes, "in Hell the Son confronts the dark mystery which is the Father's permission of sin."[91] Christ's descent into hell can be compared with the first descent into the womb of the Virgin Mary, and in the same manner, descent does not so much imply desertion of what is above, but assumption of what is below. It reflects still further Balthasar's kenotic Christology, where both becoming human and entry into hell arrive through a free act of Christ's obedience to the Father.[92] It is kenotic self-emptying taken to its ultimate extent. In other words, it takes the incarnation to a new depth.[93] The Son in hell encounters sin in all

---

89. Ibid., 174–75.

90. I have borrowed this phrase from McIntosh, *Christology from Within*, 112.

91. John Saward, *The Mysteries of March: Hans Urs von Balthasar on the Incarnation and Easter* (London: Collins, 1990), 116.

92. For discussion of this point, see Balthasar, *GL* 7, 231.

93. On one level, of course, the experience of Christ in hell does not express the incarnation, as he is now dead, and this may be one reason why Balthasar describes the process as a "removal of the whole superstructure of the Incarnation" in order to expose the eternal will of the Son within the Trinity, namely, obedience. Yet it is this eternal will that is "the substructure that is the basis of the entire event of the Incarnation." Ibid., 231. There is a difficulty with the idea that the incarnation is somehow removed in hell,

its personal, social, *and* cosmic dimensions.[94] Balthasar also is prepared to speak of hell as containing "the unfinished part of creation, that it was left to the incarnate Son to finish."[95] This implies the potential for an equally cosmic redemption.[96]

In the following section, I will discuss his sacramental approach to creation, which includes a relationship between Christ as Logos and the created order. It therefore makes sense to speak of hell—and Hades, for that matter—as an undoing of that creation and to speak of the presence of Christ in that hell in order to allow for the possibility of that creation to be restored. Although Balthasar takes bold steps to avoid the kind of mythology of hell as depicted in the discussion of earlier Christian centuries, some commentators still find in his imagery a certain gnostic quality. Yet given that the afterlife is completely outside human experience, the only other alternative would be silence. Certainly, the following section seeks to show the extent to which Balthasar grounds theology in an appropriate appreciation of the created order.

4.4 Cosmic Christology in Trinitarian Perspective

In this final section, I intend to counter some of the suspicions that Balthasar may have become "gnostic" in his theology, which surfaced in the previous section, by highlighting the extent to which he included affirmation of the creation in his thinking, drawing not just on Ignatian spirituality, which emphasizes finding God in all things, but also on poets such as Gerard Manley Hopkins, who was also a Jesuit, and Eastern Orthodox writers such as Maximus the Confessor. Balthasar may have followed Barth in his description of the earth as a "stage" on which the drama of

---

inasmuch as it might imply that Christ is no longer really human, but this is precisely not what Balthasar intends, for it is the *human* Christ who enters hell, as the God-man in solidarity with the dead in Hades. Balthasar's thoughts on this are therefore at best inconsistent. Mark McIntosh also comments on the loss of humanity of Christ in a more general sense as applied to his Christology as a whole, when "it is interpreted as the human translation of the infinite divine filial kenosis." McIntosh, *Christology from Within*, 8.

94. I will return to his discussion of atonement in the next chapter. Balthasar follows Aulen in naming the defeat of hostile powers on the cross to be an act of drama, rather than according to a pattern of legal justice, as in Anselm. Hans Urs von Balthasar, *Theo-Drama* 2, trans. Graham Harrison (San Francisco: Ignatius, 1990), 159–61.

95. He is influenced by Irenaeus here. See Balthasar, *GL* 7, 233.

96. I will take this up in chapter 7.

salvation was worked out, but he did not want to thereby exclude this stage from theological consideration or weaken its significance in relation to his understanding of theology in christological and Trinitarian terms. Balthasar holds to the patristic idea of the Logos actively at work in the world, even though he claims, "The law of history and that of nature is, ultimately, to be measured by the law of Christ, the final and definitive Logos of the entire creation."[97] Indeed, arguably he pressed for a retrieval of patristic theology's "sacramental view of creation as wondrous because it is a vehicle of the divine."[98]

His use of Maximus the Confessor shows that Balthasar held to a sacramental view of the world, one that was impregnated by Christ from the start, without lapsing into a collapse between Christ and evolution. His Christology is fundamentally a "Christology from above," while at the same time wanting to take the human Jesus and the earth with utmost seriousness as the work of the triune God. Maximus describes the world in terms of a great "cosmic liturgy," a term Balthasar borrows for the title of his commentary on Maximus.[99] Here he takes a strong stance against any forms of gnostic thinking in theology, declaring that in such a view, God and the world are engaged in a "tragic, radical antipathy."[100] Instead, he wants to maintain that a more biblical view holds to both God's absoluteness and the world's relativity in ways that are not mutually exclusive. Significantly, he describes this divine involvement in the world in terms of wisdom, eventually shining forth for Christian faith as the personal Word and the human Christ. It is also significant that he criticizes any notion of creation as a hierarchical "golden chain of being," believing that this "risks postponing once again the unity of a transcendence beyond all being and an immanence within all Being, in order to make room for a struggle between Being and Nothingness (or matter), light and darkness."[101] For this reason, Rowan Williams correctly interprets Balthasar's sacramental approach to creation as showing not so much "hints of transcendence," but showing the divine through creation *being itself* in a way that includes creation in its

97. Balthasar, WF, 23.

98. K. Mongrain, The Systematic Thought of Hans Urs von Balthasar: An Irenaean Retrieval (New York: Herder & Herder, 2002), 60.

99. Hans Urs von Balthasar, Cosmic Liturgy: The Universe According to Maximus the Confessor, trans. B. E. Daley (San Francisco: Ignatius, 2003) (hereafter cited as CL).

100. Ibid., 82.

101. Ibid., 84.

unfinished state, in its pain, suffering, and death.[102] As such, this opens the view of creation to a dynamic view of the world that can readily take into account the unfinished nature of an evolved world.

Maximus's understanding of God in all realms of the world includes intellect and sense, earth and heaven, which meet through a reciprocity that becomes "the place where the Transcendent appears, visible precisely in this burgeoning immanence as the One who is wholly other."[103] For Maximus, what is significant is the relatedness of everything to everything else, leading to a reciprocal giving and taking, so that even passivity is not to be viewed as an imperfection, because it is a way of imitating God even while being radically different. The divine being is in motion inasmuch as beings capable of love have an inner share in its life, while at the same time stimulating that longing by its nature. Here we find a sacramental, Trinitarian theology that reaches a new pitch and is worth quoting in full:

> Here, in the end, is the inconceivable fecundity of this divine unity; on the one hand, it is the cause of the unity of all things and of their respective differences; it makes each of them an image of the divine unity and uniqueness; it is the basis of what is most personal and immediate in each of them. On the other hand, this divine unity is, in itself, the overflowing unity and root identity of these individuals, the source of their community and their loving communion. This paradox of a synthesis that unites creatures by distinguishing them and distinguishes them by uniting them—a paradox that can be found throughout the whole edifice of the universe—takes its origin in the most original relation of all things, their relation to God.[104]

Such themes of identity, difference, and unity in community grounded in the Trinitarian relations, speaking of the image of the divine in all things, affirm the evolved, created order, but in a way that puts emphasis on cooperation rather than competition. The very variety of beings in the world—the extent of which is far greater than Thomas Aquinas could possibly have conceived—reflects God's goodness and beauty.[105] A theological perspective

---

102. Williams, "Afterword," 175.
103. Balthasar, *CL*, 84.
104. Ibid., 69–70.
105. Aquinas, *Summa contra gentiles* 2.44. For an English translation, see http://op-stjoseph.org/Students/stud/thomas. Book 2 trans. James F. Anderson (New York: Hanover House, 1957), html version ed. Joseph Kenny, O.P.

on the universe will support those evolutionary accounts that give proper weight to the importance of cooperation and, as I will discuss in the next chapter, find recognizable expression in species other than humans. The problem for a Darwinian view of the universe is how to explain cooperation in evolutionary terms. While theoretical biologists such as Martin Novak propose cooperation as one of the three principles of evolution, reaching down to the very cells of all bodies, fitting this into a Darwinian account of mutation and selection proves challenging.[106] The problem for a sacramental view of the universe is how to affirm the evolved natural world as it is, including its competitive elements, without thereby identifying competition with "evil" or romanticizing the way the natural world works.

Balthasar also chose the priest and poet Gerard Manley Hopkins as one of the great authors of natural beauty, no doubt reflecting an affinity with his Jesuit background and poetic sensibility. Balthasar recognizes, in particular, Hopkins's ability to pay attention to the natural world, especially in its pure, wild form, and his sensitivity to the way humanity has mutilated that form.[107] His twin ideas of *instress* and *inscape* are interpreted by Balthasar in terms of his theological aesthetics. Things express their instress, understood as their deep, unique act, in a way that is answered in the subject by an answering stress and an ability to hold communion with them and then find the words to express that depth of their power of being.[108] Instress, then, reflects the power of things, while inscape reflects their form in such a way that the entire world is full of inscape, including that in nature and art.

Yet it is significant, perhaps, that Balthasar is at pains to point out that inscape is not what drove Hopkins to theology, but a personal address by God. After his conversion, Hopkins viewed the natural world as a gift, rather than as a ladder of ascent, so that creation is an implication of the extent of the incarnation. Hopkins perceives Christ at work in the human heart, to turn it away from self, as well as Christ as the form of the cosmos. Grace becomes preeminent, so that the action of creaturely being, "so far as this action is God's . . . it is divine stress, Holy Spirit, and, as all is done

---

106. For discussion, see Martin Novak, *Evolutionary Dynamics: Exploring the Equations of Life* (Cambridge, Mass.: Belknap/Harvard University Press, 2006). His own game theory goes some way to trying to explain cooperation according to a theoretical model, though how far this can be applied to all cooperative events in human societies remains unclear.

107. Balthasar, *GL* 3, 359–60.

108. Ibid., 365.

through Christ, Christ's Spirit; so far as it is action, correspondence, on the creature's part it is action *salutans*; so far as it is looked at in *esse quieto* it is Christ in his member on one side, his member in Christ on the other."[109] Hopkins's powerful doctrine of grace transforms the natural doctrine of instress and inscape. Now the true inscape of all things is Christ, and God's grace is the stress in them. Such a theological approach avoids pantheism while recognizing that Christ is still at the heart of all things, for "now it is really God who has the true taste of the human self in his mouth."[110] Moreover, this recognition also leads to recognition of glory, so that "out of the glory of the incarnate Lord there breaks forth the truest and most inward glory of forms both of nature and persons."[111] In the face of objections from Nietzsche, Balthasar holds to this vision of the grace of God at work in the world, in that he believes that the revelation of divine glory in Christ is what allows for the redemption of natural beauty and makes its unity with goodness and truth possible.[112]

4.5 Conclusions

The theological approach of Hans Urs von Balthasar shows some similarities with that of Sergii Bulgakov, discussed in the previous chapter, whose kenotic Christology Balthasar cites with approval.[113] Yet while the Wisdom literature stands in the background of Balthasar's consideration of beauty, his theological aesthetics offers some guideposts for relating Christ and nature. In the first place, the discussion of how natural theology relates to special revelation demonstrates sensitivity to what might be termed beauty in the natural world, while recognizing that such sensitivity cannot lead to an understanding of God who is Absolute Beauty, but the two are related in an analogous way. This analogy is subject to a double dissimilarity, in that the finite being of the world is analogous to the Absolute Being of philosophy, but theology understands God and creaturely being through revelation and grace. Hence, Balthasar finds ways to affirm the value of the natural world without confusing it with the divine as such. This is not to

---

109. Gerard Manley Hopkins, *Sermons and Devotional Writings*, ed. Chris Devlin, 154, cited in Balthasar, *GL* 3, 385.

110. Balthasar, *GL* 3, 387.

111. Ibid., 390.

112. Mongrain, *Systematic Thought*, 60–61.

113. See R. Williams, "Balthasar and the Trinity," in Oakes and Moss, *Cambridge Companion*, 38.

say that God remains distant from creation, for Balthasar understands the incarnation in such a way that God is present through the very real fragile human nature of Jesus. Jesus is, however, more than simply an ordinary human being; he is also the form of beauty inasmuch as in him, the meaning of Absolute Beauty is made plain. This overturning of human assessments of beauty and its concentration on the Paschal mystery means that our attitude to the beauty of the natural world can also be transformed, even though Balthasar did not make this step.

A greater sensitivity to the pain encountered in evolution alongside expressions of natural, wondrous beauty is measured alongside the mystery of Christ's passion. The radical nature of identity with human beings is such that Jesus also descended into Hades, the place of the dead, and hell, where sin is found in its absolute sense. His passivity reflects the powerlessness of the dead, and the second death in hell has its corollary in a second chaos. This undoing of creation is significant, for it implies that once Christ is lifted from hell, creation is once again restored, a subject to which we will return in later chapters.

Yet the strong patristic background to Balthasar's thought allowed him to think of the world in a sacramental way, as displaying something of the image of God in all things for the eye of faith. Indeed, his fellow Jesuit, Gerard Manley Hopkins, was able to transform his own love of nature into a poetic account of God acting in the world through instress, and of Christ the ultimate expression of inscape. Therefore, this poetic account of the natural world needs to have the last word, for it opens up our sense of wonder in a way that purely evolutionary accounts do not. In one sense, Balthasar is correct in his assessment that science cannot do justice to the richness of the created world.

Balthasar has been criticized for remaining too theoretical in his discussion of theology, yet I would contend, like Gerard O'Hanlon, that he offers a powerful theological vision that can be appropriated much wider than his own thoughts envisaged. His affection for hierarchical structures in the church and its authority are not borne out in his image of the created order as such, so that while he has been severely criticized by feminists and others for his failure to appreciate sexual difference adequately, his attraction to creaturely relatedness does cohere with more ecological and feminist forms of thought.[114]

---

114. This suggestion is, of course, controversial, as some would argue that feminist theology, by definition, seeks to uncover the patriarchal and oppressive structures of

Evolution offers, then, partial insights into the nature of created reality, and inasmuch as it supports ideas of cooperation, it coheres with a religious sense. How far intuitions toward human cooperation can be explained in evolutionary terms is a subject we have discussed in an earlier chapter. However, the evolution of sin points to dimensions of sin that are not covered by Balthasar and therefore are suggestive of a complementary approach to Christology, namely, one that draws on the tradition of wisdom rather than wonder in the mode of beauty. It is to this subject that we turn in the following chapter.

---

society. My suggestion here is that once the importance of relatedness is recognized in theology, then awareness of the potential destructiveness of social structures is more likely, though of course the one does not lead inevitably to the other. Balthasar wrote out of his own context, and inasmuch as he failed to recognize the situatedness of that context, his writing can be faulted. This does not mean that elements of his thinking are not useful. Although his consideration of the sexual difference between men and women was, like that of Sergii Bulgakov, stereotypical—and in this sense, his concept of relatedness was flawed and not a useful way of thinking about women—this does not mean that his writing is impotent in other areas.

PART 2
THE DRAMA OF HOPE

5

Revisiting Atonement: The Drama of Christ and Shadow Sophia

The extent and depth of natural evil in the world have become a subject of intense theological and philosophical scrutiny. In particular, the level of suffering and loss is sufficiently acute for some theologians to argue in favor of an evolutionary theodicy. Rather less attention has been paid to the christological implications of such a theory, especially in the light of the possibility of a form (or forms) of morality in nonhuman creatures. In particular, we need to think more carefully about the significance of the atonement for the nonhuman world before moving too quickly to considerations about redemption, even if one always has to be considered in the light of the other. Discussion of the redemption of nature (human and nonhuman), with its emphasis on the resurrection promise, really makes sense only when we first allow the dark side of nature to cast its shadow on theological discussion. It is here that we understand the full meaning of redemption, what humanity and all creation are saved *from* or, perhaps more accurately, *through*.

I will consider various alternatives, suggesting that the theodramatic approach of Hans Urs von Balthasar mediates successfully between subjective and objective approaches to the atonement. I will also argue that one way of dealing with this complex issue with many different layers of theodicy is through the development of the idea of shadow sophia in engagement with the work of Sergii Bulgakov. I will take up a discussion of redemption in the following chapter.

5.1 Evolution of Sin

A great deal of attention has been paid to the evolution of altruism, as this seems to go against the stream of evolution understood in terms of competitive survival of the fittest.[1] To explain this phenomenon, various theories have been proposed, including multilevel selection theory, where gene selection is at the level of the group rather than the individual. The question in this case, however, was how this selection could work and be measurable as science, and initially many biologists abandoned the idea entirely. However, too strong a focus on individual genes also proved problematic, as groups of genes are transferred through individuals. Later elaborations, such as evolutionary game theory and tit-for-tat theories, showed how it was possible for altruism to emerge in terms of overall group benefits. The manner in which cultural factors impinge on and interact with biological factors also is a matter of considerable discussion, in particular, the relative contribution of biological and cultural factors to human behavior and their interaction with one another. Rather less attention has been paid to the evolution of what might be termed sinful behavior, possibly because it might seem self-evident that "natural" tendencies would be toward "self-ishness," even though this term, according to most biologists at least, does not have specific "moral" connotations in the way it is used to describe gene conservation.

From an evolutionary perspective, some authors argue that human behavioral tendencies that are destructive in contemporary society may have evolved to be advantageous in the history of human evolution.[2] I have suggested in chapter 2 that such theories amount to a secularized atonement theory; they allow present human beings to project onto far-flung

---

1. For a comprehensive overview of this area, see, for example, Stephen G. Post, *Unlimited Love: Altruism, Compassion, and Service* (Philadephia: Templeton, 2003); and Stephen G. Post, Byron Johnson, Michael E. McCullough, and Jeffrey P. Schloss, *Research on Altruism and Love* (Philadelphia: Templeton, 2003).

2. This aspect is discussed in Michael Chapman, "Hominid Failings: An Evolutionary Basis for Sin in Individuals and Corporations," in *Evolution and Ethics: Human Morality in Biological and Religious Perspective*, ed. Philip Clayton and Jeffrey Schloss, 101–13 (Grand Rapids: Eerdmans, 2004). I do, nonetheless, suggest that Chapman's seeming endorsement of evolutionary psychology is unfortunate, as it implies that human sinfulness is rooted in naturally selected capabilities in a manner that is itself controversial. That does not exclude, however, the possibility that some tendencies in humans may have a long evolutionary history; the point is that trying to prove an evolutionary basis for such changes is far-fetched in many cases.

ancestors tendencies that may have been useful then but that today we find reprehensible. How far such tendencies have a basis in genetics and/or social or cultural factors is a matter of some debate; evidence from evolutionary psychology is largely speculative as to how far and to what extent particular behaviors have clear evolutionary roots and a biological basis in adaptations. I am not suggesting that there is no connection between our biology and behavior; contemporary neuroscience has repeatedly given examples of mental diseases that can be traced to particular biological malfunctions. Human beings need a healthy brain as a precondition for adequate decision making, but this does not mean that we then trace all behavior, both moral and immoral, to particular mental modules. In this chapter, I am approaching the issue rather differently, namely, by asking how far non-human animal behavior as we know it and as can be observed in a present context can be said to be an appropriate area of concern in terms of a theory of atonement. This will also act as a helpful analogy for our hominid, primate, and animal ancestors, without laying claim to any speculative notions about what those ancestors may or may not have done in terms of moral capabilities or sinful behavior.

Marc Bekoff, in particular, has argued on the basis of cognitive ethology that we need to pay far more attention to non-human animal behavior in terms of what is appropriate in their world.[3] In particular, other animals experience a wide range of emotions, including joy, happiness, fear, anger, grief, jealousy, resentment, and embarrassment, as well as, importantly, an ability to show empathy and shock and, in some cases, to use language and culture. In addition, other animals display distinct personalities and idiosyncratic traits. Bekoff argues that our ways of measuring self-awareness, for example, are not always appropriate; for dogs, for example, it makes more sense to use smell, rather than mirrors, in detecting self-awareness. He suggests, based on careful observations of non-human animal behaviors, "We do not have to ascribe to animals far fetched cognitive or emotional capacities to reach the conclusion that they can make moral decisions in certain

---

3. Marc Bekoff, "Animal Passions and Beastly Virtues: Cognitive Ethology as the Unifying Science for Understanding the Subjective, Emotional, Empathetic and Moral Lives of Animals," *Zygon* 4, no. 1 (March 2006): 71–104; Marc Bekoff, *Animal Passions and Beastly Virtues: Reflections on Redecorating Nature* (Philadelphia: Temple University, 2004); Marc Bekoff, "Wild Justice and Fair Play: Cooperation, Forgiveness and Morality in Animals," *Biol. & Philos.* 19 (2004): 489–520; Marc Bekoff, *Minding Animals: Awareness, Emotions and Heart* (Oxford: Oxford University Press, 2002); and Marc Bekoff, "Virtuous Nature," *New Scientist* 174, no. 2,351 (July 13, 2002): 34–37.

circumstances."[4] But if this is the case, could we *also* say that animal behavior can equally express a form of *immorality* that is related to their capacity for flourishing? Is there a sense in which dolphins, for example, could "sin" inasmuch as they fail to realize their flourishing, becoming addicted to destructive behavior patterns, rejecting their responsibilities as parents, and so on?[5] This is certainly *not* equivalent to human sin but is related to *their moral capacity in their own world.*

I have to confess to a change of mind here. In previous work, I suggested that morality is firmly confined to humans and argued, against Michael Northcott, that non-human animals should not be held morally culpable in any strong sense.[6] Then, as now, I believe that we need to take particular care not to ignore the differences between humans and nonhumans; in other words, I suggest that *we cannot simply absorb animals into the human moral community.* But reading the recent work of Bekoff, de Waal, and other primatologists and animal behaviorists has convinced me that there is still a way of envisaging non-human animal morality that both does justice to their own behavior *in their own worlds* and also helps us understand both the similarities to and differences from human behavior. Hence, this is challenging for some philosophers, who might even view such a shift as a "category mistake," but only if one assumes that the way we construct human morality is the only way to conceive of moral (or immoral) relations. Much the same conclusion seems to be reached by the philosopher John Dupré, who argues that it makes relatively little sense to try to teach chimpanzees human language; what is far more significant is whether there are nonlinguistic means of communication that are sophisticated.[7] Further,

---

4. Bekoff, "Animal Passions," 93. I have discussed the idea of morality in non-human animals in more detail in C. Deane-Drummond, "Are Animals Moral? Taking Soundings through Vice, Virtue, Conscience and *Imago Dei*," in *Creaturely Theology: On God, Humans and Other Animals*, ed. C. Deane-Drummond and D. Clough (London: SCM, 2009), in press.

5. Michael Northcott, "Do Dolphins Carry the Cross? Biological Moral Realism and Theological Ethics," *New Blackfriars* (December 2003): 540–53.

6. "Reading into animal behaviour moral agency in a strong sense as morally culpable is a mistake, that there remain crucial differences between animals and humans that should not be underestimated so as to interpret in animal behaviour capabilities for being included as moral agents as part of human moral communities." C. Deane-Drummond, *The Ethics of Nature* (Oxford: Blackwell, 2004), 72.

7. John Dupré wants to resist what he sees as Cartesian tendencies to seek for the essence of language in nonhuman animals. The question about animal languages then, more often than not, betrays for him a form of essentialism that has been denied by

being prepared to consider the possibility of non-human animal morality is not equivalent to reading into animal behavior vice and "beastly" patterns that humans would wish to shed from their own terms of reference, a point that Mary Midgley raises in her epic book *Beast and Man: The Roots of Human Nature*.[8] She also claims here, significantly, that "everyone knows that animals are as incapable of vice as they are of virtue"; for her, such portrayals are symbolic, not real.[9] However, while we might certainly want to avoid anthropomorphisms, there is a difference between the crude renderings that Midgley speaks about in her book and the careful reflections of ethologists who have taken the trouble to, as far as possible, try and enter the world of other animals on their own terms.[10]

The consequences of being prepared to consider the possibility of moral action in nonhuman animals are highly significant in theological terms, as I discuss further in a later section. It is hardly surprising that respected theologians, including Denis Edwards, remain "uneasy" with the idea of morality in other animals.[11] I also had a sense of unease, at least until I read more closely the recent work of animal ethologists. Of course, inasmuch as this work is still being undertaken, it is a reaction to the resistance to "anthropomorphizing" that naively reads into non-human animal behavior analogous human traits. The distinctiveness different kinds of animal social life needs to be stressed, but that does not mean we exclude the idea of morality from animals, unless by definition we are resistant to this idea. This view proceeds in much the same way that animal rights are a contested area of debate in animal ethics; more convincing versions are not simply an *extension* from human rights but are adapted to the particular needs of non-human animals. Moreover, there is another sense in which

---

later philosophers such as Wittgenstein. Of course, ethologists are less likely to make this mistake, but he is also equally critical of what he believes are generalizations arrived at from anecdotal evidence, so "an inductive argument based on observation of one case to a generalisation over a population of billions is hardly deserving of the title of 'argument.'" J. Dupré, *Humans and Other Animals* (Oxford: Clarendon, 2002), 220. While I agree that it is a mistake to seek to "read into" animal behavior essential properties of animals, ethological research is rather more sophisticated than he implies here.

8. Mary Midgley, *Beast and Man: The Roots of Human Nature*, 2nd ed. (London: Routledge, 1995), 35.

9. Ibid., 31.

10. See, in particular, Frans de Waal, ed., *Primates and Philosophers: How Morality Evolved* (Princeton: Princeton University Press, 2006). See also other essays in Deane-Drummond and Clough, *Creaturely Theology*.

11. Denis Edwards, personal communication, January 9, 2007.

morality has evolved in human beings *from* animals. As creatures, we share many of the tendencies of our forebears, so that human behavior is, at least to some extent, linked with that of other animals, even if not in the "essentialist" manner that Dupré abhors.

I am not suggesting that we treat nonhuman and human animals as identical in terms of moral capability—far from it. Ian Tattersall is among those who have argued that the emergence of human uniqueness in the earliest hominids follows the punctuated evolution characteristic of Stephen Jay Gould; that is, it happened relatively quickly, fostered by sudden changes in environmental conditions, where different groups were separated from each other.[12] The assumption in this case, of course, is that human intelligence has arisen through natural selection. Yet the intelligence one speaks of in such a context is still one of degree compared with the nonhuman world, rather than absolute difference. The philosopher Peter Munz has put forward a rather different and equally plausible argument. In his critical engagement with evolutionary psychology, he suggests that the evolution of the very large human brain was in fact a liability.[13] Most other authors have suggested that the increase in brain size arose as a response to social conditions, including the size of social groups.[14] But this leaves unanswered why such social groups emerged in the first place. Others, such as Terence Deacon, argue that the ability to symbolize is related to brain size.[15] Munz argues that this does not adequately distinguish between language that relates to definable objects and language that relates to events and objects that have not yet happened and/or are not yet there. The former

---

12. Ian Tattersal, *Becoming Human: Evolution and Human Uniqueness* (New York: Harcourt Brace, 1998).

13. Peter Munz, *Beyond Wittgenstein's Poker: New Light on Popper and Wittgenstein* (Aldershot: Ashgate, 2004).

14. Such authors include, for example, Nicholas Humphrey, Robin Dunbar, and Terence Deacon. Of particular note is N. K. Humphrey, "The Social Function of Intellect," in *Growing Pains in Ethology*, ed. P. P. G. Bateson and R. A. Hinde (Cambridge: Cambridge University Press, 1976); R. Byrne and A. Whiten, eds., *Machiavellian Intelligence: Social Expertise and the Evolution of Intellect in Monkeys, Apes and Humans* (Oxford: Clarendon, 1988); R. I. M. Dunbar, "Determinates in Group Size in Primates: A General Model," in *Evolution of Social Behaviour Patterns in Primates and Man*, ed. W. G. Runciman, John Maynard Smith, and R. I. M. Dunbar (Oxford: Oxford University Press, 1996), 50; and T. Deacon, *The Co-Evolution of Language and the Brain* (New York: Norton, 1997).

15. T. Deacon, *The Symbolic Species: The Co-evolution of Language and the Brain* (New York: Norton, 1997).

type of language states meanings about what is; the latter expresses meanings about what is not. Both nonhuman and human primates can produce symbols, but only humans produce symbols about what is not.

In other words, only humans worry about their own uniqueness and other such problems. Munz characterizes these differences as two-dimensional and three-dimensional language.[16] He suggests that too large a brain does not allow simple and straightforward responses. He also suggests that the very large brain arose in the first instance because of a predominantly fishy diet.[17] In this scenario, only those who developed three-dimensional language survived, as it served to compensate for the overly large brain. The large brain was, in this case, a spandrel rather than something "designed" by natural selection. While the emergence of language also depended on suitable anatomical changes, such as upright posture and a larynx suitable to modulate and inflect sounds, the different "neural churnings" could come together into a representation. In this sense,

> the damage initially caused by too large a brain was not only mitigated, but turned into a positive advantage. With the help of three-dimensional language, it now became possible to assemble linguistically what was taking place in the brain's separate parts. It became possible to assemble the separate cerebral reactions to colour, movement, location, duration and so on into a coherent representation of something which the brain in itself had not taken in as such. The three-dimensional language does not depend for its meaningfulness on ostensive definition.[18]

Munz is arguing, then, for the importance of human cultures that made the modification of two-dimensional language into three-dimensional language possible. In this, he parts company with the view of evolutionary psychology that specific mental modules, including those for moral and religious sense, have evolved through pressures of natural selection.[19] The advantage of using language as a means to specify more precisely human uniqueness is that it shows that the difference with the nonhuman world is cultural as well as biologically related to the way human minds work. Although there has

---

16. Munz, *Beyond Wittgenstein's Poker*, 144.

17. He draws here on the work of Robin McKie as well as Finlay, Darlington, and Nicastro; see ibid., 207.

18. Ibid., 146.

19. I share his reservations about the standard evolutionary psychology model and his support for the alternative view of the mind as a general-purpose mind.

been a turn toward more relational understandings of *imago Dei* in theological discussion, this scientific discourse is a reminder that human capabilities, such as intelligence, rationality, and so on, cannot be separated from the ability to have relationships.[20] In considering the "morality" of other animals, I suggest that this need not reduce or weaken the claim for human uniqueness. In fact, it might help to clarify more precisely the difference in the moral landscape of human and nonhuman animals. For I suggest that we could perhaps speak of morality as that which is *three-dimensional* in humans but only *two-dimensional* in other animals, in that they are unable to anticipate harms and goods to the same extent as humans.

This is not the same as suggesting a pure moral naturalism, in which human behavior can simply be described or, even stronger, guided in terms that are entirely derivative from nonhuman animals. Human culture renders the picture far more complex than this. Rather, the issue at stake here is how far nonhuman animals can be described as showing not just "latent" morality that eventually finds an echo in human behavior, but also a morality that is inherent in their own life-worlds. Michael Northcott believes that such behavior exists, and he suggests that dolphins do stand in need of redemption, though far less so compared with human beings,

---

20. Wentzel van Huyssteen discusses the different theological approaches to image bearing and their relationship to evolutionary biology in "Fallen Angels or Rising Beasts? Theological Perspectives on Human Uniqueness," *Theology and Science* 1, no. 2 (2003): 161–78. He also takes this up further in his masterly book *Alone in All the World? Human Uniqueness in Science and Theology* (Grand Rapids: Eerdmans, 2006). Perhaps somewhat surprisingly, he does not seem to challenge the view of evolutionary psychology that the human mind is the way it is because of natural selection, and sees this as simply an extension of evolutionary epistemology in becoming "embodied," speaking of forms of human intelligence as "adaptations" in a way that would be quite foreign from someone of Peter Munz's perspective. While he warms to Popper's view of knowledge as that which is created by human intelligence, with the least successful theories eliminated, this version of evolutionary epistemology is very different from more biologically based theories of Henry Plotkin. Van Huyssteen even speaks approvingly of a *universal Darwinism*, which is odd, considering his discourse with postmodern theory. The crucial difference is that between a general-purpose mind and an adapted mind, and van Huyssteeen seems to lean toward the latter. See van Huyssteen, *Alone in the World?* 75–83. Munz has pointed to the underlying positivism in evolutionary psychology, which ties the mind into specific instructions, coded by genes, rather than seeing the mind as freely inventing hypotheses. Munz is therefore sharply critical of authors such as Henry Plotkin, whom van Huyssteen seems to endorse, and views the path that Popper took in his incorporation of Darwin as very different from the ultra-Darwinian stream endorsed by evolutionary psychology. See Munz, *Beyond Wittgenstein's Poker*, 156, 165–66.

especially the destructive behavior of human beings toward dolphins. I am less sure than Northcott that we can call such behavior "sin," inasmuch as this might imply a deliberate turning away from God and also implies too close a comparison with human morality. Domning and Hellwig argue that the tendency in the biological world toward selfishness eventually finds its expression in humans, so they prefer to speak of such behavior as "Original Selfishness" rather than "Original Sin."[21]

However, inasmuch as we find a morality and immorality (both latent and specific to other animals) in nonhumans, so the human capacity for sin is embedded in nonhuman animal behavior, and this behavior, I suggest, also stands in need of redemption. We could press the point here and speculate that the immorality existing in their worlds, inasmuch as it expresses some freedom of choice, also stands in need of redemption. Of course, this raises the difficult question of how far and to what extent we can really think of other animals as self-conscious beings (persons) able to make decisions, a characteristic more usually associated with *imago Dei*.[22] Certainly, many animal behaviorists are arguing in this direction, with Bekoff claiming, "It is clear that morality and virtue didn't suddenly appear in the evolutionary epic beginning with humans. While fair play in animals may be a rudimentary form of social morality, it could still be a forerunner of more complex and more sophisticated human systems."[23] In Northcott's scheme, the significance of the cross for dolphins (who have clearly not heard the gospel) is expressed in terms of the "moral priority of the weak." This assumes that the "weak" in the gospels includes other animals, which requires rather more theological justification. I suggest that we need to take a different tack in considering the possible significance of the cross for other animals.

As one might expect, perhaps, primates also show tendencies to violent, aggressive behaviors, some at times killing and eating their young.[24] Of course, this is not to make judgments about how far such behaviors in primates *legitimize* parallel human behavior, but rather to ask a different question: How deep does what seems to us to be immoral behavior or "sin"

---

21. Daryl P. Domning and Monika K. Hellwig, *Original Selfishess: Original Sin and Evil in the Light of Evolution* (Basingstoke: Ashgate, 2006).

22. The extent to which we can call animals "persons" is outside the scope of this chapter.

23. Bekoff, "Wild Justice," 510.

24. Richard Vrangham, *Demonic Males: Apes and the Origins of Human Violence* (London: Bloomsbury, 1996).

go in the evolved world? Certainly, we may be far more inclined to warm to the positive stories of ape behavior that expresses empathy and altruism;[25] some would even see such behaviors as models for human behavior, finding in other animals a naturalistic basis for ethics. Yet perhaps we need to take off our rose-colored glasses and see nonhuman animal behavior for what it is, in its full capacity for what appears to us to be good or ill.[26] I would prefer, therefore, to see such tendencies for good and ill as expressing both a form of "morality" in the worlds of nonhuman animals (if we take on board the research of Bekoff and others) *and* a *moral latency* for good and ill in humans, rather than a foundation for a strict biological moral realism.[27] But regardless of how far we see dolphins or primates as expressing moral tendencies that are good rather than evil, this issue raises a wider one of how far and to what extent we need to revise our understanding of atonement (and redemption) in the light of such ethological studies on nonhuman animals, set within an even broader compass of the sheer extent and volume of evolutionary suffering and extinction of species.

The depth and extent of suffering in the natural world throughout the history of life on the planet also call into question traditional theological

---

25. See, for example, Frans de Waal, *Good Natured: The Origins of Right and Wrong in Humans and Other Animals* (Cambridge, Mass.: Harvard University Press, 1996).

26. I am using the term *ill* here, rather than *sin*, for I think that the latter is too bound up with the history of human relationships with God to be all that helpful. The debate about which sins might be the most profound in the human community (pride and sloth have been great contenders), and how far these might be found in other animals, need not concern us here, for the direction of movement is from nonhuman animal behavior to tendencies in humans, rather than the other way around. This tendency for ill, or moral latency, eventually expresses itself in free human choices that are deliberately evil acts. This does not mean there are no distinctions between human and nonhuman animal kinds. Humanity does have a distinctive capacity for "sins" that outweighs anything remotely recognizable in nonhuman animal behavior.

27. Bekoff has criticized the idea of "quasi-moral" and "proto-moral" behavior discussed in Gregory Peterson on the basis that it is condescending to nonhuman animals to consider their behavior in such terms. For discussion, see Gregory R. Peterson, "The Evolution of Consciousness and the Theology of Nature," *Zygon* 34 (1999): 283–306; and Gregory Peterson, "Think Pieces: God, Genes and Cognizing Agents," *Zygon* 35 (2000): 469–80. The objection seems to stem from Peterson's portrayal of quasi-morality as that which emerges from instinctive behavior in nonhuman animals and has some analogies with human behavior. Proto-morality, in contrast, is more deliberate, includes a variety of cognitive skills, and would correspond approximately to what I have termed moral latency. For Peterson, genuine morality, defined as the capacity for abstraction and symbolic expression, as well as rich emotional states such as shame or guilt, is found only in human societies.

models of fall and redemption that are focused entirely on human history. There are various ways through this account. One is to scrap the account of the fall viewed as a human fall into depravity based on original sin, focusing instead on humanity as in some sense unfinished, in need of further development and maturity.[28] The "fall" is then viewed in terms of growth of human potential and self-consciousness. While the idea of a "fall upward" posits humanity in continuum with the created order, it does not seem to do justice to the radical depth of evil found in human history, including the evil effects of human action on nonhuman species, or to deal adequately with the question and extent of what might be termed evolutionary evil. The latter would also include what I would term immorality (latent and nonlatent) in social species other than humans, as well as what is commonly termed "natural evil," which has more in common with the processes in nature that are perceived as automatic and inevitable consequences of life. The danger in this case, of course, is that evil might seem to be reified and elevated as a category, giving it *too* much importance.

To avoid such a suggestion (through notions of a literal Satan, for example), we need to view the fall as a mythological rather than a historical account, epitomizing the outcome of humanity's self-assertion in claiming radical independence from God, and leading to a series of breakdowns in relationships with God, the land, and the human community. In evolutionary terms, the fall could be thought of as that sharper awareness of the capacity for negative choice that is present in the human community, with its enhanced capacity for moral action. How far and to what extent such moral or immoral capacity emerges at least in part in biological continuity with our primate cousins, or whether it is simply the indirect outcome of greater evolved intelligence in humans, is not the issue here; the point is that the "fall" reaches *behind* into the evolutionary history of the world as well as pointing *forward* as a shadow on human history.

Yet if, with Paul, we speak of Christ as a second Adam, what does this mean in evolutionary terms and in relation with nonhuman creatures that share some capacity for morality, even if the biological or psychological basis for that potentiality may or may not be different from that in humans? To probe this question in more depth, we need a short excursus on theodicy

---

28. See discussion in Gregory Peterson, "Falling Up: Evolution and Original Sin," in *Evolution and Ethics: Human Morality in Biological and Religious Perspective*, ed. Philip Clayton and Jeffrey Schloss, 273–86 (Grand Rapids: Eerdmans, 2004).

as that which can be extended in evolutionary terms. This will set the compass for various meanings of the atonement and their interpretation.

5.2 Evolution: The Theodicy Problem

Discussions about theodicy have arisen in the context of science and religion debates about God's intervention in the world. God's immanence in the world is stressed, but the issue then surfaces as to how to deal with the affirmation of a good God working within the world in spite of the extent of natural evil and suffering. What is missed, characteristically, is a theological response to theodicy by consideration of the meaning of the atonement, even though redemption is often discussed in broad eschatological terms. I am briefly reviewing this discussion here in order to situate a discussion of atonement theory, for I suggest that an enlarged discussion of atonement and redemption considered from a *christological* perspective can meet some of the challenges raised by contemporary discussions of theodicy from an *evolutionary* perspective. Christopher Southgate suggests that there are three facets of evolutionary suffering.[29] The first is an ontological issue, namely, *that* God gives existence to a world that contains nonhuman suffering, death, and extinction. Second, the teleological issue is *why* God would have chosen this means, including extinction of species, to create free, self-conscious human beings. Third, if nonhuman species are viewed in terms of redemption, then soteriological issues need to be addressed.

I agree with Southgate that to dismiss the problem is not an option for those who believe in God as Creator. Polkinghorne's "free process" defense of physical evil is elaborated further in Thomas Tracy's analysis, where sentience arises through evolutionary suffering.[30] It also has analogies with Arthur Peacocke's suggestion that suffering is a necessary aspect of the overall evolutionary process.[31] Southgate suggests that these positions will

---

29. Christopher Southgate, "God and Evolutionary Evil: Theodicy in the Light of Darwinism," *Zygon* 37, no. 4 (2002): 803–21. Christopher Southgate's monograph was published as this book goes to press. C. Southgate, *The Groaning of Creation: God, Evolution and the Problem of Evil* (Louisville: John Knox, 2008).

30. John Polkinghorne, *Science and Providence* (Philadelphia: Templeton Foundation Press, 2005; London: SPCK, 1989); and *Science and the Trinity: The Christian Encounter with Reality* (London: SPCK, 2004).

31. A. Peacocke, "The Cost of New Life," in *The Work of Love: Creation as Kenosis*, ed. John Polkinghorne, 21–42 (London: SPCK, 2001).

work when combined with redemption; that is, some ultimate good will befall such species. I am perfectly in favor of introducing a redemptive element into discussions of theodicy, and I also think it is important to avoid "thin" descriptions that confine discussion to philosophical speculation about theodicy. However, I suggest that using the language of *necessary* suffering (where this appears) is somewhat misleading, for it still implies that suffering is *required* as part of the overall process, including processes in the far-flung future, and eschatology is in danger of being misused as a way of *justifying* suffering. It is here that I think Reinhold Niebuhr's account is helpful, for his description of sin as "unnecessary, but inevitable"[32] could also be ascribed to evolutionary suffering. Hence, while I agree with authors such as Southgate who claim that "suffering is *intrinsic* to a biosphere that evolves by natural selection,"[33] I believe that the language of *necessity* used by Arthur Peacocke, for example, implies an affirmation of suffering, especially perhaps if this is then dealt with through a purely teleological model of theodicy, which might soften the horror of such suffering.

Certainly, teleological proposals that seek to address the problems in evolutionary theodicy are an essential element of the way theology might address the issues, but I suggest they are never *sufficient* to deal with the extent and depth of evolutionary ills.[34] In addition, I suggest that addressing

---

32. Reinhold Niebuhr, *The Nature and Destiny of Man*, (New York: Charles Scriber's Sons, 1941), also cited in R. J. Russell, *Cosmology, Evolution and Resurrection Hope* (Kitchener: Pandora, 2006), 31. Bob Russell also takes up this idea and enlarges it in his description both downward to the level of biology and physics and backward to the history of life on earth and the very beginnings of the cosmos. He suggests that once we reflect on the way this particular universe has made life possible, then the laws of thermodynamics and other constants offer a way of thinking about contingency that makes the reality of natural evil inevitable, without making it a principle of life. Of course, this view relies on a speculation that the laws of nature in the new creation will not be identical to the ones that pertain in this world. See Robert John Russell, "Natural Theodicy in an Evolutionary Context: The Need for an Eschatology of New Creation," in *The Task of Theology Today*, vol. 5, ed. David Neville and Bruce Barber, 121–52 (Hundmarsh, Australia: ATF, 2005). I find this suggestion very attractive in terms of how the future might be envisaged as free from evil, but I am less sure that this really eliminates the problem of natural evil being somehow necessary to life as we know it *in this world*, even if not inevitable to life in the eschaton. In other words, it is an eschatological reading of the dilemma; what is projected for the eschaton is used as a means to interpret the present.

33. Christopher Southgate, personal communication, January 5, 2007. Italics mine.

34. It is worth noting that Southgate never claims that teleological processes are sufficient, and argues for a combination approach. However, he seems to put most

the problem philosophically, such as through notions of free process defense, has the unfortunate effect of seeming to affirm suffering in the natural world. The line of reasoning is that if only we could see the overall impact of a particular evil, then it would be seen in the long run to be working for the good, in terms of affirming either free will or some other property of human nature. Unfortunately, such a line of reasoning breaks down when horrendous evils are considered, where there is no possible benefit for the individual concerned.[35] This is as true in the nonhuman world through, for example, mass extinctions as it is in the human world.

Instead of viewing future hope for qualities such as freedom or even hope for redemption as relieving the pressure of suffering, or even providing justification for it, eschatology always needs to be a theological *response* to suffering, while recognizing that the mystery of evil remains. Holmes Rolston's suggestion that the world is cruciform through being marked with suffering is an example of where the idea of necessity seems to take us, for it implies that suffering is a principle that is inevitably built into the universe in a way that cannot be challenged.[36] Southgate, in a similar manner, seems to endorse a view of the cross as that which epitomizes or represents the evolutionary suffering in the world.[37] The notion of cruciform nature, like free process defense, also seems to subtly endorse such suffering rather than giving the moral imperative to seek its amelioration. Why should we help suffering animals on the way to extinction if such processes are part of cruciform existence that cannot ultimately be changed or challenged? Why should we do anything about climate change if all is inevitably going to come right in the future?

Another strategy for theodicy is to elaborate the idea of kenosis, of God willing to risk all for the sake of an emerging beauty. I have discussed in chapter 3 arguments in favor of using kenosis confined to a christological sense. But there are helpful and unhelpful ways of using kenotic imagery in relation to the Godhead. Extending kenosis to include God is, in my view, far more problematic if it envisages some sort of spatial withdrawal

---

emphasis on teleological arguments and to accept the idea of evolutionary suffering as *necessary* for the emergence of freely conscious beings.

35. For discussion of horrendous evils, see Marilyn McCord Adams, *Horrendous Evils and the Goodness of God* (Ithaca: Cornell University Press, 1999).

36. Holmes Rolston III, "Naturalising and Systematizing Evil," in *Is Nature Ever Evil? Religion, Science and Value*, ed. Willem B. Drees, 67–86 (London: Routledge, 2003).

37. Southgate, *Groaning of Creation*, 75–77.

prior to self-involvement, as in Moltmann's account.[38] Where kenosis of incarnation speaks of an attitude of self-giving, then, arguably, the movement of the Son in relation to the Father has some parallels with the self-giving that is a permanent feature of relationships among the persons of the Trinity. But the view of theologians influenced by process thought, including John Haught, needs to be clearly distinguished from the understanding of kenosis in Hans Urs von Balthasar. The former seem to envisage the identity of God reflected in close entanglement with the world. For Haught, "The depth beneath all perishing bears the stamp of everlasting care and promise. . . . This same divine care takes into itself all of the suffering, discord, tragedy and enjoyment in biological evolution and cosmic unfolding, as well as in human history."[39] This is rather less inclined toward necessity than are other strategies I have mentioned, but it may leave the impression of a rather limp view of God as totally involved in creation but powerless to make changes.

Southgate criticizes the anthropocentrism that has dogged much discussion of theodicy, but then, perhaps surprisingly in view of this criticism, he puts humanity in a strong position as co-redeemers of suffering, evolved creation. In other words, he is highly optimistic about the intervention of humans in evolution. Much of the current suffering of nonhuman nature has emerged through human impacts on the natural world, either directly through exploitative practices or indirectly through disruption of habitats following settlement or climate change effects. I prefer then to see this as a distinct category of *anthropogenic evil*, that is, evils leading to suffering in the nonhuman sphere that arise specifically out of human actions. In this respect, repentance and reconciliation through careful balancing of the needs of the human and nonhuman world would seem to be a more appropriate stance of humanity vis-à-vis nonhuman creation, rather than aspirations toward co-redemption, even if the latter implies the *improvement* of nonhuman nature in human "partnership with God's redeeming of evolution."[40] The latter has the added unfortunate effect of lessening the depth of human sin by suggesting that we have the capacity to ameliorate the ills that confront the human and nonhuman worlds. The supposed

---

38. For more on Moltmann, see discussion later in this chapter.

39. John Haught, *Deeper Than Darwin: The Prospect for Religion in the Age of Evolution* (Boulder: Westview, 2003), 158.

40. Southgate, personal communication, January 7, 2007.

"partnership with God's redeeming" almost bypasses considerations of the cross in order to alleviate evolutionary ills.

In other words, I am arguing that from a theological point of view, many different varieties of theodicy show themselves up as inadequate, as in all sorts of ways they seem to *reconcile* us to evils, rather than deal with their awful impact.[41] Even separating evil into moral evil and natural evil does not do justice to the fact that evils may not always arise through moral choice (moral evil) or a natural effect (natural evil). I have suggested, in this section, an additional category of anthropogenic evil (evils suffered in the nonhuman sphere as a result of human activity). In addition, the idea of "soul making" in the human sphere or "free process" defense in the non-human sphere suggests that God has to withdraw in some measure in order to allow genuine freedom to be possible, setting up a clash between God's freedom and that of God's creatures. This view is very much colored by Enlightenment dreams of individualism, independence, and autonomy.

Classic Christian theology specifically addresses the problem of evil and suffering through those facets of Christology that focus on the atonement, but once that Christology is shorn of its distinctive elements, it no longer seems to be effective in meeting the challenge. While such reflection cannot explain *why* God permits evils to occur, a broadening and revision of the classic agenda of Christology opens up the possibility of co-redemption understood not from the perspective of humanity, but from the perspective of God in Christ as redeemer of all facets of creation, both human and nonhuman.

5.3 Atonement of Nature

While Southgate's treatment of atonement is very brief, I do have sympathy with his view that the atonement represents far more than simply a subjective event in the minds of human believers. Yet the way different models of atonement have been set up in order to deal with "sin" assumes that the recipients of the benefits of the atonement are only human subjects. The point here is that there is an unacknowledged disjunction between cosmic models of *Christology* that stress cosmic redemption and narrow versions

---

41. For a critical discussion, see Kenneth Surin, *Theology and the Problems of Evil* (Oxford: Blackwell, 1986); and Terrence Tilley, *The Evils of Theodicy* (Washington, D.C.: Georgetown University Press, 1991). Further discussion is in Karen Kilby, "Evil and the Limits of Theology," *New Blackfriars* 84, no. 983 (January 2003): 13–29.

of *atonement* that confine Christ's atoning work to human beneficiaries, whether in the broad objective sense or narrow subjective sense.

It is appropriate at this stage of the argument to challenge some of the traditional ways of speaking about the atonement as being woefully inadequate. In this, I share many of LeRon Shults's concerns with the traditional language of the atonement.[42] He identifies, for example, a tendency in early patristic thought to rely on dualistic Platonic notions of universal humanity, an abstract *humanum* to which the Logos is united, a *humanum* that is still in need of redemption. Aquinas modified this by supposing that universals exist in particular individuals, rather than outside them, but he leaned toward a satisfaction model. Later interpreters, following William of Ockham's nominalism, abandoned any universal ideal altogether and opted for more individualistic interpretations. Luther, for example, put emphasis on the victory of Christ over the devil. This individualism laid the burden more squarely on individual believers and their evil intentions or actions, rather than viewing atonement in social terms. Specific concepts of law and order have also influenced theories of atonement, the image of ransom being popular in the early patristic period. This uncomfortable undertow that God somehow needs legal satisfaction for sin predominates in many classic theological accounts of the atonement.

The difficulty remains in how to continue to affirm the holiness of God while avoiding images that seem to present God as vengeful, demanding violence as payment for violence though a particular penal system. Even contemporary scholars who have welcomed an understanding of God as primarily a God of love find difficulties in expressing an adequate portrait of the atonement. For example, in Moltmann's earlier account of the crucified God, he envisages Christ as one who represents the human community in an objective way, substituting for human beings through "taking our place."[43] Several questions follow: In what sense does atonement need to be revisited in the light of these classic traditions? What elements can be retained, and how might subjective elements of the atonement be married to more objective interpretations that, arguably, are more promising in their potential capacity for extension to nonhuman creatures? And in what sense can atonement be broadened to include *all creatures*, not just those with moral capacities?

---

42. F. LeRon Shults, *Christology and Science* (Aldershot: Ashgate, 2008), 68–74.
43. J. Moltmann, *The Crucified God* (London: SCM, 1974), 184.

Of course, we are bedeviled once again by the question of definitions. If we define atonement as at-one-ment with God, in the sense that there has been a deliberate turning away from purposes intended by God, then deliberateness implies a sense of freedom, which can only reasonably be found in animals. If we define atonement strictly in terms of "sin," understood as self-conscious turning away from God, then it could only apply to humans. More broadly still, if we define at-one-ment simply in terms of the hoped-for freedom from pain and unity with God in heaven, then atonement becomes virtually equivalent to redemption. There are undoubted difficulties in envisaging atonement if it means satisfaction of the wrath of a vengeful God. This may be one reason why many theologians prefer not to use the language of atonement at all when speaking about the non-human world, but instead rely on the language of redemption.[44] This is certainly a more comfortable position to adopt in many respects: after all, redemption in its breadth of transformation can take up natural as well as moral evil—indeed, all the ills of the world—in its scope. It is much easier to avoid the more uncomfortable notion of atonement altogether and to speak simply of the cross (or incarnation) of Christ as the means for the redemption of the earth. The questions then return: How and in what sense might the cross be salvific for all creation, and are atonement theories rendered redundant?

Jürgen Moltmann has, especially in his later work, more explicitly widened the scope of Christ's action on the cross as inclusive of nonhuman creation. He suggests, "If Christ is the firstborn of the dead, then he cannot be merely 'the new Adam' of a new humanity. He must also be understood as the firstborn of the whole creation. He is present not only in the human victims of world history, but in victimized nature too."[45] Such an understanding of co-suffering and co-presence with has some similarity to Ruth Page's understanding of God as "companioning" the natural world in its

---

44. This is the route taken by Denis Edwards, and in many respects I have sympathy with this position. His equation of incarnation with redemption means that difficulties associated with the cross as such do not come into the foreground. See D. Edwards, "The Redemption of Animals in an Incarnational Theology," in Deane-Drummond and Clough, *Creaturely Theology.*

45. Jürgen Moltmann, *The Way of Jesus Christ* (London: SCM, 1990), 278–79. The fact that this later view does not cohere well with his earlier work that tended toward penal substitution theory) seems to show some inconsistency, for even if we claim that penal substitution is necessary only for humans, it still creates the impression that the victims for whom Christ died are solely human, rather than other animal kinds.

suffering.[46] The difference is that Moltmann envisages such companioning in a *christological* perspective, whereas Page speaks of such companioning in terms of God. The question is, if God is merely companioning the world, to what extent is God also involved in its continuing creation? A Trinitarian perspective on creation and redemption is necessary in this respect, as the suffering or companioning in God needs to express itself christologically, for the incarnation of Christ means not just that God companions the world in its suffering, but rather also shares and enters fully into that material suffering creation in the dereliction of Jesus on the cross.

I suggest that penal substitution theories, especially represented by the earlier work of Moltmann, are unconvincing because of their tendency to view sin as that which requires punishment; here God's holiness somehow demands retribution in some form, even on an innocent victim. Yet this notion of God punishing the Son is clearly at odds with God envisaged as a God of love, so the cross of Christ instead needs to be seen in the first place as the result of human sinful tendencies, and only in the second place as the action of God in making right and reconciling the evils of the world. Atonement theories that simply highlight the distinction between those whose sins are acquitted through faith in Christ and his cross and those whose sins remain set up an unhelpful disjunction between us and them that arguably goes against the very purpose of the cross, namely, its power of reconciliation and peace making.[47] It is one reason why Jürgen Moltmann, drawing on Martin Luther's theology of the cross, has attempted to correct this impression by also seeing Christ's suffering as being *shared* by God. However, this creates other difficulties, for how can a God who simply shares in the suffering of the world also be effective as one who redeems the world? Such self-giving for Moltmann is also a process of self-emptying, a kenotic Christology that even reaches back to the earliest creation of the world, when God makes space for God in divine withdrawal.[48]

Even Abelard's classic notion of Christ as "moral example" does not seem appropriate when considering nonhuman animal behavior. Abelard's belief in Christ as moral exemplar might take us closer to the notion of

---

46. See Ruth Page, *God and the Web of Creation* (London: SCM, 1996), 81–168.

47. On a philosophical discussion of the cultural roots of us and them, see Shults, *Christology and Science*, 81–88.

48. I am less convinced by the extension of kenosis into a process of creation itself, even though this has also been a popular move among those engaged in the science and religion discussion. See J. Polkinghorne, *The Work of Love* (London: SPCK, 2001).

incipient vice and virtue in other animals, but then we are left with the problem of how and in what sense Christ can possibly be an example for non-human animals, which might be able to empathize with human beings in many respects, but could hardly be expected to conceptualize an ideal. Such is the stuff of three-dimensional language rather than two-dimensional language.

A more pressing issue that concerns us here is *what kind of atonement theory, if any,* might be most useful in consideration of the nonhuman world. Certainly, there is little sense in which the nonhuman world could be thought of as "godless," if this implies a deliberate turning away from God that often creeps into discussions of the significance of the atonement. Yet the strongest theme in Moltmann's account of the atonement seems to be that of *suffering* as a working metaphor for the atonement.[49] Suffering, of course, is sufficiently general to apply to all sentient creatures, including nonhumans. There are, however, theological problems in identifying God as paradigmatically one who suffers. In the first place, it seems that God is changed through that suffering, so that God is now dependent on external circumstances in order to be God. Furthermore, the question of theodicy is intact, for even if God suffers, then this does not necessarily diminish the responsibility of God for that suffering. In addition, Moltmann's theology needs to be interpreted in the light of his understanding of Christ's suffering from the perspective of the resurrection. This gives a stronger account of a God who acts decisively to raise Christ from the dead, and as such, it offers the possibility of hope for all creaturely beings, not just humankind.

Niels Gregersen has also drawn on Luther's theology of the cross in order to provide a commentary on evolutionary suffering.[50] He is traditional inasmuch as he divides evolutionary pain from human sin, while I have suggested that the category is more blurred in terms of recognizing the possibility of moral choice in animals and the contribution of anthropogenic sin to the evolutionary pain of creatures inasmuch as some, at least, are forced into extinction either directly or indirectly by human activities. He recognizes that while Luther himself did not extend his reflection on the significance of the cross to include evolutionary suffering,

---

49. This aspect is discussed in relation to the natural world in Dee Carter, "Foregrounding the Environment: The Redemption of Nature and Jürgen Moltmann's Theology," *Ecotheology* 10 (2001): 70–83.

50. Niels Gregersen, "The Cross of Christ in an Evolutionary World," *Dialog* 40, no. 3 (2001): 192–207.

his affirmation of the natural world is inherent in his thought, so that his theology of the cross is not so much anti-natural as anti-legalistic. He criticizes Luther's teleology inasmuch as it seems to suggest a deliberate, alien work of destruction prior to the work of grace. To view natural selection as a work of divine wrath or human agency is misplaced, so in this sense, Luther's teleological framework needs some adjustment. Luther's particular focus was on human pride that claimed wisdom for itself. While Luther's model of the cross may be appropriate in this context, Gregersen is correct to identify problems with his model when stretched to include creation, echoed in views developed by Johann Gerhardt that the created world has to be annihilated in order that new creation may come.

Nonetheless, Gregersen, while accepting that natural selection is "amoral," believes that the woes of evolutionary processes are part of a "package deal," though it is not entirely clear whether his position is constitutive, such as some models of aesthetics that include the idea of ugliness, or process, that is, including a teleological orientation.[51] His stress on complexification as that which emerges in an evolutionary context implies the latter. Gregersen also uses what he terms a Christology of identity, that is, a Christology that identifies Jesus with God in God's glory. He resolves the tension with a focus on the cross in Luther by reference to the New Testament interpretation of the eschatological vision of Isaiah, Christ as Suffering Servant. He suggests, "God's heavenly glory is stretched so as to encompass the soil of the cruciform creation." Jesus is also, according to him, "an *icon of a loser in the evolutionary arms race*."[52] He then extends this to the action of God, so that "God, the giver of life, who produced the package deal of natural order and disorder, is also the co-carrier of the costs of creation."[53]

Yet we might ask ourselves whether this is sufficient as a way of dealing with the atonement. Gregersen recognizes this inasmuch as he argues for Jesus' suffering as not just *with others*, but *for others* as well, in a way that transforms suffering. He uses Luther's concept of "happy exchange," such that all the pains and ills known to humanity, including a descent into hell, are experienced by Christ on the cross but in themselves defeated and

---

51. I have reviewed the various models of theodicy in an evolutionary context further in C. Deane-Drummond, *Ecotheology* (London: Darton, Longman & Todd, 2008), 114–29.

52. Gregersen, "Cross of Christ," 203. He also includes the idea of Jesus as outlaw in order to encompass the social dimension, those who lose out in social competition.

53. Ibid., 204. Original all in italics.

transformed. Gregersen presses for an extension of this exchange to take place between all creatures and the suffering Christ, not just humanity. Yet he still, somewhat surprisingly, uses the language of sin to describe this exchange, though he does not seem to attribute moral agency to nonhuman creatures. Hence, "what is annihilated is sin, what is preserved yet transcended is the essence of the creature. This is the logic of superabundance that follows out of the divine Spirit who is always in exchange, always communicating with creatures and always sharing itself with the creatures."[54]

This illustrates, of course, the difficulties of expressing the atonement in a way that both deals adequately with the need for *reconciliation* between a holy God and humanity, including the depths of human depravity and sin, and includes the ills that are characteristic of the evolutionary world, as discussed previously in this chapter. Moreover, how can God be thought of as holy, exercising justice, while refraining from dualistic approaches that seem to pitch evil against God, even in the work on the cross? Are such dualistic tendencies in evidence in Luther's portrait of the cross as some kind of "mighty duel" with human sin, death, and hell, through which Christ ends up as victor in the struggle?[55]

Hans Urs von Balthasar takes up the Reformed tradition as represented in the work of the Lutheran Gustaf Aulen in order to develop his portrait of Christ's dramatic struggle at the heart of atonement.[56] Aulen distinguishes the biblical and patristic type of atonement theory that he finds in Luther, and names as both classical and dramatic from the "objective" type of atonement theory found in Anselm and the subjective type found in Abelard. Aulen recognized that the idea of an alien evil in the world is harder to accept today, but even if it is accepted, God cannot defeat such an evil by an external power. Instead, God's opposition must be carried out from within, rather than outside, world history. Yet such opposition should not be thought of in dualistic ways; rather, "even hostile powers must finally serve his all embracing design for the world," so that we can think of this as an inner conflict between wrath and love in God, where love is always deeper than wrath. For Balthasar, the "dramatic" dimension is key, so that

---

54. Ibid., 205.

55. See, for example, Martin Luther, "The Freedom of a Christian," in *Martin Luther: Selections from His Writings*, ed. John Dillenberger (New York: Doubleday, 1962), 61. Gregersen also cites this passage, but he does not comment on its dualistic philosophy.

56. Hans Urs von Balthasar, *Theo-Drama* 2, trans. Graham Harrison (San Francisco: Ignatius, 1990), 159 (hereafter cited as *TD* 2).

in "Christ, God personally steps onto the stage, to engage in 'close combat' and vanquish powers that enslave man."[57] The drama of Christ is such that God is portrayed as one who "conquers by total self-surrender." Terms such as *satisfaction* used by Anselm imply that God somehow changes God's mind through a human act according to a legal pattern of justice. In the third, "subjectivist" type, adopted by Schleiermacher, redemption means moral transformation of a subject, and Jesus' action is only relevant inasmuch as he is teacher and moral exemplar. The significance of Aulen for Balthasar is that he believes the conflict between God and evil needs to be expressed in such a way that it is neither monistic nor dualistic, but is *dramatic*. Balthasar is also not troubled by the metaphorical use of battle, since, for him, even when extending this to the drama of discipleship, it always refers to a spiritual battle for the sake of the gospel of peace.[58] This dramatic possibility, it seems to me, successfully gets around some of the problems we have encountered already between a subjective atonement that is inevitably confined to humans and an objective cosmic atonement that seems to detach Christ from his ordinary human existence.

Balthasar's discussion of the atonement comes out most clearly in the fourth volume of *Theo-Drama*. Here he finds the struggle on the cross that Luther speaks about formulated in paradoxical ways. But he finds the absoluteness of Luther's concept of "exchange" troubling, for *sola fides* is not consistent with the idea of Christ as effecting an objective exchange with sinful humanity, and seems more like a human achievement.[59] He is particularly critical of Luther's "union of opposites" as that which "affects his entire theology."[60] The struggle between opposites is even within God, so that on the cross, grace is embroiled with sin, and sin imbibed with grace. In a parallel anthropology, Christ's becoming sin is matched by humanity's

---

57. Ibid., 161. Balthasar considered pride to be the root of sin, a lack of obedience to God. Ben Quash considers this to be inadequate compared with Barth, who allows for a richer conception of sin, which includes tendencies such as sloth. Although Quash posits indifference as the solution to the tendency to pride, indifference has a more active tendency than he implies, and this is epitomized in Balthasar's account of the active role of Christ in the drama of the atonement. See Ben Quash, *Theology and the Drama of History* (Cambridge: Cambridge University Press, 2005), 156–57.

58. Balthasar, *TD* 2, 165. He may also have in his mind the chivalry that is encouraged by Ignatian spirituality.

59. Hans Urs von Balthasar, *Theo-Drama* 4, trans. Graham Harrison (San Francisco: Ignatius, 1994), 288 (hereafter cited as *TD* 4).

60. Ibid., 289.

becoming righteous through faith alone (*sola fide*). For Balthasar, the illogical nature of the notion of "exchange" comes to the surface, since the act of faith is not synchronous with Christ's act, and the only synchronous event is objective change of status of humanity. In relation to what Luther terms the "first righteousness" won through faith, human righteousness only finds its expression through opposites. Hence, grace only appears in wrath, heaven is only reached by going through hell, and so on. Luther's so-called "second righteousness" is that following the call of the believer to holiness in response to the ongoing sin found in the world. In particular, Balthasar objects to the lack of attention to subjectivity in human life that seems to follow from Luther's interpretation of drama. More important, for Balthasar, Luther's drama fails to deal adequately with the other drama, which presupposes the existence of ordinary human persons, who moreover are persons constituted not just by faith alone, but in love. He also criticizes Moltmann, who draws heavily on Luther and, according to Balthasar, portrays God as the one who loads sin onto Jesus in vicarious punishment.[61]

Balthasar is equally sharply critical of René Girard and other theologians who demythologize Old Testament accounts of God, transforming God from wrathful to powerless.[62] He is particularly critical of "scapegoat" theories of Girard. Such theories have been developed by authors such as Mark Heim, but Heim arguably shares Balthasar's concern not to represent God either as one who sanctions violence or as one whose work is tied to a particular legal system.[63] He also criticizes theories, as in Pannenberg, that imply that only humans cast their sin onto the Lamb of God, as this implies that redemption was the initiative of human action.

Yet there is a tension here that Balthasar does not fully address. On the one hand, if the cross is the initiative of God, then it implies a God who is vindictive; on the other hand, if the cross is an outcome of human sin, it implies human initiative. In this respect, it is perhaps more reasonable to suggest that more anthropological interpretations represent a genuine interpretation at this level, that is, show up the atonement in terms that

---

61. Balthasar finds this tendency in Luther's portrait as well. Ibid., 295, 317.

62. Ibid., 298–313.

63. Mark Heim, *Saved from Sacrifice: A Theology of the Cross* (Grand Rapids: Eerdmans, 2006). The advantage of Heim's interpretation and others that follow in the wake of Girard is that they pay sufficient attention to cultural anthropology. For this reason, LeRon Shults welcomes such an approach. See F. LeRon Shults, *Christology and Science* (Aldershot: Ashgate, 2008), 88–93.

are reasonable at this level. The difficulty, however, that Balthasar seems to be struggling with here is that authors such as Girard seem to reduce the significance of the cross to a particular anthropological interpretation, thus suffering from the limitation of earlier theories, though cast in a different mold. Balthasar holds out against this while, perhaps, being too glib in his dismissal of alternatives and not always sufficiently acknowledging the inevitable cultural embeddedness of his own position.

Balthasar favors the Trinitarian perspective taken by Sergii Bulgakov and uses this to develop his own position on the meaning of the atonement that seeks to weave in a number of different strands from different theories.[64] For the present chapter, the most significant aspect of Balthasar's dramatic theory of the atonement is that not only does it attempt to reclaim the importance of consideration of the holiness of God; it also seeks to give due weight to human responsiveness or, as we might suggest, *creaturely* responsiveness in kinship with other creatures. The importance of this scene in the drama for Balthasar is essential; for him, "God's entire world drama hinges on this scene. This is the theo-drama into which the world and God have their ultimate input; here absolute freedom enters into created freedom, interacts with created freedom and acts as created freedom."[65]

In interpreting the cross in a Trinitarian way, Balthasar puts particular emphasis on the love of God for the world in giving up his Son, so that all that the Son suffered is understood as being attributed to this love. In particular, he intends to stress the cross as the *revelation* of the Trinity, rather than the *actualization* of the Trinity.[66] Such identification found in the latter is, for Balthasar, particularly troubling, for now death is located in God, and salvation is expressed in Hegelian terms as the negation (expiation) of the negation (sin).[67] Instead, Balthasar favors the view of the immanent Trinity that allows an eternal, absolute self-surrender that in turn explains

---

64. Moltmann also favors a Trinitarian perspective in his later work, and Balthasar would, no doubt, have warmed more to the perspectives represented in these works than to those in his earlier *Crucified God*.

65. Balthasar, *TD* 4, 318.

66. Balthasar finds the latter in Moltmann's doctrine, as expressed in *The Crucified God*, which is an inevitable result of a combination of Hegelian influence and equation of the immanent Trinity with the economic Trinity.

67. Balthasar, *TD* 4, 322. He is commenting here on Moltmann's treatment of internal divine processes being equated with salvation history, leading to language about the "suffering of God."

God's self-giving to the world as love, without suggesting that God somehow needed either the world process or the cross in order to become God. He suggests, therefore, that the Trinity exists in self-surrender in the generation of the Son in an initial kenosis within the Godhead that underpins all other kenosis. Balthasar therefore rejects the idea that God suffers in the manner of creaturely suffering, but also recognizes that God grounds the possibility of that suffering, and "something happens in God that not only justifies the possibility and actual occurrence of all suffering in the world but also justifies God's sharing in the latter, in which he goes to the length of vicariously taking on man's God-lessness."[68] While he recognizes that this means "to walk on a knife edge," his concept of suffering that is in solidarity without identity is convincing to some extent. Of course, Jesus, in his God-humanity, is also one who would share fully in human suffering to the extent that we may be able to say rather more as to what that solidarity with suffering implies.

Balthasar also resists any notion of the suffering in God as being somehow abstract, which lacks the seriousness of real pain and death. The Father does not, in other words, extinguish himself in the self-giving. He also rejects the idea that just because this drama of what he calls the "primal kenosis" is abstract, then this also leads us to compensate in some way and "imagine that the divine drama only acquires its dynamism and its many hues by going through a created, temporal world and only acquires its seriousness and depth by going through sin, the Cross and hell."[69] Such a compensation is, rather, an expression of hubris, as if it is only in a human drama that God may extract Godself from a trap God has set. Rather, "it is the drama of the 'emptying' of the Father's heart, in the generation of the Son, that contains and surpasses all possible drama between God and a world."[70] In saying this, he is attempting to avoid the difficulties of mythology that claim God has to be involved in the world process while adhering to what happens on the world stage as such. Yet concerning *what* Balthasar claims Christ to have carried on the cross, it is the load of the world's No to God—that is, an existential acceptance by Christ, rather than being imposed from the outside, so that there is "an inner appropriation of what is ungodly and hostile to God, and

---

68. Ibid., 324.
69. Ibid., 326.
70. Ibid., 327.

identification with that darkness of alienation from God into which the sinner falls as a result of his No."[71]

Yet it is also equally possible to extend the existential burden that we understand that Christ was accepting to include not just human sin in isolation, but also the negative weight of evils as understood in terms of evolved creaturely being as such. Without such extension, the death of Christ becomes expressed just in terms of human weakness and need for human reconciliation with God. While the latter should not be minimized, especially in the light of anthropogenic sin and all that this implies for creaturely suffering, I am arguing here for a more thoroughgoing compass to the scope of the atoning work of Christ, such that it takes up and includes the voice of all creaturely Nos, including and especially that of humankind. This also has the advantage of providing a link between the dramatic human history of Christ and wider significance of Christ for the cosmos, as presented in chapter 3. As indicated in the next section, in naming the wisdom of the cross as the wisdom of God, Paul had in mind the widest possible scope of Christ's reconciling and redeeming work.

5.4 Viewing Atonement through Shadow Sophia

While keeping this dramatic backdrop in view, in order to go further into the possibilities for the meaning of the atonement, I suggest we need to recover once more the sense of Jesus as Sophia. The background to this discussion is the idea of Christ as divine Wisdom, the wisdom of the cross, where the movement of creation and redemption in Christ is expressed in sophianic language.[72] This is why Hans Urs von Balthasar claims that at the crucifixion, Christ most fully expresses the Word made flesh and his full humanity.[73]

While creaturely wisdom is in concert with divine Wisdom in the creation of the world, the two come together perfectly in the person of Christ. Sergii Bulgakov used the term *shadow sophia* in speaking of the dark side of creaturely wisdom, though it is very important to stress that there was

---

71. Ibid., 334–35.

72. Colossians 1:15-23 speaks of this double movement of creation and redemption through the cross and, significantly, is inclusive of not just the human community, but the community of creation as well.

73. Mark McIntosh, *Christology from Within: Spirituality and the Incarnation in Hans Urs Von Balthasar* (Notre Dame: University of Notre Dame, 1996), 89–90.

no such shadow side to the creaturely wisdom found in Christ, for he was without sin. Shadow sophia, for Bulgakov, expresses the dark possibility of evil in the world. He also considered that evil was not ontologically in competition with the good, for that would suppose a radical dualism; rather, evil is (as in Aquinas) a privation of the good, a state of creaturely being, or rather nonbeing.[74] Yet, as in the classical account, we are not told *why* there is a privation of the good, or where this lack comes from. More often than not, he links sophia's shadow more specifically with the mission of the church, rather than a theology of creation as such, and he views shadow sophia as emerging only after the fall of humanity.[75] It is important, perhaps, to emphasize that shadow sophia is not present in any shape or form in divine Sophia. The uniqueness of Bulgakov's view is in his ability to distinguish clearly between divine Sophia and creaturely sophia, and only the latter is subject to a shadow side, not divine Sophia. Evil is nowhere present with the Creator, but rather, shadow sophia arises along with creaturely sophia.[76]

Bulgakov suggests that after the fall, humanity falls *under* the power of nature because humanity has the mistaken belief that higher spiritual knowledge can be attained through the elements of this world alone. Such a belief, he suggests, means that nature now is vulnerable to nonbeing and chaos, thus expressing the dark face of fallen sophia.[77] In consideration of the effects of the fall, Bulgakov seems to take the view that the beauty of nature is "arrested" by the darkness existing in creaturely sophia after the fall of humanity. The beauty of nature has no moral attributes; it is neither good nor evil in the sense of moral decision making. However, following

---

74. See chapter 3 in S. Bulgakov, *The Bride of the Lamb* (Grand Rapids: Eerdmans, 2002).

75. Bulgakov speaks of evil as a "shadow" and "illusion," which tends to weaken its force, for evil is associated with misdirected freedom, which "sooner or later must wither before the radiance of Wisdom." S. Bulgakov, *Sophia, the Wisdom of God: An Outline of Sophiology* (1st Russian ed., 1937; Hudson: Lindisfarne, 1993), 147.

76. I am using the lowercase *sophia* in this case to make it quite clear that the shadow side of sophia is not inherent in God, nor is it a metaphysical term, except inasmuch as the wisdom of the cross takes shadow sophia into itself, and the cross is an offering of love that counters the depths of suffering and evil in the human and nonhuman worlds. Moreover, creaturely sophia is created by God and is distinct from God in an analogous way, perhaps, to the classic idea of secondary causes used by authors such as Bill Stoeger and Denis Edwards.

77. C. Graves, *The Holy Spirit in the Theology of Sergius Bulgakov* (Geneva: WCC, 1972), 28.

the fall, humanity begins to direct undo attention to beauty in the created world, so that it becomes the object of human possession and thereby an occasion for sin. In this sense, it is impossible for the Holy Spirit to enkindle the universal spiritual transfiguration of creation until the parousia, but in the meantime, the Holy Spirit acts as the "natural grace of creation," working toward the sophianizing of the created world, when creaturely sophia will be united with divine Sophia, and God will be all in all.[78]

In the light of the earlier discussion of social behavior in animals, Bulgakov's understanding clearly needs some modification. There are, though, some elements of his thinking that are worth preserving. In the first place, we can affirm that evil is not a "substance" or a "principle" of creation in the manner implied in some more contemporary accounts, but in many situations operates as an absence or privation of the good. As discussed in section 5.2, even, for example, speaking of the natural world as "cruciform" (as is notorious in Holmes Rolston's work) has the unfortunate effect of suggesting the necessity of evil.[79] However, Bulgakov in speaking of evil as a "shadow" and "illusion" perhaps tends to weaken its force too much in the other direction, for evil according to Bulgakov is associated with misdirected freedom, which "sooner or later must wither before the radiance of Wisdom."[80] The fall, instead, needs to be seen as the *culmination* of tendencies already latent in the natural world, rather than a specific work of a mythological figure of Satan. Bulgakov does seem to hint at this possibility in statements such as these: "Creaturely creativity entails not only the possibility but also the inevitability of errors, which in themselves are not yet evil, but prepare a place for evil," and "Man, being called to perfect and create himself, is most marked by imperfection and limitation."[81] In this sense, while it is true that humanity's impact on the material world expresses the shadow side of sophia as the alternative face to human wisdom, shadow sophia is also implicit as a possibility from the very beginning of creaturely existence, just as natural wisdom in the creaturely world eventually finds its expression in human wisdom. I am less convinced that shadow sophia can be thought of as *constitutive* to creaturely wisdom, unless we read this

---

78. Ibid., 233–34.

79. Rolston, "Naturalising and Systematizing Evil." He reiterates this in a section of the introduction to the new edition of his book, "Historical and Cruciform Nature: Life Persisting in Perishing," in *Science and Religion: A Critical Survey with a New Introduction*, xxxix–xliii (Philadelphia: Templeton, 2006).

80. Bulgakov, *Sophia, the Wisdom of God*, 147.

81. Bulgakov, *Bride of the Lamb*, 149–50.

aspect in terms of original "selfishness," for it still exists as possibility, but this supplements Bulgakov's simpler idea of privation.

Is this account of evil as shadow sophia too mythological to be all that helpful?[82] Certainly, given the Orthodox background of Bulgakov's thought, I admit that his envisaging of the tapestry of evil in somewhat metaphysical terms needs to be handled very carefully. In the first place, it is not intended to substitute for other ways of responding to the idea of evil, but rather to address the polymorphic theodicies in a dramatic way that seeks to bring together the various elements so that an adequate account of atonement follows. Inasmuch as the shadow might be considered the dark brooding where the possibility of creativity emerges, then there remains a positive Dionysian dimension to shadow sophia.

I suggest that this account also needs to be grounded in Hebraic imagery as well, where the path to death and life runs as a vibrant thread through the biblical account. In its ultimate expression, alongside Dame Wisdom, we also find Dame Folly, the counterfoil to human wisdom.[83] Even the search for wisdom always includes ambiguity, the possibility of human error, or sin, as expressed graphically by Eccl. 7:23-26, where the writer claims that wisdom is beyond his reach. Why? The surprising answer is that he, the seeker after wisdom, too, has fallen captive to folly, represented by the adulterous woman. In Hebrew thought, folly is about the bogus delights that are outside the boundaries and limits set by God in the created world.[84] I prefer to retain the imagery of shadow sophia rather than folly, for the language of folly is too bound up with the human community to extend to animals in the manner suggested here. This is, I suggest, a highly realistic account about life's difficulties, for it points to the almost inevitable entrapment of human persons, even as they seek to be wise. This is, I suggest, not so much idealism as realism in the face of that difficulty. More important, perhaps, freedom in this case is a *tuning in* to divine Wisdom, an alignment of creaturely sophia *with* divine Sophia as part of the way of life, rather than naked freedom that is affirmed without such align-

---

82. This criticism was raised by Denis Edwards. Personal communication, January 9, 2007.

83. Dame Folly is a figure that appears frequently in the Wisdom literature, and it is present in, for example, passages such as Prov. 2:16-19; 5:3-6; 6:24-26; 7:5-27; 9:3-18. Ecclesiastes also speaks of how wisdom can probe the nature of folly (Eccl. 2:3).

84. See Raymond van Leeuwen, "Liminality and Worldview in Proverbs 1–9," *Semeia* 50 (1990): 111–44.

ment, and a turning away from those aspects of shadow sophia that act in opposition to God, the way of death.[85]

Shadow sophia can also be viewed christologically. The wisdom of the cross expresses a reversal of human claims for power and superior knowledge.[86] As such, it is a kenotic Christology, one that is a gift of offering, a *self-emptying love* for the sake of the other, but that other is understood to include all created existence, not just human beings. At the cross, we can envisage shadow sophia as finally being transformed through the dramatic self-offering gift of Jesus, not only for humanity, but for all vulnerable creation as well. In other words, atonement needs to be thought of not so much just in sacrificial terms, and especially not in terms of penal suffering, but as Christ's dramatic and loving self-offering, in spite of the brutality of human evil, a love that serves to dispel once and for all the negative aspects of the dark shadow of sophia. The cross is not so much one more instance of evil in the world, but a way of confronting and transforming that evil through the loving self-offering of Christ. What seems to be human folly turns out to be paradoxically an expression of God's wisdom. Original selfishness is one facet of this creaturely wisdom in Christ expressing the radiance of the love of God for all creation. With Balthasar, I suggest that we need to stay under this shadow for a period and reflect on the experience of the dark night of Holy Saturday before moving too quickly to consider the positive elements of redemption theory.[87] Accounts of the atonement that express vicarious suffering in isolation are grossly inadequate, as they seem to insulate Jesus from the rest of humanity and, arguably, from creation as

---

85. Death is understood here metaphorically rather than literally.

86. Denis Edwards also points to this reversal of human understanding of power in reflection on the cross in his thought-provoking article, "Every Sparrow That Falls to the Ground: The Cost of Evolution and the Christ Event," *Ecotheology* 11, no. 1 (March 2006): 103–23.

87. Balthasar believed that we need a period in which we wait following the death of Jesus, so for this reason, he considers the importance of Holy Saturday before moving to accounts of the resurrection, as discussed in chapter 4. Although Hans Urs von Balthasar's Christology is existential in orientation, he does acknowledge cosmic Christology as being important and, as indicated earlier, combines both elements in his dramatic account of the atonement. The difference I am urging here is that the benefits of the atonement are more self-consciously extended to include nonhuman animals. He—correctly, in my view—resists the universalizing element of Christology if it then implies that the cross is regarded as a particular instance of that which is already present in the natural world. See discussion in McIntosh, *Christology from Within*, 28.

a whole.[88] Instead, for Balthasar, it is at the crucifixion and eventual descent into hell that Jesus enters most fully into alienated human existence, and Christian discipleship is marked by sharing in the dark night of Christ's passion, the final stage of every human journey.[89]

If we are now to open out Balthasar's account to be more inclusive of nonhuman creation, we could say that it is at the crucifixion that Jesus enters most fully into alienated existence, and the dramatic existential sharing in the dark night of Christ's passion by humanity is one that is also *representative* for the whole of created existence in its suffering. Why is this helpful for nonhuman creation? It is helpful in that we can, as in Rom. 8:18-30, suggest that the whole of the created order is waiting in anticipation of human redemption, for this is the prelude to that glorious future that is to follow in the power of resurrection hope for the whole of the created order. It is in this sense that humans become "co-redeemers," not so much through positive intervention in the nonhuman world, but through a sharing in Christ's humble self-offering on the cross. What does it mean to say that Christ's work of atonement expresses God's judgment on shadow sophia? It means that suffering and evil do not have the last word, for shadow sophia as a negative force no longer has any seductive power over the natural world. Furthermore, it goes deeper than simply portraying the atonement as a shared suffering, for this would restrict its scope to sentient creatures. Shadow sophia hovers with creaturely sophia from the very beginning of created existence, allowing her to develop in creative ways.

Shadow sophia is also useful as a way of giving a response to evil inasmuch as it resists too ready an explanation as to why it exists. In other words, we are not told why it is inevitable that shadow sophia surfaces in creation in the way that is envisaged; human wisdom is confronted here by its own limitations. The evolutionary rendering of sin as "selfishness" in the manner of Domning and Hellwig, or the account of the atonement in imagery of the scapegoat, offers only a partial explanation. This is the limitation that 1 Corinthians speaks about, and also that Ecclesiastes recognizes as the danger of empirical wisdom. This is not an easy escape into the idea of evil as mystery, but a realization that the depth of evil and suffering in the world and its atonement through the cross are ultimately beyond human understanding. Denis Edwards also recognizes the fundamental mystery of

---

88. Ibid., 54.
89. Ibid., 89–91.

evolutionary and other forms of suffering in theological terms.[90] Before the mystery of evil, we need to spend time in silence, to experience the silence of the tomb after the death of the Son, rather than race too quickly to the visitation in the garden following the resurrection.

Why does it help for us to think of creatures other than humans to suffer and behave in this way? It cannot help them in a literal sense any more than redemptive categories could literally help animals. Certainly, it does not imply a "solution" to the problem of suffering and evil. Rather, it encourages us to reflect in detail on the depth to which evil and suffering reach into the biological world and to become more aware of the potential of the atonement to widen out to include such forms of ill. Our hope in the possibility of transformation is then informed by acknowledgment of the depths of ills that have afflicted both the human and the nonhuman communities.

5.5 Conclusions

The evolution of sin presents serious challenges to those who want to restrict considerations of the atoning work of the cross to human activities in isolation from human evolutionary history. While I am critical of the narratives employed by evolutionary psychologists, this does not mean that human persons are to be viewed simply as detached cultural units, sheared from their grounding in natural history. Rather, the implication is the opposite: not only are tendencies found in the human world also characteristic of social animals more generally, but once we view nonhuman animals as having in some sense moral agency, then theories of atonement need to be widened and stretched to include creaturely ills.

How far atonement also encompasses evolutionary ills that arise out of the processes of natural selection is a matter for some debate, though I argue that objective as well as subjective accounts of the atonement need to

---

90. He develops this idea in his earlier accounts. Denis Edwards, *The God of Evolution: A Trinitarian Theology* (Mahwah, N.J.: Paulist, 1999), 36–42. He has subsequently developed this theme further in "Resurrection and the Costs of Evolution: A Dialogue with Rahner on Non-interventionist Theology," *TS* (December 2006): 816–33; and "Why Is God Doing This? Suffering, the Universe and Christian Eschatology," in *Physics and Cosmology: Scientific Perspectives on the Problem of Natural evil*, ed. Nancey Murphy, Robert J. Russell, and William Stoeger (Berkeley: CTNS; Vatican City: Vatican Observatory, 2007) 247–66. I am grateful to Denis Edwards for letting me see these articles while they were in press.

be held together. Moreover, inasmuch as the future hope includes freedom of the nonhuman world from these ills, then it is also appropriate to consider that the significance of Christ's cross and resurrection also extends in a mysterious way to include such evolutionary suffering. The qualifications associated with distinctions between moral and amoral suffering, and moral and natural evils, alongside what I have termed anthropogenic sin need, of course, to be borne in mind in making the case for the atoning significance of the cross. I have argued, drawing on ethological studies, that the distinctions commonly set up between humans and higher primates are artificial in their construal of human uniqueness. I am not advocating a theory of no distinction; rather, humanity is perhaps best thought of as unique in its extent of various capacities, so that the depth of sin and betrayal possible in the human community far exceeds that in the nonhuman world.

We are left with a discussion of which theories of atonement, if any, are useful in such an analysis. Inasmuch as theories of the atonement have tried to lay the blame for casting the burden of evils onto Christ either on a wrathful God or on accidents of human history, they have failed to convince. Avoiding the issue entirely by speaking simply of Christ's redemption without reconciliation also is not a convincing strategy, as it seems to leave intact underlying problems associated with combining the justice and holiness of God with God's love. Drawing particularly on Balthasar, in dialogue with other Lutheran theories, I have argued for the primacy of love in any considerations of the atonement, especially that which relates to the self-giving of the inner kenotic movement of the Trinity, rather than kenosis as understood in a primary sense as that between Creator and creation. I have also extended Balthasar's theodrama in the life of Christ as one who chose to take on the sins of the world by suggesting that this choice also embraced not just the negativity of human sin, but also sin more generally associated with creaturely being.

In taking up Bulgakov's notion of shadow sophia, I am not so much seeking to generate a mythology as to do justice to the various facets of evil that different theodicies seek to encompass and that theories of atonement need to address. My argument is that such facets of evil can never be explained or addressed by talk of God, as if humanity is somehow answerable *for* God, but at the same time, a theological response is one that includes the cross. In particular, the wisdom of the cross is where all such reflections intersect, and as such, it can be named as the place where shadow sophia is addressed. As discussed in chapter 4, Balthasar envisaged Christ dealing with sin understood as absolute evil only after Christ's death and entry into hell. Lest we think that this evil is only present here, that is, in Christ's encounter beyond death, I would prefer an interpretation that allows some recognition of absolute evil surfacing in the drama of human and evolutionary history. Moreover, it is vitally important that all such reflections on evil ultimately take their bearing from not just reflection on the cross in isolation, but rather reflection in the light of faith in the resurrection. It is only here that the power of the cross to reconcile and redeem can be made known. Therefore, we turn to this topic in the chapter that follows.

6

The Risen Christ: A Sophianic Interpretation

Evolutionary interpretations of Christology share some of the difficulties of a purely historical interpretation of Christology inasmuch as both
tend to avoid developing an adequate theology of the resurrection. I
will develop further the idea that the evolutionary history of the world
needs to be included in the resurrection understood as theodrama, rather
than relegated to the position of the "stage." Moreover, the specific dramatic account of Mary Magdalene's encounter with the risen Christ, Jesus
Sophia, shows not only the way the Gospel of John is influenced by the
Sophia tradition, but also the importance of women in the resurrection
narrative and early Christian apostolic ministry. This account serves as an
important corrective to the more stereotypical views of women found in
the work of Sergii Bulgakov and Hans Urs von Balthasar. Sergii Bulgakov's
sophianic interpretation of the resurrection includes an interplay between
Jesus as creaturely sophia and divine Sophia. Yet the kenosis of the Son only
disappears following the Pentecost and after Christ has ascended. While
appreciating aspects of his thinking, I will explore the extent to which Bulgakov's account of the risen Christ veers too close to an epic, mythological
view that is detached from theodrama. In dialogue with his theology, I will
also argue that the role of Christ as redeemer in the evolved, natural world
needs to be qualified by due attention not just to the concrete encounter
with Mary Magdalene, but also to the apophatic tradition, symbolized in
the empty tomb.

6.1 Introduction

Viewing Christ as simply an extension of the evolved world is one way of approaching the relationship between Christ and evolution. Inasmuch as Christ shares fully in the human condition, such an evolutionary approach seems entirely appropriate. Teilhard de Chardin took this a step further in his belief that Christ represented a new stage for evolved humanity, whereby evolutionary processes became absorbed into salvation history.[1] However, Christian belief in the resurrection seems to encounter a stumbling block if this is *all* that can be said about who Christ is. Certainly, Christ interpreted according to the historical Jesus school had similar reticence when it came to speaking about the resurrection, for it is outside what can be reasonably thought of as historical experience. Part of the difficulty is the sheer variety and inconsistency in the biblical record, leading to problems of convergence of history and myth, truth and rhetoric, experience and interpretation.[2] Not only do such tensions exist between different Gospel accounts, but even within one account, there are inconsistencies. Christ both appears and eats with the disciples; he asks not to be touched yet invites Thomas to touch his wounds. Such inconsistencies are not necessarily incompatible, once we allow for consideration of the resurrection as not simply a particular event in time and space, but also one that cannot be understood just in these terms.

Wolfhart Pannenberg is well known as a theologian who has tried to circumvent these difficulties by portraying the resurrection as an event in history that is unique.[3] Certainly, for the early Christian community, the resurrection necessarily signaled the beginning of the end of all things, and this, he believes, is translated into faith in the divinity of Christ. He rejects—correctly, in my view—pseudoscientific interpretations of the appearances of Jesus as hallucinations caused by excited expectations, as

---

1. Pierre Teilhard de Chardin, "Christ the Evolver," in *Christianity and Evolution*, trans. René Hague (London: Collins, 1971).

2. See Markus Bockmuehl, "The Resurrection," in *The Cambridge Companion to Jesus*, ed. M. Bockmuehl (Cambridge: Cambridge University Press, 2001), 103. Stephen Davis argues that the different accounts of Jesus' resurrection can be harmonized. While I agree that they are not necessarily *incompatible*, the idea of harmony is too strong, as it implies that the inconsistencies are irrelevant. See S. Davis, *Risen Indeed: Making Sense of the Resurrection* (Grand Rapids: Eerdmans, 1993), 53–61.

3. W. Pannenberg, *Jesus, God and Man*, trans. L. Wilkins and D. A. Priebe (London: SCM, 1968), 67–70.

their faith was at rock bottom. Instead, he suggests that following the laws of physics, "only a part of the laws of nature are ever known," and an individual event is not completely determined by natural laws in that the validity of those laws is itself contingent.[4]

Robert Russell has followed up this suggestion in his proposal that the resurrection is the instantiation of new laws of nature for the new creation.[5] Such a resolution is both bold and appealing inasmuch as it allows for continuity in that these are laws of *nature* yet discontinuity in that this is based on *new* law. Yet in order to get around the problem of historicity, Pannenberg proposes, "The judgement about whether an event, however unfamiliar, has happened or not is in the final analysis a matter for the historian, and cannot be pre-judged by the knowledge of natural science."[6] By resisting the claim that the resurrection "breaks the limits of the merely historical," he seems to be shoehorning the resurrection into a historical explanation. There is some parallel here with Russell's interpretation of the resurrection in terms of new scientific laws; both history and science are now affirmed, but in terms that are different from those anticipated from either current scientific or historical knowledge. The difference between Pannenberg and Russell is that while the former believes that it still makes sense to claim history as an authority, the latter is readier to admit that whether the resurrection is historical or not cannot be proved either way, so the conclusion is a theological one.[7] Both raise similar problems in that for an uncommitted reader, this might seem somewhat suspect on *methodological* grounds, in that both readings are not how history or science are normally understood; certainly, they are not science or history as we know it.[8]

Russell tries to alleviate the historicity issue in Pannenberg by distinguishing between what he views as historical events, that is, the life, death,

---

4. Similar explanations can be called on in order to explain the miraculous in Jesus' narrative.

5. See, for example, Robert John Russell, *Cosmology: From Alpha to Omega* (Minneapolis: Fortress Press, 2008), 298–327. John Polkinghorne also has hinted at this idea, though in a far less detailed way, in *The God of Hope and the End of the World* (London: SPCK, 2002), where he claims, "It seems a coherent hope to believe that the laws of its nature will be perfectly adapted to the everlasting life of that world" (115). But the meaning of such an adjustment of laws is unclear.

6. Pannenberg, *Jesus, God and Man*, 78.

7. Russell, personal communication, March 10, 2008.

8. Rowan Williams raises this issue in relation to Pannenberg's interpretation of the resurrection in historical terms. See R. Williams, *On Christian Theology* (Oxford: Blackwell, 2000), 185–86.

resurrection, and appearances of Jesus, and what he views as transhistorical or proleptic historical occurrence, namely, the ongoing significance of the risen Christ. However, some problems still remain, for we might ask what we *mean* by the resurrection appearances being defined as a new instance of history or science, for the very fluid presence of the risen Jesus even as he appeared to his disciples seems to escape any such definition.[9] In addition, how far is it helpful to use the *language* of new laws of nature if such laws are drawn from theological, rather than scientific, premises? Hence, while such a view is certainly not unreasonable, and in many ways is highly attractive given the theoretical openness of both history and physics to contingency, inasmuch as it cannot be grounded on known experience, it seems to offer the promise of a concrete rendition of an event that escapes any such categorization. It is certainly not convincing to envisage some sort of literal biological or *evolutionary* continuity, given the fluidity of the various images of the post-resurrection Christ.

Of course, an alternative that is far more problematic is to leave behind the resurrection entirely and avoid the issue, either by omitting it from the discussion or by simply proclaiming the resurrection as a matter of "blind" faith where historicity or science is irrelevant.[10] Yet the historical issue is not just important in terms of the Christian community; it is also relevant for the evolutionary community, since if the resurrection is not historical in *any* sense, then the scope of that resurrection becomes reduced to existential interpretations in the minds of believers, detached

---

9. Robert Russell has discussed the issue of time and eternity in some depth from the perspective of a physicist, and inasmuch as scientific imagination allows some scope here, his suggestions are intriguing. In this respect, it is important to consider the issue of how time is understood—for example, debates about alternatives between flowing time or the "block universe" in special relativity. However, any envisaged scenario for the "new creation" seems to entail either a new interpretation or revision of special relativity. Moreover, while such speculations might help an imaginative leap into what the "new creation" might be like, they do not deal more concretely with the variegated form of the risen Christ as told in the Gospel accounts. In other words, we are left with the dilemma of radical discontinuity in evolutionary terms but speculation about continuity in terms of physical laws. Hence, while a physicist may find such speculation satisfactory inasmuch as it can legitimately deal with issues of time and eternity, a biologist is faced with a brute lack of resolution, for not only is death irreversible in biological terms, but also the biological form of Christ, while showing continuity in several accounts, escapes anything that can be reasonably identified with known biological phenomena.

10. Such a position is well known in the work of authors such as Rudolf Bultmann.

from evolutionary history and the world as we know it. It might, therefore, be sensible to describe the resurrection with a *different kind of language*, one that resists particular categorization. Bockmuehl, for example, uses *metaphor* to describe the resurrection, but unlike ordinary metaphors that use the literal to speak of the otherworldly, the resurrection redescribes earth in terms of heaven, and history in terms of eschatology. Hence, "the resurrection here constitutes the defining historical, moral and ecological reality that is the 'new creation.'"[11]

Michael Welker connects the historical Jesus with the risen Christ by pointing to the diversity of impact of the historical Jesus, and suggests that such diversity also characterizes how the life of the resurrected needs to be understood.[12] In other words, the multiplicity of expectations and experiences in historical terms opens the way for a multiplicity of symbolic representations of the resurrected one that go further than simply addressing the question of historicity as such according to what he calls the "archeologistic" mind-set. He also recognizes the tension between the incompatibility of resurrection hope and theories of emergence, alongside the dangers of abstraction where the resurrection is simply equated with theophany.

In the present context, this means that the question arises as to how evolution can be affirmed while at the same time recognizing the newness of the resurrection and the hope that this brings, not just for human beings, but for the natural world as well. I will propose first that the language of theodrama offers a way of including evolution and resurrection in an account that takes history seriously, while avoiding the difficulties discussed. Second, I suggest that the theological category of *sophia* integrates both creaturely and theological aspects; it affirms the risen Christ in a metaphorical way, but at the same time, it resists leaving nature or history behind.

6.2 Including Evolution in the Theodrama

The ability to read evolution not just as science but also as history means that through evolutionary accounts, nature as such becomes historical, a perspective that, according to some, is one of the most significant

---

11. Bockmuehl, "Resurrection," 117.

12. M. Welker, "Theological Realism and Eschatological Symbol Systems," in *Resurrection: Theological and Scientific Assessments*, ed. T. Peter, R. J. Russell, and M. Welker (Grand Rapids: Eerdmans, 2002), 42 n. 25.

discoveries of science.[13] The most common way of reading human history is according to the activities of individual human subjects in genealogies or according to the dynamics of historical change through systematic analysis in what can be termed a "grand narrative" approach.[14] This is applied most commonly to a reading of the activity of human subjects, but in evolutionary science, we find similar trends toward either tracing genealogies or constructing grand narratives such as evolutionary psychology, but also others such as Darwin's theory of natural selection, Mendel's laws, and so on. Such a reading, as applied to human history, arguably fails to give attention to exceptions to the rules, resistances to explanation, and densities of meaning that are allowed for in a more dramatic approach to history. Much the same criticism could be applied to evolutionary history. Ben Quash, drawing particularly on the work of Balthasar, has argued for the recovery of theodramatic approaches to history that concern human actions in time in relation to God's purpose.[15] For him, the concern of theodramatics is with the character of human agency, its necessary conditions in terms of place, and its relation to the wider plot over time.

Yet I suggest that the fruitfulness of this approach can also be extended, with due care, to include evolutionary history as well. Evolutionary biologist Jeffrey Schloss has noted such a possibility in describing evolution in terms of a play on an "ecological stage." He suggests, "The lines, the players and even the plot may change over evolutionary time, though they are ever constrained by the props and setting and choreographic syntax of the ecological moment."[16] While I agree with the analogy, I suggest that we can go even further than this, in that ecology is rather more dynamic than this view might suggest. Hence, ecology does not *just* represent the stage but also, for many nonhuman animals at least, includes the possibility of agency. Ernst Conradie, while rather more inclined to speak of evolutionary history in narrative terms, also hints at the possibility of dramatic language in the realization that evolutionary history makes us more aware of our finitude

---

13. J. F. Haught, "Ecology and Eschatology," in *And God Says That It Was Good: Catholic Theology and the Environment*, ed. D. Christiansen and W. Grazen (Washington, D.C.: U.S. Catholic Conference, 1996), 57.

14. Ben Quash, *Theology and the Drama of History* (Cambridge: Cambridge University Press, 2005), 6.

15. Ibid., 3–4.

16. J. Schloss takes this idea from Evelyn Hutchinson. See J. Schloss, "From Evolution to Eschatology," in Peters, Russell, and Welker, *Resurrection*, 56–85 at 58.

and that "we are nothing more than a brief episode in the cosmic drama."[17] Yet what might this drama mean in theological terms?

The profile of the dramatic includes indeterminacy and thus is inclusive of circumstance, compulsion, and decision, which most characterize human existence.[18] Such indeterminacy is also, I suggest, characteristic of life in general and becomes most intense in animals that share the capacity for decision making. Drama also works through particular events, as well as showing a social dimension through including the audience as much as those on the stage. The possibility of sharing in a *performance*, it seems to me, makes for a more readily accommodated perception of inclusiveness with other finite creatures, compared with, for example, a simple portrayal of evolution in terms of a rational system of truth claims.

As discussed in chapter 1, the idea of including evolution in human history by interpreting it as a *story* or *narrative* has become increasingly popular, especially among theologians influenced by Teilhard de Chardin, such as Brian Swimme and Thomas Berry.[19] Such a rendition transposes the account of evolution into a grand narrative, which is then baptized through theological interpretation and endorsement. In many respects, the narrative tradition is helpful inasmuch as it fosters a sense of belonging to a wider history of the earth in such a way that this can be connected with salvation history. Ernst Conradie has achieved this to good effect in his understanding of the earth in God's economy, using a more traditional account of creation, reconciliation, and redemption as signposts in the narrative. Yet it is also of interest that he cannot avoid the language of drama in places, but this drama is still contained within the overall narrative account.[20] The narrative account of evolution offered by Swimme and

---

17. Ernst Conradie, "Resurrection, Finitude and Ecology," in Peters, Russell, and Welker, *Resurrection*, 280.

18. Quash, *Theology and the Drama of History*, 35–37.

19. Brian Swimme and Thomas Berry, *The Universe Story* (San Francisco: Harper-Collins, 1992).

20. A full discussion of this is outside the scope of this chapter. A preliminary discussion is found in E. Conradie, "The Earth in God's Economy: Reflections on the Narrative of God's Labour" (Inaugural Lecture, University of Western Cape, October 24, 2007). Conradie's use of drama in an adjective sense to describe the texture of the narrative is perhaps an attempt to defend against postmodernist opposition to "grand narratives." Narrative is, however, still primary and comes to the surface in his discussion of the Protestant tradition, including the assertion that "plot is best captured by the Christian symbols of the cross and resurrection of Jesus Christ." Ibid., 31. I am arguing,

others bears some *analogy* to the literary concept of epic, whose concern may be about God's actions but with an abiding universal significance presumed. A description of evolution as narrative rarely goes as far as rendering nature as in some sense inert, or reifying regularity in the manner of accounts deemed to be "epic," but inasmuch as it follows the trend of modernity that a "view of nowhere" is possible, it commits the same fallacy.[21] At its worst, epic includes an element of necessity and represents the "genre of false objectification."[22]

The advantage of theodrama, by contrast, is that it envisages an *encounter* between God and creation, where the freedom of the creature is preserved without resorting to pantheistic interpretations of the relationship between God and creation, which surface in many renditions of evolution as narrative.[23] This is where Rosemary Radford Ruether's account of the resurrection fails miserably, for it simply incorporates humanity into the cosmic cycle without any possible reference to a drama as such, for God is equated with the stage rather than being the drama's director.[24] In theodrama, the tragic is recognized fully, rather than absorbed and neutralized in the manner that more often than not happens in an epic account. The tragic has been the pattern for the drama of evolutionary history for millennia, as witnessed in the paleontological record. Interpreting evolution in theodramatic terms has a further advantage in that anticipation still plays a vital role, but it does not take the form of resignation, as is characteristic of purely secular accounts of evolutionary science, but rather encourages further interpretation and engagement. Theodrama also resists tendencies toward epic description in natural theology, while avoiding equally problematic mystical "lyric" accounts, where "the whole substance of an action is transposed into a highly volatile, highly individual, immediate and emotionally coloured mode of

---

instead, for a much more self-conscious appropriation of drama, rather than narrative, and the dramatic, rather than the epic.

21. For a discussion of epic in these terms, see Quash, whose discussion of epic draws on Hegel and Balthasar. Quash, *Theology and the Drama of History*, 41–42, 47–49.

22. Ibid., 42.

23. Exceptions include, for example, Conradie's interpretation of narrative, which includes a more Barthian interpretation of the action of God in history. Given this, it is worth asking if his theology is more consistent with theodrama than with the narrative approach.

24. Rosemary Radford Ruether, *Sexism and God Talk: Towards a Feminist Theology* (London: SCM, 1983), 257–58.

response and expression."[25] Such lyric accounts are particularly tempting in speaking about resurrection hope, but ultimately such lyric accounts open the way for escapist approaches to the earth.

Quash suggests that theodrama fills the rift opened up between the "brutally given" and "banally free"—the former referring to many sorts of natural theology, and the latter to certain appeals to mystic experience.[26] Yet I would argue that viewing nature as merely the "brutally given"—or even as the stage, for that matter—forces a rift to be opened up where it is not due between the human and creaturely being as such; in other words, it suffers from an anthropocentrism that is equally epic in its attempt to regulate material according to a particular formula. Quash seems to be aware of this difficulty in that he, citing Stephen Clark, acknowledges that in liturgical practice, other creatures are "fellows in relationship to God," springing from "God's love and regard."[27] Yet he does not link this clear sense of "creation's whole ecology of praise" explicitly with theodrama in the way I am indicating here, though he hints at this possibility in his reflection on the Eucharist.

Narrative accounts of evolution, inasmuch as they include the evolutionary world, avoid anthropocentrism, but in versions such as that inspired by Teilhard de Chardin, the concentration on the human more often than not proves irresistible, hence falling back once again into anthropocentrism.[28] In addition, there may be a place for the mystic, but the context needs to be set firmly within theodrama, that is, in the context of a community. Certainly, in considering Christ's resurrection, there is a need to avoid tendencies toward both objective closure and mystical individualism, and placing the resurrection in the context of the drama of God's activity in the world takes some steps toward this possibility.

Yet given the importance of the resurrection, it is perhaps surprising that Balthasar pays relatively scant attention to the particular event of the resurrection in his *Theo-Drama*, even though arguably his discussion

---

25. Quash, *Theology and the Drama of History*, 42.

26. Ibid., 50.

27. Ben Quash, "Offering: Treasuring the Creation," in *Blackwell Companion to Christian Ethics*, ed. S. Hauerwas and S. Wells, 305–18 (Oxford: Blackwell, 2006), esp. 312, 315.

28. The cosmic dimensions in Teilhard's original work counter this to some degree. See also discussion in C. Deane-Drummond, ed., *Teilhard de Chardin on People and Planet* (London: Equinox, 2006).

presupposes its crucial importance.[29] Yet the drama becomes clear in that the resurrection and cross are still bound together inasmuch as they are included in the dramatic action of God in the world. Hence, the cross is not so much a "manifestation of God's reconciliation with the world, a reconciliation that is constant, homogeneous and always part of the given: rather we should say that God, desiring to reconcile the world to himself (and hence himself to the world), acts dramatically in the Son's Cross and Resurrection."[30] Such a dramatic action does not "entangle" the immanent Trinity in the world but lifts the world to "the level of the economic Trinity." His focus, nonetheless, is on the open wounds of Christ, even in the resurrected state, and he implies that this woundedness continues in time, for the drama is "constantly actual" and "embraces all past and future points of world time" in such a way that "not only is this definitive event being continually rendered concrete from below, as it were, by continued sin: it is continually being implanted from above into all times, in the sacrament instituted by Christ."[31] Such a reading shows Balthasar's difficulty in confining the passion narrative to theodramatics, in that he displays a tendency for an epic reading of the passion narrative that is also overlaid by mystical attention to Christ's wounds.[32] Of course, the problem faced in any interpretation of the resurrection is how to point to future hope without collapsing time and history.

Moreover, while Balthasar is highly critical of Moltmann's tendency, as he sees it, to "entangle" the history of the world with the economic Trinity, his eschatological approach does bring with it something of the dramatic that Balthasar attempts to convey. For Moltmann, the resurrection is "an eschatologically determined happening—the raising of a dead person into the eternal life of the new creation, and the transformation of his natural,

---

29. Balthasar includes a discussion of the resurrection in the fourth volume of *Theo-Drama*, but the specific attention to the risen Christ as such occupies only six pages. See Hans Urs von Balthasar, *Theo-Drama: Theological Dramatic Theory*, vol. 4, *The Action*, trans. Graham Harrison (San Francisco: Ignatius, 1994), 361–67 (hereafter cited as *TD* 4). He does cover this aspect more fully in his *Mysterium Pascale*, trans. Aidan Nichols (Edinburgh: T&T Clark, 1990) (hereafter cited as *MP*).

30. Balthasar, *TD* 4, 362.

31. Ibid., 363.

32. Ben Quash has criticized both the epic and lyrical tendencies in Balthasar, especially in his reading of literature, inasmuch as it moves Balthasar away from his project of interpreting theology as theodrama.

mortal body into the body of God's glory, interpenetrated by the Spirit."[33] In a way not fully explained, this does not so much "interrupt the natural laws of mortal life" as it changes its "whole quality," including the "laws of its mortality."[34] This begs the question of how its laws might be changed, and in what sense this might be rendering an objective interpretation in biological terms where it is not due; even though he acknowledges this is outside "objective proofs," why use the language of objectivity, namely, laws, and why use the language of mortality?

Like Balthasar, Moltmann uses analogy to describe the transformation effective in this mortal life compared with that anticipated in eternity, yet he does not just restrict this analogy to that of the life of the church, but welcomes the inclusion within it of the experiences of the Spirit "in the rhythms of nature" and "the fertility of life," including incorporation of festivities that worshipped the "goddess of the sunrise."[35] Yet it is doubtful that such analogies serve the purpose to which they are intended, namely, an encounter of the believer with the risen Christ, inasmuch as they imply a universal religious experience through encounters with nature, detracting from the drama of the encounter of God with the world in Christ. Indeed, by viewing the rhythms of nature as parables of the new creation, Moltmann has set up what Balthasar has described as the idea of constant, uniform reconciliation of God with the world. The absence of any real analogy between Jesus' resurrection and pagan parallels is reinforced by the difficulty of preaching the message of the resurrection to the pagans in the nascent church, suggesting that this message is not simply a construct evolving out of prior images and myths, a view that is the logical end point of drawing on such analogies in this context. Such a rendition is also problematic in that it could easily lead to the concept of the natural world as *cruciform*, in such a way that such images and myths seem to be rendered as somehow necessary or expressive of what is then experienced in the Christ event. This is especially the case since Moltmann argues that the analogy works in "both directions," so that "eternal life is prefigured in these natural events."[36] But can we really say that human conceptions of the

---

33. Moltmann, *The Way of Jesus Christ* (London: SCM, 1990), 250 (hereafter cited as *WJC*).

34. Ibid., 250. Moltmann also talks about mortality being overcome by immortality. Ibid., 252.

35. Ibid., 250–51.

36. Ibid., 252.

"goddess of the sunrise" or the "rhythms of creation" in some sense pre-figure eternal life? Is not this the very kind of conception that Christ came to challenge rather than reinforce? Certainly, other strands in Moltmann's thinking point in the opposite direction, so he has also been criticized for speaking about the new creation in such a way that its radical newness, including a loss of mortality, seems, in effect, to separate the new creation from the creation in too drastic a manner.[37] This shows an inconsistency with his emphasis on natural cycles that is hard to reconcile. Such criticisms do not, however, take sufficient account of his insistence on enduring somatic identity in death and the persistence of personal relationship to God *through* death.[38]

Instead, inasmuch as it is possible to include others in the drama of history, the drama is not just acted out through human religious consciousness or nature mysticism, but begins with and widens out to include non-humans as subjects. For although Moltmann uses the language of nature with great liberality, its grounding in a more detailed discussion of, for example, ecology or evolution is largely absent.[39] The real issue, it seems to me, is rooted in a deeper one of Moltmann speaking in detail about the new creation in a manner that is not sufficiently qualified, its elaborate speculations moving outside the boundary of what can be asserted with any confidence.

Jeffrey Schloss has argued more specifically that there is an analogy between "ideal" and "actualized" niches found in evolutionary history and that which can be expected in an eschatological future "heaven."[40] Most species occupy theoretically "suboptimal" niches due to competitive displacement by other, more dominant species. Yet while some biologists resist any language of the "ideal"—the "optimal" niche always being a compromise in terms of physiology and availability of resources, competition, and so on—the meaning of "optimal" is equally under dispute. The use of terms like *optimal* and *ideal* implies teleology, a future to which species aspire. Yet Schloss is critical of those attempts to endorse evolutionary accounts through a developed teleology inasmuch as many of the assumptions in

---

37. See, for example, Conradie, "Resurrection, Finitude and Ecology," 279.

38. Moltmann, *WJC*, 261. He also speaks here of mortality being "overcome" by immortality, which, strictly speaking, might not imply mortality is abolished.

39. Such a criticism also applies to Balthasar in his use of history and represents a tendency to theorize that pulls against claims to be concrete. See also C. Deane-Drummond, *Ecology in Jürgen Moltmann's Theology* (Lewisham: Mellen, 1997).

40. Schloss, "From Evolution," 65.

such stories do not appear to be true. For example, there is no real evidence for an increase in complexity over time, and ever since the Cambrian Period, morphological diversity has stayed more or less constant. There is also no evidence that parasites or other harmful organisms gradually become more mutualistic.[41] Such benign readings of nature characterize much natural theology, especially those that seek to find a continuum between evolution and eschatology.

Schloss draws on Richard Dawkins's idea of the extended phenotype as operative in evolution, where the phenotype extends beyond the immediate "skin" of a given organism to all its fitness-enhancing influences on the environment.[42] Such a move breaks down an organism's identity, rendering it fluid, in such a way that there is an ambiguity over "whose" body a body is. He uses this model as analogous to the resurrection, in that while some accounts are literal, others are less so. Yet this seems to assume that Dawkins's account of natural selection working primarily through genes is correct, a view that I had some reason to call into question in chapter 2. Dawkins would no doubt shudder to see his views expounded in support of claims for the resurrection, but this is perhaps beside the point. In addition, if Christ becomes rendered through his resurrection as some kind of "superorganism" in the manner of Dawkins's extended phenotype, what might this mean for individual encounters? Perhaps a key insight here is that the boundary of what might be termed ontology of being is rather more fluid than used to be considered the case, but it is a kind of fluidity that is still bound by existing laws of nature, rather than operative outside it.

In evolutionary terms, there are trends to be observed, such as increase in body temperature, increase in body size, episodic jumps in energy intensiveness, increases in developmental cascades, increases in hierarchical integration, as well as levels of organization. But there are also increases in competition, rather than evasion and powers of cognitive processing.[43]

---

41. Schloss, for example, questions more saccharine accounts of evolution in a number of ways, not least challenging the myth that infectious agents coevolved with hosts in order to "minimise pathogenicity"; this view, he suggests, is false on both "theoretical and empirical grounds. . . . Pathogenicity often increases over evolutionary time, depending on infectiousness and host density." Ibid., 73.

42. R. Dawkins, *The Extended Phenotype: The Gene as the Unit of Selection* (Oxford: Oxford University Press, 1986); and R. Dawkins and D. Dennett, *The Extended Phenotype: The Long Reach of the Gene* (Oxford: Oxford University Press, 1999).

43. The three basic life history strategies are those that evade competition, those that win competition by efficiency or defense, and those that win by sabotage, that is, taking

A future hope *tied in with* such processes becomes problematic in that "a critique of eschatologies based on evolutionary aesthetics is that we have fashioned God after our own fallen image, at precisely the cultural moment when theology needs to recall us in eschatological hope to the renewal of his moral image within us."[44]

I suggest that including evolution in a theodrama not only avoids problems associated with an apparent endorsement of evolution, but also gives due weight to the significance of the risen Christ as one who challenges humanity not just through an encounter, but also through the gift of the Spirit in the transformation of our moral and inner life. A way of envisioning that encounter is through the language of Sophia or, we might prefer, her performance.

6.3 Scene 1: Mary Magdalene and Jesus Sophia

How might Christ as risen be related to the natural world? One window on this comes through a closer examination of the dramatic encounter of Mary Magdalene and the risen Christ in John's Gospel (John 20:1-18). This account also serves to introduce the theme of Sophia, inasmuch as John was heavily indebted to this tradition. While the number and variety of accounts of the resurrection in the Gospels are considerable, this particular story illustrates aspects of how Jesus as risen came to be perceived in the early Johannine community. Hence, rather than attempt a survey of all the different accounts in scripture, the purpose of its inclusion here is to "flesh out" one particular scene in the drama and to serve as a sounding board for the more developed sophiology in the theology of Sergii Bulgakov.

The story in its present form illustrates a combination of a number of different accounts connected with both the traditions of the empty tomb and the appearances of Jesus.[45] Mary discovers the empty tomb and calls

---

more than they might "need" physiologically and in this sense enhancing their potential competitive impact. Some evolutionary biologists argue for an escalation rather than an attenuation of competition over time. See G. J. Vermejj, *Evolution and Escalation: An Ecological History of Life* (Princeton: Princeton University Press, 1987).

44. Schloss, "From Evolution," 77.

45. At least two or three traditions are likely to be involved. See C. K. Barrett, *The Gospel According to John*, 2nd ed. (London: SPCK, 1978), 560–62; R. E. Brown, *The Gospel According to John* 11 (London: Doubleday, 1966), 998–1004; B. Lindars, *The Gospel of John* (London: Marshall, Morgan & Scott, 1972), 595; and R. Schnackenburg, *The Gospel According to St. John* 3 (London: Burns & Oates, 1982), 302–7.

Peter and "the other disciple," but in the rush, she seems to be left standing apart, while the disciples return home. John 20:8 claims of "the other disciple" that "he saw and he believed," but there is an inconsistency: Why did Mary report her later sighting as if no one knew anything about it?[46] Moreover, why did this disciple not apparently show any excitement about this knowledge or share it with the other disciples or even Peter, who was with him at the time?[47] R. Schnackenburg argues that the underlying story here is one where Mary and Peter visit the tomb, and the Gospel writer reworks this in order to include the beloved disciple.[48] Martin Scott suggests that this is significant in that it allows Mary to be singled out in a special way so that she is the first to see the risen Christ. However, woven into this account is one that also stresses the importance of faith,[49] given that the Johannine community was some distance historically from the original events. All four Gospel accounts portray Mary as present at the empty tomb, but John gives her the most significant mission, where Jesus calls her by name and she is given a "double apostolic role," both calling Peter and the other disciple as witnesses to the empty tomb and, following her encounter with the risen Christ, taking this message to the other disciples.

The singling out of Mary in the Johannine account is surprising, given that John's contemporaries may not have accepted the validity of a woman as a reliable witness, according to second-century Jewish traditions.[50] Scott suggests that this may be a *second* instance in the Fourth Gospel where a woman replaces the apostolic role of Peter, the first being Martha's confes-

---

46. Martin Scott points to this inconsistency in his commentary, *Sophia and the Johannine Jesus* (Sheffield: JSOT, 1992), 223. The angel motif in vv. 1-13 also seems to represent duplication of material of Mary weeping and her reply. Bultmann argues that this is "entirely superfluous," and Scott seems to accept this explanation, though I am far less convinced. R. Bultmann, *The Gospel of John* (Oxford: Blackwell, 1971), 682. It seems to me that such duplication was deliberate, as it increases the dramatic intensity; one who is grieving regularly repeats a lament.

47. Scott disagrees with Schnackenburg here, and I am more convinced by Scott's analysis. See Scott, *Sophia and the Johannine Jesus*, 227.

48. This is more convincing than alternatives that suggest this tradition simply builds on accounts of women visiting the tomb, adding both the story of Peter and the beloved disciple, as in Bultmann, *Gospel of John*, 681–83.

49. This view is attested to by a several commentators; see, for example, Barrett, *Gospel According to John,* 652; Lindars, *Gospel of John,* 598.

50. See discussion in B. Witherington, *Women in the Ministry of Jesus: A Study of Jesus' Attitudes to Women and Their Roles as Reflected in His Early Life* (Cambridge: Cambridge University Press, 1984), 9–10.

sion in 11:27.[51] The belief spoken about in 20:8 is more likely a reference to belief in Mary's account of the empty tomb and, as such, would enhance Mary's status as a reliable witness.

Mary initially fails to recognize who Jesus is, supposing him to be a gardener, in common with many other accounts of his post-resurrection appearances. Mary's eventual recognition follows her name being spoken in a way that parallels the Good Shepherd parable (John 10:3). She is given here as an example of how faith works in a believing community when physical touch is no longer possible, reinforced by 20:17, where she is commanded not to touch. Her faith also progresses from viewing Christ as teacher (*Rabbouni*) in 20:17 on hearing her name, to subsequently confessing him as Lord in 20:18. Scott suggests that the first title afforded to Jesus, namely, Teacher, is associated with the need to hold on to Jesus in a bodily fashion that Jesus refuses. Instead, his mission is much wider and can only be effected through his breathing of the Holy Spirit on the disciples, reported in 20:22. The subsequent appearance of Jesus to his disciples need not detract from Mary's role as witness to a personal encounter with Jesus. Her confession to "have seen the Lord" is one of the hallmarks of apostleship in the early Christian church, repeated in 1 Cor. 9:1.[52]

In this context, it is important to clarify the way that Balthasar interprets these verses. In the first place, he accepts John's testimony of belief as acknowledgment of the risen Christ in John 20:8, just discussed, and elaborates this further to suggest that this has priority over the appearance of Jesus to Mary Magdalene, even suggesting that she becomes the witness to this faith without appearance.[53] He also interprets the mission given to the disciples as "decisive," apparently ignoring the significance of Mary's encounter with Jesus by explaining his later appearance to them as an encounter *in facto esse*, compared with Mary, who merely becomes a witness to the supposedly superior *resurrectio in fieri* of John, for "she is sent with this vision to the disciples," even though the account speaks of her telling of her personal encounter with Christ.[54] The story of Magdalene itself is interpreted in his hands as one where Mary "returns" from a gesture of clasping to testifying to the other disciples, but her role is mirrored

---

51. Scott, *Sophia and the Johannine Jesus*, 226.

52. For a discussion of the link between seeing the Lord and apostleship in 1 Corinthians, see H. Conzelmann, *1 Corinthians* (Philadelphia: Fortress Press, 1975), 152.

53. Balthasar, *MP*, 258.

54. The manipulation of the text here is somewhat remarkable; see ibid.

in the command given to the disciples not to look to heaven following the ascension.[55] He explains the enhanced role of women in the accounts of the crucifixion, burial, and appearances and developed in John as an allegory for the femininity of the church, so that "what is in question is the delicate equilibrium between the Church as 'bride' of Christ and the Church as hierarchical institution."[56] Mary is thus denied any aspostolic role in his rendering of this account and becomes reduced to an allegory of the church as feminine symbolic bride of Christ or a mirror for the faith of the disciples.[57]

Martin Scott has argued vigorously for the significance of Sophia in the Christology of John, and this is illustrated more indirectly in the account of Jesus' appearance to Mary Magdalene. While John draws on traditional resources, he develops these in a way that shows his indebtedness to the Sophia tradition. The question that Jesus uses to address Mary ("Whom do you seek?") is one that only Jesus asks, even though he repeats the angels' question about why she is weeping. This has some parallels with John 8:21, where Jesus is sought following a withdrawal in a way that parallels the Wisdom traditions, such as Prov. 8:17.[58] Seeking after God as Sophia holds out the possibility of success, in much the same way that Mary Magdalene in her love for Jesus sought him and searched him out in the empty tomb. Jesus is also described in the role of teacher in this account, an attribute that is also commonly given to Sophia.[59] Both Jesus as teacher and Sophia as teacher are pointers to the revelation of God, but Jesus' presence as teacher takes the form of the gift of the Holy Spirit following his departure (John 14:26). Yet it is highly significant that this attribution is not sufficient, for

---

55. Ibid., 250–51.

56. Ibid., 257.

57. In the following chapter, I will develop in more detail a critique of Balthasar's stereotypical approach to women, which runs throughout his work and represents what Quash has termed epic thinking. In this context, it also seems to do violence to the text.

58. Scott, *Sophia and the Johannine Jesus*, 159–62.

59. Ibid., 152–57. Jesus' authority as teacher is based on his relationship with God, and it is open rather than gnostic teaching. See John 7:16-17; 18:20. Sophia as teacher also shows parallels in Prov. 8:22-31, where her credentials come from her relationship with God, and in Sir. 24, she embodies the very words of God; like Jesus' ministry, Sophia is available to a wider public (Prov. 1:20, 21; 8:1-3). Finally, like Jesus' teaching, that of Sophia marks a separation between those who accept and those who reject the teaching, most vividly expressed through Dame Folly. Those who refuse to listen (Prov. 1:24-25) are also culpable, as in John 8:21.

Magdalene also later confesses Jesus as Lord. The purpose of the Spirit is both to reveal things of God and, ultimately, to bring the confession of Jesus as Lord (John 20:18) or as Son of God (John 20:31). Scott remarks, "Just as the initial recognition of Sophia as teacher leads on to a knowledge of God, so too the recognition of the risen Jesus Sophia, the teacher, must lead on to a confession of his true identity."[60] The calling of Mary Magdalene by name also echoes the tradition of the Good Shepherd. The influence of the Sophia tradition is also in evidence through parallels with the parable of the Good Shepherd, where the intimacy between Sophia and her disciples expressed in passages such as Wis. 7:27; 8:2-16; and Sir. 24:19-22 parallels the intimacy found between the Shepherd and the sheep.

It is worth noting that feminist theologian Elisabeth Schüssler Fiorenza names Mary Magdalene as "the primary witness to the resurrection," though, of course, not to the resurrection itself.[61] She notes how Paul omits reference to women in his account and interprets this omission as a way of reinforcing male dominance in the church.[62] Her analysis here is correct; the marginalization of the place of women seems to have crept into the earliest Christian discourse; however, it also makes the Johannine account all the more remarkable. Whether we can conclude, with Scott, that the author of John's Gospel may also have been a woman[63] is, perhaps, to take speculation rather too far, in my view. Schüssler Fiorenza is wary, however, of any accounts that speak of Christ's ascension into heaven; rather, for her, the resurrection simply means that "Jesus, the Living One, goes ahead of us," and "the imaginative space of the 'empty tomb' leads to the proclamation of the Resurrected One who has been vindicated."[64] For her, the tomb tradition of the women is significant inasmuch as it presents an image of

---

60. Scott, *Sophia and the Johannine Jesus*, 234.

61. Elisabeth Schüssler Fiorenza, *Jesus: Miriam's Child, Sophia's Prophet; Critical Issues in Feminist Christology* (London: SCM, 1994), 122.

62. Balthasar has also noted this shift but believes that this endorses the hierarchical structure of the church, which of course, amounts to male dominance, though he does not specifically note the latter or find it objectionable in any way. *MP*, 256–57. Rather, he sees the hierarchical male structure complemented by the femininity of the church. In a somewhat remarkable way, he interprets John as setting up a dual allegory of the church in the two disciples running to the tomb: Peter represents the male church of office, and John the female church of love, hence reducing the role of women still further by collapsing them into a Johannine parable and taking something from the genuine role of women in the early experiences of the resurrection of Jesus. *MP*, 258–59.

63. Scott, *Sophia and the Johannine Jesus*, 240.

64. Schüssler Fiorenza, *Jesus*, 123.

the risen Christ as one who is ahead, in contrast with the male "confessional articulation of resurrection that served as a visionary legitimation of authority."[65]

Yet to assume that such accounts of the resurrection legitimize political authority seems to me to take the exclusion of women in, for example, Pauline accounts too far. In the Johannine tradition, Mary Magdalene both encounters Jesus in visual terms and subsequently confesses Jesus as Lord prior to the confessions of the other disciples. Such confession can therefore hardly be equated in a simple way with male authority. Moreover, while Schüssler Fiorenza sees any theology of the cross as an endorsement of suffering, she still finds in that suffering the presence of the Resurrected One, "in the struggle for survival of those impoverished, hungry, imprisoned, tortured and killed, in the wretched of the earth."[66] Yet as we noted in earlier chapters, a theology of the cross is just as much about a presence of Christ *with* those who suffer, in the light of the resurrection hope, and cannot be considered apart from that hope. It need not and should not be interpreted so much as an *endorsement* of such suffering as *solidarity* with that suffering.

Hence, while I agree that the empty-tomb tradition carries theological weight, and I will return to this in more detail, Schüssler Fiorenza objects in principle to the attribution of the titles of Lord and Son of God to Jesus Sophia. She also believes that not only is the title Lord masculine, but the title also expresses mythological features that represent Christ as divine Sophia, exalted as cosmic Kyrios, and such a rendition of Jesus Sophia "came to function in the Christian community as a foundational myth that created its own cult."[67] It is this, she suggests, that "lends itself in the long run to legitimise Christian domination in christological terms."[68]

Her preoccupation with power and authority has prompted Rowan Williams to suggest that her approach "suffers from the pressure to construct an 'ideal type' of what she calls 'kyriarchal' theology (theology preoccupied with domination and its legitimacy)."[69] Yet I suggest that there is

---

65. Ibid., 123.
66. Ibid., 126.
67. Ibid., 148.
68. Ibid., 149.
69. Williams, *On Christian Theology*, 191.

no reason to assume, in the way that Schüssler Fiorenza suggests, that the exalted Christ automatically legitimizes oppression, since what is crucial is the way that Christ's lordship is interpreted. Certainly, if this lordship is connected with the apostolic ministry of women and named in the imagery of Sophia, it need not lead to oppressive attitudes toward women or marginalized others in the way that she suggests.

Finally, mention needs to be made of the way that the cross and resurrection are held together in the thinking of Elisabeth Johnson. For her, the cross is integral to the birthing process, so that "the cross is part of the larger mystery of pain-to-life, of that struggle for the new creation evocative of the rhythms of pregnancy, delivery and birth so familiar to women of all times."[70] While this might seem appealing on one level, in that it is grounded in women's experience, I have more doubts about its credibility. In the first place, it seems to essentialize women's experience in a particular way, to the exclusion of men. In the second place, it seems to collapse the experience of crucifixion and resurrection into one and thereby could endorse the very suffering that feminist scholars criticize in theologies of the cross. If suffering is *inevitably* a means to birth, in the way she suggests, then surely it should be accepted as part of nature, part of life, and so endorse an unavoidable fatalism. Instead, the story of Magdalene shows that her suffering arose through her loving solidarity with the suffering of Jesus, even before she knew that he was risen from the dead or that the promise was on the way. Hence, suffering needs to be resisted and fought against where it is avoidable or possible to resist, rather than viewed as inevitable and somehow "natural." Yet, paradoxically, in the struggle against injustice, which is the mission of the new community, suffering may occur, and this "unnatural" suffering is where the Spirit of the risen Christ can come and give consolation.[71] Johnson does, however, recognize the key role of women and Mary Magdalene in particular as key witnesses to the resurrection, and unlike Schüssler Fiorenza, following the biblical record, Johnson is prepared to appropriate the possibility of a cosmic Christology as the widest possible scope of the risen Christ's significance.[72]

---

70. E. Johnson, *She Who Is* (New York: Crossroads, 1994), 159.

71. I will return to a discussion of this topic in relation to Balthasar's theology in the following chapter.

72. Johnson, *She Who Is*, 162.

6.4 Sergii Bulgakov: Sophia and the Risen Christ

While the account of Mary Magdalene shows how the Gospel writer John understood Jesus as illustrative of Sophia, the Wisdom of God, Sergii Bulgakov uses the Sophia tradition to develop his account of the resurrection. Bulgakov's risen Christ is woven together with his understanding of the role of the Holy Spirit.[73] To hold to the traditional account of Christ's unity as divine and human, Bulgakov expresses this unity in the way he develops an understanding of the resurrection. For him, the God-man, Jesus, is found "worthy of resurrection," so in this sense, he "raises Himself" by the Holy Spirit reposing on him. This action of Christ Bulgakov holds in parallel with the way Christ raised others from the dead during his earthly ministry, but as in this case, it represents only a partial victory over death, since those he raised also subsequently died. Humanity, even in the original form created by God, could not yet receive the full power of resurrection. Hence, Bulgakov insists that creaturely humanity "would not have been capable of encompassing the power of the raising," as it would have been simply destroyed by the new creation.[74] Human nature has to be elevated both by liberation from sin and through inner deification. This path to deification and immortality through human freedom is offered to Adam, who failed through sin, but is accomplished only in Christ.

This is one reason why Bulgakov can claim that the resurrection of Christ can be understood only according to Christ's high priestly ministry; by high priest, he means the beginning of the end of Christ's kenosis.[75] Yet such cessation of kenosis is in one sense also a "crowning" through the full deification of his human nature, and in this context, Bulgakov speaks of glorification being received by the Son from the Father. The resurrection is not simply an isolated event; rather, it makes sense for Bulgakov only as part of a tapestry of other events connected with glorification, including the ascension, sitting at the right hand of the Father, and sending down of the Holy Spirit at Pentecost. Christ in glory is not, for Bulgakov, simply a return to the preexistent Logos before the incarnation; rather, Christ's human nature is "deified here to such an extreme degree that it is capable of becoming an inseparable part of the divine life of the God-man, and in

---

73. S. Bulgakov, *The Comforter*, trans. Boris Jakim (Grand Rapids: Eerdmans, 2004), 254–55 (hereafter cited as *TC*); and S. Bulgakov, *Lamb of God*, trans. Boris Jakim (Grand Rapids: Eerdmans, 2008), 382–83 (hereafter cited as *LG*).

74. Bulgakov, *LG*, 383.

75. Ibid., 380.

Him, an inseparable part of the life of the Holy Trinity."[76] Moreover, in its deified state, Christ's humanity, "sanctified in him in all its life and in all its being, was deified and acquired the *potency* of actual immortality."[77] God thus bestows immortality on humanity that is both capable and worthy to receive it, and this is found only in Christ. For Bulgakov, "resurrection is a new creation of man in which man himself participates; it is the second and concluding act of creation."[78] Christ's resurrection is a "raising" from the perspective of divinity, but a "resurrection" from the perspective of humanity. Bulgakov is also therefore careful to suggest that the work of glorification is a work of the Holy Trinity, even if it is initiated by the will of the Father.

The resurrection of Christ represents for Bulgakov his glorification, but not in a definitive sense. Indeed, Christ's glorification is definitively *not* a "self-glorification" by the God-man, and in this sense, it includes kenosis.[79] Bulgakov also expresses the action of the Spirit in the Son in kenotic language:

> This increase of the action of the Holy Spirit in power corresponds to a diminution of His kenosis. In raising Christ, the Holy Spirit manifests Himself as Glory in the glorification of the God-man, the kenosis of the Holy Spirit's action in Christ approaches its end, as does the kenosis of the Son.[80]

The grace of the Spirit now comes to Christ himself, in his power to give the Holy Spirit not just through his works, but in a sending of the Spirit onto his disciples. Bulgakov believes that this represents the full deification of the human nature of the God-man. Moreover, the extension of the power of Christ's resurrection to the "entire human race" and the "entire world" was possible only through the activity of the Holy Spirit.

For Bulgakov, there is a difference between the work of the Spirit in the creation of the world or in the Old Testament accounts and the presence of the Spirit following the incarnation. In the former case, the Holy Spirit is present externally, while after the incarnation, the Holy Spirit becomes present "inwardly, for the incarnation has already prepared a place for it

---

76. Ibid., 381.
77. Ibid., 383.
78. Ibid., 384.
79. Ibid., 382.
80. Bulgakov, *TC*, 255.

in the world."[81] The abiding presence of the Spirit in the sacraments shows how, in matter, the power of the Spirit is manifested, albeit in a mysterious, hidden manner. This means that, for Bulgakov, the "fate of the world has already been decided—in the sense of its final salvation and transfiguration," though "not without tragic opposition," because the world still "yearns to be delivered from the bondage of corruption."[82]

For Bulgakov, the Holy Spirit following Pentecost works as much in the natural world as in the human world, for all has already been accomplished for this. His understanding of eschatology is telling here:

> The special character of "the last times" or of the New Testament, consists in this lack of conformity between the fullness of the accomplishment in the heart of creation, on the one hand, and the absence of this accomplishment in the world, or, more precisely, the failure of the world to perceive it and receive it, on the other.[83]

He describes this inaction of the Holy Spirit as the kenosis of the Spirit in its descent into the world. This kenosis is not simply concealment, but represents the inability of the world to receive the Holy Spirit. In other words, the transformation of the world that is anticipated needs a period of kenotic preparation, just as the Pentecost represents the kenosis of the Spirit prepared by the kenosis of Christ. The kenosis of the Son is, in this way, continued in the kenosis of the Spirit, even though the kenosis of the Son is limited in one sense, since the Son is glorified following the ascension into heaven. For Bulgakov, this period of waiting is for the benefit of the world, since, like the reception of the possibility of immortality,

> divinity in all its power and glory cannot enter the world without destroying it or ontologically melting it, as it were. The world must be brought to a state where it can receive the coming of the God-man in glory and where God will be all in all. Until then, the deification of the world which is the descent of the Holy Spirit can only be in part.[84]

---

81. Ibid., 347.
82. Ibid.
83. Ibid., 348.
84. Ibid., 350–51.

In this way, the kenosis of the Spirit is not a self-emptying through removal of divinity, but self-limitation for the sake of the world, "in the subordination of the immeasurable to measure." This is a "kenosis of love, of divine condescension, where the Divine absoluteness enters into connection with creaturely relativity."[85] It is an adaptation of God, not just to the finite being of the world, but to its rejection and alienation from God as well.

The resurrection and ascension of Christ, the God-man, are significant for Bulgakov in other ways, for in Christ we find the unification of creaturely sophia with divine Sophia, and a creaturely sophia that is deified to the fullest extent only after the pouring out of the Holy Spirit following Pentecost. In this way, Bulgakov can claim that Divine-humanity is not complete in the incarnation in a way that would be so if Sophia was only a revelation of the Logos, but the reunification of divine Sophia and creaturely sophia is *both* accomplished in the Logos and anticipated in the Holy Spirit. Hence, for him, "the descent of the Holy Spirit is just as necessary and essential for the sophianization of the world or the accomplishment of the Divine-humanity as the incarnation itself."[86]

Bulgakov's account of the resurrection bears some similarity to that of Balthasar in not just holding together cross and resurrection, but also insisting that it is inclusive of ascension and Pentecost.[87] He also gives a place to Christ's descent into hell as an aspect of his sacrificial ministry.[88] Yet there are important differences as well. Bulgakov places more emphasis

---

85. Ibid., 351.

86. Ibid., 357.

87. Balthasar, *MP*, 199.

88. Admittedly, Bulgakov's account of the descent into hell is less developed than that in Balthasar. See Bulgakov, *LG*, 372–79. Like Balthasar, however, Bulgakov does insist that the descent into afterlife is an integral aspect of the kenosis of the Son. He gives Christ a more active role in hell, preaching to the dead, and for him, Christ's death was not an outcome of the necessity of mortality, but accepted willingly, while being *unnatural* in that it was the result of murder. Bulgakov also considers that Christ suffered the naked power of sin on the cross, which seems to be kept for Holy Saturday in Balthasar's account. In Bulgakov, Christ on the cross receives the torments proper to hell in their intensity; for him, eternity is a quality, rather than duration. God's anger is present against this sin, rather than against the sinner. Bulgakov is also prepared to speak more freely than Balthasar of the suffering of the Holy Spirit as well as the Father, allowing him to speak of co-crucifixion and co-passion of the Love-Spirit, extending this to "the entire Trinity [which] is co-crucified with the Son." Bulgakov, *LG*, 371; see also 356–71, 384.

on the role of the Spirit and on the importance of Jesus in his humanity in the resurrection, even if understood in kenotic terms, as an aspect of his high priestly ministry, rather than the more exclusive role of the Father in Balthasar. He is also less attached than Balthasar to the notion of obedience and has a greater place for the Spirit, especially the work of the Spirit in creation and the new creation. Nonetheless, Balthasar does give to the risen Christ a freedom that is his own in his decision to show himself to chosen disciples, but it is still a freedom that is marked by obedience and that "reveals, ultimately, the freedom of the Father."[89] The Spirit is also given a somewhat lesser role than in Bulgakov, for it is simply a milieu in which the resurrection takes place.

It is also important to note that Bulgakov, in his discussions of Jesus as divine Sophia and creaturely sophia, does not intend to create a "timeless" sense of God's actions in the world. Eternity is not so much the *negation* of time as "the foundation and depth of time. The fullness of eternity is actually disclosed in temporality, which has its power of being only from eternity."[90] Eternity and time are related through divine Sophia and creaturely sophia. Creaturely sophia is, for Bulgakov, a *dvoica* (yoking together) of Word and Spirit active in creation, where the Word represents deep Wisdom and the Spirit the Glory of the unity. The Word as deep wisdom represents the "masculine" element of Sophia, while the Spirit as glory (and beauty) represents the "feminine" element.[91] Bulgakov also incorporates the theme of motherhood, both in the engendering of different species of the natural world in the womb of heaven and as expressed in the God-motherhood of Mary. He extends this imagery to conclude that the Son brings to the Trinity "manhood," while the Spirit brings a "feminine" element to the Godhead. Even so, there are two parts to this heavenly "manhood," namely, the Logos and the Holy Spirit. Bulgakov, like Balthasar, sets up a typology of male and female, where idea/truth is masculine, and reality/beauty is feminine; I will consider this critically in the following chapter. Creaturely sophia is, for him, the all-unity of the creaturely world, while divine Sophia is the all-unity of the divine world. Creaturely sophia is the revelation of the love of the Father in creation as such.

---

89. Balthasar, *MP*, 207, 209.
90. Bulgakov, *LG*, 135; see also 131–35.
91. Ibid., 140.

6.5 Seeking Wisdom and the Empty Tomb

Both Bulgakov and Balthasar use the language of the "soul" to describe what happens to Jesus in his sojourn in hell after death while his body laid in the tomb, prior to the resurrection of both his body and soul. This use of traditional language of "soul" is especially problematic where it pertains to a description of present existence, in that it implies a dualism that works against what we know of neurological science.[92] However, in that the resurrection entails embodiment that is a different kind of "physical" body than that known on earth, there must be a transition from one to the other. Nancey Murphy speaks of this as a "temporary interval" between decay of the earthly body and new creation,[93] though, of course, in Jesus' case, the empty tomb implies that there was no such decay as such, but sheer transformation. Could "soul" still be used in a metaphorical sense to describe the continuity of what happens in this "interval" or in a metaphorical way to describe the existential passage of Jesus in hell?

While I agree that Murphy is correct to point to the philosophical limits of our language in describing the resurrection, it may be that some aspects of traditional theological language can be retained, as long as they are used with sufficient care.

However, there are deeper problems connected to wider theological speculation about the resurrection and future hope that relate not just to the limits of philosophical knowing, but to the limits of theology, as well as the limits of how to incorporate scientific discourse. In offering a critical analysis of Bulgakov's contribution to the debates about the significance of Christ's resurrection, I am returning once again to the problem I addressed at the start that surfaces in the context of biblical discourse, namely, that of the empty tomb. Rowan Williams is, I believe, correct in his assertion that the empty tomb has profound theological significance, beyond any debate as to its authenticity in the historical record.[94]

The question that comes to mind is whether Bulgakov's detailed account of the resurrection and high priestly ministry of Christ goes beyond what can be usefully said about Christ and the new creation. In a way analogous to that identified in the historicization of the resurrection,

---

92. N. Murphy, "The Resurrection of the Body and Personal Identity: Possibilities and Limits of Eschatological Knowledge," in Peters, Russell, and Welker, *Resurrection*, 202–18.

93. See ibid., 215.

94. Williams, *On Christian Theology*, 183–86.

do such speculations give sufficient weight to the apophatic tradition? Are we left with a sophiology that is now no longer seeking, no longer "on the way," subject to a complex theological model that is abstracted far from the simple encounter of Mary with a gardener who turns out, through her seeking, to be Jesus Sophia, the risen Christ? Has the universalism implicit in Bulgakov created a grand, epic narrative that resists revision or awareness that this represents an interpretation appropriately aware of its own situatedness in history? It is also necessary not only to appraise the extent to which Bulgakov's sophiology suffers from such limitations, but also to give due credit to the creativity of his thought and the insights that it brings to the difficult question of how to think about a risen Christ in a creaturely, evolutionary world. Moreover, while taking into account the dangers of metanarrative, to imply that Christ has *no* universal importance or that nothing can be said that offers the widest possible scope to his significance is limiting in the opposite direction, for it empties out and makes vacuous the content of Christian hope.

In the first place, I welcome Bulgakov's inclusion of the work of the Holy Spirit as a key player in the dramatic account of the resurrection of Jesus. This account takes its bearings from his understanding of Jesus as God-man, where divine Sophia and creaturely sophia are united in a single hypostasis, united in one life,[95] and following the resurrection, united in new life. His discussion of Christ's human nature in somewhat ontological terms does, however, need some adjustment in the light of more fluid evolutionary conceptions of human being and becoming. The theodrama enacted between God and humanity reaches its pitch in Bulgakov's account; the resurrection and ascension in this way need not be excluded from theodrama, but rather serve to heighten the climax of the drama felt at the scene of the cross.

Of course, the offering of immortality to Adam need not imply a literal Adam figure in the manner that seems at times to be implied by Bulgakov, though his insistence that immortality is *offered*, rather than given, to Adam in the gift of human freedom provides a way out of more traditional, unrealistic theological accounts of Adam as enjoying the fruit of immortality before the fall.[96] Such mythological stories are clearly outside

---

95. Bulgakov discusses the two natures of Christ in sophianic language. See *LG*, 196–98.

96. I will come back to a discussion of Christ as the second Adam in the context of a Wisdom Christology in chapter 8.

history but give expression to that hazy period in the evolutionary journey of humanity that still escapes full definition. In other words, we can never know precisely when the first *Homo sapiens* appeared, if, indeed, we choose to confine humans as made in the image of God to that species. I am not suggesting that Adam is created by God through divine fiat; rather, the ways of God with the earliest humans cannot be set out in any definitive manner. We have to be content, in other words, with the use of metaphorical language.

Any notion of a literal paradise is out of the question in the light of evolutionary science, but the myth of Adam is saying something different about God's potential relationship with human beings. This is where drama succeeds and where narrative fails, for while authors such as Ben Quash resist any notion of time that fails to fit in with historical time, I suggest that there may be places in a dramatic account where nailing history to a specific time frame falls short, as it is prehistory.[97] In much the same way, while as a matter of faith, we might be prepared to admit that the resurrection of Christ is a concrete event, inasmuch as it fails to fall within our own understanding of the physical cosmos, it makes more sense to use metaphorical language. What does need to be resisted is the introduction of epic language that takes over the dramatic *as if* it were concrete and acts as the primary hermeneutic for the resurrection, such that the concrete accounts of Jesus' encounter with ordinary human mortals fall from view.

It is here that the resurrection of Christ brings us up sharply with the difficulty of theological discussion about the afterlife and future hope. It does, I suggest, make sense to use the language of deification by the Holy Spirit to speak about the resurrection of Christ in his human nature. I am also convinced that, in speaking in this way, something happens in God inasmuch as human "nature" is, in a mysterious way, incorporated into the

---

97. Quash is particularly exercised by Balthasar's account of Jesus' descent into hell as that which is outside what can be envisaged as ordinary time, and considers this a good example of unhelpful "epic" tendencies in his thought. However, it seems to me that keeping such an account *framed* in that of dramatic history helps qualify such "epic" speculations and keep them in their place, as it were. In other words, including "myth" in a dramatic account is not quite as devastating as Quash implies, as long as this thinking does not take over completely. Certainly, the resurrection narrative, which Quash does not attempt to deal with, does not fall into known history, and its significance reaches out beyond what is normally understood as time. Quash, *Theology and the Drama of History*, 194–95.

divine "nature" and opens up the possibility of access to others who also participate in Christ.

The theodrama includes the ascension and Christ as high priest. But the priestly language attributed to Christ is marked by kenosis, or self-offering. This seems to me to be crucial, for without this qualification, the language of priesthood could imply a coercive dominance, rather than a love offering to the world and beyond the world to include the cosmos. While it is understandable, given Bulgakov's background, that he speaks frequently of the primacy of the Father, and this may be troubling to some feminists, it is also the case that he softens this by giving due weight to the work of the Holy Spirit. I do, however, challenge his more stereotypical understanding of the feminine and the transfer of these attributes to the Spirit, rather than to the other two persons of the Trinity. The Trinitarian dance in bringing about the resurrection and ascension of Christ and the pouring out of the Spirit on Pentecost resists any attempt to construe Christ's resurrection as a simple dramatic duo of Father and Son. While there are times when Bulgakov says rather more than could be confidently asserted, it is hard to deny the Trinitarian basis for divine action during and after the resurrection.

Bulgakov presents us with a cosmic vision of present and future hope, where eternity is the foundation of time, and the divine Sophia indwells creaturely sophia. This helpfully avoids the problem of thinking of eternity as simply the evolutionary continuity of time. Drawing on Ernst Conradie's discussion of finitude, where eternity is viewed as a new dimension of time and space,[98] it is possible to understand divine Sophia as incorporating creaturely sophia insofar as it moves beyond the dimensions of time and space in which creaturely sophia is expressed on earth. Bulgakov does offer what amounts to a mythological view of time; his understanding of the period on earth following the Pentecost being a time of waiting and preparation for the time when God will be all in all alleviates any tendency toward what might be termed fully "realized" eschatology. The gradual evolution of the world could be viewed as preparation for the incarnation, and this is set in parallel with waiting for full expression of the new creation that has begun in the resurrection and been made possible by Christ as risen in glory. The theodrama is not over yet. Bulgakov does, nonetheless, at times talk about the Spirit and time in terms that seem somewhat Hegelian in tone.[99]

---

98. Conradie, "Resurrection, Finitude and Ecology," 289.

99. Analysis of this aspect of his work is outside the scope of this chapter and could

Bulgakov also draws the line between animals and humans too sharply in his reflections on human distinctiveness, which makes me wonder as to the real content of future hope that he insists is cosmic in scope. This brings up the very difficult theological issue of the fate of all creatures, including those long since made extinct in evolutionary history. To ignore speaking of the possibility of future hope for the whole earth on the basis of a renewed resistance against metanarratives of any sort is, I suggest, profoundly mistaken. Instead, the basis for the broadest possible hope as that expressed in the third chapter of the epistle to the Colossians gives us reason to hope for such a universal and cosmic experience in the future,[100] even if it would be somewhat foolhardy to make this expectation a matter of *theological* obligation. The gap between the angels alluded to in Rowan Williams's account in order to symbolize the incomplete nature of our knowledge of the meaning of the resurrection remains a gap, so that at the tomb, as in this case, it is not necessary to fill in all the details.[101]

It is tempting, nonetheless, to suppose some creatures might be considered more capable than others of being incorporated into divine life, at least in the sense that not every creature is either individuated or conscious. Ernst Conradie and other ecotheologians such as Denis Edwards have suggested that many beings are retained in God as a kind of memory, rather than in individuated existence in the manner hoped for in human immortality.[102] This in many respects seems an entirely reasonable way of appropriating the tradition in Colossians, and I find it theologically persuasive on many counts. However, I am also challenged by the discourse on the resurrection to remain ultimately open-minded about the extent and scale of future hope for the cosmos. In this sense, Conradie's speculation that God retrieves specific memories, which Conradie makes analogous with human "photos" or "videos," that then go through the judgment and mercy of God

be the topic of further research. Rowan Williams also has drawn attention to this issue in his anthology of Bulgakov's work. See R. Williams, "General Introduction," in *Sergii Bulgakov: Towards a Russian Political Theology*, ed. R. Williams (Edinburgh: T&T Clark, 1999), 19.

100. For further discussion in ecological terms, see C. Deane-Drummond, *Ecotheology* (London: Darton, Longman & Todd, 2008), in press.

101. Rowan Williams, "Between the Cherubim: The Empty Tomb and the Empty Throne," in *On Christian Theology* (Oxford: Blackwell, 2000), 183–96.

102. Conradie, "Resurrection, Finitude and Ecology"; and D. Edwards, "Every Sparrow That Falls to the Ground: The Cost of Evolution and the Christ Event," *Ecotheology* 11, no. 1 (March 2006): 103–23.

goes rather too far. What does inscription mean for God, and how can such memories be "relived" in the manner he suggests?[103] Human life is more than just a collection or assemblage of memories. While I do agree that it is important not to deny the value of the ecodrama in which human drama plays its role, the ending does not mean an eternal recovery of specific memories, but a completion, and one that is perhaps best left as an admission of ignorance. Such an admission need not be escapist if one recognizes the significance of the resurrection of Christ in the accounts that stress the physical aspects of his life after death, such as eating and drinking.

But life in the eschaton is both connected to such a concrete history of Christ and moving beyond its bounds. The mystery of the one who created the world is so much more than our imaginations can conceive that attempts to constrain the nature of what might happen in specific ways are not necessarily all that much of an improvement on the highly speculative accounts that insist on a "re-volution," an individual salvation for all creaturely beings throughout the history of evolution.[104] Reflection on such futures brings a sense of vulnerability in unknowing, but that need not diminish our hope, even if we are tempted to fill that gap with concrete, or not so concrete, images. In keeping with creaturely sophia, the

---

103. Conradie, "Resurrection, Finitude and Ecology," 294–95. He qualifies this speculation by suggesting that one might also think of inscriptions as a drama that then allows for improvisations. While I remain convinced that drama is a valuable metaphor, I am rather less sure about inscription, for it seems to tie God to a certain process through which memories are retained in order to assure that the memory of bodily material existence has some place in the eschaton.

104. I have in mind Moltmann's speculative account in *WJC*:

> It is the divine tempest of the new creation, which sweeps out of God's future over history's fields of the dead, waking and gathering every last created being. The waking of the dead, the gathering of the victims and the seeking of the lost bring a redemption of the world which no evolution can ever achieve. This redemption therefore comprehends the redemption of evolution itself, with all its ambiguities. In this redemption, evolution turns and becomes re-volution, in the original sense of the word.

Moltmann, *WJC*, 303. Not only is a future where all creatures that have ever lived envisaged, but also Moltmann seems to suggest here that the process of evolution as such stands in need of redemption. This coheres with his previous account of God as one who works in evolution through a suffering presence in history, rather than supernatural intervention. Moltmann, *God in Creation* (London: SCM, 1985), 211. Yet elsewhere he concedes that through "his Spirit God is present in the very structures of matter." Ibid., 212.

human search is necessarily left open-ended, even if we might hope for full divinization through divine Sophia. Somehow, it seems to me, we have to learn to accept that vulnerability after the pattern of the one who showed forth divine Sophia in that he emptied himself. Perhaps we should think of such futures more in line with how we think about the resurrection of Christ; namely, that while we can be confident that there will be a new creation, one that is to some extent in continuity with the present world, it also far exceeds and is beyond our expectations and imaginings. We wait in anticipatory hope for what we know not, except that, in a mysterious way, God will be revealed as all in all, and this revelation will be an act of divine condescension, of grace. Seeking wisdom remains open to the possibility of mistake, so that the schemes rendered in the name of Christ are not necessarily of Christ at all. Our hope in Sophia is opened up and opened for the possibility of wonder, a wonder that is not a reflection of scientific knowing as much as poetic appreciation of unknowing.

6.6 Conclusions

I have argued in this chapter for the need to reconsider the significance of Christ's resurrection not just for humanity, but for the wider cosmic community of creation as well. In the discourse on the resurrection of Christ, it becomes relatively easy to adopt a stance that either ignores the significance of this event due to a problematic history or constricts the discussion along lines known to science or history, in other words, in conjunction with known historical and scientific methodologies. While on one level, such a discourse may prove fruitful, inasmuch as it seems to avoid some of the real theological difficulties emerging in analysis of the biblical record, it proves rather more problematic.

I have argued instead that we need to find ways of weaving the observations pertinent to evolutionary discourse *into* a theodramatic account of the resurrection and draw on metaphorical language in order to achieve a certain distance from methodologies more appropriate to history and science. While Jürgen Moltmann attempts to achieve this by speaking of the significance of the resurrection in eschatological terms, his attraction to viewing the resurrection as both an analogy to natural cycles and a sharp discontinuity between the creation and new creation is inconsistent. In addition, his speculations about the content of future life are unconvincing, in that they are not suitably grounded in knowledge of evolutionary biology. I have also suggested that considering the dramatic encounter of Mary Magdalene with the risen Christ illustrates both the drama of the resurrection and its ability to overturn preconceived notions about authority and revelation. Her seeking after Jesus Sophia represents a model of the journey of faith in relation to the resurrection, one that does not easily find closure but is still prepared to admit to naming Christ as Lord.

In considering the sophiological work of Sergii Bulgakov, I have suggested that his understanding of the resurrection of Christ, the Lamb of God, is of one who remains humble even in his exaltation. I also argued that his work is significant inasmuch as he draws on a pneumatological understanding of Christ's resurrection and its significance. While I am critical of aspects of his work—in particular, his tendency to use mythological and epic narrative description, his naive view of animals, his stereotypical view of women, a view of the Trinity that gives the Father primacy, and an unchallenged metaphysics that seems reliant on a certain Hegelian metanarrative—such problems should not obscure his constructive contribution to debates on the significance of the resurrection in an evolutionary context. In particular, reflection on Jesus as creaturely sophia and divine Sophia invites further reflection on wonder as that open space where we can come to know the mystery of God in the community of the saints. To fill out a little further what that mystery might mean, I will turn to the work of Balthasar in the next chapter.

7

Revisiting the New Community: Christ in Eschatological Wonder

This chapter returns once more to the theme of wonder introduced in chapter 4: How might wonder as that experienced by humanity be connected with Christian expectation of a new community grounded in an experience of faith in Christ? Drawing particularly on a critical appreciation of the work of Hans Urs von Balthasar, I will argue for the importance of wonder in the mode of glory as a realistic Christian hope. This way of thinking about the future is in marked contrast to that expressed in evolutionary psychology, and offers both a rebuttal and a challenge to its secularized eschatology. Balthasar's work identifies an important dimension in any discussion of Christ and evolution, namely, that Christian eschatological expectation treats time in a different way, and that future hope includes participation in the life of the Trinity. The relationship between Christ and the new creation includes due attention to the Holy Spirit, who is also the Spirit of Christ, and it is through this Spirit that a mirror of the wonder and glory of God becomes visible. Such wonder has within it the marks of suffering, yet it is now experienced as fruitfulness. While I will have reason to challenge certain aspects of Balthasar's thinking, especially in the light of a feminist critique, the inclusion of a cosmic aspect to his understanding of future hope parallels his attention to Christ understood in cosmic, concrete terms.

7.1 Wonder at Being

Balthasar reinstates the importance of wonder in his metaphysics, boldly claiming, "Wonder at Being is not only the beginning of thought, but, as Heidegger sees it—also the permanent element . . . in which it moves."[1] But contrary to Heidegger, it is "astonishing" that existent beings can wonder at Being in distinction from Being, and also that Being itself "causes wonder, behaving as something to be wondered at, something striking and worthy of wonder."[2] Metaphysics is built around this "primal wonder."[3]

Yet this is different, again, from the kind of wonder that scientists experience in their discoveries. For Balthasar, this feeling of scientists is related to Plato's loss of a sense of wonder and metaphysics, and its replacement by "admiration" and a fixed cosmology, so that "the sciences now soar proudly aloft in their joy of intellectual discovery."[4] Underlying this philosophy is the thought of some kind of necessity, which removes the primal wonder that there is something rather than nothing. This elevated feeling is also removed from love, which is a priori a love of Being; hence love informs a sense of wonder, for he believes that "no science will track down the ground of why something exists rather than nothing at all."[5] I am less convinced than Balthasar that at least some scientists experience the kind of love and contemplation that he believes are necessary in order to achieve metaphysical wonder, though it is fair to suggest that Richard

---

1. Hans Urs von Balthasar, *The Glory of the Lord*, vol. 5, *In the Realm of Metaphysics in the Modern Age*, trans. O. Davies, A. Louth, B. McNeil, J. Saward, and R. Williams (Edinburgh: T&T Clark, 1991), 614 (hereafter cited as *GL* 5).

2. Ibid., 615.

3. Balthasar has been criticized for a somewhat "idiosyncratic" approach to metaphysics by many contemporary critics. See, for example, Fergus Kerr, "Balthasar and Metaphysics," in *Cambridge Companion to Hans Urs von Balthasar*, ed. Edward T. Oakes and David Moss (Cambridge: Cambridge University Press, 2004), 224. However, the category of wonder may become rather more fashionable again in contemporary philosophy. As the philosopher Jerome Miller suggests—ironically, perhaps—in a postmodern context, wonder itself might seem to kill reasoning, but at the same time, it opens up a space where the impossible can be conceived. See Jerome A. Miller, *In the Throe of Wonder: Intimations of the Sacred in a Post-modern World* (Albany: State University of New York Press, 1992), 3–6.

4. Balthasar, *GL* 5, 647.

5. Ibid. Of course, Balthasar may have been unaware of the attempts by scientists to do just this through theoretical physics, though his point remains intact in that such explanations are not "final" in any sense of the word.

Dawkins's sense of wonder, by being tied to specific rationalistic formulas in evolutionary science, is certainly not wonder in the Balthasarian sense.[6]

Balthasar also argues against the sufficiency of evolutionary and biological explanations of existence, even though he recognizes evolutionary forms as helpful for classification purposes.[7] Balthasar's critique is most appropriate in the context of human life and, in particular, reducing personal love to "either transcendental, biological and evolutionistic or materialistic process," for such a reduction leads to forms of human existence that "lack all radiance and meaning, and there is no longer any reason why it should be better that something exist rather than simply nothing at all."[8] His remarks make most sense in the context of evolutionary psychology's attempt to explain all aspects of human behavior, including aesthetics, in evolutionary terms, though his reduction of evolutionary accounts to "a fertile and fertilizable cell within the whole organism, who can enjoy only a prospective intuition of an invisible evolutionary goal," is itself perhaps surprisingly naïve. Even though evolutionary psychology speaks of "design," Darwinian evolution, at least, knows of no teleology. His comments are less convincing inasmuch as I would urge rather more weight to be given to evolutionary science than to render it simply as a "classification system." On the other hand, giving evolution too much significance through attempts to formulate a grand narrative or through the opposite tendency to stress contingency, opening up the possibility of nihilistic denial of meaning, is equally problematic compared with Balthasar's somewhat thin conception of evolution.

Balthazar also resists a more Leibnizean philosophy of Spirit and Hegelian dialectic in resolving the problem of the relationship between Being and beings. The Christian, for Balthasar, has a role in the secular denial of the ultimacy of Being and so is the "guardian of that metaphysical wonderment which is the point of origin for philosophy."[9] He argues that once we assume the dependence of Being on beings, it is impossible to attribute to Being the responsibility for the essential forms of entities. Closing the circle, as it were, between Being and beings shuts out the metaphysical category of glory, dissolving either into the beauty of the order

---

6. For more discussion of wonder in science, see C. Deane-Drummond, *Wonder and Wisdom* (London: Darton, Longman & Todd, 2006).

7. Balthasar, *GL* 5, 620.

8. Ibid., 644.

9. Ibid., 646.

of the world or a self-explication of Being governed by no ultimate form of freedom.[10] Hence, while we might think we encounter "glory" in such instances, what we actually encounter is "inauthentic" versions, which are inauthentic inasmuch as majesty is always more than our perception of it. Rather, he argues, through the freedom of Being, the "radiance of glory is justified, that radiance streams intangibly through everything that is."[11] This freedom also entails a "letting be" that opens up the possibility of either alien Being and nihilism or Being appearing to us as glory, so that all "power," "light," and "grace" are gathered into it. For us to secure nonsubsisting Being in glory, it needs to be grounded in the subsisting freedom of Absolute Being, which is God.[12] This metaphysical approach to wonder in the mode of glory forms both the background to his understanding of the glory of Christ and his particular approach to eschatology.

7.2 The Glory of Love

Balthasar is not content to stop at a metaphysical account of wonder transcribed as glory in theism, but rather seeks to embed it in his reading of biblical texts drawn from both the Old and New Testaments. He believes that biblical theology and identification of its "central concerns" should form the criterion through which to test other accounts of glory.[13] While it might be disputed how far he has achieved such scriptural reasoning, his intention, at least, seems sincere enough, and his retrieval of the biblical category of glory goes further than what he claims is Scholasticism's "pagan" account of it as honor, praise, fame, or renown.[14]

Rather, beginning with the Hebrew Bible, he seeks to recover a biblical sense of *kabod* (glory) with its root in *kbd*, the physically heavy. He also seeks to distinguish between human *kabod*, which includes an inseparability of biological, spiritual, and personal potency, from *kabod* of God. God's *kabod* is no longer simply submerged in the biological sphere, but there are also no purely "spiritual" manifestations. God's *kabod* is also inseparable from, while not coinciding with, holiness, the manifestation of God's

---

10. Ibid., 621.
11. Ibid., 622.
12. Ibid., 623–25.
13. Hans Urs von Balthasar, *The Glory of the Lord*, vol. 6, *Theology: The Old Covenant*, trans. Brian McNeil and Erasmo Leiva-Merikakis (Edinburgh: T&T Clark, 1991), 20 (hereafter cited as *GL* 6).
14. Ibid., 26.

name, and the might of spiritual actions.[15] Any form or epiphany of God seen in the Old Testament account is an indication or hint of God's *kabod*, rather than the full *kabod* of God, so that it is veiled from human eyes.

In the intertestamental period, there existed a "long twilight" without any encounter with or even hints of God's glory. Yet Balthasar is positive about strands in Judaism that are, he believes, indispensable mediators to the New Testament account, including messianic, apocalyptic, and Wisdom theology. While he is critical of the "lack of distinctiveness" in Wisdom literature, he also admits that the book of Wisdom is close to Torah.[16] Such a possibility seems to be reached by stages, so that divinity as immanence in the world expresses God's majesty, divinity as free elevation above the world expresses God's sublimity, and God's glory in the strongest sense is expressed only through the free turning of God's personal divinity to the creature. Such free turning becomes expressed as word and deed, in the creation of God's image in the created order, and definitively in the face of Jesus Christ.[17]

Once we come to the new covenant, Balthasar is able to spell out more specifically his understanding of Christ as the revelation of God's glory. Drawing particularly on the passage in Col. 1:19 that speaks of the "fullness of the deity [that] dwells bodily" (Balthasar's translation), he presents Christ as expressing not just an image of God's glory, but God's glory as such:

> The previous distinction between the archetype of divine glory and its reflection in the human image, and finally the reciprocity between archetype and image in the glory of the covenant of grace, is bypassed and dissolved, so that the one of whom we must now speak becomes in an unheard of manner the joint founder of all periods and indeed the "effulgence of the glory" and "imprint of the substance" of God himself (Heb. 1.3).[18]

Yet the task of Christ is also to go down into the "absolute contradiction of the glory of God, into the night of abandonment by God and the formless

---

15. Ibid., 33–34.
16. Ibid., 302–3.
17. Hans Urs von Balthasar, *The Glory of the Lord*, vol. 7, *Theology: The New Covenant*, trans. Brian McNeil (Edinburgh: T&T Clark, 1989), 269 (hereafter cited as *GL* 7).
18. Ibid., 13.

chaos of Hell," so that he may establish the indivisible form that joins God and the world in the new and eternal covenant.[19] Perceiving such a glorious "vision of the form" is for Balthasar possible only with the eye of faith, the "simple eye" that recognizes that the unique form of Christ is also what he terms an expression of the mystery of the "superform" within the Godhead, showing forth the Trinity as "absolute love," and thereby the "essence" of God is made known. The glory and wonder that are perceived are therefore the glory and wonder of love made manifest in Christ. Moreover, it is a glorious love with a "radiance that has its source in the momentum of the obedience on the Cross."[20] It is in giving himself away that Jesus becomes the perfect icon of the Father, who has given himself away in generating the Son.[21] Here the relationship between the economic and immanent Trinity becomes clear, for although God did not need the form of Jesus Christ to be the triune God, there is nothing "accidental" in this act of making Godself known. Citing 2 Cor. 4:6, Balthasar is able to claim that the light and knowledge of the glory of God are made evident in the face of Jesus Christ.[22]

7.3 Glory as Participation in Love

Although it might be possible to see the radiant glory of Christ as mirrored in the Trinitarian relationships of love, the question then becomes how this might be accessed by creatures. Balthasar relies heavily on Jesus' departure discourse in John 16 to link Jesus' departure with the coming of the Holy Spirit. It also allows him to develop an eschatology that veers on the side of "realized" in the present, rather than not yet in the far-flung future, even though both elements are present. Yet he does not want to collapse all eschatology simply into a fulfillment of Old Testament promises, for "the presence of what belongs in the future is the true source of beauty in the New Testament."[23] Moreover, the future is not simply a restoration of an idealized beginning, but a drawing in of both the new community of the church and the world "into the light of the trinitarian love."[24]

---

19. Ibid., 14.

20. Ibid., 256.

21. Hans Urs von Balthasar, *Mysterium Pascale*, trans. Aidan Nichols (Edinburgh: T&T Clark, 1990), 153.

22. Balthasar, *GL* 7, 17–18.

23. Ibid., 19.

24. Ibid., 260.

Before coming to reflect on the manner of deification that Balthasar envisions for the new community, we must pay some attention to his understanding of Christ "in the concrete," that is, in his lived, material existence.[25] In the first place, God enters into dependence and neediness on a human mother, so transcendence cannot mean an abstraction that cannot enter into a relationship with humanity.[26] It is therefore only as *incarnate* that the Son can provide a measure of the relationship between God and the world, from above and from within.[27] In addition, Mary, as *Theotokos* (God bearer), by giving birth to the Son of God, in some sense participates in the divine life. The influence of patristic teaching on Mary comes to the fore here; she symbolizes the life of the church that now becomes the womb where God and humanity are united, an ongoing "assumption" of all created being.[28]

The self-giving that Balthasar finds expressed in Mary is also taken up in his interpretation of the Pauline idea of death in Christ, which implies a depth of self-surrender "which he makes his aim in the act of faith," expressing a longing to appropriate for himself that "total self-giving of God."[29] This is not a passive activity, but one that is "driven" by the Spirit, in a manner of sonship rather than slavery. Our spirit is borne by the Pneuma, who is also the Pneuma of the Son, and this allows a deeper entering into "the event of the eternal generation of the Son (Jn 1.13)."[30] Balthasar draws an analogy between this experience of giving and yet finding oneself and that of sex, though he believes that where a single reality is shown up, this amounts to a loss of personality. His somewhat stereotypical portrait of the psychology of sex is problematic, and he overworks this in other ways. For example, he draws a further analogy between sex and the Eucharist as "pneumatological bodiliness of the Son" while resisting all forms of anonymity that such an analogy might imply.[31] While I will have occasion to comment more fully on his understanding of the relationship between the sexes in the next section, for the moment the most important issue is to stress that this analogy is his

---

25. See, for example, Hans Urs von Balthasar, *A Theology of History* (London: Sheed & Ward, 1963), 13 (hereafter cited as *TH*).

26. For discussion, see Nicholas J. Healy, *The Eschatology of Hans Urs von Balthasar: Being as Communion* (Oxford: Oxford University Press, 2005), 99.

27. Balthasar, *TH*, 65.

28. See Brendan Leahy, *The Marian Profile in the Ecclesiology of Hans Urs von Balthasar* (London: New City, 2000).

29. Balthasar, *GL* 7, 405.

30. Ibid., 406.

31. Ibid.

way of expressing the enduring "bodiliness" of the divine love between God and the world in such a way that "the historical and sexual existence that includes birth and death can be taken up eschatologically and given a home in the absolute triune love."[32] Hence, he finds that the "inchoate creaturely forms of finding oneself" are justified through God, who expropriates them and gives them a home in the one who loves all things. The life of God comes through the "inmost indwelling of Christ in the believer."[33] Yet such participation rests in the incarnation, through the double act of the Father's sending and human consent by the virgin Mary.[34]

The love that is possible within the church by the grace of God's free bestowal is, for Balthasar, truly a "miracle of God's glory," so that, citing Eph. 1:6, a person has truly become "the glorification of the glory of the grace of God."[35] Moreover, he returns again and again to the theme of the miracle of God's appearing in what God is not, so that in human fellowship, we find the presence of God made manifest:

> It is the dawning of the divine love in what is not God and what is opposed to God, the dawning of eternal life (as resurrection) in utter death: not the dawning of the divine I in the non-divine Thou, but the dawning of the divine I-Thou-We in the worldly, creaturely, I-Thou-We of human fellowship.[36]

In this, he is resisting individualism and pointing to the corporate nature of eschatological expectation. The future hope for which humanity longs is more than just a vision, for it is "a participation in the very surging life of God."[37] The participation in the life of the Trinity allows humanity to enter into the Trinitarian relationships. According to John of the Cross, the soul on earth can only grasp a shadow of the wisdom, beauty, and power of God.[38] The breathing of the Holy Spirit is united with that of the mystic, so

---

32. Ibid.

33. Ibid., 407.

34. Hans Urs von Balthasar, *Theo-Drama: Theo-Dramatic Theory*, vol. 5, *The Final Act*, trans. Graham Harrison (San Francisco: Ignatius, 1998), 467 (hereafter cited as *TD* 5).

35. Balthasar, *GL* 7, 431.

36. Ibid., 432.

37. Hans Urs von Balthasar, *Explorations in Theology*, vol. 4, *Spirit and Institution*, trans. Edward Oakes (San Francisco: Ignatius, 1995), 442 (hereafter cited as *ET* 4).

38. Glory-shadow does not have the same connotations of negativity as shadow sophia in chapter 5, and is the language used by John of the Cross. Balthasar, *TD* 5, 431.

that the same breathing received in grace amounts to collaboration in the work of the Trinity, given for the sake of the new community. The mystic experiences portray for Balthasar a borderland between earth and future glory, so that, in the case of John of the Cross, "only a thin veil separates what he portrays from heaven; once the veil is rent, the mutual breathing of the Spirit by Father and Son will be the most intimate bliss."[39]

7.4 Glory in Fruitfulness: The Eucharistic Feast

The mystery of eternal life finds expression for Balthasar in the images of meal and marriage. I will concentrate on the former here, though both are linked with his notion of fruitfulness, and commenting on "the inner connection between meal and marriage," he remarks, "Even in earthly life they are situations of self-surrender, reciprocal nurturing, fruitfulness and joy."[40] This takes up his image of fruitfulness as a theme running through the New Testament in a way that is connected with glorification in the image of the vine.[41] It is in Christ's Eucharist that we find the full meaning of fruitfulness, as expressed in a biological metaphor, so that "in this thanksgiving he definitively becomes the grain of wheat that falls into the earth in order to bear much fruit."[42] It expresses, in other words, the abundance of God's grace in the midst of suffering, so that "when God throws himself away (as seed and Word), he shows not only the principle of all fecundity and all generosity, but also the essence of his glory."[43] Balthasar also believes that it is through identification with the suffering of Christ that human suffering and pain can be transformed, so that "the entire futility and decay of earthly existence can, as such, be transformed into fruitfulness, if it understands itself as the 'pangs' of the new aeon, and a sharing in Christ's sufferings."[44]

Yet it would be incorrect to surmise from the discussion thus far that Balthasar's understanding of suffering simply glorifies it.[45] It is, in the first

---

39. Ibid., 469.
40. Ibid., 471.
41. Balthasar, *GL* 7, 416.
42. Ibid., 418.
43. Ibid., 432.
44. Ibid., 519.
45. This position is evident in Sarah Coakley's dismissal of the spirituality of Balthasar as amounting to a "pedestalized place of suffering" in an otherwise sensitive treatment of the topic of power and spirituality in the Christian tradition. S. Coakley, *Powers and Submissions: Spirituality, Philosophy and Gender* (Oxford: Blackwell, 2002),

place, a transformation of suffering through identification with the suffering of Christ in response to divine mission. In the second place, suffering as such is not welcomed for its own sake, but human goals are qualified in relation to the hope anticipated in the future. Hence, he suggests, "Every attempt to establish freedom, peace and brotherhood on earth must go in the *direction* which the Christian hope indicates," and that hope includes absence from suffering. His resistance to evolutionary or linear accounts of the coming kingdom raised his hackles against most forms of political theology, but that does not mean he considered Christian mission to be *isolated* from social goals; rather, he failed to develop in concrete terms the direction that his thinking indicates.[46] In the third place, he is clear that the cross and all suffering express humanity's *alienation* from God, and he accuses Moltmann of identifying the cross *as* life in God in a way that is unacceptable.[47] Fourth, the permission of God to act through the bestowal of grace in human lives is "the opposite of lazy passivity"; it is not simply a grim embracing of suffering in a passive sense, but the inevitability of suffering coming to the surface where Christ's disciples seek to realize the kingdom.[48] The greatest depravity of sin occurs, for Balthasar, *after* the divine has made known the depths of its love through coming in Christ.[49] Moreover, "the triune love of God has power only in the form of surrender (and in the vulnerability and powerlessness that is part of the essence of that surrender)."[50] Similarly, for him the church is unlikely to bear fruit through power and strength, but weakness in worldly terms is the true

---

xx. Only a superficial reading of Balthasar would lead to such a conclusion; suffering in Balthasar's spirituality is not so much sought after but embraced for the sake of one who suffered for the love of the world. In addition, his attention to kenosis understood as an embracing of vulnerability and powerlessness is a view that Coakley believes can withstand a feminist critique toward victimization. Nonetheless, like Coakley, I also have reason to challenge Balthasar's particular view on sexuality and women.

46. Gerard O'Hanlon is helpful here in his suggestion that Balthasar lacks a real engagement with the concrete, though I am less convinced that Balthasar is as neutral toward patriarchy as he suggests, and while his theodrama could, as he implies, be hijacked to support unjust structures, it could equally be expanded toward social goods. G. O'Hanlon, "Theological Dramatics," in *The Beauty of Christ*, ed. Bede McGregor and T. Norris, 92–111 (Edinburgh: T&T Clark, 1994), 108–11.

47. For a careful discussion of Balthasar's treatment of Moltmann, see Kevin Mongrain, *The Systematic Thought of Hans Urs von Balthasar: An Irenaean Retrieval* (New York: Herder & Herder, 2002), 175–79.

48. Balthasar, *GL* 7, 530.

49. Balthasar, *ET* 4, 435.

50. Ibid., 435–37.

mark of the church, so that through the pouring out of the Spirit, God's grace is sufficient. Fifth, the suffering of the church and those called to imitate the mission of Christ enters into the dialectic of the cross and resurrection, suffering and joy. This is a mystery known to Christian experience, so that "the Christian leaves the world's rhythms in which joy and suffering alternate, and enters a sphere that is mysterious for all men, and for himself, into a possibility of affirming suffering in joy, with God and in God, while nevertheless not depriving suffering of its depths of abandonment by God."[51] Such a position is not something that can be argued for in a logical way; rather, it is born of Christian experience. For Balthasar at least, the church can never resemble the bright glory of God but must always be content just to reflect this glory as the moon reflects the sun's light.[52]

The eternal future for humanity is also one in which the gift of divine freedom is realized, but this does not amount to a loss of freedom; rather, it is "a divine freedom in one's own freedom."[53] His account of human freedom draws heavily on Ignatius, but it is an attitude of surrender that is encompassed by the freedom of God, rather than adding on "something unimaginably new." Hence, he believes that our preference for the divine will still gives full play to our own will, and the essence of the eternal begins to be perfected in mortal life.

While it is certainly true that the language of obedience Balthasar uses can be off-putting, it is worth considering how far this focus leads to suppression of human creativity in the manner indicated by some critics.[54]

---

51. Balthasar, *GL* 7, 539.

52. Ibid., 543.

53. Balthasar, *ET* 4, 439.

54. Quash, for example, comments that with respect to freedom, obedience has the last word in Balthasar, comparing him unfavorably with Barth in this respect, suggesting that Balthasar interprets obedience in an ecclesial way that leads to a lack of human creativity. Ben Quash, *Theology and the Drama of History* (Cambridge: Cambridge University Press, 2005), 158–59. I agree that obedience in Balthasar comes over at times as cold and institutional, even claiming in a quite horrifying way that "every 'dialogue-situation' was excluded—by a corresponding agreement of Adrienne's soul—so that it became experientially clear that the obedience of the Church can and at times must have all the reality and relentlessness of the Cross itself, both in the authority which commands and the faithful who obey." Hans Urs von Balthasar, *First Glance at Adrienne von Speyr*, trans. Antje Lawry and Sergia Englund (San Francisco: Ignatius, 1968), 70. However, obedience is not as strict as it may appear, in that, like his mentor Ignatius of Loyola, his did not cohere with the language of obedience that he enunciated. Aidan Nichols comments on the "cold-shouldering" of Balthasar by church authority, perhaps related to his own decision to leave the religious life. See A. Nichols, *The Word*

How far he is successful in practice in allowing that creativity to emerge is a moot point, one that we will return to in section 7.7, but he resists any mechanical adoption of spiritual practices, including either a deliberate "plunging downward" or a deliberate seeking after the divine unity through adherence to ascending mystical "techniques."[55]

Balthasar does not shy away from speaking about eschatological judgment, but it is one in which the figure of Christ in his glory still bears the marks of the wounds he has received and his work of reconciliation. Gazing on the wounded judge shatters any preconceived notions of glory and proves what the sin of the world has done to God. The lament is for the one wounded, rather than fear of judgment as such, so his authority presupposes his powerlessness.[56] While the outcome of judgment cannot be known in advance, those who are to be judged can hope in the grace of solidarity of Christ with sinners and the lost. The church stands as co-judge rather than co-redeemer. Such judgment is not so much a breaking in at the end of time, but a vertical dimension that becomes manifest in a dimension commensurable with world-historical time.[57] Hence, even here, we still have the Eucharistic feast, so that the Father continues to surrender the Son in the form of the Eucharist, and the divine Spirit continues to groan for our redemption. In this way, Balthasar admits to a mysterious co-suffering of the whole of heaven with the world, "pathos" in God.

Yet the image of eternal life in the Eucharistic feast shows more clearly than other images the mystery of the relationship between Christ's body and the believers' body as both somatic and pneumatic.[58] The earthly and heavenly are not simply compared through transience and eternity, but there is a "vertical" connection between the two that is best expressed through nuptial imagery.[59] It is a mystery of body and spirit both now and

---

Has Been Abroad: A Guide through Balthasar's Aesthetics (Edinburgh: T&T Clark, 1998), xv–xvi. In addition, any tendency toward rigidity and conservatism is not the only note in his theology, since elsewhere he speaks much more positively about future hope, including creativity. I will have reason to comment later on the *content* he envisages for that creativity, insofar as it needs to be enlarged, but human creativity is still affirmed, even though he views this as a corporate affair, rather than the "lonely" isolation of the genius. See Balthasar, *TD* 5, 487.

55. Balthasar, *ET* 4, 440.
56. Ibid., 448–49.
57. Ibid., 457–59.
58. Balthasar, *TD* 5, 471.
59. Ibid., 472.

in eternity; hence, the bodily aspects are affirmed rather than negated. At the same time, Balthasar resists any suggestion that there might be a literal need for nourishment in eternity; the analogy needs to give way to the analogy made possible by Christ's resurrection, where the bodily need for nourishment, as well as death, suffering, mourning, and marriage, will no longer hold sway. The command for eternal fruitfulness does not apply to procreation, for in Balthasar's view it is expressed in eternity purely in the spiritual-intellectual dimension. This dimension is not possible for non-humans as it is rooted in the knowledge of God.[60]

Of course, the question now arises as to why Balthasar has seemingly reified the "spiritual-intellectual" dimension of fruitfulness in the eschaton, without considering, for example, other, affective aspects more fully. This may be related to his particular concentration on *freedom*, interpreted as *obedience*, and understood as the essence of *imago Dei*, and his particular— and, in my view, flawed—way of engaging human interpersonal and sexual relationships. The transcendence of the meal is expressed through allowing God to give us what we need and experiencing a sense of dependence, accepting it with gratitude. Yet, citing John 4:34, the meal becomes its most "ascending analogy" to eternal life by relating the exchange taking place in the Eucharistic meal to the task of obedience to the Father. Christ no longer has any need to suffer in the bodily sense, but "by the operation of the Holy Spirit he has become a eucharistically fruitful Body for the reconciled world."[61] Yet the "wounds in Christ's body remain open" in response to the divine love of the Father, in such a way that devotion to the "Blood of Christ" is "at the heart of dogmatics."[62]

Yet it is important for Balthasar to express a reciprocity that is involved in the Eucharist; it is not simply a passive receiving, but a freely given response and acceptance of it by the church through the power of the Holy Spirit.[63] In eternal life, following Erich Przywara, he urges that our vital bodies will receive nourishment through the Eucharist, even though our mortal bodies have perished. Yet, as on earth, the Eucharist "as an event of love will remain reciprocal."[64] It is important therefore for

---

60. Ibid., 474.

61. Ibid., 477.

62. The influence of the mystical thought of Catherine of Sienna is in evidence here, and many will balk at this seemingly crude way of expressing the love of God.

63. Balthasar, *TD* 5, 478.

64. Ibid., 481.

the individual to be respected in eternity; thus, "[divine triune freedom] does not override or infringe the area of mystery of each individual's creaturely spontaneity."[65] The free availability of each person to the other comes through the distinctiveness of each, so that "what is offered to the other is thus always an unexpected and surprising gift."[66] The creative elements of disparate redeemed human freedoms come together in a synthetic way, and such coincidence is an aspect of "eternal blessedness" yet beyond all predictions.[67]

7.5 The Breadth of Glory

Discussion of Balthasar's eschatology has more often than not concentrated on the extent to which he resisted or endorsed universalism, understood as an openness of salvation to all.[68] In the context of the present study, however, the main focus is the extent to which he understands how nonhuman creatures might share in the eschatological promises given to the church. This area has been neglected in analysis of his works in secondary sources, no doubt reflecting an anthropocentric bias assumed by his contemporary interpreters. Indeed, the thrust of his thinking is such that creation is not so much "left behind" as "gathered in," so that he can ask, "How could God forget his 'evolutionary' creation when he plans to make ready for it a definitive place in his triune love?"[69] Balthasar is clear that the processes of evolution of

---

65. Ibid., 485.

66. Ibid., 486.

67. He follows Hegel here in his admission that creativity necessarily involves an overcoming of alienation, which he views as the deeper reason for the Hegelian project as a whole. For Balthasar, this has already taken place through the cross and resurrection. How far Balthasar is being consistent with his earlier staunch attack against all forms of Hegelian thinking is questionable. Certainly, he wants to distinguish between creaturely creativity and that in God, which he believes is opposed to all forms of Hegelian synthesis. Hence, he argues later that in God, "the decision to create is purely gratuitous, and we cannot get 'behind' or 'above' it to find some external necessity. The whole thrust of this book has been to show that the infinite possibilities of divine freedom all lie within the trinitarian distinctiveness and are thus free possibilities within the eternal life of God that has *always been realized*." *TD* 5, 508. Hence, while he seems to admit to a measure of Hegelian appropriation in the matter of human creativity, he resists this suggestion for God. How far he is entirely successful in removing all traces of Hegelian thinking in his project as a whole is open for discussion.

68. See, for example, Geoffrey Wainwright, "Eschatology," in Oakes and Moss, *Cambridge Companion*, 113–30.

69. Balthasar, *GL* 7, 518.

the world are insufficient to bring about the kingdom of God. However, this does not lead to a denial of the material order, for he insists that it is through the vehicle of concrete realities of bread and wine that the gift of God can be fully recognized as such. Balthasar's strong resistance to all tendencies in theology toward Gnosticism refers back to his thorough grounding in the incarnational theology of Irenaeus, Ignatian spirituality, and his desire to keep creation and redemption firmly woven together.[70] He also rather too readily accuses others of displaying what he calls "epic" theology that is ahistorical, or accuses them of undue influences such as that of Hegelianism, which he detects particularly in the thinking of Jürgen Moltmann.[71]

While he is somewhat hesitant in spelling out the eschatological future in any detail, he is clear that creation as a whole is the object of future glory while also sharing in a "radical dying and rising." Yet while there are "different ways in which man and the world will enter eternal life," such life will be "transparent" for a life that will "possess the infinite determination of the trinitarian process of love."[72] How this might happen is related to Balthasar's concept of time. In the last part of his *Theo-Drama*, he spells out the way historical and, by implication, evolutionary time is woven into what he terms the "vertical" theodrama, giving horizontal time "meaning and form." Yet this is not "nontime," or the timelessness that is sometimes attributed to God, but a time above every time, a "supertime," shown by the recapitulation of world time in Christ's time.[73] Balthasar believes it is an "open question" as to whether the "little while" of Jesus' absence is both up to his resurrection and his coming again, though he urges that both elements are likely to be present, even though John's Gospel favors the former.

This vertical theodrama is, as far as he is concerned, distinguished from any "epic" account inasmuch as it is grounded in the fulfillment of

---

70. For a discussion of the influence of Irenaeus, see Mongrain, *Systematic Thought*.

71. Does Balthasar's somewhat unnecessarily vicious attack on Moltmann display a certain lack of proper attention to Hegelian strands in his own thinking, a view that Ben Quash seems to endorse? Or is his affinity with Irenaean grounding in creation sufficient to counter any such tendency, in the manner held by Kevin Mongrain? Quash identifies Balthasar's attachment to indifference as betraying Hegelian habits of thought and, for him, thereby suppressing creativity in individuals' response to God. See Quash, *Theology and the Drama of History*, 132ff.

72. Balthasar, *ET* 4, 438.

73. Balthasar, *TD* 5, 30.

Yahweh's covenant drama with Israel[74] and, we might add, the whole of evolutionary history. For this reason, Balthasar ultimately resists any linear image of the "last day," and, heavily influenced by Johannine eschatology, he overstates somewhat categorically, "The New Testament no longer entertains the idea of a self-unfolding horizontal theo-drama; there is only a vertical theo-drama in which every moment of time, insofar as it has christological significance, is directly related to the exalted Lord, who has taken the entire content of history—life, death and resurrection—with him into the supra-temporal realm."[75] Yet he resists the idea that this damps down a sense of expectation that is characteristic of the Christian life. Such expectations should bypass extensions of anthropocentric time, leading to simply an extension into the future or, rather, christological time, where time is "assumed into the divine form of duration" and thus becomes Trinitarian time. This is one reason why he resists the notion of "realized" eschatology, as for him, this implies an anthropocentric reading of time, even though assumption does not mean annihilation.

Balthasar's discussion of "supertime" and "divine time" is not intended to remove Christian hope from the hopes in this world. Rather, "it does not pass it by," but "takes the world with it on its way to God" in such a way that it is never individualistic and goes beyond hope for worldly well-being.[76] His understanding of the future of creation is built upon his understanding of the world as embedded in Trinitarian relationships, building on Aquinas's

---

74. Ibid., 32. How far he is successful in this grounding is open for discussion. For a commentary on epic thinking in Balthasar, see Quash, *Theology and the Drama of History*. Ben Quash describes Balthasar's own definition of epic thinking as "an element of *necessity* at the heart of events and happenings that take place. . . . This is one way to choose to read the interaction between God and his creatures. . . . At its worst . . . epic is the genre of a false objectification." Ibid., 42. Quash subsequently proposes that Balthasar has fallen into this trap of epic thinking himself, in spite of his denials. Kevin Mongrain argues that Balthasar is successful in avoiding epic thinking through his use of Irenaeus, while Ben Quash believes that he still slips into epic discourse. It is easy to see how both authors can come to such disparate conclusions, and it seems to me that while Balthasar's intentions are thoroughly Irenaean, his stereotypical views of nature and women in particular work against his overall project and reinforce the kind of epic thinking that Quash has pointed to in other aspects of his work.

75. Balthasar, *TD* 5, 48. Italics in original. Balthasar relegates the horizontal dimension to "unimportant and incidental vestiges of Jewish eschatology" (48). This is clearly overdrawn, but his intention is clear enough, namely, to stress the fulfillment and transcendence of previous categories that relied on Jewish and pagan ideas of the "End." His opposition to pagan ideas relates to his equal resistance to Gnostic tendencies.

76. Ibid., 176.

real distinction.[77] There is an analogy between the real distinction and the distinctions among the person of the Trinity; the Trinitarian relations, following Thomas Aquinas, find their echo in creation as such.[78] This echo is expressed in created beings as particularity in relation to the Logos, participation in nonfinite being in relation to the Father, and "vocation of self-surrender" in relation to the Spirit, the embodiment of "love's generosity."[79] Within the Godhead, we find "eternal movement" and "process," rather than "becoming"; in other words, this is a dynamic, "eternal movement" and the "fountain of life" as such.[80] Drawing on Adrienne van Speyr, Balthasar suggests that the world, in its pain, also shows forth a prefiguring or premonition of the cross that is to come.[81] For this reason, Balthasar can describe creation as such as *imago trinitatis* (image of the Trinity)[82] without entangling the world in God, for he holds on to the real distinction. On this basis, Balthasar refuses to speak of the eschaton as a movement of the world "outside" God to "inside" God; rather, it is a change in the condition of the world while remaining equally close to an immanent God.[83] The distance, in other words, is between earth and heaven, rather than heaven and earth.

It would be incorrect, however, to suggest that, by this, Balthasar has no notion at all of heaven in terms of an afterlife as such. However, his picture of what this entails is relatively tentative, and he supports the idea that the new heaven and earth spoken about in the book of Revelation are not *new* in the sense of explosion into this world from above, but a *renewal* of the present world, so that in heaven the life we have led on earth will remain "an abiding presence," rather than a memory. Such a life will have gone through the "renunciation of death and the purifying fire of God's judgement," and gratitude for grace given is uppermost, rather than any residual guilt.[84] Heaven is also where the frustrations that were present on earth are no longer present, so "in heaven we shall live the full and eternal

---

77. The real distinction means that every limited being (*essentia*) participates in real being (*actus essentia*), without the limited beings ever exhausting real being.

78. Balthasar, *TD* 5, 63.

79. Ibid., 76.

80. Ibid., 77–78.

81. The idea of premonition comes close to the notion of "cruciform" creation discussed in chapter 5 but is subtly different from it, for it is an anticipation interpreted as a *warning* rather than an affirmation. See ibid., 99–100.

82. Ibid., 105.

83. Ibid., 395.

84. Ibid., 415.

content of what on earth was only a transcendent, unsatisfied longing."[85] A person's earthly mission, discussed in section 7.4 above, will also be fulfilled in heaven, but this movement toward mission does not arise out of any sense of incompleteness of the mystical Body, but out of the plenary fullness of the mission of Christ.[86]

In keeping with the main thrust of his eschatology, Balthasar resists any idea that only the final stage of the earth's history will acquire a place in eternal life. Just as "all ages" in an individual life will be present in eternity,[87] so all positive elements in the world's history will participate in "God's eternally new event. Then we shall see that what seemed primitive and undeveloped could have greater latency and potency than what was highly developed."[88] Yet he resists any notion that there might be some kind of overall grand synthesis; rather, differences between peoples will be kept intact, and divergences still allowed to coexist.[89] While he believes that theological discussion of earth and heaven is "utterly untouched by all scientific considerations of the world," the effectiveness of the change wrought through the resurrection is cosmic, rather than simply confined to humanity.[90]

He seems to want it both ways here. On the one hand, he is hostile toward bringing scientific discourse into a discussion of heaven. On the other hand, he disagrees with Vögtle, inasmuch as the latter seems to resist the cosmic significance of Christ, a theme that Balthasar appreciates in the thought of Teilhard de Chardin, even though he is critical of other aspects of Teilhard's thought. Balthasar insists that the ultimate lordship of Christ does not make sense without considering the mutual interdependence of humanity and the environment. In Rom. 8, the whole creation longs for redemption. Even though Balthasar believes that the theological center of

---

85. Ibid., 413.

86. Ibid., 414.

87. In this respect Balthasar comes close to Jürgen Moltmann's understanding of all times of life being gathered up in eternity. See, for example, J. Moltmann, *The Coming of God* (London: SCM, 1996), 116–18; J. Moltmann, *Science and Wisdom* (London: SCM, 2003), 98–110. The difference, however, between Balthasar and Moltmann relates to the greater stress of the latter on the prospect of an intermediate state, partly related to Moltmann's greater appreciation of the importance of taking account of a scientific discourse on the fate and future of the universe.

88. Ibid., 418.

89. Ibid. Balthasar's repeated desire to maintain diversity against any kind of higher synthesis shows his overt resistance in this instance to Hegelian patterns of thought.

90. Ibid., 419.

this passage is human redemption, the cosmic scope of future hope leads him to comment that any thought, as found in Aquinas, of only humanity entering the resurrected world is something of a "chimera."[91] He even goes on to suggest:

> This cruel verdict contradicts the Old Testament sense of the solidarity between the living, subhuman cosmos and the world of men (Ps 8; Ps 104; Gen 1, and so on), the prophetic and Jewish ideas of divine salvation in images of peace among the animals (Is 11.6-9; 65.25), and it also goes against a deep Christian sense that Joseph Bernhart has vividly expressed in his work *Heilige und Tierre* (Saints and animals); finally, one can refer (with Wolfram von den Steinen) to the role of animals in the biblical heaven—the lamb, the dove, the living creatures with animal faces before the throne of God—and to their indispensable employment in Christian art.[92]

He also goes further than simply affirming the animals; rather, drawing on the book of Revelation, he claims, "Cosmic pre-history can attain salvation together with him [man] in God's world, which will ultimately achieve wholeness: God's creation, in all its multiplicity, is one."[93]

Importantly, the final form of the earth in heaven will "bear a christological stamp." While Balthasar hesitates over the idea of the possibility of "reconciliation" in the universe other than humanity, he believes that the insertion of the cross and the church into the relatively static image of the cosmos supposed by Col. 1:15-20 brings dynamism into a static cosmic picture.[94] Of course, there is now no need to envisage the cosmos in static terms; dynamic history includes the evolutionary history of the cosmos and, as I have argued in chapters 5 and 6, the possibility of redemption does need to be broadened out beyond that of humanity alone. While Balthasar makes some bold steps in the direction of a future hope that is inclusive of creation, rather than in dismissal of it, his ideas need to be broadened in relation to our knowledge of evolutionary forms in their richness, variety, and diversity.

---

91. Ibid., 419–21.

92. Ibid., 421.

93. Ibid., 422.

94. I have discussed the significance of this passage for the future of creation in more general terms in C. Deane-Drummond, *Ecotheology* (London: DLT, 2008), 100–103, 170.

Balthasar has consistently been criticized for his relative lack of attention to concrete instances of history, even while intending to speak in the concrete through his insistence on the concrete Christ. Rather less attention has been paid to his relative lack of attention to the forms of creation as such from an understanding of evolutionary biology and science, even though he also wants to stress the bodiliness of Christ and pay some attention to sexuality, which I will return to in section 7.6 below. His failure in this respect is common inasmuch as it is also characteristic of his sparring partner, Jürgen Moltmann, who, in spite of introducing Trinitarian language heavily laden with ecological symbolism, largely fails to discuss creation in concrete terms.[95] Of course, his resistance to Moltmann's interpretation of the Trinity in ecological and historical terms reflects his own intention, through his analogy of being, to speak of God in a way that recognizes the significance of God's immanence without thereby entangling God in the world in the way that Moltmann's position suggests.[96]

His attention to creation is, at least, a step away from a historicity that is common among most contemporary theologians. However, he seems to veer somewhat uneasily at times between a thorough sacramental and affirming notion of creation, which he gleans from Thomas Aquinas, Ignatius, and elsewhere, and a balder picture of the earth as simply a stage on which the drama of human history is played out. At times, his metaphysical discussion of the analogy of being can also seem to make creation remote from language about God. His eclectic and somewhat idiosyncratic approach, in my view, softens his attention to metaphysics and makes it rather more palatable. It is a pity, though, that in his *Glory of the Lord*, his attention to the scientists was confined to a discussion of Blaise Pascal (1623–1662).

It is appropriate, therefore, to broaden his understanding of the evolutionary forms of the universe as a whole in order to present an adequate picture of future hope. The new community is, in other words, inclusive of the evolutionary history of creation, not just the history of individual human beings. The question of which form(s) may or may not have their place in heaven—do dinosaurs enter the kingdom?—is impossible to answer, but with Balthasar, we can affirm a universal hope for the whole cosmos. Our own human understanding of what is important in relation to nearness to

---

95. See J. Moltmann, *God in Creation* (London: SCM, 1985); and C. Deane-Drummond, *Ecology in Jürgen Moltmann's Theology* (Lewisham: Mellen, 1997).

96. For this reason, ultimately, Balthasar's position, for all its difficulties, is more convincing theologically in relating Christ to evolution.

human species also is unlikely to be correct in the context of Trinitarian time, for the diversity of form is at its most intense in species that we pay little attention to but that may nonetheless be vital for the health of the planet as a whole. Looking back into the vast eons of evolutionary history and, before that, planetary and stellar history puts the relatively short history of the human race into perspective. It is, I suggest, an analogy for that supertime that is experienced in God.

How the history of the planet and of species might retain more than a memory in God goes beyond the scope of this chapter.[97] Rather than speculate as to this future, we must return again to the concrete living history of the planet and human responsibility within it.

7.6 Overform of Sex and "Superform"

The integration of the use of sexual analogies into Balthasar's understanding of the Trinity and of the relationships between the church and Christ could be viewed as both a blessing and a curse. Certainly, it seems appropriate that he draws on this most biological and bodily of analogies in order to express what, for him, is the depth of the incarnation wrought in Christ and the shape of things to come in the future of the new community. However, it is unfortunate that the way he expresses earthly sexual relationships betrays a stereotypical view of women in particular that has rendered his theology the object of severe attack by feminist scholars. This would not be so serious if it did not at the same time inform the way he thinks about Trinitarian relationships and relationships in general, and also has a bearing on what he thinks human existence will be like in eternity.

Just as there is a certain lacuna in his thinking on the concrete historical situation of humanity, as well as the concrete evolutionary history of the world, so, too, I suggest that the lacuna in his understanding of sexuality is most likely to be related to his particular cultural context, rather than expressing any specifically misogynist attitude toward women.[98] His

---

97 For a short review of this topic, see C. Deane-Drummond, *Ecotheology* (London: Darton, Longmann & Todd, 2008), ch. 12.

98. In this, I part company with the analysis of Tina Beattie, who claims to find abusive forms of sexuality in much of his writing, endorsing such practices as "rape" through a spiritualization of the relationship between Christ and the church. However, the popular text from which this accusation emerges does not, to my reading at least, deliver the "rape" scene that she envisages. Quoting Balthasar's *Heart of the World*, Beattie finds evidence (194–97) for the nuptial love between Christ and the church as

link between male sexuality and death has also been subject to criticism, though again, there is little evidence of anything more sinister in terms of sadomasochism.[99] Tina Beattie considers that the way Balthasar links sexuality with death means that he is trapped in "necrophiliac stereotypes," where sex is the "terrible origination of the inevitability of death."[100] This, it seems to me, somewhat overstates the case in that, as I have discussed, his attention to joy, fruitfulness, and glory along with sexuality runs like another thread in the thinking of this subtle and complex theologian. It is the *contingency* in the sexual process that seems to be ambiguous for Balthasar, not sex as such.[101] Moreover, in other works, he points to this contingency as a source of wonderment/awe, as is clear from his wonder that human existence comes from a "chance hit" but at the same time cannot interpret itself as simply a product of that chance.[102]

His attention to Eucharist is a way of trying to affirm the importance of concrete bodiliness, rather than deny its validity. His relationship with

---

represented through "a sado-masochistic 'blood wedding', consummated in an act of rape during which the woman's body is conquered by the Bridegroom" (174). Tina Beattie, *New Catholic Feminism* (London: Routledge, 2006), 174. Yet in the text itself, he seems, in my reading at least, to be asking not so much for an affirmation of such violence as for a transformation of any hint of violence so that it becomes "the white bridal bed of divine love." I do agree, however, that such imagery is, at best, ambiguous and, while it is treated with rather more nuance in his subsequent works, represents a serious flaw in his overall project.

99. Sarah Coakley, with some justification, treats with considerable caution the way that Balthasar links the Eucharist with male sexual release, thereby associating death and sexuality. While she does not accuse him of sadomasochism, her attention to this in the next paragraph introduces the suspicion that this is underlying his work. It is also important to note that she drew on his more popular work, *Elucidations* (150), for this analysis. Coakley, *Powers and Submissions*, 63. He is rather more careful in his other works to stress in a more nuanced way that sexuality is *analogous* rather than *directly linked* with the self-giving of the Son. Nonetheless, his association between the eternal generation of the Son by the Father and the kenotic self-giving of the Son in the incarnation and death is drawn into an analogy with sexuality in a way that is highly problematic, for it seems to reinforce and embed through his theological structure the stereotypical views of women that he presupposes. I have my doubts, however, whether this amounts to any form of sadomasochism in his case.

100. Beattie, *New Catholic Feminism*, 157.

101. See, for example, Hans Urs von Balthasar, *Explorations in Theology*, vol. 3, *Creator Spirit*, trans. Brian McNeil (San Francisco: Ignatius, 1993), 19 (hereafter cited as *ET* 3). Here his wonder takes the form of dread/awe that God's creative act is so linked to "nature's chance act of generation."

102. Balthasar, *GL* 5, 615.

Adrienne von Speyr was clearly an intimate one, though there is no real evidence for the presumption either that this relationship was necessarily sexual or that he was necessarily a misogynist.[103] The influence of von Speyr's mystical thinking on his theology is clear enough and self-professed, and the closeness born of living in the same community and acting as her spiritual director was bound to have some influence. He was also rather more "precious" in his attitude to her work than one might have expected from a purely "platonic" relationship. However, the main issue in the present context is not so much his personal story, but how he portrayed the relationships between men and women in his theology, and the impact this had on his theology as a whole, including eschatological aspects.

Nonetheless, it is not hard to find plenty of clear evidence in Balthasar of a naive and stereotypical view of women in relation to men, and of sexuality in particular. In interpreting 1 Cor. 11:2-16, he cites Rom. 7:2 as portraying woman "below the man" and becoming the "glory of the man," and while he admits to the image of God being in both sexes, he considers, astonishingly, that there is a "gradation of the *doxa* [glory]." In other words, women are considered glorious only *in relation to men*, whose glory they reflect, and in which God "establishes in the order of creation the basis for the mysterious interplay of sexual fruitfulness in the opposition of personal partners with equal rights."[104] Yet his admission of "equal rights" hardly extends to the way he treats women in theological terms, extending into the analogy he uses for describing the relationship between Christ and the church. Consider, for example, his comment on the Son:

[He] sheds his blood as a human being and as a man for his bride—which is undeniably a feminine bride—in order to give her from himself the form that

---

103. Tina Beattie, for example, claims that Balthasar's relationship with Speyr, "even if it did not find physical sexual expression, was in no small measure responsible for the growing sexualisation of his work after their relationship began in the early 1940s." *New Catholic Feminism*, 13. She also speculates whether their relationship was a form of "sado-masochistic 'marriage' which condemns a woman to solitary hell so that a man's theology can bear fruit? A woman who even takes on his physical illnesses, despite herself being apparently at death's door? A body whose body must be marked with a wound that is a sign of a man?" Ibid., 166. While these questions are certainly worth airing, and show the extremely ambiguous nature of the relationship between Balthasar and von Speyr, I am less sure that his arguably negative sexual stereotyping also included the malicious streak that Beattie suggests.

104. Balthasar, *GL* 7, 479.

is to be hers for ever. Since human sexuality serves this mystery, it is sanctified sacramentally, but at the same time, it is transposed above itself. It leads to the nuptiality between God and the world—the red line of life—the colour of sex and of flowing blood—but only to pass away, in itself, and to enter the greater sphere of which it is the "mystery".[105]

The important point to note here is that the Son imprints on the female church her form. In other places, he recognizes that there is a difference between sexual relationships and the relationship between Christ and the church, in that the church is not his partner, but his "fruit," and the "fruit" of the woman is "something new" rather than simply given by the "form" of the man. However, this weak concession does nothing to prevent the analogy from reinforcing the stereotype that he has already set up both of women being subordinate to men and of man as epitomizing the Word and woman as essentialist Answer to that Word, expressed as fruitfulness rather than as active answer.[106] As Rachel Muers points out, "If silence is their nature, it cannot be their act. It cannot be a vocation they accept or a role they play. . . . Woman's silence marks this indispensable difference. But, at the same time, woman's silence is constructed, interpreted and controlled, assimilated to the monologue."[107]

Quite apart from extending into the way Balthasar interprets the relationships within the Trinity,[108] this sexual stereotyping also has implications for his eschatology. Here, the more earthly metaphor of fruitfulness is simply retained as a "spiritual-intellectual" dimension, a reification of those aspects of human life that he considers to be most evident in the male, so

---

105. Ibid., 453.

106. Balthasar raises this on a number of occasions. See, for example, Hans Urs von Balthasar, *Man in History* (London: Sheed & Ward, 1968), 306; and *TD* 3, 283–90, 356.

107. Rachel Muers, "The Mute Cannot Keep Silent: Barth, von Balthasar and Irigaray on the Construction of Women's Silence," in *Challenging Women's Orthodoxies*, ed. S. Parsons (Surrey, UK: Ashgate, 2000), 116–17. Lucy Gardner and David Moss make much the same comment in "Something Like Time: Something Like the Sexes," in *Balthasar at the End of Modernity*, ed. Lucy Gardner, David Moss, Ben Quash, and Graham Ward (Edinburgh: T&T Clark, 1999), 86–88.

108. Rowan Williams accurately comments on the problematic aspects of this in relation to the Trinity and suggests, "What Balthasar does is both to open up some extraordinary new insights which thoroughly and usefully confuse our assumptions about love and action, and to link them with a set of far more problematic 'fixings' of gender roles." Williams, "Balthasar and the Trinity," in Oakes and Moss, *Cambridge Companion*, 47.

that even while he acknowledges and accepts diversity and difference, it is a difference circumscribed by a particular stereotypical attitude to women, and even within that stereotype, more affective qualities seem to disappear. The creativity and joy seem to lack grounding in ordinary life that he believes is the basis for the incarnation. Again, by drawing an analogy between the relationship between men and women (as inferior) and that of God and creation, the place of creation as such is thereby weakened and becomes liable to forms of oppression that have characterized patriarchal relationships.[109]

I also consider that his use of sexual stereotypes to describe relationships has additional drawbacks that he does not consider adequately. Certainly, the appearance of sexuality in evolutionary terms is something of a puzzle; cooperation and biological fruitfulness are not tied in with sexuality in the way that he implies. Active maternal love, for which he finds a place in the mysterious awakening of self-consciousness expressed, he claims, through the baby's smile, still ties the role of woman to motherhood, and even if it seems rather more active than simply the silent answer to man's active word, such motherhood reflects the stereotypical expectation for women by men: her place is in the home.[110]

This is particularly problematic if we consider that Balthasar's project is intended to counteract the positivism and nativism we have already identified in evolutionary psychology, which also stereotypes the role of women and men in particular essentialist terms, ironing out individual differences and ignoring the cultural diversity that speaks of the variety of forms of relationship and family life. This tendency to construct an "innate stability in the constitution of human life," which Quash detects and associates with Hegelian thought,[111] extends, I suggest, more generally to his

---

109. Associations such as these have been pointed out by ecofeminists for some time. See, for example, Rosemary Radford Ruether, *Gaia and God: An Ecofeminist Theology of Earth Healing* (London: SCM, 1993). It is significant in Balthasar's case, however, as it is inconsistent with other aspects of his theology that are much more affirmative toward nature and creation.

110. It could be questioned whether a baby's smile signals the start of an independent self-consciousness. The ability of a baby to smile at the mother about six weeks after birth is a result of face recognition rather than any independent sense of the self, which comes much later. See, for example, Annette Karmiloff Smith, "Why Babies' Brains Are Not Swiss Army Knives," in *Alas Poor Darwin: Arguments against Evolutionary Psychology*, ed. H. Rose and S. Rose, 144–56 (London: Cape, 2000). Smith claims, for example, that face recognition reaches that of an adult after twelve months.

111. Quash, *Theology and the Drama of History*, 163.

understanding of creation as such, where contingency is seen as a threat rather than a blessing. Hence, one could argue that this way of thinking about women works against his overall project of theology in the mode of openness and wonder that he intends and that correctly aligns itself against the excesses of evolutionary psychology.

The essentialism that creeps in here ties the role of women in with a particular task: an active role of mother and a more passive role as man's answer, one that is also idealized and epitomized for Balthasar in his portrayal of the virgin Mary. Yet the vocation and mission of Christian love has become too closely related by the use of this analogy to those biological functions that are transcended in the life of the church. The evolutionary world shows itself up in two respects. On the one hand, evolution allows for cooperation to exist at the level of the cell and beyond; it is not simply defined by evolutionary competitiveness through natural selection and sex selection. If Balthasar had realized this point, perhaps he would not have restricted his understanding of the analogy of fruitfulness to fertility and to sexual productivity. On the other hand, by confining the material analogy in this way, his intention to resist envisaging the future as the transition from the evolutionary world to the next world begins to look rather thin, for his theology points in this direction, even though it is protected from any direct extension by his use of the analogy of being. It might have been more appropriate, in other words, to insist more on radical difference here—that the mission of the Christian to love one's enemies goes far beyond any sexual and kinship ties that dominate the evolutionary world. Christ's self-giving, which we are also called to imitate, goes far beyond any self-giving professed in kinship and sexual relationships.

7.7 A Return to Silence

Balthasar has occasion to speak of the mystery of being, especially where he draws parallels between what happens in the human sphere and what happens in eternity. However, it is worth considering again the kind of silence that women can offer in this respect, a silence that is not so much imposed but actively sought after and showing significance as a pointer to eternal life. Such silence recognizes that in God, especially in considering the glory and wonder in God, there cannot be one answer, one discourse, or one philosophical system.[112] Indeed, this openness to new truth was something that Balthasar himself seemed to endorse in theory, even if in practice his authoritarian attitudes largely prevented him from fully appreciating alternative ways of doing theology.[113] While he was cautious about what might be said about the future and eternity in any detail, what he did say was grounded in his own perception of God as in some sense like the world but having a "superform" and glory that can only be dimly appreciated in the present and that are most likely to be found in the experiences of mystics.

Certainly, the mystical tradition is replete with the apophatic awareness of what cannot be said about God. It seems to me that the last word should go to this tradition, for while understanding God in the superlative may make sense to some, there is still the nagging doubt that God cannot be so ascribed, especially once one considers the future of the cosmos. The silence, as understood in Balthasar, seems to be that mute silence of no response, in the silence of the womb and culminating in the silence of the tomb.[114] As Denys Turner suggests, true apophaticism is not saying nothing, or saying God is nothing; rather, it "is the encounter with the failure of what we must say about God to represent God adequately."[115]

7.8 Conclusions

Balthasar's interpretation of eschatology as one marked by wonder in the mode of glory in a realm that seems to be both connected to time yet moving in another sphere that is "God's time" offers an important way of thinking about the relationship between the creation and new creation. For Balthasar, wonder is the context in which all theology is developed, and this unfashionable attention to metaphysics sets his face against those tempted by modernity's explanation of existence as that which runs according to

112. Rachel Muers follows Irigaray in making this point. Muers, "The Mute Cannot Keep Silent," 118.

113. He claims, for example, that "this openness is what keeps a Christian alive. He will constantly be able to receive new truth from God, and not be blocked by patterns or prejudices, spiritual or worldly, which are products of yesterday, and which, though justified then, cannot recur or suffice in the same form today." Balthasar, *TH*, 118.

114. See Raymond Gawronski, *Word and Silence: Hans Urs von Balthasar and the Spiritual Encounter between East and West* (Edinburgh: T&T Clark, 1995), 102.

115. Denys Turner, "Apophaticism, Idolatry and the Claims of Reason," in *Silence and the Word*, ed. Oliver Davies and Denys Turner (Cambridge: Cambridge University Press, 2002), 18.

necessary laws or as the combination of chance and necessity characterized by the account of evolutionary history. Indeed, the positivism that emerges as the philosophical basis for much evolutionary psychology represents the kind of approach that Balthasar is most keen to resist,[116] though he also has equally sharp words to say about those who might alternatively be tempted by gnostic tendencies toward the separation of matter and spirit. Balthasar's reading of scripture is similarly resistant to the historical-critical methods that he believes have arisen from too close attention to the agenda of modernity, and the breadth of his use of biblical sources on glory, ranging from the Hebrew Bible to the New Testament, is breathtaking.

In all, he attempts to build up an account of God who displays glory most profoundly through the personal address of love, the self-gift and bestowal culminating in the address of the Son to the world in his life, death, and resurrection. Participation in God through the mediation of the Holy Spirit becomes possible following the death and resurrection of Christ, so that humanity is caught up in the life of the Trinity, sharing through grace in its life of relatedness. Here Balthasar shows his preference for associating the work of the Holy Spirit with the church, and with the Eucharist in particular. It would be easy to criticize him for an ecclesial narrowness here, including an idealization of the church and of the virgin Mary in particular. However, any such criticism is softened somewhat by his determination to include creation in a sacramental way in the life of God, immanent in creation, including, it seems, the future life of the new community.

This affirmation of creation, which he draws primarily from his attention to patristic and medieval authors such as Irenaeus and Aquinas, and also in the formative influence of Ignatian spirituality, is confronted by another stumbling block within his thinking, namely, a stereotypical view of the relationships between men and women and his caricature and at times seemingly negative view of sexuality and of the role of women in particular. His association of women with subordination and with a stereotypical role defined by men, along with his seemingly authoritarian approach to the church, delivers an eschatology that is less grounded than it might have been if he had followed through more consistently his attention to an Irenaean sense of the value of creation and the concrete Christ. The glory that is to be revealed in eternity through the biological image of

---

116. Balthasar did not write at a time when evolutionary psychology had become established, but its emergence could, he would argue, be anticipated as an outcome of modernity's arrogant self-assurance.

fruitfulness becomes reified into human spiritual and intellectual creativity. This flaw in his thinking represents the very temptation toward epic that he desires to resist. While he claims to have an important place and role for creation in heaven, no longer left behind, as in the somewhat abhorrent claims of traditional medieval writers, it is hard to envisage precisely what such role might comprise, given his particular account of women in relation to men on earth, and presumably also in heaven. The silence of women and creation is a mute silence, imposed by authority, rather than a creative silence that recognizes the multiplicity and complexity of created forms and their inadequacy in lending expression to divine glory. The new community, in other words, needs to be opened out in a more explicit way to include women, non-human animals, and the dynamic natural orders of creation while recognizing that words are inadequate to describe in what sense creation will be true to itself yet live in the glorious light of eternity. Humanity has reason to be silent again in the face of the massive destruction it has wrought on the evolutionary history of the earth. In its groping toward life and its complexification over millions of years, we are left once again with a sense of wonder at this world and its continued existence.

While I agree with Balthasar that to view the eschaton in a linear sense is misguided and that the responsibility to work for the coming kingdom is grounded in this life, and this life only, a deeper appreciation of where we have come from in evolutionary terms helps ground an eschatology by reminding humanity once again of its limited capacities even to know itself, let alone the God who is beyond all knowing. Such limitation, as applied to God, issues in an apophatic liturgical silence of all creation before God, an image of God's glory in the mode of wonder. But humanity, at least in this life, does not merely wait in that expectation and premonition of silence, but moves from such silence to active engagement with the world. The expression of this engagement, and how it might be related to an understanding of Christ, is the subject of the chapter that follows.

8

The Future of the Human: Transhuman Evolution or Human Identity as *Imago Christi*?

This chapter engages and critiques what might be termed an evolutionary trajectory that leaves the biological realm and projects transhumanity as the goal of life toward the poshuman condition. I will argue that, like evolutionary psychology, discussed in chapter 2, this form of evolutionary reasoning uses a grand narrative in order to convince its audience. However, not only is it at odds with the Christian eschatological future, discussed in the previous chapter, but it also undermines human identity understood in a christological perspective. Instead, the identity of Christ, best depicted in the drama of his own particular narrative and through personal encounter, informs a theological anthropology that remains anchored in history and nature and is respectful of the great drama of evolutionary history now expressed in the present scene as ecological diversity and complexity. From a Christian perspective, Christology does not just speak about reconciliation, but also tells about a positive vocation, a vocation best expressed in terms of living out the drama of our lives as *imago Christi*, in service not only to humanity in its widest possible sense, but also to our creaturely companions.

8.1 Transhuman Evolution

Christian engagement with transhuman discourse has more often than not been situated in the context of ethical debates about the legitimacy of particular technologies championed by transhumanists in their goals to achieve a form of humanity that is not just freed from those mortal ills that weigh down ordinary human lives, but also aims toward additional qualities deemed desirable to attain. Ted Peters, for example, engages with transhumanism in the light of related alternatives such as therapy and enhancement.[1] Transhumanism is the view that humans should be permitted to use technology in order to remake human nature, offered as the next stage in human evolution.[2] It differs from posthumanism inasmuch as the posthuman condition is largely concerned with an idealized future where such transitions have already happened. Many see transhumanity as an intermediate stage on the way to a full-blown posthumanity, and as such, transhumanism draws on the technologies currently available in order to justify its position. Transhumanism also assumes that intelligence is the mark of what makes us human.

The concern in this present chapter is to explore more specific claims of transhumanists that their project represents a new stage in the evolution of humanity. This supposedly evolutionary process is affected by human application of a variety of technologies, including smart drugs, nanotechnology, prosthetics, computer-assisted communication, and genetic modification; through these, humanity becomes superhumanity.[3] Transhumanism promises to create a new species that is beyond *Homo sapiens,* so that "humans have beaten evolution. We are creating intelligent entities in considerably less time than it took the evolutionary process that created us. Human intelligence—a product of evolution—has transcended it."[4] Such ideas have filtered into popular consciousness through magazines that flourished in the 1990s, such as *Mondo* and *Wired,* appealing to an

---

1. Ted Peters, "Perfect Humans or Transhumans?" in *Future Perfect? God, Medicine and Human Identity,* ed. C. Deane-Drummond and P. Scott, 15–32 (London: Continuum, 2006). See also other essays in this volume that deal with the goal of perfection in transhumanity, such as C. Deane-Drummond, "Future Perfect? God, the Transhuman Future and the Quest for Immortality," 168–82.

2. This definition is taken from Heidi Campbell and Mark Walker, "Religion and Transhumanism: Introducing a Conversation," *J. Evol. & Technol.* 14, no. 2 (August 2005): 1.

3. Tiziana Terranova, "Posthuman Unbounded: Artificial Evolution and High Tech Subcultures," in *FutureNatural: Nature/Science/Culture,* ed. G. Robertson (London: Routledge, 1996), 165.

4. Ray Kurzwell, "The Coming Merging of Mind and Machine," *Sci. Amer.* 10, no. 3 (1999): 60. Such ideas of having overcome the chanciness inherent in natural selection were also uppermost in the early enthusiasm expressed for the human genome project. For discussion, see C. Deane-Drummond, ed., *Brave New World: Theology, Ethics and the Human Genome* (London: Continuum, 2003).

audience enthralled by cyberculture. Machinic evolution, according to such writers, completes the task of natural selection, endorsing not just salvation through technology, but a "licence for exponential self-improvement."[5]

Not all transhumanist writers are unsophisticated or simply working at the level of popular culture. Nick Bostrom, writing from the philosophy department at Oxford University, is arguably one of the founders of transhumanism. For him, the future of human evolution lies in technology. His argument in a nutshell is as follows.[6] He suggests that the apparent "progress" in the evolutionary story toward increasing complexity, consciousness, and so on cannot be guaranteed; indeed, it seems highly likely that it will not achieve desirable progress for the human species as we know it. He also considers a future society where computerized modules have replaced human beings.[7] Yet it is telling that he believes that the issue is not that the mind is on silicon processors rather than biological neurons; rather, "the catastrophe would be that such a world would not contain even the right kind of machines, i.e., the ones that are conscious and whose welfare matters."[8] In other words, there would be no personal identity. The paradox implicit in transhumanism is not lost on its commentators. Elaine Graham, for example, aptly remarks, "To become posthuman—to be radically dependent on technology for future evolution and survival—actually entails the erosion of the very categories of bodily integrity, autonomy and personal subjectivity that define liberal 'human nature.'"[9] Yet the way Bostrom speaks of future evolution in terms of "uploads" means that he in effect endorses technological life forms that have lost their essential connection with biological processes of reproduction, though he retains this as an "option," while retaining the language of "fitness" in describing the fate of such creatures.

---

5. Elaine Graham, *Representations of the Post/Human: Monsters, Aliens and Others in Popular Culture* (Manchester: Manchester University Press, 2002), 159. Graham is properly concerned with the political implications of transhumanity.

6. Nick Bostrom, "The Future of Human Evolution," in *Death and Anti-Death: Two Hundred Years after Kant, Fifty Years after Turing*, ed. Charles Tandy, 339–71 (Palo Alto: Ria University Press, 2004), accessed at www.nickbostrom.com/fut/evolution.html, March 19, 2008.

7. While such futuristic trends may seem far-fetched, they have been discussed by physicists such as Frank Tipler in *Physics of Immortality* (New York: Doubleday, 1994).

8. Bostrom, "Future of Human Evolution," 5.

9. Elaine Graham, "In Whose Image? Representations of Technology and the 'Ends' of Humanity," in Deane-Drummond and Scott, *Future Perfect?* 60.

He has to engage in mental gymnastics to argue the case for the social engineering of conditions such that what he terms "eudaemonic" types are preserved. Such eudaemonic types of creatures are most concerned with hedonistic patterns of life that are largely obsolete in terms of selective "fitness" in a computerized world. He suggests, further, that the capacity to control evolution be given over to a "singleton," defined as a "democratic world government, a benevolent and overwhelmingly powerful superintelligent machine, a world dictatorship, a stable alliance of leading powers, or even something as abstract as a generally diffused moral code that included provisions for ensuring its own stability and enforcement."[10] Such a horrifying vision takes no account of the possibility of evil, is totally naive in its projection of the use of political power, and is presumptive in its assumption that such a singleton would benefit the global human race as such. While there may be no guarantee that human evolution according to natural biological processes will enable the survival of the human race, Bostrom's vision is ultimately dehumanizing, for it is based on a preconceived understanding of the good according to a particular narrowly defined transhuman utopian model, which is then tied in with a manipulative political structure.[11]

More recently, Nick Bostrom and Anders Sandberg have approached the topic of human evolution in a somewhat different way by speaking of the "wisdom of nature" as a way of identifying some of those enhancements that are justified.[12] It is also important to point out that while enhancement may be theoretically distinct from transhuman goals, transhumanists develop a case for their projects through currently available enhancement technologies. Hence, just as there is clear evidence for a slide from therapy toward enhancement, so, similarly, I am rather more wary of the slide from enhancement to transhumanism than are authors such as Ted Peters.[13]

---

10. Bostrom, "Future of Human Evolution," 17.

11. It is barely an improvement on the physical futures envisaged by Frank Tipler, *Physics of Immortality*.

12. N. Bostrom and A. Sandberg, "The Wisdom of Nature: An Evolutionary Heuristic for Human Enhancement," *Enhancing Humans*, ed. Julian Savulescu and Nick Bostrom (Oxford: Oxford University Press, 2008), in press, accessed at www.nickbostrom.com, March 19, 2008.

13. For a discussion of the way therapy has moved toward enhancement in practical, ethical contexts, see Deane-Drummond, "Future Perfect?" For a discussion of the differences between enhancement and transhumanism, see Ted Peters, "Perfect Humans or Transhumans?"

Bostrom and Sandberg portray evolutionary processes as the positive ground for enhancement, such that

> "evolution is a process powerful enough to have led to the development of systems, such as human brains—that are far more complex and capable than anything that human scientists and engineers have managed to design. Surely it would be foolish . . . to suppose that we are currently likely to be able to do better than evolution, especially when so far we have not even managed to understand the systems that evolution has designed and when our attempts even just to repair what evolution has built so often misfire!"[14]

The use of the language of design in evolutionary terms mirrors almost exactly its use in evolutionary psychology. The supposed "wisdom of nature" is in reality a reading of the natural world according to evolutionary psychology. Like many transhumanists, Bostrom and Sandberg also assume, in common with evolutionary psychologists, that "natural" evolution of humans stopped in the hunter-gatherer societies of the African savannah. Yet even if they use the language of wisdom, Bostrom and Sandberg give the evolutionary heuristic that implies that "nature often knows best" only very limited scope, and it seems that they are using this rhetoric in order to undermine the arguments of opponents to transhuman projects. The starting point for interventions is one that reflects the "wisdom of nature," but posing what they term is the *evolutionary optimality challenge*—namely, if the proposed intervention would lead to an enhancement—why have humans *not* evolved in this way?

They also align their tasks with that of evolutionary medicine in order to endorse the project still further. However, they are anxious to go further than simply finding ways to enhance particular "natural" capacities such as eyesight, for the good in terms of selective fitness to a given environment is likely to be different from that which humans value as good, such as mathematical capacity. Of course, it is particularly poignant that mathematical ability as such is picked out in this context, given the importance of this skill for the whole transhuman project. The important point for the transhumanists is not whether the reduced fitness is a good, but whether there are sufficient reasons for overriding this reduced fitness. The social good is up for consideration in this context as well as the individual good, but

---

14. Bostrom and Sandberg, "Wisdom of Nature," 2.

the focus remains on individual traits, such as increase in compassion, that contribute to the good of society.

In the final analysis, Bostrom and Sandberg believe it is permissible to go beyond the fundamental limitations of evolution, caused either by physical incapability (as in the case of diamond teeth) or by being "locked in" through genetic processes such as heterozygote alleles giving an advantage to a homozygote lethal condition. In such cases, the human engineer has a specific aim in view, and so works backward in order to propose possible enhancements. This process of human engineering takes account of the evolutionary knowledge already gained but is also able to override ignorance in that Bostrom and Sandberg believe there may be some justification in making interventions where the evolutionary function is unknown. In the final analysis, it seems that the goal of transhuman evolution is simply made more palatable by the rhetorical use of the evolutionary heuristic wrapped up in the language of the "wisdom of nature." Bostrom and Sandberg's approach is about as far away from a Hebraic understanding of human wisdom as one could imagine possible, for it speaks of the attempt of human beings to exercise their individual powers of control over their own futures. The belief that we might have within our power the ability to reformulate ourselves shows up transhumanism as the counterfoil to anything recognizable as human wisdom.[15]

The above concerns also reinforce the idea that there is a strong marriage between transhumanism and evolutionary psychology. Elaine Graham's critical comment on the transhumanist project is particularly apt in this context:

> Like socio-biology, which appropriates "cultural" behaviours in order to describe "natural" processes (such that human traits such as "selfishness" become projected on to the destiny of genes), so too humanity's deployment of technology becomes its means of transcending nature yet simultaneously remains in thrall to its logic of survival and adaptation. The result is a confusion of anthropocentric triumphalism and evolutionary determinism: "Evolution's grandest creation—human intelligence—is providing the means for the next stage of evolution, which is technology."[16]

---

15. I have developed this aspect in an address entitled "What Is Human Wisdom? A Challenge to Transhuman Evolution" (Metanexus Conference, Madrid, July 15, 2008).

16. Graham, *Representations of the Post/Human*, 160. Citation referenced here is Ray Kurzweil, *The Age of Spiritual Machines* (London: Orbis, 1991), 35.

The transhuman project is geared toward a perfectionist ethic that offers a secularized transcendence that taps into religious instincts while rejecting formal religious ideas and concepts. In this sense, Friedrich Nietzsche becomes the prophetic figure, as foretold in his will to power and *Übermensch*.[17] Yet some of those enthralled by such technologies are also—ironically, perhaps—drawn to use more explicit spiritual imagery to reinforce their position. Such spirituality is more often than not dualistic inasmuch as the technologists are those who use a spiritual imperative in order to inspire technological intervention. Cruder versions of this thesis can be found in Michael Lieb's reading of the book of Ezekiel, where the ineffable comes to be expressed in a technological imperative.[18]

Associations of technology with an idealized evolutionary future of humanity are not new, for they are also clearly evident in the endorsement of technology by Pierre Teilhard de Chardin. In his case, however, while he qualified the social character of the new humanity using the language of "Super-charity," his particular attraction to evolutionary progress held sway, so that he was able to greet even horrendous ills, such as the atomic bomb, with approval, on the basis of some undefined evolutionary good. He claims, therefore, "In exploding the atom we took our first bite at the fruit of the great discovery, and this was enough for a taste to enter our mouths that can never be washed away, the taste for super-creativeness."[19] Philip Hefner follows Teilhard in his approval of technology, even citing with approval Teilhard's admiration for the atomic bomb,[20] though he qualifies the progressive activity of human evolution through technology by suggesting that it needs to pay sufficient attention to a future "that is

---

17. In this context, it is significant perhaps that this is only a loose and rather inaccurate reading of Nietzsche, since, as Graham points out, Nietzsche would have had no time for the transcendent visions or metaphysical speculation that appear to come to the surface in transhumanity. As Graham comments, "In its logic of immortality, invulnerability and omniscience, transhumanism exposes its vestigial craving for a perfect, transcendent world." *Representations of the Post/Human*, 174.

18. Michael Lieb, *Children of Ezekiel: Aliens, UFOs, the Crisis of Race and the Advent of End Time* (Durham: Duke University Press, 1998). For further commentary, see Graham, *Representations of the Post/Human*, 167.

19. Pierre Teilhard de Chardin, "Some Reflections on the Spiritual Repercussions of the Atom Bomb," in *The Future of Man*, ed. Norman Denny (London: Collins, 1964), 144.

20. Hefner comments on the purpose that Teilhard had in using this example, but he does not question its appropriateness. Philip Hefner, *Technology and Human Becoming* (Minneapolis: Fortress Press, 2003), 43.

most wholesome for the nature that has birthed us," including the "evolutionary and ecological reality in which and to which we belong."[21] In this way, his views lack what might be termed the bald anthropocentrism and individualist tendencies in transhuman discourse. The difficulty, of course, is that there is a clash of values presented by cyborg futures and those of ecological responsibility, which he does not adequately address. Like Teilhard, he uses a Christian mandate in order to identify the way forward, but he resists the Christomonism apparent in Teilhard's writing and uses a looser term of "God's ends" in order to press for technological development. It is worth probing a little more what he might mean by such ends.

Hefner holds to a sociobiological model of biocultural evolution that views religion as simply the next cultural phase of evolution. Significantly, freedom is what marks the human person as one who can legitimately engage in cocreation such that a new evolutionary phase will emerge. Hefner insists that technology need not be simply death-denying in the manner of transhuman desires for immortality, but rather "a means to create an alternative state of life."[22] For him, the imaginative visions of alternative futures are forms of spirituality, and in this way, technology becomes an exercise of spirituality also. Yet he believes that what surfaces in such an exploration of imaginative technological futures are feelings of freedom and vulnerability, woven together through the telling of particular dreams and stories. This attitude of vulnerability at first sight seems poles apart from the more self-confident "will to power" inspired by Nietzsche in the transhuman activists previously discussed, but if we probe in more depth as to what this vulnerability might entail in Hefner's account, it seems to be related to the creative exercise as such, rather than any admission of weakness.

Yet based on what Hefner perceives as spiritual analogues in technological quest, he claims, "Techno-human, cyborg and technosapiens are terms that describe the form or shape of religion."[23] He argues that it is necessary to view technology in this way, as to banish religion from its processes is to exclude the religious from the most significant development in human becoming. For him, technology represents the next stage of natural evolution; the two are so intimately intertwined that "humans and their

---

21. Philip Hefner, *The Human Factor: Evolution, Culture and Religion* (Minneapolis: Fortress Press, 1993), 27.

22. Hefner, *Technology and Human Becoming*, 39.

23. Ibid., 75.

technology are a set of nature's possibilities. . . . The religion of cyborgs and technosapiens, therefore, is also a religion of nature."[24] Even more explicitly, "Cyborg is created in the image of God. . . . Technology is now a phase of evolution, and it is now creation, a vessel for the image of God."[25] While agreeing to an ethical mandate of such technologies according to that based on humanity as created cocreator, he believes that religion must *encompass* and embrace the new humanity that we are becoming through such creative processes. His argument necessarily leads to the conclusion that God is intimately involved in the technological processes: "God is a *participant* in the technological process, since the purposes of God are now embodied through technology and techno-nature."[26] The question, then, for him is not whether God is involved, but how to understand God's involvement. It turns out that God's ends are simply aligned with the ends of human creativity. Moreover, it follows that the cyborg as the freely given image of God tells us something about God, and that the mandate for transcendence as given in the figure of the cyborg also tells us something about God and God's desired future for nature.

Elaine Graham also comes down in support of Hefner's theological interpretation of transhumanity: "The possibility of human evolution continuing through technologies is not to be rejected. . . . It is possible to argue that a quintessential aspect of our very humanity is realised in and through our relationships with our tools and technologies."[27] Yet her somewhat benign reading of Hefner's interpretation of the place of God in his theology means that the danger of hyperhumanism, a belief that humanity is in control of its own history, which she recognizes rather more clearly than Hefner, does not take hold. I am less convinced that his theological construction is adequate to defend itself against a slide toward human elevation, which she recognizes as a danger in transhumanism. I do agree with Graham's suggestion that the image of humanity is more properly considered through the image of God revealed in Christ.

Yet all this reasoning makes two presuppositions that are worth challenging at the outset. The first is that technological evolution and natural evolution form part of a seamless web, a view that depends on a projection of the grand narrative of sociobiology, which I have had reason to

---

24. Ibid., 77.
25. Ibid., 77.
26. Italics in original, *Technology and Human Becoming*, 79.
27. Graham, "In Whose Image?" 65.

challenge throughout this volume. Moreover, as noted earlier in this section, more aggressive advocates of transhumanism seek to disentangle themselves from such evolutionary roots where it is justified, often on the basis of particular views that rest on narrow political ideals that are likely to benefit only a small minority of individuals. Hefner seems to have no sociological or political instinct as far as cybertechnology is concerned, and lacks awareness that it is tied up with a particular view of human becoming that has flourished in the intellectual domain of the Western world.

The second presupposition is that technology as such as a means to further human evolution is inherently desirable and God given, what Hefner terms a "sacred space." Yet this seems to be a religious endorsement of basically anthropocentric goals: Who is to say that "God" is involved in such a process at all, other than a remnant of religious instinct toward transcendence? Whether or not the cyborg is the image of God is not open to human inquiry, for the only image that we have been given, one that points beyond what might loosely be termed human nature, is Christ, who is the manifestation of God and humanity. The question then becomes whether the kind of perfection sought in the cyborg can or cannot be aligned with the clues given to us already in the drama of Christ's coming. While Hefner does speak of Christ as the paradigm of being human in earlier work, his particular model of sacrifice on which his christological reflection rests is simply this: "The person engaged in sacrifice believes that he or she is acting in harmony with the way things really are. . . . Jesus stands as a symbol of one whose identity was drawn from the process of nature and history in which he emerged."[28] This sacrificial model bears no dramatic content; it simply endorses what is, lacks due attention to atonement, and describes simply how we live. Moreover, it is doubtful that such a sacrificial model interpreted simply as the way things are is all that helpful, given the tendency to oppression of minorities and women throughout human history.[29] Given this, it is hardly surprising that, as Hefner believes that technology is emergent in human cultural history, any vulnerability felt in human creating is simply that vulnerability associated with God's *creative* work in nature and the coming of Christ, rather than Christ's sacrifice as such.[30]

---

28. Hefner, *Human Factor*, 245.

29. For further discussion of the significance of Christ's action as sacrifice, see chapter 5.

30. Denis Edwards's critique of Hefner's approach to sinfulness is particularly telling

Brent Waters's critique of posthuman discourse also is relevant in this context. He claims that the lack of a clear eschatology means that providence remains vacuous, "enslaved to an infinite regress of historicist cultural construction and posthuman self-creation."[31] Yet I am less convinced than Waters that the kind of radical openness and contingency that he finds in posthuman discourse is as evident in transhuman discussion as he implies, for as remarked already, that seems to be set on more modern particularized goals of perfection and perfectibility, blurred with discourse on medical enhancement, even if the dreams and visions are aired in a freewheeling "postmodern" manner. The difficulty in this case is that posthuman futures are entertained by what might be termed "postcritical" posthumanists, on the one hand, who draw heavily on postmodern reconstructions, including the challenge of reconstructing the human, and by evolution-oriented transhumanists, on the other hand, who more often than not identify with Enlightenment ideals of progress and perfection. In other words, in a manner unlike evolution by natural selection but more akin to the rhetoric of evolutionary psychology, transhumanity begins with an ideal design or trait in mind and then works out ways of achieving that design. In this sense, it attempts to construct a grand narrative and is rather more aligned with *modernism* than postmodernism, even if Philip Hefner adopts a thoroughgoing postmodern theology and feminist theorists such as Donna Haraway use the cyborg as a literary basis for challenging what might be termed the "ontological hygiene" characteristic of "modern" distinctions between non-human animals, human, and machine.[32]

I am also far less troubled than Waters by the prospect of contingency in postmodern discourse, for I believe it can still be married to a more

---

here. Hefner seems to equate original sin with a difference between genetic and cultural information. As Edwards points out—correctly, in my view—drawing on Karl Rahner, bodiliness and finitude are not, as such, something to be overcome, but part of God's good creation. It is also significant, perhaps, that Hefner is attracted to posthuman futures that move away from biologically grounded nature, in spite of his rhetoric of ecological responsibility. See Denis Edwards, "Original Sin and Saving Grace in Evolutionary Context," in *Evolutionary and Molecular Biology: Scientific Perspectives on Divine Action*, ed. R. J. Russell, W. R. Stoeger, and F. Ayala (Vatican City: Vatican; Berkeley: CTNS, 1998), 381.

31. Brent Waters, *From Human to Posthuman: Christian Theology and Technology in a Posthuman World* (Basingstoke: Ashgate, 2006), 123.

32. See, for example, her controversial essay, D. Haraway, "A Manisfesto for Cyborgs: Science, Technology and Socialist Feminism in the 1980s," in *The Haraway Reader* (New York: Routledge, 2004), 7–45, first published in *Socialist Review* (1985).

rigorous theological position through theodrama, as discussed in earlier chapters. Yet while Waters begins with posthuman discourse and ends with a christological affirmation informed by Oliver O'Donovan's *Resurrection and Moral Order*, the direction of the present work moves the other way around. In other words, the purpose in this context is to view post- or transhumanity through the lens of a Christology informed by theodrama and the motifs of wisdom and wonder that have already largely been thrashed out and developed in the context of evolutionary thought.[33] I am also inclined, within this christological framework, to take up aspects of what might be termed Christ as moral exemplar, which Waters so roundly rejects, for while this is not adequate on its own as a basis for Christology, it still gives useful pointers in the development of theological anthropology. The question then becomes how an understanding of who Christ is should be related to Christian anthropology, and particularly to human becoming.

8.2 Relating Christology and Anthropology

For Immanuel Kant, Jesus became the moral exemplar, an understanding taken up further by Albrecht Ritschl, who described the vocation of Jesus to be the founder of a new moral community.[34] The nineteenth-century "lives of Jesus" failed because Jesus came to be identified with the particular cultural traits of the time; he became gentle Jesus and a moral teacher. Such readings were exposed by Albert Schweitzer and others as projections of human needs and wishes, leading to the demise of any quest for the historical Jesus and the emergence of what might be termed nonincarnational

---

33. Some convergence is evident, however, in that I also develop the idea of obedient freedom while using the category of analogy, rather than "objective moral order," as the defining characteristic of the natural realm. In addition, I am more inclined to the view that natural law, for example, is a useful heuristic tool for associating *some* evolutionary theories and theological treatments of nature, rather than viewing it as an "objective moral order," which implies lack of flexibility. Indeed, as I have discussed elsewhere, the only principles of natural law that cannot be changed according to Aquinas are that good is sought and evil avoided, so it is rather more flexible than some Protestant commentators assume. See C. Deane-Drummond, "Plumbing the Depths: A Recovery of Natural Law and Natural Wisdom in the Context of Debates about Evolutionary Purpose," *Zygon* (2007): 981–98.

34. A. Ritschl, *The Christian Doctrine of Justification and Reconciliation* (Edinburgh: T&T Clark, 1902), 449–51.

Christologies that focus on the Christ of faith rather than the Jesus of history.[35]

It is in such a context that we find Karl Rahner developing Christology that emerges from his understanding of anthropology.[36] Rahner unites Christ's identity with that of evolved human being and becoming. In his thinking, the only difference between the figure of Christ and that of humanity seems to be that Jesus appears at that pivotal moment in history when the world takes a different turn toward God. Hence, he claims that the hypostatic union "must not be seen as much as something which distinguishes Jesus our Lord from us, but rather as something which must happen once, and once only, at the point where the world begins to enter its final phase in which it is to realise its final concentration, its final climax, and it radical nearness to the absolute mystery called God."[37] But if this is the case, then the encounter with Christ is identified more with his humanity than his divinity, and the possibility of a radical transformation of self fades, for why should we believe that divinization of the world has now begun with the appearance of Christ in the manner he suggests? While he wants to resist what he terms the "Platonic" tendencies of separating matter from Spirit, the lack of adequate distinction between spiritual and material means that he is left with a somewhat limp form of the meaning of the Spirit as simply humanity "conscious of himself."[38]

For Rahner, human becoming is about "becoming more," rather than "becoming Other." Yet he also envisages, somewhat confusingly, the idea of self-transcendence as that which takes place through "the power of absolute fullness of being," but coming from "within," as "interior" to finite being, without being the "constitutive principle of the essence of this finite being achieving itself."[39] He seems to want to have it both ways. On the one

---

35. Space does not permit discussion of this topic here. A leading exponent of non-incarnational Christology is John Hick. For discussion and critique, see Oliver Crisp, *Divinity and Humanity* (Cambridge: Cambridge University Press, 2007), 154–84.

36. For further discussion of Rahner's work, see chapter 1.

37. Karl Rahner, "Christology within an Evolutionary View of the World," *Theological Investigations* 5, trans. Karl H. Kruger (London: DLT, 1966), 160. We should note that although Rahner titled his essay "Christology," much of his discussion in this chapter is about humanity. Of course, his reasons for this were different from the intent of the present chapter, which is to highlight the need for a theologically oriented understanding of Christology in order to elaborate further the meaning of a theological understanding of the human person.

38. Ibid., 163.

39. Ibid., 165.

hand, being human is about being more than we are already, but on the other hand, it is not constitutive of the finite being as such, for he believes that if it were so, being human would not be capable of any "real becoming in time or history."

As an alternative approach, I suggest that in order to understand humanity, we need to understand who Christ is, and that encounter with Christ need not separate us from either the Jesus of history or the community of creation. Although Karl Barth reacted against his liberal colleagues in proclaiming the importance of the human encounter with the Word, with which I have some sympathy, he neglected historical aspects of the story of Jesus and tended to isolate salvation history from the history of creation. The work of Christophe Schwöbel inasmuch as it is heavily influenced by Barth is worth considering in this context. He proposes twelve theses for a Christian anthropology. His first thesis is that Christian anthropology needs to define itself in terms of relationality. In secular terms, this is expressed as biological, social, cultural, or self-reflexive relationships. He argues that Christian theological anthropology needs to be grounded in the relationship of the triune God to humanity. Moreover, the implicit awareness of God is made explicit through Christ:

> The revelation of God in Christ is the foundation of what it means to be human. This implies, secondly, that the true humanity of Christ is understood as the paradigm for true knowledge of human beings. . . . The true pattern for understanding human being is not the factual existence of humanity, but the new humanity of Christ in whom humanity is recreated and restored.[40]

Although Schwöbel does not use the language of theodrama, it is the drama of God's action in Christ that sets forth the pattern of what humanity is to become. Moreover, in this drama, human actors are placed in such a way that their freedom is honored and their context is respected. Schwöbel is critical of authors such as Wolfhart Pannenberg who seem to view theology as a way of *adding* something to a basically secular anthropology. For Schwöbel, becoming human is about having faith and recognizing not only epistemologically, but also ontologically, the new mode of being in which humanity actualizes its relationship with God. Hence, this is not

---

40. Christophe Schwöbel, "Human Being as Relational Being: Twelve Theses for a Christian Anthropology," in *Persons Divine and Human*, ed. Christophe Schwöbel and Colin Gunton, 141–54 (Edinburgh: T&T Clark, 1991), 144.

just a "new stage" in the development of humanity, in the manner also implied by Karl Rahner, as discussed earlier, but a renewal of relationship with God and fulfillment of that relationship begun in Christ. For Schwöbel, the opposite of faith is not unbelief, but sin, for it represents a violation of relationship.[41] Hence, through faith, we find that "the destiny of humanity to live as created in the image of God is recreated as life in the image of Christ."[42] He goes further to suggest, "The image of Christ is the only way in which human beings are enabled to recognise their created destiny as the image of God. . . . The humanity of Christ is therefore the pattern for rediscovering the image of God."[43] In other words, the definition of humanity is not derived so much from "natural stereotypes" of what it means to be human, but from "the revelation of true humanity in the humanity of Christ which in this way becomes the criterion for assessing any natural understanding of human 'nature.'"[44] The resulting question, which Schwöbel does not adequately answer, is this: What is meant by the humanity of Christ, and how far is it possible to arrive at such an understanding?

Schwöbel also rejects the idea of the image of Christ as being the pattern for redeemed humanity, *imitatio Christi* (imitation of Christ), believing that conformity to the humanity of Christ (*conformitas Christi*) is through faith by God's grace. In view of the legacy of Kant with respect to viewing Christ as moral pioneer, and Protestant suspicion of "good works," it is hardly surprising that Schwöbel rejects any concept of *imitatio Christi*. I suggest that his contrast between *imitatio* and *conformitas Christi* is too stark. Moreover, he seems to portray the work of grace in a Lutheran sense as wholly through faith, without any initiative at all on the part of the human person.[45]

---

41. I suggest that this focus on faith as a basis for defining sin is problematic, not least because it implies that those who do not believe are sinners regardless of their treatment of others. While sin reflects a breakdown of relationship, I suggest it would more properly be aligned to a deliberate turning away from God and others, as well as including structural or communal sin of oppression and misuse of power, along with human pride and arrogance, which Schwöbel's definition would apparently fail to include, since for him, the defining characteristic is lack of faith in God.

42. Schwöbel, "Human Being as Relational Being," 151.

43. Ibid., 152.

44. Ibid., 152–53.

45. He seems to be following Barth in approaching the starting point of anthropology as from "above," rather than from "below," as in Rahner, or "from the end," as in Pannenberg, or "from the Three," as in Gunton. For discussion of these alternatives, see Kevin Vanhoozer, "Human Being, Individual and Social," in *The Cambridge Companion*

While I think that an important strand of any Christian theological anthropology is recognition of the importance of Christ and faith, we need to probe far more deeply four issues in order to explore the relationship between anthropology and Christology. The first issue is what we mean in speaking of the humanity of Jesus in the context of what humanity is to become. The second is what it means for humanity to engage with Jesus and in what context(s) we might expect human flourishing according to that relationship. Third, the idea of conformity to the image of Christ cannot be considered apart from the work of the Holy Spirit, for it is through the Spirit that such transformation is possible. Fourth, and finally, Schwöbel's position is too individualistic; the context of humanity as created and the context of Christ's lordship as universal speak of humanity as becoming through relationship to *all creatures*, not just those in the human community. Theological anthropology is therefore ultimately ecological in orientation.

8.3 Hans Frei and the Identity of Jesus

Much ink has been spilled on trying to uncover who Christ is from the Gospel accounts, and the relationship between the Jesus of history and the Christ of faith in the early church, with something of a revival in returning to the specifically historical dimensions of Jesus' life in more recent decades.[46] A more promising approach is offered by Hans Frei, who sought to probe the particular narrative of the Gospels and thereby uncover something about the identity of Jesus Christ as portrayed in the story. This is not so much a "grand narrative" that turns into an epic reading as it is a particularized account that allows us to probe rather more clearly what it means for Christ to have lived and served on earth at a particular moment in evolutionary history. Frei's work is important for two reasons. First, his analysis of human identity offers an account of the human person that is helpful

---

to *Christian Doctrine*, ed. Colin Gunton, 158–88 (Cambridge: Cambridge University Press, 1997).

46. Those familiar with the revived discussions about the Quest for the Historical Jesus will sense the somewhat endless arguments about who Jesus was historically and how interpreters have, in the past, read into their portrait something of their own cultural and social prejudices. The liberal Protestant school that sought to find in Christ a moral example gave way either in neo-Barthian thought to more strident rejections of the importance of any historical reference or to more existential readings in Bultmann and Kierkegaard.

in unraveling what it means for human futures. Second, his portrayal of Christ bears witness to what the writers of the gospel wanted to achieve in communicating the story, regardless of how far and to what extent individual events might be deemed historical as such. In other words, it helps to fill out a concrete image of Christ in a way that is useful in developing a theological anthropology as an alternative to transhuman futures.

What then does human identity mean? Frei suggests, "Loosely speaking, the word indicates the very 'core' of a person toward which everything else is ordered, like spokes in a wheel."[47] It is "specific uniqueness," and while it is in relation to an abstract model, such a reference does not constitute that uniqueness. Identity also includes self-awareness, so that, for Kierkegaard, identity becomes the self in relation to self, though for this model, it is not clear what constitutes the relating factor in the self.[48] In addition, identity of self may be thought of as inferred from observations and physical patterns, but it can also be intuitive, so that there is a clear distinction between knowing *about* a person and knowing *a* person. Identity can also be thought of as moral responsibility, so that conscience is that which directs a person and helps shape his or her identity. The problem in this case is the source of conscience: Is it the inner self, God, or society? Frei—correctly, in my view—resists the idea of identity as a "ghost in the machine," the idea that there is a mysterious factor X beyond physical and personal characteristics. He believes that all such characterizations end up in metaphysical debates that take away from the core issue at hand— namely, how to describe the identity of Jesus Christ from the perspective of faith.

Frei therefore ends up with two key probes for investigating identity: "intention-action" and "self-manifestation." The first is based on his argument that "a person is not merely illustrated, he is constituted by his particular intentional act at any given point in his life."[49] It answers the question "What is he or she like?" The second, self-manifestation, addresses "Who is he or she?" in a way that shows continuity through different changes and becomes manifest in particular actions, bodily patterns, names, and words. Self-manifestation is also characterized by elusiveness as well as persistence, so that it is not always clear who a person is until sometime after events

---

47. H. Frei, *The Identity of Jesus Christ: The Hermeneutical Bases of Dogmatic Theology* (Eugene: Wipf & Stock, 1997), 95.

48. Ibid., 96ff.

49. Ibid., 100.

have taken place. Moreover, self-manifestation implies ultimacy; that is, it goes beyond simple description of characteristics—biological, psychological, and so on. This is an important point when engaging in dialogue with the biological and social sciences, for such sciences may be able to tell us something *about* a person, but they cannot in the end, simply by description, tell us *who* someone is, so that we are forced to give indirect answers.

If we turn to the figure of Jesus in the Gospel stories, then "his identity is given in the mysterious coincidence of his intentional action with circumstances partly initiated by him, partly devolving on him."[50] He also argues that just as intention is directly linked with action,[51] so self-manifestation also has an outward aspect, so that the body is not just the self in manifestation; it *is* the self. Has Frei gone too far here in trying to avoid the "ghost in machine" idea? Certainly, the self cannot be separated from the body, but wrapping up *identity* too closely with physical manifestation is problematic in other ethical ways, for it might seem to exclude or devalue those whose physical form is challenged by birth or accident. Bearing in mind these limitations, Frei reminds us of the character of Jesus that slowly emerges in the Gospel accounts, most poignantly in the passion narrative. Here we find that his love for humanity was not his only or most predominant quality; rather, it is obedience to God, which included love for all.[52] Obedience to the will of God, then, seems to be the "hallmark" that allows us to glimpse something of the pattern from intention through to action found in the person of Jesus, spelled out most graphically in the Garden of Gethsemane. Moreover, as we reach the climax of the passion narratives, the powerlessness of Jesus on the cross mysteriously becomes the means of salvation for others. Only at the resurrection does the identity of Jesus become fully manifest, and not as a mythological figure, but as the human Jesus, "regarded as an unsubstitutable individual in his own right,"

---

50. Ibid., 138.

51. Of course, Frei realized that it is quite possible to have intentions without actions, or actions that do not follow from intentions, but he suggests that these are unimportant in defining a person's identity. While I agree that the passage from intention to action shows us what a person is like, it seems to me that a person's identity could also be drawn on the basis that intentions rarely, if ever, are devolved into actions—in other words, the possibility of inauthentic existence. Frei does not consider this problem. Actions that are without intentions are, for him, just "overt behaviour," but again, repeated thoughtless behavior could also, arguably, define what a person is like. See ibid., 136–37.

52. Ibid., 145–46.

and in this sense "most fully historical."[53] In other words, the identity of the risen Jesus allows the possibility of identity in others.

8.4 Jesus as Lord and Exemplar: Phil. 2:5-11

Pauline sayings point to the insight just suggested, namely, that Jesus Christ is the true image or manifestation of God (2 Cor. 4:4; Col. 1:15; and Heb. 1:3). Christians are encouraged to conform to Christ's image in Rom. 8:29; 1 Cor. 15:49; 2 Cor. 3:18; and Gal. 4:19. Yet while these passages all endorse the possibility of transformation into Christ's image, for us to understand its practical meaning for human vocation, or what Balthasar would term human mission, it is important to understand how Christ was perceived in the early Christian church. Most biblical scholars believe that the letter of Paul to the Philippians expresses an early Christology.[54] It is also less relevant whether the hymn to Christ in Phil. 2 is a separate source or not, for it is clear that by using this hymn, Paul intends to provide not only a summary of the significance of Christ for Christians, but also an example for them to imitate.[55]

James Dunn attributes an Adam Christology to the hymn, comparing Christ as in the "form" (morphē) of God with humanity as the image (eikōn) in Genesis.[56] While there are epistles that do make this analogy and treat Christ as a "second Adam" repairing the damage wrought by the sin of the first humans, this interpretation has unfortunate consequences. For either Christ becomes a perfect human, resisting temptation, or he is identified with the shadowy prehistorical and mythical figure of Adam, who seems somewhat disconnected from human evolutionary history, even if in general terms the theological tradition of the fall can be reinterpreted in order to embrace a wider evolutionary compass. I would therefore be rather

---

53. H. Frei, "Theological Reflections on the Account of Jesus' Death and Resurrection," essay included with *The Identity of Jesus Christ*, 33.

54. I am assuming that Paul is the author of this epistle, as do many biblical scholars; see Ralph Martin and Brian Dodd, *Where Christology Began: Essays on Philippians 2* (Louisville: Westminster John Knox, 1998).

55. For the present purposes, I am leaving aside debates about whether this hymn denotes Christ as preexistent. It seems to me that the balance of evidence favors this interpretation, which was also that of the early church fathers.

56. James Dunn, "Christ, Adam and Pre-Existence," in Martin and Dodd, *Where Christology Began*, 74–95.

more cautious than some scholars in relying on an Adam Christology to make concrete links between Christology and anthropology.[57]

Instead, the Christology portrayed in Phil. 2 echoes the Suffering Servant figure in Deutero-Isaiah. Richard Bauckham has argued against Dunn—convincingly, in my view—that Phil. 2:10-11 alludes to Isa. 45:22-23, and that the latter is prefaced by "I am God, there is no other." This means the text should be interpreted to mean that equality with God was not something to be used for Christ's advantage. He suggests that Christ "renounced the splendour of the heavenly court for the life of a human being on earth, one who lived his obedience to God in self-humiliation, even to the point of the particularly shameful death by crucifixion, the death of a slave."[58] Most important, perhaps, is the subsequent exaltation of Christ, so that, as in 1 Cor. 8:6, "the purpose is to include Jesus completely in the unique identity of God."[59] Hence, the question for Paul in the context of first-century Judaism, with its belief in God as universal emperor, was not so much, How can the immortal God become a human creature and take on human limitations? Rather, it was one of status: Can one who inhabits the heavens lower himself to such a life, culminating in death? Bauckham therefore concludes, in a way that reinforces discussion in the early part of this book, "His humiliation belongs to the identity of God as truly as his exaltation does. The identity of God—who God is—is revealed as much in self-abasement and service as it is in exaltation and rule."[60]

---

57. An example of this tendency is found in, for example, Schwöbel, "Human Being as Relational Being." His preconception is the importance of faith in Christ and a Reformed view of justification by faith, which means that a somewhat stylized understanding of who Christ is remains inherent in his thought. I would agree with the author inasmuch as he also claims that human personhood cannot be understood apart from Christ. However, I would want to put more emphasis on the importance of grounding such a discussion in contemporary biblical studies, which tries to discover the meaning of Christ's human identity in the narrative.

58. Richard Bauckham, *God Crucified: Monotheism and Christianity* (Carlisle: Paternoster, 1998), 58.

59. Ibid., 40.

60. Ibid., 61. Of course, this opens up the difficult contemporary debate as to the passibility of God, that is, whether God might suffer and the manner of God's suffering. Although the shift in this direction has gained in popularity in recent years, and the suffering of the world and God becomes virtually equivalent in process thought, I have become more inclined to resist too strong a shift in this direction, in that it implies too strong an equivalence between God and humanity and thereby weakens the means for salvation. Where is hope when God becomes just a feature in the process of world suffering? Christ becomes an example of that suffering rather than the means

Yet Phil. 2 is also important in another sense: it tells us something about the character of Christ's obedience. Against the background of Christ's identification with humanity, the letter shows "the shaping of a Christian phronēsis, a practical moral reasoning."[61] Practical moral reasoning is, of course, the way in which intentions become expressed in actions, and follows in the tradition of prudence or practical wisdom.[62] Christ is portrayed as one who is vindicated and exalted in spite of suffering, humiliation, and shame, and this pattern can also be expected in the Philippians' own context of persecution. Paul urges them to unite in one spirit and mind, so that Phil. 2:5 could be translated, "Base your practical reasoning on what you see in Christ Jesus."[63]

Philippians 3:2-16 also gives an account of how Paul's own way of thinking was transformed by his encounter with Christ. What seems to be encouraged here is not so much literal imitation of the life of Christ in its precise details, but seeing by analogy the kind of pattern that might be appropriate in each case. Stephen Fowl puts the point forcefully: "Rather than a difference obliterating sameness, Paul's language of imitation in Philippians is designed to produce an ordered, harmonious diversity."[64] It is also important to note that the imitation of Christ does not constitute the essence of a believer's relationship with Christ. Rather, Paul speaks of being

---

for its restoration. I would want to insist that Christ genuinely suffered in taking on human flesh, and in this sense, Christ as Suffering Servant becomes incorporated into the divine mystery of the Trinity, bearing in mind that this is the economic, rather than the immanent, Trinity.

61. Wayne Meeks, "The Man from Heaven in Paul's Letter to the Philippians," in *The Future of Early Christianity: Essays in Honor of Helmut Koester* (Minneapolis: Fortress Press, 1991), 333.

62. Space does not permit detailed discussion of practical wisdom or prudence in this context. I am referring to it here to indicate that the kind of intention-action dynamic that Frei speaks about could equally describe prudential reasoning. Furthermore, authors who have developed this line of thought through virtue ethics are rather more aware than Frei seems to be of the possibility of distortions at any stage. For discussion, see C. Deane-Drummond, *The Ethics of Nature* (Oxford: Blackwell, 2004). It also ties in with Josef Pieper's claim that the practice of prudence gives us an insight into human identity. Hence, "the intrinsic goodness of man, and that is the same as saying his true humanness, consists in this, that 'reason perfected in the cognition of the truth' shall inwardly shape and imprint his volition and action." J. Pieper, *Prudence*, trans. R. Winston and C. Winston (London: Faber & Faber, 1957), 16.

63. Stephen Fowl, "Christology and Ethics in Philippians 2.5-11," in Martin and Dodd, *Where Christology Began*, 140–53, following Meeks, "Man from Heaven," 147.

64. Fowl, "Christology and Ethics," 149.

"in Christ" and of the adoration of Christ as the means through which Christians gain their inspiration.[65] In other words, while in one sense Christ performs the function of moral exemplar, he means much, much more than this, for to be related to Christ is not simply to follow Christ, but in a mysterious sense to allow Christ through faith to indwell the human person. As suggested in the previous chapter, this indwelling of Christ in the person cannot be separated from the work of the Holy Spirit, but now it is the Spirit given by Christ as promised in the farewell narrative in John's Gospel. In other words, being conformed in some sense to the image of Christ is pneumatological as much as it is Christological.

8.5 Facing Jesus Christ

The idea of facing Jesus Christ can usefully be woven into a theological anthropology.[66] It is also helpful in that it picks up something of the style of postmodern discourse while challenging its secular trajectory. I also believe that such a representation fills out what might happen in a particular scene of the theodrama in a way that is consistent with evolutionary history inasmuch as evolution can be viewed as a series of encounters between God the Father, Son, and Spirit and creatures, rather than an overarching epic. It is appropriate, therefore, that in the encounters with the risen Jesus, we find a disturbance of ordinary recognizability, which "provokes fear, bewilderment, doubt, joy and amazement."[67] I would call such an encounter one that provokes wonder. Yet it is not the kind of enthralled wonder at the potential capacity of humanity to recreate itself in transhuman evolution, but the awesome wonder at the presence of God beyond human imaginings and dreams. In the risen Christ, we gain a vista on the true "transhuman" face, one who is earthed in concrete scars of bodily life yet moves in a sphere that no longer is restricted to what is known of evolutionary becoming. Yet, as I

---

65. For discussion of this point, see Brian Dodd, "The Story of Christ and the Limitation of Paul in Phil. 2–3," in Martin and Dodd, *Where Christology Began*, 154–61.

66. I am drawing here on David Ford, *Self and Salvation: Being Transformed* (Cambridge: Cambridge University Press, 1999), especially chapter 7. Although the main focus of this book is on the doctrine of salvation, I suggest that an understanding of human identity, a theological anthropology, also can usefully draw on this theme. Indeed, from a Christian perspective, who we are should not be separated from who we become in Christ.

67. Ford, *Self and Salvation*, 172. I have also discussed in chapter 6 the particular encounter of the risen Christ with Mary Magdalene.

suggested in chapter 6, trying to capture precisely what this new humanity signifies is an attempt to make the encounter with the risen Christ concrete in an illicit way, just as it is illicit to seek those particular goals of perfection that are aimed against mortal life and ordinary bodiliness.

An encounter with the face of Jesus also vindicates to some extent any worry about the vagueness of the concept of face. Such vagueness can signify something more profound than intellectual "impoverishment of reference," for it can point to "unimaginable intensity and inexhaustible abundance."[68] Furthermore, as David Ford comments profoundly:

> It is the openness of the hospitable face, the good underdetermination of not being self-contained. This face is alive with the life and glory of God, so its openness has all the capacity for innovation and surprise which belong to God. It is so orientated to others that knowing and loving this face means being called to know and love them. Its self-effacement constantly urges those who look to it that they should route their seeking the face of Christ through other people. This is the long detour of recognising Christ in others, not one of whom is irrelevant to knowing and loving him.[69]

Ford suggests that by the time the letters to Timothy and Titus were written, the idea of "living before the face of the risen Jesus Christ had by then become the normality of Christian living."[70] Christ is described in Heb. 12:1-2 as the "pioneer and perfecter of our faith," with the hoped-for full vision of Christ expectantly awaited in the future. Furthermore, the face of Christ in worship becomes identified with the glory of God. The facing of Jesus is a reminder of an encounter, and encounter through liturgy and worship, so that radical regard for others becomes an expression of love for Christ. It is also embedded in Ignatian spirituality, which marks out the distinctive contribution of Balthasar that I have drawn upon throughout this book.[71] We need to ask, in addition, who might be included in

---

68. Ibid., 171. Ford develops his notion of facing in dialogue with postmodern philosophers. A discussion of postmodernity is outside the scope of this chapter, but the connection with this cultural stream is worth noting in this context.

69. Ibid., 172–73.

70. Ibid., 173.

71. Such imagery culminates in the meditation on the two standards on the fourth day of the second week, where the retreatant is invited to picture Christ as a commander and to envisage a specific encounter with Christ, following the close consideration of different aspects of the narrative of Christ's life on earth earlier in the week. See Louis

this "other" where Christ is present. David Ford seems to assume that this must mean other human persons. I suggest an expansion of those others in the presence of Christ in order to include a wider concern for the whole created order, including the memory of those others now captured in the evolutionary record.

8.6 Christian Identity in *Imago Christi*: Toward an Evolutionary, Ecological Mandate

The example of Christ, portrayed in dramatic terms as one who gives until he is empty, shows the possibility of a radical altruism that goes far beyond any evolutionary explanations of altruism through, for example, game theory. I am not suggesting that game theory is entirely irrelevant to understanding behavioral tendencies in human societies; human persons are evolved, social beings, grounded in the natural capacities of all creatures. Hence, it may be relevant to understanding the evolution of language and other cultural traits.[72] However, radical Christian altruism speaks of a radical transformation of self so that self-identity becomes so caught up with the drama of Christ that selfless behavior becomes both a possibility and a vocation. This radical model of human becoming counters the self-absorption expressed through transhumanist visions for the future of humanity.

Gerd Theissen has argued that Christ needs to be considered under the biological categories of "mutation," "selection," and "adaptation" as a way of coming to terms with clash between modern evolutionary consciousness and Christology.[73] Jesus in this way shows forth the possibility of a new development in humanity, but whereas selection marks the natural world, Christ shows a break with such selection in instituting the principle of solidarity instead. In him, we see "a possible goal of evolution," and a new form of humanity appears in Jesus, where the new feature is love, expressed as solidarity with the weak. Of course, Theissen recognizes some problems with this metaphor inasmuch as naming Christ as a "mutation" might

---

J. Puhl, *The Spiritual Exercises of St. Ignatius* (Chicago: Loyola University Press, 1951), 49–67.

72. See, for example, a recent discussion in Carl Zimmer, "In Games: An Insight into the Rules of Evolution," *New York Times*, July 31, 2007, accessed at http://www.nytimes.com/2007/07/31/science/, August 2, 2007.

73. Gerd Theissen, *Biblical Faith: An Evolutionary Approach* (London: SCM, 1984), 86.

imply something impermanent, though inasmuch as a "mutation" suggests a new combination of prior elements, it is consistent with the teaching of Jesus. Moreover, for Theissen, the Spirit is also a "mutation" insofar as a Spirit-filled humanity resists patterns of behavior that have biological or cultural foundation, though he aligns the work of the Spirit with cultural rather than biological evolution.

This strange amalgam of biological and theological imagery fails not so much because it is illicit to relate Christology, evolution, and humanity, but because they are related in a way that distorts each realm. Christ is, for example, more than simply a "mutation" in humanity that arguably could happen again, in order to produce the superhumanity projected by transhumanists. The term *mutation* is also inappropriate inasmuch as it assumes a commonality between biological and cultural evolution that is at best tenuous. While Theissen does not intend this language to be literal, but uses it metaphorically, it is important to ask what the metaphor is achieving. Is it really encouraging its readers to live as Christ lived, in humble obedience and self-offering, or not? Certainly, his rejection of selection as derived from natural selection in all its various forms in opposition to the New Testament teaching on self-giving shows the limitations of his metaphor, but the metaphor is forced in the first place, reliant on an outmoded and simplistic understanding of the role of mutations in evolutionary processes. Further, envisaging the Spirit as a "mutation" that seems to work against the biological processes of the natural world implies a dualistic approach to the natural world that is unhelpful; such a "mutation" would not survive long, shorn from its material boundedness.

I agree with both Theissen and Hefner in their desire to connect Christology with evolutionary history in working out an adequate anthropology, and in this respect, their efforts are entirely appropriate. The difference I envisage is, rather, the way these three areas intersect and interrelate. If Christology becomes absorbed simply into an evolutionary epic in the manner that Theissen and Hefner suggest, in spite of what might be termed a "postmodern" attitude to theology that seeks to defy more classical traditions, then Christology has very little to say about what kind of "posthuman" future one might anticipate. We are simply left with a weak sense of responsibility toward evolutionary history, thrashed out in the context of human creativity, with all the expectation, risks, and vulnerability that this entails. However, replacing the evolutionary epic with a grand Christian narrative that is abstracted from specific encounters with the divine is equally problematic, as is fusing the evolutionary and Christian narrative together, because both types of accounts no longer seem to connect with lived reality or make sense with respect to the diversity of cultures that make up the global context of our shared earth.

I have argued throughout this book for an approach to evolutionary history that makes good use of theodrama, and inasmuch as this helps mirror the evolutionary and ecological histories we share with other creatures, it can serve a useful task in offering a vision for human futures as well. The lust for power and defiance of mortality associated with transhumanism need to be resisted, for our human task needs to be far more keenly identified with our responsibilities for the earth and for each other. While Hefner pays lip service to ecological responsibility, it is not clear how his cyborg future enables such responsibility to be achieved.

While I recognize that cyborg anthropology, which uses a human/machine boundary as a basis for challenging preconceived assumptions about human nature, differs from transhuman evolutionary aspirations, I have focused more specifically on transhuman discourse in this context. I also believe that the boundary between the cyborg anthropology and transhumanism is rather more fluid than authors such as Elaine Graham suggest; in other words, I would be much more cautious of affirming the cyborg on the basis of critical posthuman discussion, while taking up aspects of postmodern discourse in other respects. Thus, I am arguing against the use of the *evolutionary* trajectory, where it appears, whether in transhuman or cyborg discourse; this aspect in particular needs to be challenged, even if there may be some useful ways of thinking about how new technologies can become incorporated into human persons. Hence, what is at stake here is not a Luddite reaction against all application of technology, but the motivation behind transhumanism, which is driven by idealized and misplaced ideas about human becoming.

Indeed, the transhuman project can be challenged not just from a theological perspective, but also from an evolutionary perspective. The complexity of evolution is such that different "configurations can cascade in innumerable directions, each crucially dependent upon tiny differences in the antecedent states[;] we regard these subsequent outcomes as unpredictable in principle (as an ontological property of nature's probabilistic constitution, not as a limitation of our minds, or as a sign of the inferior status of historical science)."[74] Yet it is only *after* the occurrence that they can be explained as the actual result among numerous different possibilities. In much the same way, transhuman evolution, were it to be attempted, would contain far too many variants in order to be fully anticipated in terms of risk and benefit in the manner suggested by many of its advocates, even if a measure of explanation after the event might be possible—and by then, it may be too late, as humanity has itself changed and subverted itself through such tinkering.

In other words, the remarkable features of evolution are not so much the outcome of a grand design as an improvised script of a grand drama. This makes evolutionary history and that of humanity no less awesome. Admittedly, debates continue about the extent to which evolution is constrained in physical terms, or whether constraint also includes, in some sense, a directional signal, in which case evolution works beyond or in addition to the weak driving force of natural selection. Nevertheless, the place of contingency is still of uppermost importance as a way of interpreting evolutionary history. There need be no violence done to this contingency in order to affirm belief in a God who is active through theodrama, most specifically in the drama of Christ's coming, for just as an explanation becomes possible after the event, so belief in the sacramental presence of God in the natural world is inclusive of evolutionary and cosmological history, as well as the history of humankind.

It is tempting, further, to assume that the workings of God in cosmological processes are identical to those in the biological realm. An expression of faith that it is *God* working in the evolutionary processes themselves falls readily off the tongue of those imbided with theology and natural science.[75] While this is true to the extent that biological events are constrained

---

74. S. J. Gould, *The Structure of Evolutionary Theory* (Cambridge, Mass.: Belknap/Harvard University Press, 2002), 1333.

75. Arthur Peacocke safeguards his view from pantheism by claiming that God *acts* in evolutionary processes, rather than identifying God as such with the processes. He resists any idea of God as some "additional factor" supplementing the processes of evolution. See, for example, A. Peacocke, "Biological Evolution: A Positive Theological Appraisal," in *Evolutionary and Molecular Biology: Scientific Perspectives on Divine Action*, ed. R. J. Russell, W. R. Stoeger, and F. J. Ayala (Vatican City: Vatican Observatory; Berkeley: CTNS, 1998), 359. The question then arises: Why use the language of God's *action* at all if God is, in effect, redundant? Or perhaps we need another way of saying the same thing—one that respects the freedom of creaturely being while acknowledging the Creator as the source of all that is. Denis Edwards, in the same volume, comments that McFague's distance from evolution by natural selection and the Christ figure

by physical laws, I am less convinced that we can know or define precisely *how* God works or acts in such contexts, even if we might want to resist forms of "vitalism" that suggest there is a "life force" in the biological world that tends toward particular ends in a way that is entirely different from that in the nonbiotic world. The advantage of theodrama as a metaphor for God's working in the world, including creation, is that it allows God to be present to creation through the Holy Spirit and in the person of Jesus Christ without violating the freedom of creatures or the contingency of individual events and encounters. In other words, the affirmation of God's action in the narrative of Jesus is such that his humanity is rendered divine in a way that is impossible for other creatures. Yet Jesus does not simply become divine; there is a sense in which he is divine from the beginning, even if we might argue that through his obedient love, his humanity was divinized over the course of his human history.

The response of humanity in viewing such a marvelous play spelled out through eons of evolutionary time is necessarily one of awe and wonder, and that awe is not diminished by viewing it in evolutionary as well as theistic terms. Indeed, there is no need to feel a sense of threat by the contingency so keenly felt by evolutionary biologists such as Stephen J. Gould. Alternative evolutionary theories, such as those of Simon Conway Morris, which put rather more emphasis on the possibility of a directional signal in evolution, may seem more compatible with theological insights on purpose, but I suggest that such concepts are not strictly *necessary* in order to affirm the compatibility of evolutionary and theistic ideas. Indeed, inasmuch as Gould's position on contingency is a strong rejection of any "grand narrative" in evolutionary terms, it serves as an important guarantor

---

is troubling; for him, the "Christic paradigm" serves to "define not only God's action in Jesus Christ, but also God's creative action in and through natural selection." Edwards, "Original Sin and Saving Grace in Evolutionary Context," in Russell et al., *Evolutionary and Molecular Biology*, 381. Yet I would be more reluctant than Edwards to use the language of *Christic* to define how God works in evolutionary history, as it implies an affirmation of the oppressive aspects of natural selection that McFague is attuned to in her writing. This does not mean that there is some sense in viewing the significance of the risen Christ in cosmic terms, or that God works in the creation of the world after the pattern that is eventually expressed in the coming of Christ, namely, through theodrama. The advantage of theodrama here is that it lends itself to finding *analogous* relationships among the different ways of God acting in the theater of the world without presupposing identity in all cases; different scenes call for rather different players, even if the Director is the same, and even if that Director acts largely through improvisation rather than a set text.

of something crucially important. Gould's sense of wonder is spelled out toward the end of his great work on evolutionary theory, and it is worth citing in full, for it calls to mind the possible attention that all humanity needs to pay to the evolutionary world in which we live:

> And something almost unspeakably holy—I don't know how else to say this— underlies our discovery and confirmation of the actual details that made our world and also, in the realms of contingency, assured the minutiae of its construction in the manner we know, and not in any one of a trillion other ways, nearly all of which would not have included the evolution of a scribe to record the beauty, the cruelty, the fascination and the mystery.[76]

Just as the explanation for particular events can be named after a particular evolutionary event has taken place, so God's purpose in evolution and in human history is really clear only in retrospect. Yet for a Christian, much more can be said, because prophetic voices reach out toward unknown futures glimpsed intuitively as if from ahead. A Christian has one foot in history and nature and one in the hoped-for future, but if it is to be a future that expresses the kind of eschatology articulated in the previous chapter, it includes the natural history with human history, rather than envisaging a transhuman future severed from biological and historical roots.

In the light of such awareness of evolutionary history and the drama into which our human lives are called, the Christian vocation and responsibility become extended not just to include animals that we might invite to be our kin, but beyond this to the ecological community as well. Such responsibility is best expressed through the exercise of love and wisdom in imitation of Christ, but also is empowered by the gift of the Spirit. A way of reinforcing the dramatic connection between our lived biological and historical reality and that of the history of Christ, along with an ethical mandate to imitate Christ in all things, comes through liturgical celebration, found most profoundly in the Eucharist. Here wine and bread, the fruit of the earth, but also the fruit of human technological labor, become transformed through the Holy Spirit into the body and blood of Christ, so that Christ can be said to dwell in the hearts and minds of those who receive in faith, the believers. In this sense, humanity has already become

---

76. Gould, *Structure of Evolutionary Theory*, 1342.

transhuman; there is no need to search for the Holy Grail elsewhere or presume that a cyborg future will be wholesome for people and planet.

Of course, the practical, ethical task of how to express the wisdom learned of coming close to Christ, the Wisdom of God, and sharing in his prudence cannot be developed here, except to suggest quite simply that it necessarily will fulfill the mandate to express justice and to walk humbly with God, obedient in all things after the pattern of Christ named as Lord. Perhaps we have created the cyborg from our own imaginings, and it is time to give it the *qualified* place that it needs, namely, as a creation of human ingenuity but one that needs to be firmly kept in its place: technology needs to remain our servant, not our master or our goal. In other words, we need not totally reject such technology, but appreciate its proper limits according to particular goals that express the common good. While the cyborg may be useful in challenging preconceived notions of self, subject and object, mind and machine, it should not become so enlarged in our human consciousness that other human responsibilities fade from view, in particular, those relating to evolved, biological worlds in which we are embedded, including the suffering of human and creaturely others. There is much work to be done in naming and understanding the evolutionary history in which human life is situated, let alone keeping and preserving what remains of the biodiversity that much misdirected human technology seems bent on destroying at will.

Even a cursory pause at one snapshot scene in evolutionary history makes us realize how precious and yet precarious each evolutionary lineage now existing really is, surviving against the odds. Whether human futures go the way of other species or not is not for our own making and remaking; such scenarios smell of the odor of eugenics rather than a positive future becoming. In evolutionary terms at least, our life span is simply too short to make accurate predictions about our particular place in human evolutionary history. An attempt to overcome that history can just as easily lead to nihilism as to learning to accept what can and cannot be done. Hence, while I would concede that some technologies may be suitably constrained in order to contribute to the common good, it would be a mark of intense hubris marked with political overtones of eugenics to expect that humans can control their own evolution.

8.7 Conclusions

This chapter has looked more specifically at the development of a theological anthropology amid cultural trends toward a posthuman future. I have argued strongly against those who press for the legitimization of posthumanity in transhuman projects as the next stage of evolution. Such legitimization presumes the rhetoric of evolutionary psychology but takes it further into practical mandates that have social as well as political implications. Transhumanity more often than not assumes that the basis for being human persons is our intelligence, and that intelligence can be improved through technologies. Also, while transhumanity claims to find a basis for its arguments in science, it is still mixed up with idealistic and utopian speculation about a perfected humanity.

Against such a view, I have argued that the only figure in history who can be claimed to be more than human in a positive sense is the figure of Jesus Christ. In him, we find an example of what perfected humanity really means. Once we explore a little more closely what that identity might be, we find that it is characterized by the dramatic action of God within the contingencies of his own particular narrative, one that he expressed through overriding obedience to God's purposes. These purposes did not lead so much to his idolatrous self-aggrandizement, but to a humble path of suffering, where he emptied himself for others, including, I suggest, the other of evolved creation as such. This pattern of self-emptying may not seem all that palatable in the face of the hubristic claims made by transhumanists, but it is vital if human evolution is not to become dehumanized and dis-incarnate. Indeed, I have severe doubts whether we have the wisdom or love to project what such constructions might entail, apart from limited uses of technology that make a much lesser claim of being a servant to humanity, rather than seeking to reconstruct that humanity.

In the encounter with Jesus in the drama of our own lives, we find the basis for a new humanity, a new creation; this is a theodrama that began not just two thousand years ago, but many millennia before this in the dawn of life and the dawn of the cosmos. As such, this longevity should caution us to respect that which evolutionary biologists are now claiming, namely, that the way to preserve evolutionary diversity and richness of relationships is by giving a place for contingency, rather than seeking to manipulate and control our futures. Therefore, human responsibility is less about seeking new evolutionary pathways for itself than it is a matter of engaging in practices that will help sustain the biodiversity on which human life as we know it depends. Transhumanism represents a callous escape from that responsibility and a severing from evolutionary history in the guise of the rhetoric of evolutionary psychology, and as such, it also shares in the limitations of evolutionary psychology. Instead, there is no need to search vainly for the Holy Grail in recreated humans; the transformation we might anticipate toward true perfection comes from offering our technology at the altar under the form of bread and wine, for the new creation in Christ offered to humanity begins in this life, even if the hope we speak of includes a new and transformed creation.

Index

complexity, *continued*
and Darwinian evolution, 2, 16
n.39, 17, 27–28, 44, 58, 281
and directionality, 17
and intelligent design, 25
and progressive evolution, 30
Conradie, Ernst, 199–200, 222–24
constraint, 23
contingency, 24, 283
convergence, 19–20, 21–22
Conway Morris, Simon, 20–24,
21–22, 283
Copernican revolution, 3
Copernicus, Nicolaus, 90
Cosmides, Leda, 63, 67
cosmos
and Christology, 105, 129,
149–53
history of, 41–42, 45
and redemption, 105–6, 174,
244–45
and resurrection, 244
creatio ex nihilo, 47
creationism, 15, 25
cross
and atonement, 179–83, 191–93
beauty of, 140–41, 143
and resurrection, 99 n.10
and sin, 177
and suffering, 183–85, 189–90
theology of, 178–79, 181
transformation of, 104
and Trinity, 183–84
cruciform, 45, 57, 172, 179, 187, 204
Cunningham, Conor, 9
cyborgs, 263–65, 281, 285
Cyril of Alexandria, 34

Daniel (biblical figure), 72
Darwin, Charles
Descent of Man, 4, 5
on evolutionary cycle, 2–3
influence of, 1

misappropriated ideas, 90
and modification, 82
on morality, 5
and natural selection, 199
On the Origin of the Species, 1, 3
prejudice of, 89
prejudices, 81, 89
on Spencer's interpretations, 5
Darwinian evolution
adaptive vs. neutral, 12
and Christology, 29, 34–48
and complexity, 2, 16 n.39, 17,
27–28, 44, 58, 281
constraints, 6
as controversial, 5–6
core principles, 1, 4, 5
and environmental conditions,
10
and incarnation, 38, 40–41
and kenotic Christology, 53–59
and materialistic philosophy, 3
as narrative vs. drama, 10–24
patterns, 15
and purpose, 46–47
and redemption, 37, 48
religious quandaries, 24–30
and theodrama, 33, 48–53, 198–
207, 277, 281, 286
See also natural selection
Dawkins, Richard, 11, 25, 60–62,
228
and Beattie, 89
and genetic components, 75–76
God Delusion, The, 88
and meme theory, 82, 93
and Theism, 90
Deacon, Terence, 164
Dembski, William, 25
Dennett, Daniel, 82
design
intelligent, 2 n.2, 22, 25, 29
language of, 260
and natural selection, 2, 80

Holy Spirit
as female principle, 56, 119, 123, 222
and Pentecost, 216
and resurrection, 220
See also Sophia/sophia; Wisdom/wisdom
hominids, fossil, 8–9
homology vs. homoplasty, 19–20
Homo species, 8
Hopkins, Gerard Manley, 149, 152, 154
Hurtado, Larry, 108–11
hypostasis
of God, 42, 115–19
and incarnation, 113, 135, 268
of Logos, 114–15, 123 n.101
of Sophia, 119, 220
of Wisdom, 102
of Word, 97, 114

identity
Christian, 279–86
of Jesus Christ, 271–74
idolatry, 60, 89
Ignatius of Loyola, 52, 131, 137, 145, 149, 237, 246, 278
imprinting, 6, 10
incarnation
and creation, 47, 87, 104, 112, 115
deep, 95, 100, 107, 128–55
defined, 108, 110
and ecologization, 96
and evolution, 38, 40–41
and faith, 111
and human soul, 34
and kenosis, 44 n.71, 113, 173
and Mary, 95, 114–15, 122–25
and redemption, 113
and Sophia, 117
and transcendence, 42, 97
of Wisdom, 100–107

individuals
adaptations by, 10, 19
and allopatry, 16
and evolutionary patterns, 15
and groups, 8
Ingold, Tim, 78
intelligent design, 2 n.2, 22, 25, 29
Irenaeus, 241, 254
Israel
God's alignment with, 72
repudiation of Jesus, 101

Jesus Christ
as archetype, 34–35
as evolutionary psychologist, 69–72
facing, 277–79
followers of, 72
as form of beauty, 138–43
in hell, 143–49
historical, 70–71
as human/divine, 35, 90, 94–100, 107–11, 120–21
humanity of, 270
identity of, 256, 271–74
imago Christi, 256, 270–71, 272, 277, 279–86
as Lord and exemplar, 274–77
as Omega, 48
as prophet, 93–94
resurrection, 146
as second Adam, 169, 274
and Sophia, 55, 101–7, 124, 126, 127, 207–19, 226
suffering of, 235–36
as wisdom, 101–2
and Wisdom motif, 107–11
See also Christology; incarnation
John (apostle), 71, 104, 107–8
of the cross, 234–35
gospel of, 112, 194, 207, 211
and logos, 111
and Matthew, 126